Capacity Management Reprints

Revised Edition

© 1987 The American Production and Inventory Control Society, Inc.
International Standard Book Number: 0-935406-99-9
Library of Congress Catalog Number: 87-072931

No portion of this publication may be reproduced by any means without prior permission from the publisher. Contact society headquarters at the address below for information concerning reprint policies. The society will not be responsible for any statements, beliefs, or opinions expressed by individuals in this publication. The views expressed are solely those of the individual and do not necessarily reflect endorsement by the society.

American Production and Inventory Control Society, Inc.
500 West Annandale Road
Falls Church, Virginia 22046-4274

Stock No. 05009, 8/90, 2,400

CAPACITY MANAGEMENT REPRINTS
Table of Contents

Capacity Management Committee v

"40 Days to the Due Date" by Willy Makeit:
The Role of Capacity Management in MRP II
Lloyd Andreas, CFPIM 1

Integrating Capacity Planning and Capacity Control
Bill Belt 6

Rough-Cut Capacity Planning—What It Is and How to Use It
Kenneth L. Campbell, CPIM 20

Vendor Capacity Planning: An Approach to Vendor Scheduling
Phillip L. Carter, CFPIM, and Chrwan-jyh Ho, CPIM 24

Capacity Management
James T. Clark, CFPIM 35

Capacity Management—Part Two
James T. Clark, CFPIM 39

Scheduling the Job Shop
R. L. Lankford, CFPIM 46

Short-Term Planning of Manufacturing Capacity
R. L. Lankford, CFPIM 66

Job-Shop Scheduling: A Case Study
Ray Lankford, CFPIM, and Tom Moore 98

Priority Fixation Versus Throughput Planning
Hal Mather, CFPIM, and George Plossl, CFPIM 106

Capacity Planning and Control
George W. Plossl, CFPIM, and Oliver Wight 131

Resource Requirements Planning and Capacity Requirements Planning—
The Case for Each and Both
F. John Sari, CFPIM 168

Why the Process Industries Are Different
Sam G. Taylor, Samuel M. Seward, CPIM, and Steven F. Bolander 171

Input/Output Control: A Real Handle on Lead Time
Oliver Wight 187

CAPACITY MANAGEMENT REPRINTS
Table of Contents

Capacity Management Committee
No Icing on the Cake Does It, With Motion
the Role of Capacity Management in Mfg. II
Lloyd Andreas, CPIM 1
Integrating Capacity Planning and Capacity Control
Bill Bell ....
Rough-Cut Capacity Planning—What It Is and How to Use It
Kenneth L. Campbell, CPIM 20
Vendor Capacity Planning: An Approach to Vendor Scheduling
Phillip J. Carter, CPIM, and Chwen-Yh Ho, CPIM 24
Capacity Management
James T. Clark, CPIM 33
Capacity Management—Part Two
James T. Clark, CPIM 39
Scheduling the Job Shop
R. L. Lankford, CPIM 46
Short-term Forecasts of Manufacturing Capacity
R. L. Lankford, CPIM 56
Job Shop Scheduling: A Case Study
Ray Lankford, CPIM, and Tim Moore 98
Priority Rhythm versus Thompson Planning
Hal Mather, CPIM, and George Plossl, CPIM 106
Capacity Planning and Control
George W. Plossl, CPIM, and Oliver Wight 131
Resource Requirements Planning and Capacity Requirements Planning—
The Case for Each and Both
E. John Sari, CPIM 158
Why the Process Industries Are Different
Sam G. Taylor, Samuel M. Seward, CPIM and Steven F. Bolander 171
Input/Output Control: A Real Handle on Lead Time
Oliver Wight 187

Capacity Management Committee
W. Bergen Junge, CFPIM (Chairman); George P. Adams, CPIM; Rick Bruun, CPIM; Merle L. Ehlers, CFPIM; Arthur Hill, Ph.D., CFPIM; Jerry A. Katz, CFPIM; Richard Kust, CFPIM; Ronald Pannesi, Ph.D., CPIM; Andrew Totten, CFPIM; Kenneth L. Trask, CFPIM

"40 DAYS TO THE DUE DATE" BY WILLY MAKEIT: THE ROLE OF CAPACITY MANAGEMENT IN MRP II
Lloyd Andreas, CPIM*
IBM Corporation

INTRODUCTION

Capacity is nothing more than a constraint on a manufacturing facility. In far too many cases, the impact of this constraint is not recognized or properly planned for. The pressures to sell more, produce more, and ship more product are constantly with us. In a growth environment, these are valid objectives. Management can and should be involved in a continuing process of planning these objectives and analyzing the requirements for resources needed to achieve the plans. The purpose of this paper is to present those areas of the planning process where capacity constraints need to be evaluated and to outline some of the techniques used in these evaluations.

CONTRASTING "CAPACITY" AND "LOAD"

The APICS Dictionary defines capacity as "the highest reasonable output rate which can be achieved with the current product specifications, product mix, work force, plant and equipment". Capacity in the manufacturing environment is a measure of output, usually expressed as the number of hours of production available over a specific time period such as a shift, day, week, or month. Facilities producing only a few products requiring equal resources per unit may define capacity in terms of units of production per period. In both cases, this rate of output must be achievable over extended periods, and it must be reasonable. If overstated or understated, plans may be implemented that either cannot be met or result in poor utilization of resources.

Capacity must be available to handle the load imposed by the manufacturing plans. "Load" is the amount of work scheduled to be done by a manufacturing facility. It is typically expressed as hours or units of production. Simply stated, load is work input to a resource. The capacity of the resource determines how much time is required to complete the work. The implication of these definitions is basic, yet often ignored: a manufacturing plan that exceeds capacity will not be achieved!

FACTORS AFFECTING CAPACITY

Capacity is rarely constant over time. A major function of management is to change capacity as required to meet the short, medium, and long-range plans of the company. To accomplish this, the requirements for capacity must be known, together with the available capacity. The required capacity can be derived from the business plans, production plans, master schedule, and the material requirements plan. Available capacity must be defined for a facility or each specific resource. There are many factors which affect capacity that can be planned. Other factors impacting capacity cannot be planned, but must be monitored continuously.

Planned factors include:

Land and space	Tooling
Labor force	Days worked per week
Facilities	Shifts worked per day
Machines	Overtime
Technology changes	Subcontracting
Manufacturing/Process changes	Alternate routings
	Preventive maintenance
Learning curves	Number of setups

Monitored factors include:

Unplanned orders	Absenteeism
Scrap and rework	Labor performance
Material shortages	Machine breakdowns
Excessive tooling problems	

The consequences of not planning or monitoring these factors carefully results in poor capacity plans and manufacturing schedules, usually evidenced by the following problems:

Bottlenecks	Late orders or shortages
Low productivity	Higher labor cost
Higher WIP investment	Extended lead times
Long progress meetings	Poor labor relations

The net effect of poor capacity management, however, is a decrease in profits and lowered return on investment!

CAPACITY MANAGEMENT AS A SYSTEM

Within the framework of MRP II, capacity management plays a vital role. By validating the feasibility of the manufacturing plans with respect to capacity in each stage of the planning process, major problems can be anticipated and avoided. This does not imply that capacity problems will not occur on a regular basis; they usually will. Through the use of effective capacity management techniques, however, these problems can be minimized and dealt with in an efficient manner.

Figure 1 outlines the major elements of capacity management and their place in MRP II. Each of these "subsystems" is employed at a different level of planning or execution. Only the first three will be discussed in this paper, even though all should be included either on a manual or automated basis to achieve the greatest benefit from an MRP II system.

CAPACITY MANAGEMENT IN MRP II
FUNCTIONAL RELATIONSHIPS

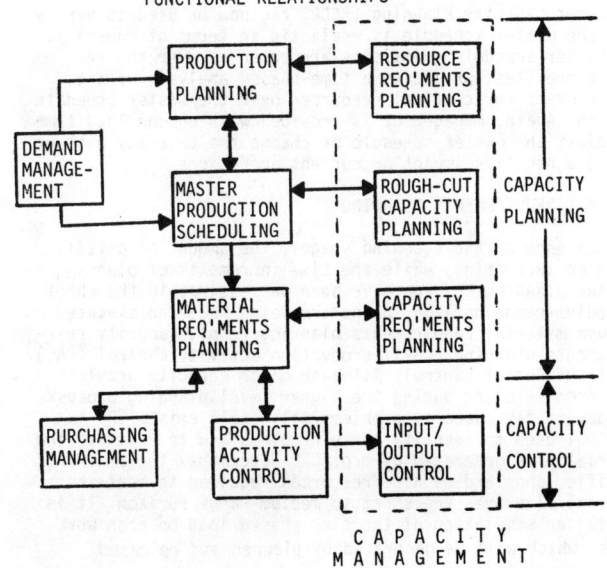

Figure 1

RESOURCE REQUIREMENTS PLANNING

The objective of Resource Requirements Planning (RRP) is to identify the aggregate level of major resources required to meet the Production Plan. The Production Plan is top management's operating lever; used to control the level of inventory or backlog, the stabilization of the work force, and the long-range direction of the business. These plans are reviewed and updated on a monthly or quarterly basis, with data aggregated at the product family level in monthly or quarterly time periods. Resource definition at this level is also an aggregation, with the critical groups of key resources being included in a resource profile. For example, rather than including each machining operation in the profile, the machining hours might be expressed as a total for a unit of the product family, weighted according to the average mix of the family's production. Other resource constraints which could be specified in the profile include labor hours, critical material, cubic feet of warehouse space, and transportation requirements. The construction of resource profiles requires experience and judgement together with analysis of the detailed routings for the items in a product family.

By extending the production plan quantities over the resource profiles, top management is presented with a picture of the requirements for critical resources throughout the planning horizon. This visibility allows management to adjust the plan or to procure additional resources with sufficient lead time, rather than "reacting" to severe resource limitations later.

ROUGH-CUT CAPACITY PLANNING

The Master Production Schedule is the implementation of the Production Plan. Where the Production Plan involved product families, covered a long (1-5 years) horizon, and planned in monthly or quarterly increments, the master schedule is much more detailed. The planning horizon is shorter, usually covering a period somewhat longer than the longest cumulative lead time of any product. The production quantities, timing, and mix of specific products is defined in the master schedule. With this increased level of detail, a more comprehensive capacity analysis can be made.

Resource profiles can be constructed for each master scheduled item, similar to the profiles used in RRP, but having a finer breakdown of resource groupings and the timing of their need relative to the master scheduled item. A resource profile can be generated using bill of material explosion logic and accessing the routing for the master scheduled item and each of its manufactured components at all levels of the product structure. Work centers in which the operations are performed can be grouped together under a "resource ID". As each routing is accessed, the scheduling of a standard lot size is simulated, and resource profile records created which specify the resource ID, quantity, and timing offset relative to the master scheduled item.

Rough-cut Capacity Planning (RCCP) can now be used to verify that the master schedule is realistic in terms of capacity. The master schedule quantities are extended over the resource profiles, producing a time-phased analysis of the requirements for critical resources over the master schedule horizon. Again, management is provided with enough lead time to adjust the master schedule or change the capacity without having a negative impact on current operations.

CAPACITY REQUIREMENTS PLANNING

Through each of the planning stages, the amount of detail has been increasing, while the time increments of planning and the planning horizon have been decreasing. In the short to medium-range horizon, plans are being made and executed through material requirements planning (mrp), capacity requirements planning (CRP), production activity control (PAC) and Input/Output Control. Although major capacity problems have been resolved during the higher level planning process, the day-to-day capacity problems will still exist. CRP is the tool used to identify those problems and to validate the material plan generated by mrp. CRP determines the amount of specific labor and machine resources required to meet the material plan over the short to medium-range horizon. It is a detailed simulation of the time-phased load on each work center which will be generated by planned and released (open) manufacturing orders.

INPUT TO CRP --- ORDER STATUS

Capacity requirements planning must deal with both planned and open orders to be most effective. If only one type or the other is used in CRP, an incomplete load picture will result. Exclusion of open orders distorts the analysis of capacity requirements in the near term. If planned or firm planned orders are not included, the load picture will become increasingly distorted from the present time through all future planning periods.

The open order data required by CRP includes:

- Order due date
- Order quantity remaining to be completed
- Operation status

Planned and firm planned orders should specify:

- Planned order release date
- Order due date
- Order quantity

INPUT TO CRP --- ROUTING DATA

CRP uses the standard routing for planned orders of an item and the specific routing for open orders currently in work-in-process. Routing data required by CRP includes:

- <u>Operation sequence</u>. The order in which the operations will be performed.
- <u>Planned work center</u>. The work center in which the operation will be performed. For open orders, the actual work center should be specified if the operation has started.
- <u>Performance standards</u>. These include the standard setup time, run time per unit, operation yield, and the time required to move the order to the operation from the previous operation.
- <u>Tool requirements</u>. Tooling required by an operation can be noted in the routing so that it can be included in a time-phased capacity plan.

The status of each operation on a released order must be known. This status should be continuously updated through feedback from the shop floor, and should specify whether or not the order has arrived at the operation, is being worked at the operation, or if the operation has been completed. If the operation is currently in process, the quantity yet to be completed must be specified.

CRP INPUT --- WORK CENTER DATA

The following information must be available for each work center:

- Rated capacity
- Primary scheduling constraint
- Performance standards
- Capacity allocation method
- Planned queue time

CRP determines the requirements for capacity by scheduling the operations of each order through the individual work centers. This requirement for capacity is then compared to the "available" capacity to identify potential overloads or underloads. A distinction must be made between "theoretical" capacity, "demonstrated" capacity, and "rated" capacity. If a machining center has 2 machines, and the company works one 8-hour shift, the "theoretical" capacity of the work center is 16 hours per day. By evaluating historical work center performance, it is found that over an extended period of time an average of only 10 standard hours of work per day have been produced by the work center. This is sometimes used as a measure of "demonstrated" capacity, but it can be misleading. The historical average really represents <u>output</u> of the work center. Actual or average output may not be a realistic measure of capacity because it is dependent not only on the capacity of the work center, but also on the input of work to the work center. If work does not exist at a work center, there will be no output. "Demonstrated" capacity should be evaluated over periods when a backlog of work was available at the work center.

"<u>Rated" capacity</u> can be calculated for use by CRP, and should approximate the demonstrated capacity. Figure 2 is used to illustrate the first step in these calculations.

CALCULATING WORK CENTER CAPACITY

WORK CENTER: W016 EFFICIENCY: 90% UTILIZATION: 80%
SCHEDULING CONSTRAINT: LABOR PLANNED QUEUE: 3 DAYS

SHIFT NO.	HOURS	NO. OF EMPLOYEES	NO. OF MACHINES	SHIFT CAPACITY
1	8	6	6	48 HOURS
2	8	4	6	32 "
3	0	0	6	0 "

"THEORETICAL" AVAILABLE CAP'Y   80 HOURS/DAY

Figure 2

The primary scheduling constraint in this work center is labor. Even though 6 machines are always available, an operator is needed full-time to run one machine. Only four machines are used on the second shift, and none on the last.

Producing 80 standard hours of work in this work center over any length of time is an unrealistic expectation. To determine an achievable rated capacity, <u>performance factors</u> must be applied. The first factor is <u>efficiency</u>.

$$\text{EFFICIENCY} = \frac{\text{STANDARD HOURS EARNED}}{\text{DIRECT LABOR HOURS}}$$

Efficiency can be monitored through feedback from the shop floor. Efficiency for both the current production period and an average over time can be maintained. In calculating rated capacity, however, a "planned" efficiency is typically used. This technique allows management to use efficiency as a policy variable, and to plan increases (or decreases) in efficiency.

A second factor which should be applied to available capacity is <u>utilization</u>.

$$\text{UTILIZATION} = \frac{\text{DIRECT LABOR HOURS}}{\text{ATTENDANCE HOURS}}$$

A common mistake in determining utilization based on historical data is the inclusion of time when no work was available. If a work center sits idle because of lack of work, its utilization will be lowered. In reality, its <u>capacity</u> was not affected. In the calculation of rated capacity, "planned" utilization should be used, taking into account the time allotted to breaks, rework, maintenance, and other activities resulting in a loss of production.

If the primary constraint in a work center is machine time rather than labor, then the direct labor hours and attendance hours should be replaced by the machine hours used in direct production and the available machine hours in the formulas for efficiency and utilization.

Applying efficiency and utilization to the "theoretical" capacity yields the rated capacity which is used by CRP. Using the data from Figure 2:

AVAILABLE CAPACITY	=	80 HOURS/DAY
X EFFICIENCY (90%)		.90
		72 HOURS/DAY
X UTILIZATION (80%)		.80
= RATED CAPACITY		57.6 HOURS/DAY

Two more data elements associated with work centers are required by CRP in order to schedule each operation: the <u>capacity allocation method</u> and the <u>planned queue time</u>.

In the example being used, 57.6 daily hours of capacity are available in work center W016. The capacity allocation method specifies how much of that capacity, <u>on the average</u>, will be allocated to a single order for CRP scheduling purposes. The amount of capacity actually used by an order on the shop floor will vary based on the order's priority. CRP has to make an assumption as to the number of hours that will be spent working on a single job in each work center.

<u>Average daily scheduling hours</u> is a very effective approach for most machine-oriented work centers, and some assembly centers. This method allocates the rated daily capacity equally to the largest number of orders that can be run concurrently in the work center, assuming one order per machine or employee. In the example from Figure 2, based on a labor constraint, 6 orders can be run on the first shift. Dividing the rated daily capacity of 57.6 hours by the largest number of concurrent jobs (6) yields average daily scheduling hours of 9.6 . Using this method, an operation scheduled through this work center having 19.2 hours of work to be completed would require 2 days of operation time to be scheduled.

In work centers where multiple people or machines are normally assigned to a single order, scheduling may be more realistic using a specific <u>number of resources per job</u>. This method calculates daily scheduling hours by multiplying the resources/job times the sum of the active shift lengths. Efficiency and utilization are then applied. Again using the example in Figure 2, with a capacity allocation of 2 people per job:

SHIFT 1	=	8 HOURS
SHIFT 2	=	8 HOURS
TOTAL SHIFT LENGTHS	=	16 HOURS
X RESOURCES PER JOB		2
		32
X EFFICIENCY (90%)		.90
		28.8
X UTILIZATION (80%)		.80
= DAILY SCHEDULING HOURS		23

The result of these calculations should always be checked to ensure that it does not exceed the rated daily capacity.

A third method of capacity allocation for CRP scheduling is the use of the <u>sum of the rated shift lengths</u>. This approach is similar to the average daily scheduling hours technique in that it assumes that an order will be run on only one machine or worked on by only one person. If the number of people or machines is the same on all active shifts it will yield the same result. In calculating this number, the sum of the active shift lengths is multiplied by the work center efficiency and utilization. In the previous example, the result would be 11.5 daily scheduling hours.

The objective of using daily scheduling hours in CRP is to smooth the load in a realistic manner based on how each work center usually works on jobs. It is not "finite" loading, but merely an attempt to apply some limits to CRP's infinite loading techniques. This subject will be addressed further in the discussion about scheduling rules.

The last element of work center data required by CRP is the <u>planned queue time</u>, normally expressed in days. Simply stated, the queue is the backlog of work present at a work center, waiting for work to be started. The amount of time that an order waits in the queue is the queue time. This time will vary in actual practice. The actual queue time of an order is a function of the work center capacity and the priority of the order. From a CRP perspective, priorities are not considered in scheduling and the actual queue time for any order is not known. CRP therefore uses a planned queue time. Even though current queue times and average queue times can be updated for each work center by constant feedback from the shop floor, these values should not be used by CRP. Planned queue time can be used as a management policy variable to aid in controlling queues and lead times. Planned queue time is the "average" length of time that management wants any order to sit in a queue at a work center.

CRP INPUT --- SCHEDULING RULES

In addition to the data discussed previously, CRP requires a set of <u>scheduling rules</u>. Two major approaches to scheduling orders are most often used in automated CRP systems; <u>forward scheduling</u> and <u>backward scheduling</u>. Both methods have advantages and disadvantages. Before addressing the detail of each method, a few misconceptions regarding CRP should be discussed.

<u>CRP uses infinite loading techniques</u>. CRP is <u>not</u> a "finite" scheduling system, but does use limits in its scheduling process. Obviously, if capacity were truly infinite, queues would not exist and an order would be completed in the time required to make one piece, even if millions of pieces were required. Infinite loading refers to the approach in which <u>CRP schedules individual orders without regard to order priority, other orders planned or in process, or the load generated on any work center by other orders</u>. Almost every aspect of the planning and execution of MRP II systems is centered around "due dates". To be effective as a planning tool, CRP should provide a picture of capacity requirements that:

- Is aligned to order due dates
- Has no "past due" load
- Is based on work being performed according to standard move, queue, setup, and run times.

In effect, CRP should answer the question: "If all planned and open orders are to be completed by their due dates, assuming current status and planned work standards, what capacity is required by each work center over the time span from today until the end of the planning horizon?". CRP's scheduling and loading process determines the amount and timing of these requirements.

In forward scheduling (Figure 3), each order is scheduled beginning "today" or, if not yet started, on its future planned start date. Using the order status, routing, and work center data, CRP schedules move, queue, setup and run time for each operation. Setup and run time for an operation is accumulated for the work center in which the operation is performed. The duration of the setup and run time in days is based on the capacity allocation method specified for the work center.

A major problem exists when CRP uses a forward scheduling technique: the load of orders ahead of or behind schedule is not aligned to the order due dates. If all orders were be-

CAPACITY MANAGEMENT REPRINTS—Revised Edition

FORWARD SCHEDULING

```
TODAY                           DUE        SCHEDULED
                                DATE       COMPLETION
                                           DATE
┌──────┬──────┬──────┬──────┬──────┬──────┐
│ MOVE │OPN 10│ MOVE │OPN 20│ MOVE │OPN 30│
│  &   │SETUP │  &   │SETUP │  &   │SETUP │
│QUEUE │& RUN │QUEUE │& RUN │QUEUE │& RUN │
└──────┴──────┴──────┴──────┴──────┴──────┘
SCHEDULING PROCESS ──────────────►
                              └─ INVALID LOAD ─┘
                                    TIMING
```
Figure 3

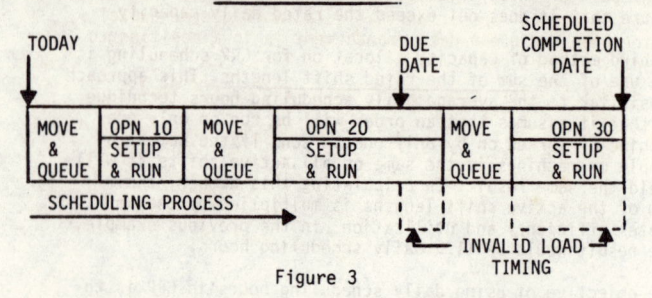

hind schedule as in Figure 3, a load picture might result which shows no overloaded or underloaded work centers. To meet the due dates, however, all work scheduled later than the due dates would have to be performed prior to those dates, resulting in severe actual overloads. In the example, the load from all 3 operations would have to occur earlier than shown if the due date is to be met. CRP ignores due dates when forward scheduling, resulting in the projected load being shown in earlier or later time periods than it will probably occur for orders ahead of or behind schedule.

BACKWARD SCHEDULING

```
                                            DUE
          TODAY                             DATE
┌──────┬──────┬──────┬──────┬──────┬──────┐
│ MOVE │OPN 10│ MOVE │OPN 20│ MOVE │OPN 30│
│  &   │SETUP │  &   │SETUP │  &   │SETUP │
│QUEUE │& RUN │QUEUE │& RUN │QUEUE │& RUN │
└──────┴──────┴──────┴──────┴──────┴──────┘
     └─ INVALID LOAD ──┘
          TIMING          ◄────── SCHEDULING PROCESS
```
Figure 4

Backward scheduling is similar to forward scheduling, except that it begins scheduling an order on the order due date, schedules the last operation first, then each preceding operation, as shown in Figure 4. This is the reason backward scheduling is usually recommended for CRP; all load is aligned to the due dates of the orders. As illustrated in Figure 4, however, backward scheduling also has some drawbacks. Orders that are behind schedule, or planned for release with inadequate lead time, may have some of their work scheduled prior to "today"; in the past. Contrary to continuing beliefs and efforts, work cannot be done on an order "yesterday". To meet the due date in the example, operation 10 will have to start today, resulting in a shift in timing of the later operations. A distorted picture of projected load can easily be developed using backward scheduling, although there is an advantage to this approach. The identification of "past due load" can assist management in evaluating short-term capacity problems.

QUEUE ADJUSTMENT

The problems associated with forward and backward scheduling can be resolved through the use of queue adjustment. These techniques are based on the concept that actual queue time is a function of priority. Orders ahead of schedule have a lower priority and will tend to spend more time in queues. Orders behind schedule will be expedited, spending less time in queues. Priorities are developed for released orders by the production activity control system, using forward or backward scheduling techniques similar to CRP. As mentioned previously, the objective of CRP is to schedule all orders so that 1) all load is aligned to order due dates, and 2) no load is scheduled in the past. Queue adjustment is used to accomplish these objectives. To use queue adjustment, orders must be scheduled twice. The order is first scheduled in either a forward or backward manner to determine the following:

- *Scheduled queue time.* This is the sum of the planned queue time for all operations that are not completed or in process.
- *Days off schedule.* This value represents the number of days the order is ahead of or behind schedule. In forward scheduling, it is the difference between the order due date and the forward scheduled completion date. In backward scheduling, it is the difference between the backward scheduled start date of the first non-completed operation and "today". This value may be negative.
- *Total slack.* The total slack is the sum of the scheduled queue time and the days off schedule. It is the amount of time that an order can actually sit in queues and still meet the due date based on using standard setup and run time.
- *Queue adjustment factor.* This is defined as the total slack divided by the scheduled queue time. It can be viewed as a percent of planned queue time that the order can actually incur and still meet the due date.

Figure 5 is an example of queue adjustment calculations for several orders which have been forward scheduled.

ORDER NO.	DUE DATE	SCHEDULED COMPLETION	DAYS OFF SCHEDULE	SCHEDULED QUEUE	TOTAL SLACK	Q ADJ. FACTOR
1	12/18	1/14	-20	15	-5	*
2	11/30	12/04	-4	10	+6	.60
3	11/28	11/28	0	12	+12	1.00
4	12/20	12/16	+4	8	+12	1.50
5	12/14	11/20	+18	14	+32	2.29

Figure 5

In scheduling the orders a second time, the planned queue at each operation is multiplied by the order's queue adjustment factor. This results in scheduled queues being expanded or compressed so that the order fits between "today" (or its future release date) and its due date. If total slack is negative, as in order no. 1 of Figure 5, the order cannot be expected to complete on time without special handling. Such an order should be forward scheduled without scheduling any queue time, and flagged for management attention.

Using the queue adjustment factor in CRP scheduling will compress or expand planned queues by a constant factor. Another queue adjustment technique may be used based on the days off schedule.

If an order is ahead of schedule (orders no. 4 and 5 in Fig. 5), the days ahead of schedule can be added to the planned queue for the first operation not started. Scheduling would use the planned queue for successive operations. For those orders behind schedule, no queue time would be scheduled by CRP until the days behind schedule are recovered. For example, if order no. 2 has 4 operations remaining, with planned queue times of 3 days for the first operation and 2 days for the second, no queue time would be scheduled for the first operation and only 1 day for the second. The third and fourth operations would be scheduled with the planned queue time for each.

Through the use of queue adjustment techniques in CRP, a more realistic picture of projected load on each work center can be constructed. These techniques can be applied using either a forward or backward scheduling method, and consider to some degree the priority of each order.

Figure 6 illustrates the effect of queue adjustment on an order that is in process and behind schedule. Figure 7 shows the same effect on an order that is ahead of schedule. The result of forward scheduling, backward scheduling, and the application of queue adjustment using both a factor and the days off schedule is shown in each example.

QUEUE ADJUSTMENT --- ORDER BEHIND SCHEDULE

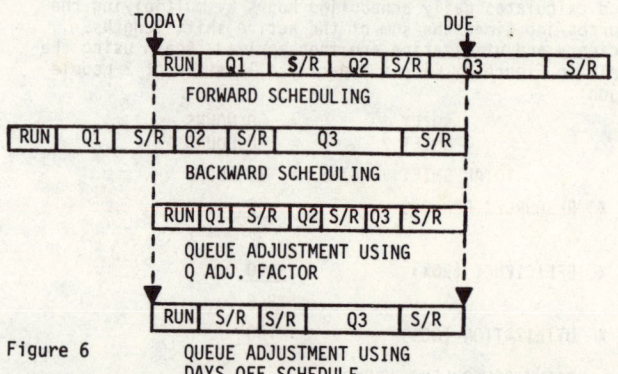

```
       TODAY                                    DUE
        │                                        │
        ┌───┬───┬───┬───┬───┬───┐
        │RUN│ Q1│S/R│ Q2│S/R│ Q3│ S/R
        └───┴───┴───┴───┴───┴───┘
           FORWARD SCHEDULING
┌───┬───┬───┬───┬─────┬───┐
│RUN│Q1 │S/R│Q2 │ Q3  │S/R│
└───┴───┴───┴───┴─────┴───┘
           BACKWARD SCHEDULING
        ┌───┬──┬───┬──┬───┬───┬───┐
        │RUN│Q1│S/R│Q2│S/R│ Q3│S/R│
        └───┴──┴───┴──┴───┴───┴───┘
           QUEUE ADJUSTMENT USING
           Q ADJ. FACTOR
        ┌───┬───┬───┬─────┬───┐
        │RUN│S/R│S/R│ Q3  │S/R│
        └───┴───┴───┴─────┴───┘
Figure 6    QUEUE ADJUSTMENT USING
            DAYS OFF SCHEDULE
```

QUEUE ADJUSTMENT --- ORDER AHEAD OF SCHEDULE

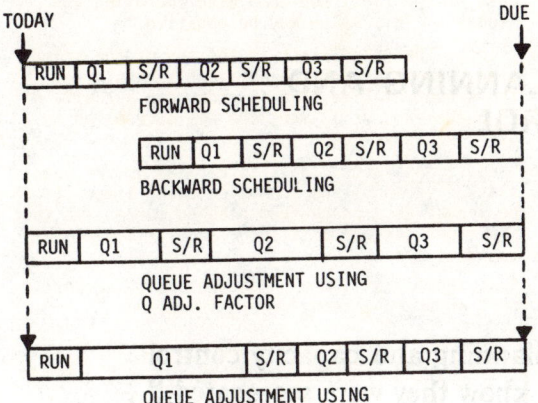

```
TODAY                                           DUE
 |                                               |
 | RUN | Q1 | S/R | Q2 | S/R | Q3 | S/R |
         FORWARD SCHEDULING

        | RUN | Q1 | S/R | Q2 | S/R | Q3 | S/R |
                BACKWARD SCHEDULING

 | RUN | Q1  | S/R |  Q2  | S/R |  Q3  | S/R |
         QUEUE ADJUSTMENT USING
         Q ADJ. FACTOR

 | RUN |  Q1  | S/R | Q2 | S/R | Q3 | S/R |
         QUEUE ADJUSTMENT USING
         DAYS OFF SCHEDULE
```

Figure 7

OUTPUT OF CAPACITY REQUIREMENTS PLANNING

At the completion of CRP's scheduling process, the time-phased load calculated for each work center can be presented in various numerical and graphical formats. The potential overload and underload conditions at each work center can be easily identified, as shown in Figure 8.

LOAD PROFILE
WORK CENTER: W016

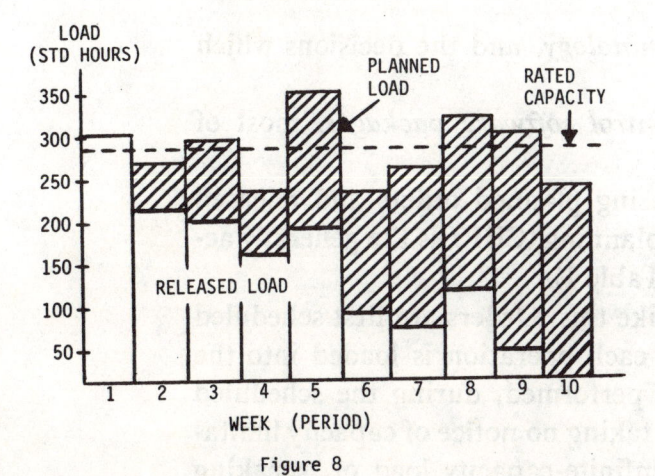

[Bar chart showing LOAD (STD HOURS) on y-axis from 0 to 350, WEEK (PERIOD) on x-axis from 1 to 10, with PLANNED LOAD, RELEASED LOAD, and RATED CAPACITY indicated]

Figure 8

In addition to showing a summarized load profile, CRP should also present the detail that makes up the load. This data should be available in a report or through online inquiries, and for each work center should identify by time period each order and operation that was scheduled. By having available the order status, operation load data, work center capacity, performance and queue data, management is in a position to answer the questions:

- Which orders (and operations) make up the load?
- Where are the orders currently?
- Which orders can be pulled up quickly, or deferred?
- Where are the bottlenecks?
- Are order due dates valid and realistic?
- Are planned queue times realistic?
- How much load is "past due"?
- <u>Is overall capacity available to meet the materials plan</u>?

If an effective job of managing capacity has been done at the higher levels of planning (Resource Requirements Planning and Rough-cut Capacity Planning), the problems identified through CRP should be minor, and should not prevent the materials plan from being achieved. The overload/underload conditions discovered using CRP can usually be resolved by "fine-tuning". Only in rare instances should changes be required in the master schedule or production plans.

CHANGING CAPACITY

Capacity or resource problems encountered at any level of planning can easily be resolved by changing the production plan or the master schedule. In fact, changing the timing or the levels of production is a fundamental part of the planning process. The role of capacity management is to verify that these plans are realistic. The point remains, however, that the master schedule and production plans are put in place to meet the overall business plans of the company. If capacity constraints prevent that, then capacity must be increased (or decreased). Common approaches used to vary capacity, based on the lead time available, include:

LONG RANGE (PRODUCTION PLANNING/RRP)
  Change land or facilities
  Change capital equipment
  Change work force level or skills

MEDIUM RANGE (MASTER SCHEDULING/ROUGH-CUT)
  Change make/buy decisions   Reallocate work force
  Plan alternate routings   Change work force level
  Subcontract (long periods)   Add additional tooling

SHORT RANGE (MRP/CRP/Input-Output Control)
  Schedule overtime   Select alternate routings
  Subcontract (short periods) Reallocate work force

SUMMARY

MRP II systems allow a company to <u>plan</u> for the future in an intelligent manner; to resolve major crises before they happen, rather than <u>reacting</u> after they occur or at a point in time when corrective action becomes counter-productive. Capacity management plays a vital role in MRP II, providing all levels of management with <u>visibility</u> into the future and a better understanding of what is required to meet the short, medium, and long-range plans of the business.

About the author

Lloyd Andreas is currently a product planner in the Industrial Sector Product Planning Department of IBM in Atlanta, Georgia. In this position, he is responsible for defining and validating the functional content of IBM's MAPICS manufacturing software. A graduate of California Lutheran College, Lloyd has been with IBM for fifteen years. He has worked with a wide range of manufacturing clients in previous positions in Sales, Systems Engineering, and as a Manufacturing Industry Specialist. Lloyd has made numerous presentations on manufacturing topics at local seminars and national conferences sponsored by IBM. He has attained APICS certification at the Fellow level, and has conducted certification workshops on mrp and production activity control for the Atlanta chapter. In addition, Lloyd serves on the Inventory Management Committee of the APICS Curricula and Certification Council.

INTEGRATING CAPACITY PLANNING AND CAPACITY CONTROL

Bill Belt
Honeywell
Paris, France

When the question of integrating capacity planning and capacity control arises, someone may remark, "Really? I didn't know they were segregated." In fact, those production control practitioners who seek to integrate the capacity *planning* function using the technique of machine loading/capacity requirements planning with the capacity *control* function using the technique of input/output control find that some problems pop up in trying to mesh the former's load-vs.-capacity graphs with the latter's inputs, outputs, and deviations.

A look at integration, then, would be helpful for three reasons:
1) *Uniting the techniques* used for the capacity planning and capacity control functions;
2) *Straightening out some snarled terminology*, and the decisions which flow from it; and
3) *Enhancing standard production control software packages*, most of which offer only Machine Loading.

Machine loading to infinite capacity using planned orders and released orders, also called capacity requirements planning (CRP), is the generally accepted method of capacity planning. (See Table 1).

Briefly, Machine Loading/CRP works like this: Orders are first scheduled by operation, then the work content for each operation is loaded into the work center where the operation will be performed, during the scheduled time period. Doing this for all orders, and taking no notice of capacity limitations of the work centers, produces an infinite-capacity load or, speaking more modernly, a capacity requirements plan. Table 2 shows such a plan.

	Priorities	Capacities	
Plan	Material Requirements Planning	Capacity Requirements Planning	(= machine Loading planned and released orders to infinite capacity)
Control	Dispatching	Input/Output Control	

Table 1 — Basic Techniques of A Production Control System

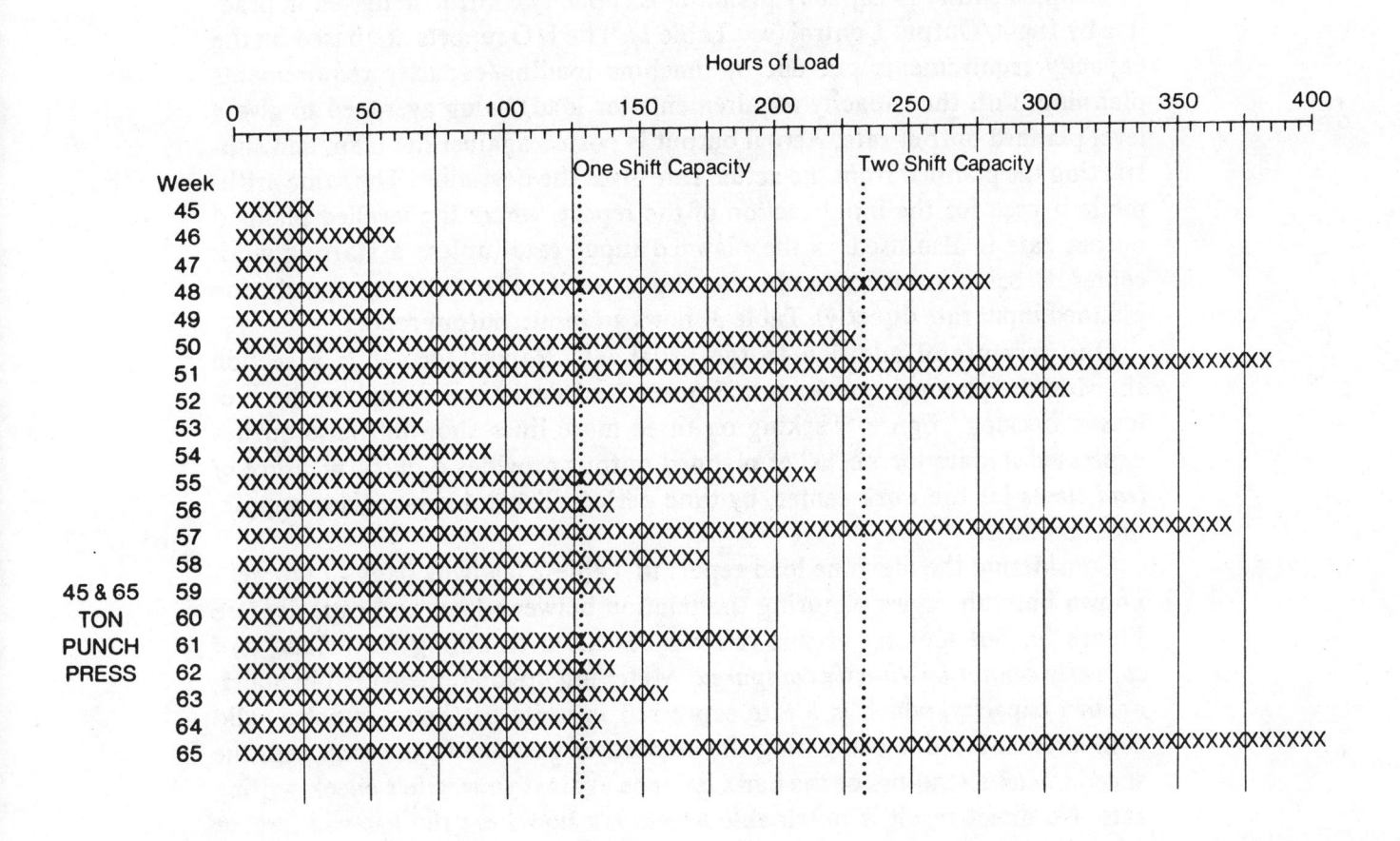

Week	Load Hours
45	32
46	64
47	37
48	284
49	69
50	232
51	389
52	311
53	74
54	99
55	216
56	142
57	374
58	179
59	142
60	105
61	200
62	142
63	163
64	137
65	405

Table 2 — Infinite Machine Load Projection or Capacity Requirements Plan

Complementary to capacity planning is capacity control, achieved in practice by Input/Output Control (see Table 1). The I/O reports are based on the capacity requirements put out by machine loading/capacity requirements planning, with the capacity requirements (or load) being averaged to give a level planned output rate. Actual output is posted against the plan, and subtracting the planned from the actual rate gives the deviation. The same arithmetic is used for the input section of the report, where the levelled planned output rate is also used as the planned input rate (unless a starting work center is being measured, wherein the capacity planner may specify the planned input rate directly). Table 3 shows an input/output report.

One very useful addition to the usual I/O Report format is a section showing the planned queue, actual queue and deviation to replace the "released backlog" figure. Tacking on three more lines showing these queues expressed in days (or weeks) of planned output provides *a quick measure of lead times* for the work center, by time period. Table 4 shows these supplementary lines.

Considering the machine load report in Table 2 leads us back to the well-known bathtub figure picturing the relation between load and capacity (see Figure 5). But looking at this relation reveals a troubling fact: *Load and capacity cannot be directly compared.* Matching up load, measured in hours, against capacity, which is a rate expressed in units per hour, is not a valid comparison. It's like comparing the amount of gasoline in the tank with the speedometer's reading, or the bank balance against your wife's check-writing rate. No direct result is obtainable unless it's how long the gas will last, or when it will be time to leave town, and each of these conclusions even requires an additional calculation.

Load, measured in unit hours or pieces or jobs, means only one thing: the amount of work resident in a work center. It is the waiting line, the queue or backlog, the level of water in the tub. Planned (or actual) load corresponds to the planned (or actual) queue and, when divided by the output rate, gives the planned (or actual) lead time. From Tables 3 and 4:

$$\frac{\text{Planned Queue}}{\text{Planned Normal Output Rate}} = \frac{320 \text{ hours}}{160 \frac{\text{hours}}{\text{week}}} = \frac{2 \text{ weeks planned}}{\text{lead time}}$$

What then do the numbers on the machine load report represent, if not load? Recalling their origin, we see that they are the rate at which material requirements planning will input work to the shop. These figures may be seen as *additions* to a work center's load (not the load itself) and properly speaking, they should appear as planned input on the input/output report, in the time period when the work arrives in the work center to become part of the queue thereafter.

	End of Week	45	46	47	48	49	50	51	52	53	54
Unreleased Backlog 0	Planned Input	160	160	160	160	160	160	160	160	160	160
	Actual Input	160	155	140							
	Cumulative Deviation	0	-5	-25							
Released Backlog* 420 hours	Planned Output	300	300	300	160	160	160	160	160	160	160
	Actual Output	305	260	280							
	Cumulative Deviation	+5	-35	-55							

Note: 1. Planned output rate is an average of recent performance.
    2. Normal capacity is 160 hours per week, but overtime is planned in the first three weeks to work off excessive backlog.
    3. Planned input rate has been set equal to the normal planned output rate, as is customarily done.

*Above desired level of work-in-process (standard queue) at this work center as of start of plan.

Table 3 — Input/Output Report

End of Week	44	45	46	47	48	49	50	51	52	53	54
Planned Queue	320	320	320	320	320	320	320	320	320	320	320
Actual Queue	740	595	490	350							
Deviation*	+420	+275	+170	+30							
Planned Queue in Weeks of Output	2.0	2.0	2.0	2.0	2.0	2.0	2.0	2.0	2.0	2.0	2.0
Actual Queue in Weeks of Output	4.6	3.7	3.1	2.2							
Deviation*	+2.6	+1.7	+1.1	+0.2							

*Cumulative deviation is not meaningful for queues, which are not rates of flow like input and output, but simply the "level" of work.

Table 4 — Supplementary queue measurement section to input/output report

CAPACITY MANAGEMENT REPRINTS—Revised Edition

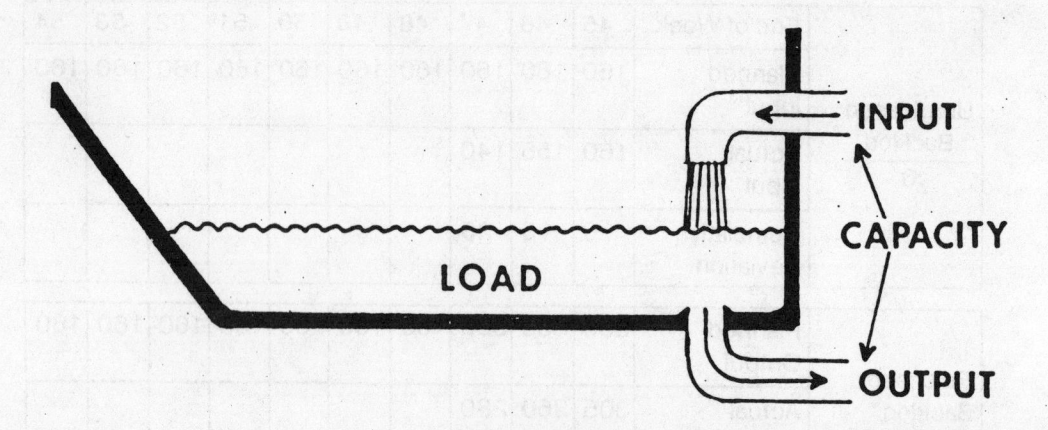

Figure 5 — Relating Load and Capacity

Capacity, on the other hand, is the rate of production, equivalent to the planned output line on the I/O Report. These definitions are summarized in Table 6:

Machine Loading Terminology	Input/Output Terminology
load	planned input
capacity	planned output

Table 6 — Relating machine load and input/output terminology

So what is really being measured on machine load reports is planned input (called load, which it certainly is not) and planned output (called capacity) vs. time. The object is to match "load" and capacity, which really means equating the planned input with the planned output rate. Is this a valid objective? *Only if the backlog should remain fixed at its present level.* Because that is the only possible result if the amount of work that is input to a work center is made equal to the work that is output.

The problem with using machine loading to plan capacity then is twofold: 1) it confuses in the capacity planner's mind the ideas of load, capacity and input, and 2) it more or less ignores the existence of backlog and its planned evolution in the future. Input/output reports used to control capacity avoid these problems entirely because they show all the information required, in a concise and understandable format, by time period, as illustrated in Tables 3 and 4.

The question that must be asked is the following: since input/output is used to control capacity, and since machine loading shows some obvious defects in planning capacity, *why not adapt the input/output technique to plan capacity as well as to control it?* At least, nothing will be lost; we have seen that machine loading is a subset of I/O reports; the information appearing on a machine load report (basically "load" and capacity) is also found on an input/output report as planned input and planned output. And the I/O Report gives future backlog visibility in addition, through its planned queue line (see Table 4).

As a first exercise using this new tool, which might be called input/output planning, as the planning counterpart to input/output control, let us slot the machine load data in Table 2 directly into the I/O format. Table 7 shows the results of doing this.

Here a rather difficult problem appears. Notice the way the planned queue/planned lead time jumps around (see Weeks 44 and 47 in Table 7). A perceptive production planner would recognize that the fixed planned lead time of two weeks in the MRP system would not really be valid anytime during the period from Weeks 44 through 50, and that system lead times should be altered accordingly. Of course this means that the MRP system would have to replan the schedule and the load using the new planned lead times, thus producing a new and different line of planned input on the I/O Report and a new and different line of planned queue/planned lead time! If this logic were followed unwaveringly, endless iterations would result (see Figure 8).

This vicious circle is characteristic of the necessity of fitting a variable workload into the finite capacity of the shop. The fact is that we are faced with this kind of self-reinforcing difficulty because inventory planning systems generate work to be done at a rate which has little to do with the rate at which the plant can do it (with the possible exception of very highly engineered flow shops). Because the thousands of input rates represented by the amount of work to be performed by time period on each operation of each production order are just plain different from the thousands of output rates possible on the hundreds of machines in the factory, with different tooling possibilities, different operators, varied maintenance schedules, different age of equipment, etc., exact matches between requirements and capacity are impossible to achieve. So finite-loading logic seeks refuge in complex priorities, so input/output planning presents us with the round-robin of problems in Figure 8.

But, after all, that is reality, we should be expecting it, capacity needs and capacity availability are going to clash directly somewhere. It's where the rubber meets the road.

The advantage of input/output planning is that it states the problem in terms of essentials, leaves out nothing of importance, and presents the alter-

INPUT/OUTPUT PLAN—WORK CENTER 100
(all figures in standard hours except where noted)

PLANNED LEAD TIME: 2 WEEKS ± 1 WEEK   TODAY'S DATE: END OF WEEK 44

End of Week	44	45	46	47	48	49	50	51	52	53	54
Planned Input	—	32	64	37	284	69	232	389	311	74	99
Planned Output	—	300	300	300	160	160	160	160	160	160	160
Planned Queue*	740	472	236	0	124	33	105	334	485	399	338
Planned Queue in Weeks of Output	4.6	3.0	1.5	0.0	0.8	0.2	0.7	2.1	3.0	2.5	2.1

Source of numbers: Planned Input = standard hours (load) from Table 2
Planned Output = planned output (capacity) from Table 3 (based on history)
Planned Queue = Previous week's queue + Planned Input − Planned Output
Planned Queue in weeks of Output = Planned Queue ÷ normal Planned Output

*Equals actual queue for the first week of the plan

Table 7 — Input/output plan

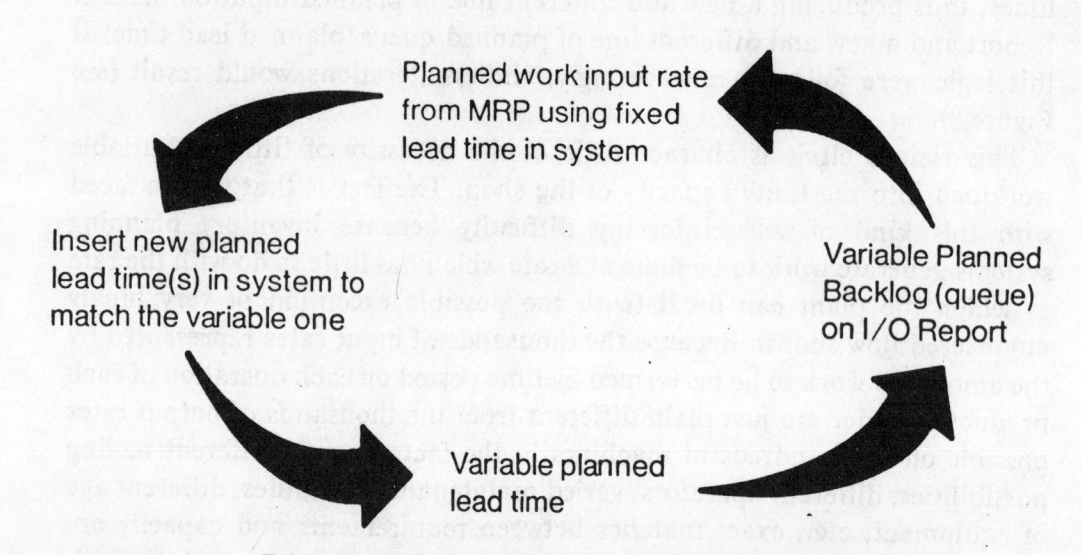

Figure 8 — A Vicious Circle to Avoid in Capacity Planning

(Cycle: Planned work input rate from MRP using fixed lead time in system → Variable Planned Backlog (queue) on I/O Report → Variable planned lead time → Insert new planned lead time(s) in system to match the variable one → ...)

natives to the human capacity planner in a straightforward and precise format that he can comprehend readily **and act on.**

Returning to the numbers in Table 7, which depict an undesirable situation—but one which will occur in work center 100 unless action is taken—and the vicious circle in Figure 8, which underlines the difficulty of taking action, what should the capacity planner do?

First, he should take the only way of breaking vicious circles—attack them at every point he can. Second, he should keep in mind the fundamental incompatibility among the inventory system's rates and those of his production facilities and seek not the impossible exact solution but a reasonable one which will do the job. One which does not let backlogs change excessively, which keeps lead time variability within reasonable bounds, which doesn't invalidate planned lead times in the MRP system by too much, and which doesn't require a whole lot of pulling in and pushing out of orders created by MRP. Rather than running and diving straight at the "greased pigs" of capacity planning, the sensible planner surrounds them and closes in step by step, and stops when they are sufficiently cornered!

Capacity-planning Work Center 100 based on the data in Table 7 might proceed as follows:

1) Planned lead time is two weeks, which means that the planned queue should be brought down to around 320 standard hours:

$$\genfrac{}{}{0pt}{}{\text{Planned Lead}}{\text{Time}} \times \genfrac{}{}{0pt}{}{\text{Planned Normal}}{\text{Output Rate}} = \genfrac{}{}{0pt}{}{\text{Planned}}{\text{Queue}}$$

$$2 \text{ weeks} \times 160 \frac{\text{hours}}{\text{week}} = 320 \text{ hours}$$

2) A lead time variability of plus or minus one week is considered tolerable. So the planned queue in weeks of output can vary from one week to three weeks (160 – 480 hours). Any greater variability is unacceptable. Hence Weeks 44 and 47 – 50 are tagged for rectifying action.

3) The existing backlog of 740 hours (in Week 44, the week of the report) is more than double the desired queue of 320 hours. Overtime in the first three weeks has already been scheduled to work off the 420 excess hours. But this is also a period of low input, and the backlog will soon be driven below the minimum of 1.0 weeks worth of work.

4) A trial is made to stabilize backlog fluctuations by eliminating overtime in Weeks 46 and 47. The planner calculates the new input/output plan, probably by hand since the computations are simple (see Table 9).

5) Now the backlog in Weeks 51–54 is excessive. Perhaps the planned input of 389 hours in Week 51 could be reduced by moving forward some orders into other weeks, if their components are available, or by rerouting some jobs to alternate work centers. But increasing planned output is simpler at this point, particularly in a week nearly two months in the future, since the next MRP run may produce a different input schedule. (Close-in weeks should not show excessive variation from one MRP run to the next if demand changes are buffered at the master schedule level.) So the capacity planner tests the results of planning overtime in Week 51, again by making the calculations manually (see Table 10).

6) Capacity planning probably would stop at this point since the planned queues in Weeks 52 – 53, some two months in the future, exceed the maximum tolerance level of three weeks but slightly, and planned input drops off in Weeks 53 – 54. Even on the shop floor, a temporary slight

INPUT/OUTPUT PLAN — WORK CENTER 100
PLANNED LEAD TIME — 2 WEEKS ±1 WEEK
(All figures in standard hours except where noted)

TODAY'S DATE: END OF WEEK 44

End of Week	44	45	46	47	48	49	50	51	52	53	54
Planned Input		32	64	37	284	69	232	389	311	74	99
Planned Output		300	160	160	160	160	160	160	160	160	160
Planned Queue	740	472	376	253	377	286	358	587	738	652	591
Planned Queue in Weeks of Output	4.6	3.0	2.4	1.6	2.4	1.8	2.2	3.7	4.6	4.1	3.7

Source of numbers: same as in Table 7 except for capacity planner's trial elimination of overtime in Planned Output in Weeks 46 and 47.

Table 9 — Revised Input/Output Plan

End of Week	50	51	52	53	54
Planned Input	232	389	311	74	99
Planned Output	160	300	160	160	160
Planned Queue	358	447	598	512	451
Planned Queue in Weeks of Output	2.2	2.8	3.7	3.2	2.8

Table 10 — Revised Input/Output Plan

excess of load such as that could properly be handled inside a work center by sequencing jobs using the shortest processing time rule or by running back-to-back all jobs using the same setup.

This example showed the easy way out, by adjusting output (capacity) rates. Had this not been possible, the planner would have been obliged to shift input backwards or forwards by a few time periods (smoothing). This is done by first picking out some jobs whose combined workload equals the reduction or addition in load necessary to drive the queue into its allowable range. If the jobs are moved *in*, the planner must look *down-level* to verify the availability of components to start the parent orders sooner than originally planned. If the jobs are pushed *out* in time, the planner must look *up-level*, tracing the where-used cases of the jobs to find out whether the delay can be absorbed at the sub-assembly or assembly level or whether a reschedule out is required there too. Such an analysis could lead all the way up to the master schedule due dates, in the case where the intermediate-level queues would be pushed out of their allowable range of variation in attempting to absorb the delay. Also, lead times cannot be compressed below the minimum time needed to perform the work! In any case, the planner fixes the new due date or start date at the highest level affected, and this date modification must be reexploded by MRP to update the due dates of all the lower-level orders in the particular replenishment "network".

Consider the difference between the input/output planning approach and machine loading. To identify overloads and underloads, machine loading would compare only the "load" with capacity. That is, it would line up the planned input line in Table 7 with the planned output line. If input exceeds output, an "overload" is signalled. If output is more than input, an "underload" results. I/O Planning, on the other hand, recognizes overloads and underloads when the planned queue goes above or below the target level—which is the way the shop sees it too.

Compare the action recommended by the two methods week by week, using the data in Table 7. The results of this comparison are shown in Table 11.

Week	Diagnosis of Machine Loading/ CRP (input—"load"—vs. output)	Diagnosis of I/O Planning (Planned Queue in Weeks of Output vs. Planned Lead Time)
44	overload — increase capacity	overload — reduce future input or increase capacity
45	underload—bring in work or reduce capacity	overload, but in tolerable range—do nothing
46	underload—bring in work or reduce capacity	slight underload—do nothing
47	underload—bring in work or reduce capacity	underload—bring in work or reduce capacity
48	overload—push out work or increase capacity	underload—bring in work or reduce capacity
49	underload—bring in work or reduce capacity	underload—bring in work or reduce capacity
50	overload—push out work or increase capacity	underload—bring in work or reduce capacity
51	overload—push out work or increase capacity	slight overload—do nothing
52	overload—push out work or increase capacity	overload, at limit of tolerance range—do nothing
53	underload—bring in work or reduce capacity	slight overload—do nothing
54	underload—bring in work or reduce capacity	slight overload—do nothing

Table 11 — **Comparison of Actions Resulting from Machine Loading vs. I/O Planning**

We see that:
1) In Weeks 48 and 50, machine loading/CRP signals overload when the work center is really underloaded. Hence machine loading recommends taking precisely the wrong action.
2) In Weeks 45, 53 and 54, machine loading cries, "Underload" when in reality an overload exists. Once again, machine loading suggests doing exactly the opposite of what should be done.
3) Input/output planning calls for action only when queue variation is excessive, in Weeks 44 and 47 – 50. Machine loading could well precipitate shifting orders and/or capacity *every week* based on the "load" (input) vs. capacity (output) comparison alone, without looking at queue.

But even if machine loading does not acknowledge the function of backlog, shop personnel will. It is an indisputable fact that a minimum level of work-in-process inventory is required both to permit a smooth physical flow of parts and to provide psychological security to workers. When queues grow too long, workers will speed up their output rate to return the backlog to normal size. Conversely, if the amount of WIP is too small, actual output will fall off until backlog builds up to the normal security level. The manufacturing manager of one large company made use of this phenomenon by intentionally keeping his factory jammed with work so that shop personnel, seeing a mountain of WIP around them, would maintain the highest possible production rate.

In summary, reconciling machine loading for capacity planning and the input/output technique for capacity control has shown that input/output includes everything machine loading does and gives a more complete picture of what happens in the shop. So the proposal was made to use input/output planning, which is nothing more than the input/output method adapted for capacity planning, in addition to using it for capacity control (see Table 12, compare with Table 1).

	Priorities	Capacities
Plan	Material Requirements Planning	Input/Output Planning
Control	Dispatching	Input/Output Control

Table 12 — New Line-up of Production Control Techniques

Employing the I/O techniques for both capacity planning and control means that a single report format as shown in Table 13 can serve both functions. Production Control software packages can easily be remodeled to

INPUT/OUTPUT PLANNING AND CONTROL REPORT –
WORK CENTER 100
PLANNED LEAD TIME: ___ WEEKS (OR DAYS)   TODAY'S DATE:
ALLOWABLE VARIANCE: ± ___ WEEKS (OR DAYS)
(All figures in standard hours except where noted)

End of Week (or Day) 46 47 48 . . .	
Planned Input	Source: Scheduled work content of planned and released orders from MRP
Actual Input	Source: Actual work content input
Cumulative Deviation	Equals Actual minus Planned, plus previous period's deviation
Planned Output	Source: Average of Planned Input or average of recent Actual Output, including any future capacity changes
Actual Output	Source: Actual work output
Cumulative Deviation	Equals Actual minus Planned, plus previous period's deviation
Planned Queue	Source: Average of recent backlogs; or planned lead time multiplied by normal Planned Output rate; or management judgement
Actual Queue	Source: Actual amount of work content located in the work center, both in a waiting line and being worked on*
Deviation	Equals Actual minus Planned (not accumulated)
Planned Queue in Weeks of Output	Source: Planned lead time; or Planned Queue divided by Planned Output rate; or management judgment
Actual Queue in Weeks of Output	Source: Actual Queue divided by Actual Output rate
Deviation in Weeks of Output	Equals Actual minus Planned (not accumulated)

*Work actually being run could be identified separately if desired.

Table 13 — Combined Capacity Planning and Control Report

handle input/output planning and control since the logic is identical for both, and is far simpler than finite-loading logic.

Input/output planning is superior to machine loading for the following reasons:

1) It focuses on *stabilizing the planned queue or backlog as the primary capacity-planning objective*, thus recognizing the true role of backlog in the shop. Backlog is stabilized to a preplanned level equivalent to planned lead time by adding capacity, reducing input, or some combination of the two, and true capacity needs are defined easily as a result. Machine loading tries only to match input ("load") with output, and ignores queue fluctuations.

2) *I/O planning validates the lead time used in inventory planning*, by seeking to stabilize queues around the inventory-control system's planned lead time value. Machine loading does not try to do this.

3) *I/O planning recognizes that backlogs will always vary somewhat* and seeks stability within a certain tolerable range of variation. Machine loading, in trying to equate input with output, attempts to keep the backlog size rigidly fixed and not permit it to fulfill its proper function of a physical and psychological buffer.

4) *I/O planning offers more flexible alternatives to the capacity planner* by giving him visibility as to future input, future output, and future queue variations by time period. Capacity planning becomes more precise and more realistic than the numbers-matching approach of machine loading.

5) *I/O Planning is useful for intermediate as well as starting work centers* since it clearly shows the evolution of backlog time period by time period, based on the scheduled input rate from MRP. Directly modifying the input rate to intermediate work centers remains a difficult proposition. But seeing the peaks and valleys of input and queues, rather than an average input for all time periods, helps the planner to decide when to change the planned output rate. Machine loading offers only the possibility of equating "load" with capacity for both intermediate and starting work centers.

6) *Changes to planned lead times are easier to implement with I/O Planning*, which will show the results clearly, in terms of queue variations, by time period. Machine Loading has no provision for showing this.

7) *An integrated I/O format may be used for both capacity planning and control functions* in production control systems, both tailor-made as well as standard packages, rather than having machine load reports for the one and input/output reports for the other.

One may wonder why, if machine loading is so unsatisfactory, shops manage to utilize it. I recall visiting a machine shop using machine loading, where capacity was adequate on the average but the shop displayed all the common symptoms of poor planning—very large backlogs, unpredictable input, frequent overtime for rush orders, harried department managers. Amid all the firefighting, the grinding department stood out as an oasis of ordered production. Although subjected to the same problems and pressures as other departments, Grinding was less chaotic, rush jobs were not often found stagnating there, and the manager was less harassed than his comrades. I asked him what his secret was. He showed me his machine load report, which luckily showed "Total Hours in Department", in other words, the backlog.

"I divide the total hours by last week's output," he explained. "When the backlog goes beyond a week's worth of work, I get help—either by going on overtime or by subcontracting." He was in effect practicing a crude kind of backlog and lead-time stabilization, which permitted him to stay a jump ahead of crises. Input/output planning, based on planned and released orders from MRP, with forward visibility of queue size, recognizes the stabilizing function of backlog in the shop and reduces capacity planning to the essentials—planned input, planned output *and* planned queue.

BIBLIOGRAPHY

Belt, Bill. "The New ABC's of Lead Time Management," *Production and Inventory Management*. XV:2 (Washington, D.C., 1974).

Gomersall, Earl. "Bloated Backlogs—Why They Happen and What To Do About Them," *Factory*. (March 1967).

Plossl, George W. and Wight, Oliver W. *Capacity Planning and Control*, presentation at 1971 APICS International Conference.

Wight, Oliver W. "Input/Output Control: A Real Handle on Lead Time", *Production and Inventory Management*. XI:3 (Washington, D.C., 1970).

Jackson, John S., "Can You Trust the Computer to Reschedule?", *APICS 1974 Conference Proceedings*. (Washington, D.C., 1974).

About the Author—

BILL BELT *holds an M.B.A. in Production Systems Management from Columbia. He has worked for West Virginia Pulp and Paper Co. (WEST-VACO) in Purchasing, and spent four years in Production Control with two divisions of IBM. For the last three years he has worked with Honeywell Bull in Paris, visiting French and European companies and counseling them on their Production Control applications.*

Reprinted from the APICS 1982 Conference Proceedings.

ROUGH-CUT CAPACITY PLANNING—
WHAT IT IS AND HOW TO USE IT

Kenneth L. Campbell, CPIM
Digital Equipment Corporation

OBJECTIVE

The purpose of this presentation is to describe what Rough Cut Capacity Planning (RCCP) is, how it fits into a closed loop manufacturing system, what is required to make it work and why one should include it in their operations.

BACKGROUND

For many of us, the phrase "closed loop manufacturing systems" conjures up a vision of a series of geometrical figures and arrows, one of which is labeled "MRP". (See Figure 1)

The increased use of material requirements planning (MRP) has brought such systems to front stage center and they are the focal point of many of the other presentations at this conference.

This diagram (Figure 1) is meant to portray the importance of feedback - of a system that detects "unsafe" conditions and emits warning signals to alert the user. They are considered the early warning systems of the manufacturing world. In this diagram, there are two feedback loops.

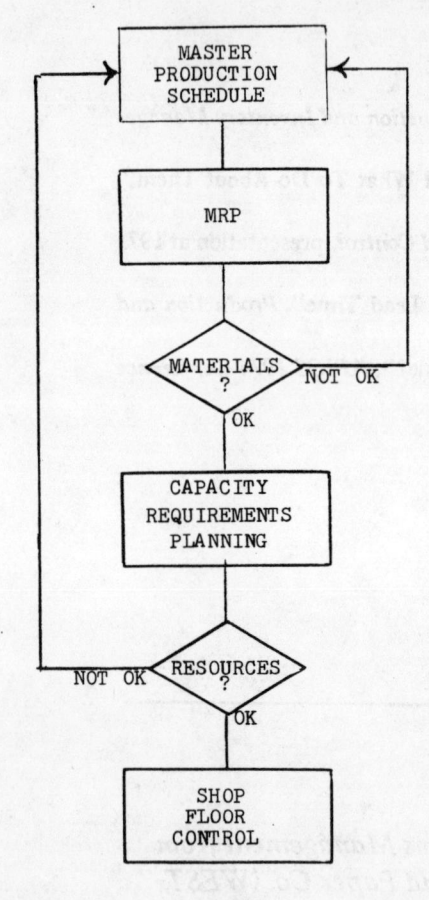

FIGURE 1

The first is from MRP to the Master Schedule. This loop warns of any imbalances of material. The method reporting the imbalance is generally an action report giving move-in, move-out, order and cancel messages.

The second feedback loop is of more interest to us since it concerns capacity. It is the one shown flowing from the block titled Capacity Requirements Planning (CRP) back to the Master Schedule. This loop warns of problems with resources: machines, tools and people.

However, as systems were developed which contained these two loops, it became evident that there must be a better way to test the validity of the Master Schedule relative to the availability of resources.

The problem which surfaced was the long "turn around" time required to validate the availibility of resources. Both MRP and CRP are relatively long runs: both in elapsed time and computer usage. If it was necessary to adjust the Master Schedule, another lengthy loop was required.

Rough Cut Capacity Planning is the technique which has been recognized as an alternative to these lengthy loops. This presentation will explore RCCP in detail.

RCCP AND THE CLOSED LOOP SYSTEM

When RCCP is introduced, the familiar diagram takes on a new appearance. (See Figure 2)

In this diagram, we see a feedback loop between the block titled "RCCP" and the Master Schedule. Since this occurs before MRP, it is obvious that considerable time can be saved in detecting resource problems.

Perhaps we should look first at how Rough Cut Capacity Planning differs from Capacity Requirements Planning.

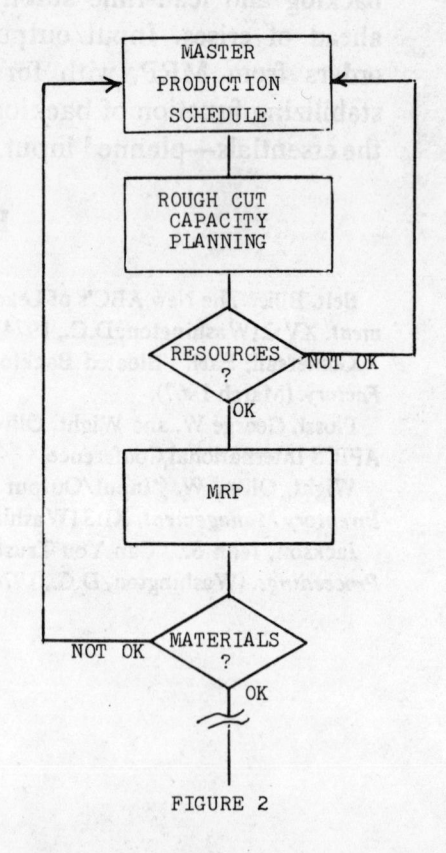

FIGURE 2

Because CRP occurs after the MRP, it (CRP) can be considered a "netted" system that works directly from the Planned Orders, Firm Planned Orders and Scheduled Receipts associated with the MRP programs. These are the result of extensive level-by-level processing.

Rough Cut Capacity Planning is, as the name implies, unnetted. It does not take into consideration any existing inventory. It simply explodes the quantities in the master schedule.

Because it is unnetted, RCCP is not as accurate, and therefore not as reliable, for the short term planning interval. However, in most cases, the Master Schedule extends out well beyond the lead time for most self-manufactured components and products. For this reason, netting has little effect. Consequently, Rough Cut Capacity Planning is considered a medium to long range planning tool.

BASIC DEFINITIONS

Before attempting to further discuss Rough Cut Capacity Planning, a few terms should be defined.

Capacity -
The ability to do work. Sometimes stated as the calculated value. In other cases, it is considered the demonstrated output of a work center. It is usually expressed in hours.

Load -
The work to be done and for which capacity is reserved. It is the equivalent of demands or requirements in a material situation. Load is generally expressed in hours.

Bill of Resources -
A list of the resources required to produce a product. It defines the resources required and the quantity (hours) of those resources. It may also contain a "lead time off set" value.

Master Schedule -
A statement of what is to be manufactured. It is expressed in terms of product units and time periods.

FUNDAMENTALS OF RCCP

The concepts of Rough Cut Capacity Planning are straight forward.
1. Determine the Capacity of the Resources (Work Centers) involved.
2. Determine the Load by time period, represented by the products and quantities in the Master Schedule.
3. Compare the Capacity and Load, time period by time period, noting any significant differences.
4. Report the Differences.

The calculation of the capacity of a resource is not difficult.
It is the product of such variables as:
1. Number of units (people, tools, machines) in the work center.
2. The hours per day when the work center functional.
3. The number of working days in the period.
4. Allowances for personal fatigue, machine maintenance, etc.

In the literature, some authors suggest that the demonstrated capacity averaged over several time periods should be used.
Others suggest using the calculated capacity using the factors shown above. The allowances can be used to adjust for inefficiencies.
In either case, it is the same capacity as you would use for Capacity Requirements Planning.
Determining the load is somewhat more complicated and does require a different data base than is used in CRP.
In general, the data required is contained in a file known as a Bill of Resources. The make-up of this Bill will depend upon what is in the Master Schedule. If you master schedule options, the Bill of Resources would be based on options. If you master schedule major product families, the BOR would be based on these product families.
If the Master Schedule includes an independent demand for service parts and components, the process sheet or master routing data for those items may also be used for RCCP as they are in CRP.
Later in this presentation, we will examine how a BOR for a product family can be developed. However, before we get to that, we will continue the discussion of how the load is generated

THE EXPLOSION PROCESS

From the Master Schedule, we extract a list (ie. Computer File) of identification numbers, dates and quantities. Using the identification number, the appropriate BOR can be located for processing.
Since the BOR identifies each of the resources (work centers) required and the time per piece (or other appropriate unit), one can calculate the total extended time required of the resource. If present, the time required for setup can be added to the extended time.

Also, if present, the lead time set back value can be used to "adjust" the Master Schedule date. Then the extended values and adjusted dates, along with the work center identification, can be outputted to a file (computer record) for later processing.
The process just defined is called "exploding".

THE REPORTING PROCESS

When the entire Master Schedule has been exploded, the resulting records are sorted by work center and date. They can then be summarized by work center and week and the summarized load compared to the planned capacity for the work center.
When a significant difference exists between the summarized load and the work centers planned capacity, the user should review his options.
If the load is somewhat less than capacity, it indicates that the work center is not likely to be fully utilized. Perhaps the capacity of the work center can be adjusted downward by working fewer shifts or re-assigning personnel to other work centers. Another alternative would be to adjust the Master Schedule to provide more of a load to the work center for the week(s) in question.
If the load is significantly greater than the work center's capacity, it indicates that work will not be done on schedule and the user is obligated to take action.
Again, there are two basic options, If practical, the capacity can be increased, perhaps by adding overtime or re-assigning personnel from an underloaded work center. If the overload is indicated to be present for a number of periods, the user may find it necessary to increase capacity by adding machines and/or tools.
When there is no other practical solution to the overload, the user should alter the Master Schedule to eliminate the overload.

TEST THE ADJUSTED MASTER SCHEDULE

When the user has found it necessary to adjust the Master Schedule, a new Rough Cut Capacity Planning run is advisable. This is particularly true if the quantities have been shifted or if any new quantities have been added.
Even if quantities were only reduced, the user may wish to re-run RCCP in order to determine if any work center(s) is significantly underloaded.
It is this re-running that makes Rough Cut Capacity Planning advantageous as compared to Capacity Requirements Planning.
As previously pointed out, to re-run RCCP, it is not necessary to go thru the entire MRP run.
Also, since RCCP employees Bills of Resources (as compared to routing files or process sheets) it is a "single level" explosion process and requires much less time than CRP.

STRUCTURING A BILL OR RESOURCE

As mentioned earlier, the make-up of the Bill of Resources (BOR) will depend upon what is Master Scheduled. If the master scheduling is done by product family, the BOR's should represent the same product families. If the Master Schedule includes options, the RCCP should include BOR's for options.
Of course, the Master Schedule is most frequently stated in specific products. In this case, the BOR will represent the specific product.
Before getting into more specifics about the structure of a BOR, it should be stated again that in all cases, the BOR is a "single level" structure. Even if the unit master scheduled is the upper level of a multilevel Bill of Material, the corresponding BOR will include the resources required for fabrication and assembly of all levels of the BOM.
To illustrate the steps in structuring a BOR, we will borrow an example used by another author in one of the trade journals. In that article, the author selected the (hypothetical) Little Red Wagon Company which could produce nearly 6500 different end products from 32 basic parts and some common hardware.
For example, the company offers a small red wagon with wheels of four(4), five (5), or six (6) inch diameter. It also offers this same wagon with different handles, some of which are painted and others are plated with chrome.

CAPACITY MANAGEMENT REPRINTS—Revised Edition

For planning materials, the company developed a Planning Bill of Materials based on the popularity of each of the various options.

In doing this, they might determine that the popularity of wheel size could be charted as shown in Figure 3.

Since all wagons require wheels, it is understandable that the sum of the popularities for wheels (21+56+23) must represent 100% of all wagons assembled.

Likewise, since each wagon requires one handle, the popularity of the painted handles (74%) and the popularity of chrome handle (26%) represents 100% of all the wagons assembled.

They also offer cushions as an "optional extra". Only 8% of the wagons have cushions.

```
POPULARITY CHART
SMALL RED WAGONS

    OPTION              % of
                      SHIPMENTS

4" Wheels                21
5" Wheels                56
6" Wheels                23
       TOTAL            100

Painted Handles          74
Chrome Handles           26
       TOTAL            100

Cushion                   8
No Cushion               92
       TOTAL            100

    (Note: Partial List)
```

FIGURE 3

In a planning BOM, the "per quantities" for the items mentioned would appear as follows:

ITEM	QTY/1 WAGON
4" Wheels	.21
5" Wheels	.56
6" Wheels	.23
Painted Handles	.74
Chrome Handles	.26
Cushions (Purchased)	.08

This same concept can be used to develop a Bill of Resources for the small red wagon.

If we review the "routings" for each of the items previously listed, we might find the following:

WORK CENTER	DESCRIPTION	TIME(hours)
4"WHEELS		
S1	Stamping	.01
W2	Welding	.04
P3	Painting	.05
5"WHEELS		
S1	Stamping	.01
W2	Welding	.05
P3	Painting	.06
6"WHEELS		
S1	Stamping	.01
W2	Welding	.05
P3	Painting	.07

WORK CENTER	DESCRIPTION	TIME(hours)
PAINTED HANDLES		
S1	Stamping	.01
F1	Forming	.02
W2	Welding	.05
P3	Painting	.06
CHROME HANDLES		
S1	Stamping	.01
F1	Forming	.02
W2	Welding	.05
E4	Electroplating	.10

CUSHIONS
Purchased; therefore no routings

Given the popularity of the various options, as used in developing the planning BOM, and remembering that each wagon has four wheels, the Bill of Resources (as related only to the items listed) would be developed as follows:

For the Stamping Work Centers (S1), the required time for one small red wagon would be:

4" Wheels: 4 x .21 x .01 = .0084

5" Wheels: 4 x .56 x .01 = .0224

6" Wheels: 4 x .23 x .01 = .0092

P-Handles: 1 x .74 x .01 = .0074

C-Handles: 2 x .26 x .01 = .0026

TOTAL   .0500 hrs/wagon

For the Welding Work Center (W2), the required time would be:

4" Wheels: 4 x .21 x .04 = .0336

5" Wheels: 4 x .56 x .05 = .1120

6" Wheels: 4 x .23 x .05 = .0460

P-Handles: 1 x .74 x .05 = .0370

C-Handles: 1 x .26 x .05 = .0130

TOTAL   .2416 hrs/wagon

When the same pattern is used for the other options and work centers, a BOR will result. The completed BOR (relative to the items listed) would appear as shown in Figure 4. It should be noted that the times shown are related to one (1) small red wagon.

```
BILL OF RESOURCES

PRODUCT: SMALL RED WAGON

WORK   OPERATION         STANDARD
CTR    DESCRIPTION       HRS/WAGON

S1     Stamping          0.0500
W2     Welding           0.2416
F1     Forming           0.0200
P3     Painting          0.0444
E4     Electroplating    0.0260
(Partial List)
```

FIGURE 4

A similar BOR could be developed for other families: for example, a large red wagon. If we refer to the article mentioned, we would note that not all the wagons offered by the Little Red Wagon Company are red. Some are painted blue, some green and some black. If we make the assumption that the times required for production are independent of color, one BOR for each size (small and large) sould be practical.

If they should require different resources because of color, for example a different paint booth for black paint, it would then be necessary to factor in the popularity of color.

REPORTING FORMATS

There are three basic reporting formats which can be conveniently applied to Rough Cut Capacity Planning.

The first is a tabulated report as shown in Figure 5. This format reports more precisely than the others since it shows the actual numbers derived for each time period.

The second format is a simple graphic display as shown in Figure 6. This format suggests that the load is a "continous" function. However, since it is generally summarized in time periods, a graphic display is not as representative as is the bar graph shown in Figure 7.

In either of these last two forms, the planned capacity of the work center is shown as a dashed horizontal line. When the planned capacity is changing, the dashed line is not as convenient. In this case, and if color is available, it might be useful to represent the planned capacity by a different color. This can be done by shading the background or, in the case of the bar graph, a second bar representing the capacity in the period.

WORK CENTER: P3 PAINTING

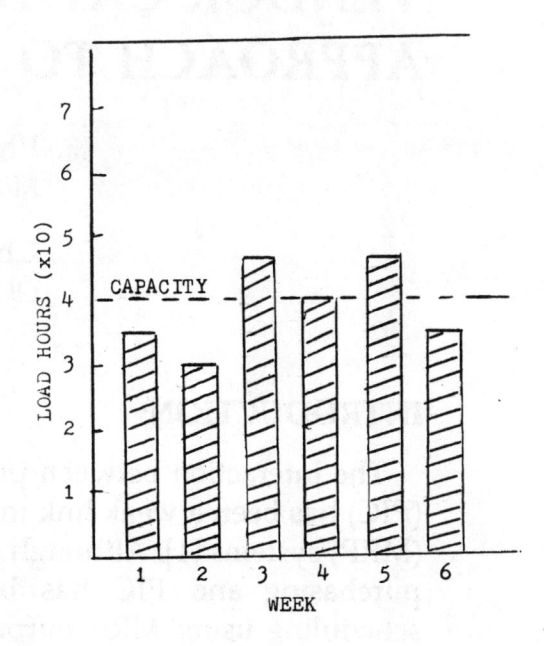

FIGURE 7

ROUGH CUT CAPACITY REPORT
WORK CENTER: P3 Painting

	\multicolumn{6}{c}{WEEK}
	1	2	3	4	5	6
CAPACITY	40	40	40	40	40	40
LOAD	35	30	45	40	45	35
VARIANCE	-5	-10	+5	0	+5	-5
% (L/C)	88	75	125	100	125	88

FIGURE 5

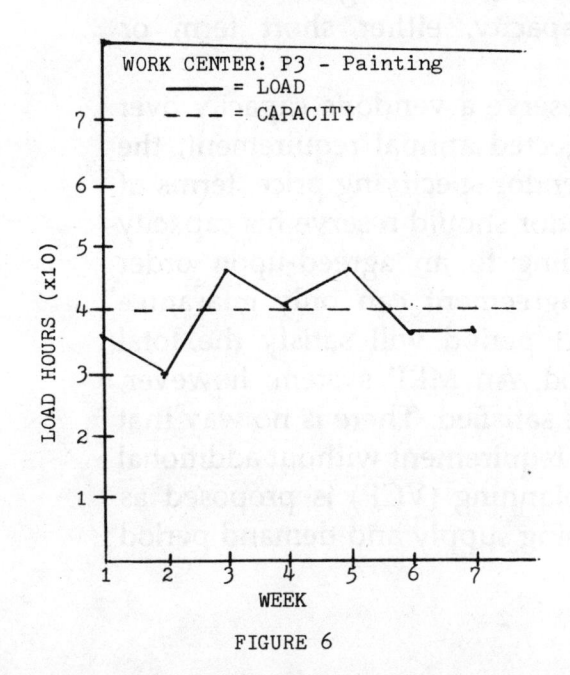

SUMMARY

Rough Cut Capacity Planning is rapidly becoming one of the planner's best tools. Since it can be executed prior to the MRP programs, it is less time consuming than Capacity Requirements Planning. For medium to long range planning, RCCP can be as accurate as CRP.

References

1. Richard C. Ling, "MASTER SCHEDULING in a MAKE-TO-ORDER ENVIRONMENT", Inventories & Production (July-August 1981), pg. 17

FIGURE 6

ABOUT THE AUTHOR

Kenneth L. Campbell has been active in APICS for over fifteen years. He has spoken at several other National Conferences and has contributed articles to the Quarterly. Ken is a Past President of the Worcester County (MA) Chapter. He is employed as a Manufacturing Systems Consultant by Digital Equipment Corporation.

VENDOR CAPACITY PLANNING: AN APPROACH TO VENDOR SCHEDULING

Phillip L. Carter
Michigan State University   East Lansing, Michigan

Chrwan-jyh Ho
Oklahoma State University   Stillwater, Oklahoma

INTRODUCTION

The interaction between purchasing and production/inventory control (PIC) has been a weak link in closed-loop material requirements planning (MRP) systems [1]. Although the significance of bridging the gap between purchasing and PIC has been well recognized [1], [2], [8], vendor scheduling using MRP output has apparently been successfully implemented in only a few companies [5], [11], [13]. One reason for this is the difficulty in matching short-term customer requirements (as calculated by MRP) with short-term vendor capacity. This paper presents a planning mechanism which can be used to achieve a better match between customer requirements and vendor capacity and thereby facilitate the implementation of MRP in purchasing.

VENDOR CAPACITY PLANNING

The major reasons for purchasing parts instead of manufacturing them in house include cost, the vendor's unique technology, and a shortage of in-plant capacity [6]. From a PIC perspective, purchasing can be viewed as a means to supplement in-plant capacity, either short term or long term.

Purchase agreements are one way to reserve a vendor's capacity over a period of time [4], [7]. Based on a projected annual requirement, the buyer can negotiate a contract with the vendor specifying price, terms of delivery, and so on. Theoretically, the vendor should reserve his capacity to meet the annual requirements according to an agreed-upon order release pattern. Practically, a purchase agreement can only guarantee that the total supply within the contract period will satisfy the total estimated demand within the same period. An MRP system, however, requires that the demand in each week be satisfied. There is no way that a purchase agreement can accomplish this requirement without additional terms in the contract. Vendor capacity planning (VCP) is proposed as one way to achieve the objective of matching supply and demand period by period.

Figure 1 illustrates the role of VCP in a production planning system. VCP requires inputs from the purchase order schedule (POS) and vendor capacity report (VCR). The VCR is a time-phased production schedule for each part or part family provided by the vendor. The POS is a time-phased schedule of requirements for each part or part family derived from the MRP output.

Following a review of the MRP output by the buyers or purchase part planner, a POS is sent to each vendor. The vendors use the POS and their own master production schedule (MPS) to prepare the VCR. The VCR, in turn, is sent to the buyers. The VCR received from the various vendors are then aggregated by the buyers into a VCR summary which serves as input for VCP. The details of the POS, the VCR, and VCP as well as their relationships are discussed below.

FIGURE 1
Production planning incorporating vendor capacity planning

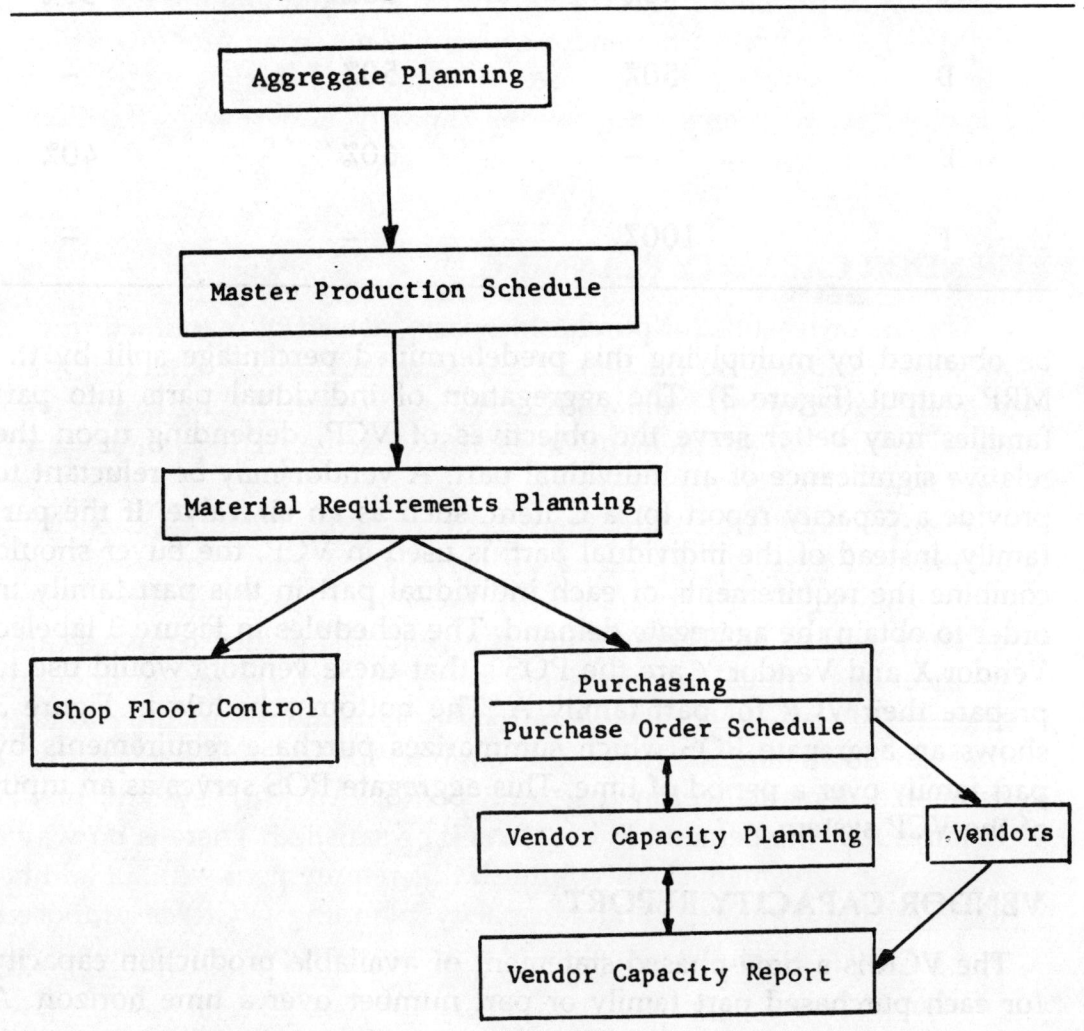

```
        Aggregate Planning
                |
                v
    Master Production Schedule
                |
                v
    Material Requirements Planning
            /       \
           v         v
    Shop Floor    Purchasing
     Control      Purchase Order Schedule
                        |
                        v
                Vendor Capacity Planning  <---> Vendors
                        |
                        v
                Vendor Capacity Report
```

Purchase Order Schedule

The POS can be derived from the MRP output and shows the time-phased requirements by vendor. If the total quantity required is split among several qualified vendors (Figure 2), the POS for each vendor can

FIGURE 2
Distribution of percentage split

Part Family Number	Vendor X	Vendor Y	Vendor Z
A	60%	–	40%
B	70%	30%	–
C	40%	30%	30%
D	50%	50%	–
E	–	60%	40%
F	100%	–	–

be obtained by multiplying this predetermined percentage split by the MRP output (Figure 3). The aggregation of individual parts into part families may better serve the objectives of VCP, depending upon the relative significance of an individual part. A vendor may be reluctant to provide a capacity report for a C item, such as an air valve. If the part family, instead of the individual part, is used in VCP, the buyer should combine the requirements of each individual part in this part family in order to obtain the aggregate demand. The schedules in Figure 3 labeled Vendor X and Vendor Y are the POS's that these vendors would use to prepare their VCR for part family A. The bottom schedule in Figure 3 shows an aggregate POS which summarizes purchase requirements by part family over a period of time. This aggregate POS serves as an input of the VCP system.

VENDOR CAPACITY REPORT

The VCR is a time-phased statement of available production capacity for each purchased part family or part number over a time horizon. A

FIGURE 3
Purchase order schedule

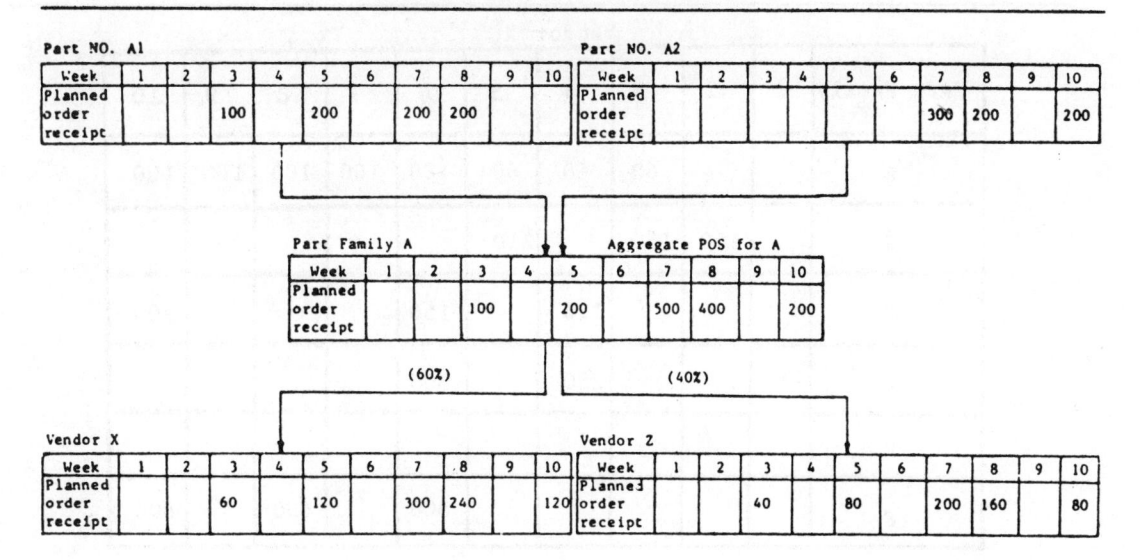

Part NO. A1

Week	1	2	3	4	5	6	7	8	9	10
Planned order receipt			100		200		200	200		

Part NO. A2

Week	1	2	3	4	5	6	7	8	9	10
Planned order receipt							300	200		200

Part Family A — Aggregate POS for A

Week	1	2	3	4	5	6	7	8	9	10
Planned order receipt			100		200		500	400		200

(60%)　　(40%)

Vendor X

Week	1	2	3	4	5	6	7	8	9	10
Planned order receipt			60		120		300	240		120

Vendor Z

Week	1	2	3	4	5	6	7	8	9	10
Planned order receipt					40		80	200	160	80

Aggregate Purchase Order Schedule

Part Family	1	2	3	4	5	6	7	8	9	10
A				100		200		500	400	200
B		200	200		300				500	
C				300		400				800
D				500		600				
E					400		400		700	
F						800		600		600

vendor should consider the VCR as a marketing tool, not just a disclosure of his capacity information to his customers. An appropriate implementation of VCP would help vendors establish a long-term relationship with the buyer. As for the buyers, the production strategy of the vendors can be detected through a careful examination of the VCR. For instance, the requirements for vendor X in periods of 3, 5, and 7 of part family A are 60, 120, and 300, respectively (refer to Figure 3). However, vendor X tries to smooth out his production rate by quoting 60, 60, 60, and 100 for periods 3 through 6 (see the top schedule in Figure 4). Vendor Z adopts a different production strategy and reports more available capacity

CAPACITY MANAGEMENT REPRINTS—Revised Edition

FIGURE 4
Vendor capacity report

Vendor X

Part Family	1	2	3	4	5	6	7	8	9	10
A			60	60	60	100	100	100	100	100
B		150	150		210				350	
C				120		150				300
D				250		300				
E										
F						800		600		800

Vendor Y

Part Family	1	2	3	4	5	6	7	8	9	10
A										
B		80	80		100				150	
C				100		150				250
D				300		300				
E					160		160		300	
F										

Vendor Z

Part Family	1	2	3	4	5	6	7	8	9	10
A			50		100		200	160		80
B										
C					100		120			250
D										
E					250		250		300	
F										

than the POS requires. Vendor Z may induce more business to supplement the expected low demand at these periods. Thus, the buyer should take advantage of the extra information conveyed in the VCR for planning the placement of future requirements of purchased items.

Actually, the VCR can be viewed as the difference between the vendor's aggregate production plan and the vendor's MPS. From the MPS, the vendor knows the committed capacity and the open capacity in his shop. Through an appropriate adjustment in order to incorporate the production plan, a VCR can be prepared. The following features, which are quite comparable to the master production schedule, are discussed to illustrate this basic characteristic of VCR.

Expression of Vendor's Capacity

Capacity is usually expressed in terms of production resources, such as machine hours or labor hours, available over a period of time. In the VCR, capacity is expressed as the amount of each part number that can be supplied per week. If this level of detail is too difficult for vendors to deal with, the available capacity for a part family can be reported instead. However, the degree of detail in the VCR depends upon the importance of the item. The capacity report for an A item, such as a generator, could be by part number, while for a C item, such as an air valve, the capacity report could be by part family. In order to obtain a capacity report for a part or part family, the vendors can determine the unit production time on the critical facility for each item. By comparing the available (i.e., uncommitted) production resource and the MPS time period by time period, the VCR can then be prepared. The VCR should be expressed in terms of delivery dates in order to be consistent with the MPS and POS.

Time Fences in the VCR

A vendor should establish time fences in the VCR similar to the establishment of a time fence in a master production schedule. Typically, capacity would be fixed from current time out to the first time fence. Between the first time fence and the second time fence, capacity could be changed by short-run adjustments such as overtime, second shift, or subcontracting. Beyond the second time fence capacity could be changed by plant expansion, new plant, new equipment, etc.

Updating the VCR

The VCR should be updated on a weekly basis after the vendor has received the latest POS and updated the MPS. The planning horizon should correspond to that in the MPS.

Vendor Capacity Planning

Two levels of VCP will be illustrated. The aggregate level of VCP is used for overall planning of purchasing requirements. The cumulation of all the vendors' capacity reports by part number or part family (as shown in Figure 4) is called the VCR summary. Figure 5 gives an example of the VCR summary. By comparing this VCR summary with the aggregate POS, the deviation between required and actual capacity can be identified throughout the planning horizon, as shown in Figure 6.

FIGURE 5
Vendor capacity report summary

Part Family	1	2	3	4	5	6	7	8	9	10
A			110	60	160	100	300	260	100	180
B		230	230		310				500	
C				320		420				800
D				550		600				
E					410		410		600	
F						800		600		600

FIGURE 6
Aggregate level of vendor capacity planning

Part Family A

week	1	2	3	4	5	6	7	8	9	10
VCR			110	60	160	100	300	260	100	180
POS			100		200		500	400		200
Cumulative Deviation			+10	+70	+30	+130	-70	-70	+30	+10

When a negative deviation occurs (i.e., insufficient capacity), the detailed level of VCP can be used to help identify corrective actions.

The purpose of the detailed level of VCP is to identify the capability of an individual vendor to conform with the POS issued by the buyer. An example is given in Figure 7, which shows a positive deviation of part family A for vendor Z. Figure 6 shows that a negative cumulative deviation occurs in period 7 at the aggregate level of VCP. Combined with the detailed level of VCP of vendor X, the other supplier of part family A, the buyer can determine how to allocate the requirements during shortage periods. In this example, vendor X estimates that he cannot meet the buyer's purchasing requirement after period 7, while vendor Z has slack capacity for not only part family A but also part families C and E. It is obvious that this problem can be resolved by re-allocating requirements from vendor X to vendor Z without forcing vendor X to change his production plan.

EXPECTED ADVANTAGES OF THE VCP

Several advantages, derived from sharing information in the POS and the VCR with the vendors and buyers, can be expected from implementing VCP.

Forward Visibility

VCP projects purchasing requirements into an intermediate future through the use of the VCR and MRP's revised POS. With this forward visibility, PIC and purchasing people can work together to make the adjustment necessary to narrow the gap between the vendors' available capacity and the planned purchase order schedule. If insufficient vendor capacity develops over a period of time, the planned purchase requirements can be adjusted accordingly through other alternatives, such as in-plant manufacturing.

Effective Communication

Current purchasing practice has been criticized for a lack of responsiveness to unexpected changes [3]. It is suggested that a buyer-planner be used to take control of the direct communication between PIC and vendors about the due dates and requirements of the needed items [12]. The communication can be further enhanced with the use of VCP. The buyer can contribute considerably to the overall planning system through the impact of VCP on the MRP system.

Mutual Benefits

Through the VCR, vendors can inform purchasing about any potential or actual supply disruptions, allowing the buyer to react to these unexpected events promptly. The vendor also knows the future purchase requirement and can determine his own strategies for capacity adjustment. The vendors can initiate their production planning to best utilize their capacity. The POS also provides a basis for estimating annual requirements, which gives vendors a better estimate of how much long-term capacity is needed to meet the estimated annual requirement of the customer.

FIGURE 7
The detailed level of the vendor capacity planning

Part Family A — Vendor Z

week	1	2	3	4	5	6	7	8	9	10
VCR			50		100		200	160		80
POS			40		80		200	160		80
Cumulative Deviation			+10		+30		+30	+30		+30

Part Family C — Vendor Z

week	1	2	3	4	5	6	7	8	9	10
VCR				100		120				250
POS				90		120				240
Cumulative Deviation				+10		+10				+20

Part Family E — Vendor Z

week	1	2	3	4	5	6	7	8	9	10
VCR					250		250		300	
POS					160		160		280	
Cumulative Deviation					+90		+180		+200	

Part Family A — Vendor X

week	1	2	3	4	5	6	7	8	9	10
VCR			60	60	60	100	100	100	100	100
POS			60		120		300	240		120
Cumulative Deviation			0	+60	0	+100	-100	-240	-140	-160

PREREQUISITES AND LIMITATIONS OF THE VCP

As with an MRP system, there are several important prerequisites of a VCP system.

VCR Availability

The most important prerequisite may be the availability of the VCR. Some vendors may not be willing to reveal their capacity information in detail, given the effort required to obtain these data. Just as vendor education is necessary to extend the MRP system into the vendor's shop [10], vendors can be educated about the advantages of preparing an adequate VCR for the buyer. The extra effort to prepare the VCR will be compensated by the expected advantages of VCP for the vendors.

POS Conformation

Large vendors may not want to conform with the buyer's POS. They may only be willing to provide a predetermined available capacity for each customer based on their own production schedule and marketing strategy. Faced with this situation, the buyer would need to modify the POS to meet the suppliers' VCR. In the extreme case, the buyer needs to inform PIC to adjust the master production schedule to cope with an anticipated shortage.

POS Stability

The objective of MRP's rescheduling capability is to keep priorities up to date and valid [9]. However, this may change the actual need date or quantity within the firm portion of the POS. In turn, open purchase orders tend to change from time to time. This nervousness will cause problems with the buyer's POS and, eventually, will obscure the future VCR such that VCP will be invalid for planning purposes. Therefore, trade-offs exist between constantly rescheduling purchase requirements and planning vendor capacity. A mutual agreement about the treatment of purchase order changes must be developed in order to ensure a better performance of VCP.

SUMMARY

As MRP systems become the dominant production scheduling technique, an effective two-way communication between PIC and related functions becomes essential. This article stresses the significance of the purchasing function in an MRP system and describes how purchasing can play a more effective role in vendor scheduling using VCP. Because effort and persuasion are required to obtain a valid and realistic VCR, the purchasing manager is the best person to be responsible for implementing VCP. On the other hand, to make VCP work best, PIC should be responsible for providing stable purchase requirements within the firm portion of POS. The VCP concept cannot be achieved without cost, but the additional effort and cost can be justified by the advantages of implementation.

REFERENCES

1. Aiello, J. L., "Successful Interaction Between Purchasing and Production and Inventory Control," *APICS Annual Conference Proceedings 1979*, pp. 234–236.
2. Benson, R. J., "Can Purchasing Supply Tomorrow's Factory?" *APICS Annual Conference Proceedings 1981*, pp. 355–359.
3. Brunelle, P. E., "Controlling the Outside Factory by Purchasing Manager," *APICS Annual Conference Proceedings 1977*, pp. 148–155.
4. Burlingame, L. J. and Warren, R. A., "Extended Capacity Planning," *APICS Annual Conference Proceedings 1974*, pp. 83–91.
5. Carter, P. L. and Monzka, R. M., "Steelcase, Inc.: MRP in Purchasing," in E. W. David, ed., *Case Studies in Materials Requirements Planning*, APICS, Inc., Washington, DC, 1978, pp. 105–129.
6. Leenders, M. R., Fearon, H. E., and England, W. B., *Purchasing and Material Management*, Richard D. Irwin, Inc., Homewood, IL, 1980.
7. Morency, R. R., "A Systems Approach to Vendor Scheduling under Contract Purchasing," *APICS Annual Conference Proceedings 1977*, pp. 458–466.
8. Olsen, R. E., "Bridging the Purchasing-Production Control Credibility Gap," *APICS Annual Conference Proceedings 1977*, pp. 450–457.
9. Orlicky, J. A., *Material Requirements Planning*, McGraw-Hill, Inc., NY, 1975.
10. Papesch, R. M., "Extending Your MRP System into Your Vendor's Shop," *Production and Inventory Management*, Vol. 19, No. 2, 1978, pp. 47–52.
11. Pellegrini, D., "Vendor Scheduling: It Really Works," *APICS Annual Conference Proceedings 1982*, pp. 358–363.
12. Plossl, G., *Manufacturing Control: The Last Frontier for Profits*, Reston Publishing Co., Inc., Reston, Virginia, 1973.
13. Smolens, R. W., "MRP II Systems: Does The Purchasing Function Change?" *APICS Annual Conference Proceedings 1982*, pp. 355–357.

About the Authors—

*PHILLIP L. CARTER, CPIM,** is professor of management and Chairman of the Department of Management in the Graduate School of Business at Michigan State University. Dr. Carter is a past cochairman of the APICS Academic Practitioner Liaison Committee.

CHRWAN-JYH HO, CPIM, is assistant professor of production management at Oklahoma State University. He holds an MBA from the University of Georgia and expects a PhD from Michigan State University. He is a member of APICS, AIDS, and TIMS.

Reprinted from the APICS 1979 Conference Proceedings.

CAPACITY MANAGEMENT

James T. Clark
IBM Corporation
Manufacturing Industry Education
Poughkeepsie, N.Y.

Capacity management is receiving attention today that rivals the attention given to materials management during the MRP crusade of a decade ago.

And for good reasons:

o   Capacity, like inventory, represents one of the largest manageable assets of a manufacturing company.

o   Many MRP systems today still are not successful because of inadequate capacity management in the production plan and in the master schedule.

o   Problems in the operational capacity management system downstream from MRP are diminishing MRP's effectiveness because of an inability to execute MRP reschedules.

o   The economic climate and lack of government policy and direction on such key issues as incentive tax credits and energy have discouraged capital expansion in the United States. (It is interesting to note that even though we are entering a recessionary period, many manufacturers will continue to be confronted with capacity problems. Consumer spending and housing will be effected more than other economic areas, but manufacturers of capital equipment will be buffered by two facts: prior to the downturn earlier this year, capital spending had lagged dramatically the unprecedented 51 months of sustained growth in the U.S. economy and inventory to sales ratios had also failed to stay in step with this growth.)

o   And . . . .the payoff for good capacity management is substantial.

This paper will address the following areas:

A. Capacity management . . . .the payoff.

B. Capacity management . . . .a closed loop system, and its relationship to priority management.

C. Capacity management techniques in the various capacity management systems.

A. CAPACITY MANAGEMENT . . . . THE PAYOFF

Figure 1. is a DuPont chart of a manufacturing company. The top portion of the tree diagram starts with the balance sheet items on the far right. These are split into current assets and depreciated plant and equipment, or net fixed assets. The bottom portion of the chart represents the income statement.

Examination of the chart establishes inventory as the largest manageable asset of this company; specifically 40.7% of all assets. Accounts receivable are 28.8% and net fixed assets are 25.0%.

Net fixed assets relate to capacity. Obviously office buildings, furniture, etc. do not represent capacity but there is one capacity item that is not on the balance sheet: the direct labor force. If somehow this could be quantified on the balance sheet and combined with plant, equipment and tooling, then productive capacity might prove to be the largest manageable asset of many manufacturing companies.

You will also notice that it is the depreciated fixed assets that have been referred to. If this company had to increase capacity to increase output, that capacity would certainly not be purchased at a depreciated amount. Based on this, one can easily argue that capacity is related to the replacement cost of plant and equipment and this might elevate capacity to the largest manageable asset.

The data outside the boxes, associated with the dotted lines on the DuPont chart resulted from a simulation assuming: 1% increase in output (net sales) accompanied by a 1% increase in accounts receivables and a 1% increase in inventory. (Good inventory management might easily produce additional sales with no increase in inventory, so assuming an inventory increase presents a conservative position). Additionally the simulation assumes that an increase in output is accomplished with the same plant, equipment, burden and labor force. Consequently net fixed assets is unchanged. Cost of sales has been increased only by a 1% increase in material costs, assumed here to be 50% of cost of sales.

Figure 2. Is a plot of the ROI (or return on total assets, which is calculated by multiplying profit margin by total asset turns) for a range of assumed output increases.

This contrasts sharply with Figure 3. which is a plot of the result of inventory reduction simulations. The inventory simulations were based on assumptions of 16% inventory carry costs. A reasonable range for small increments of inventory change ranges from 10% or 11% up to 16% for carry cost. This is predominantly the cost of money.

Simulation....1 % increase in output (sales) assuming a 1 % increase in a/r, inventory, and material costs and assuming material costs are 50 % of cost of goods sold

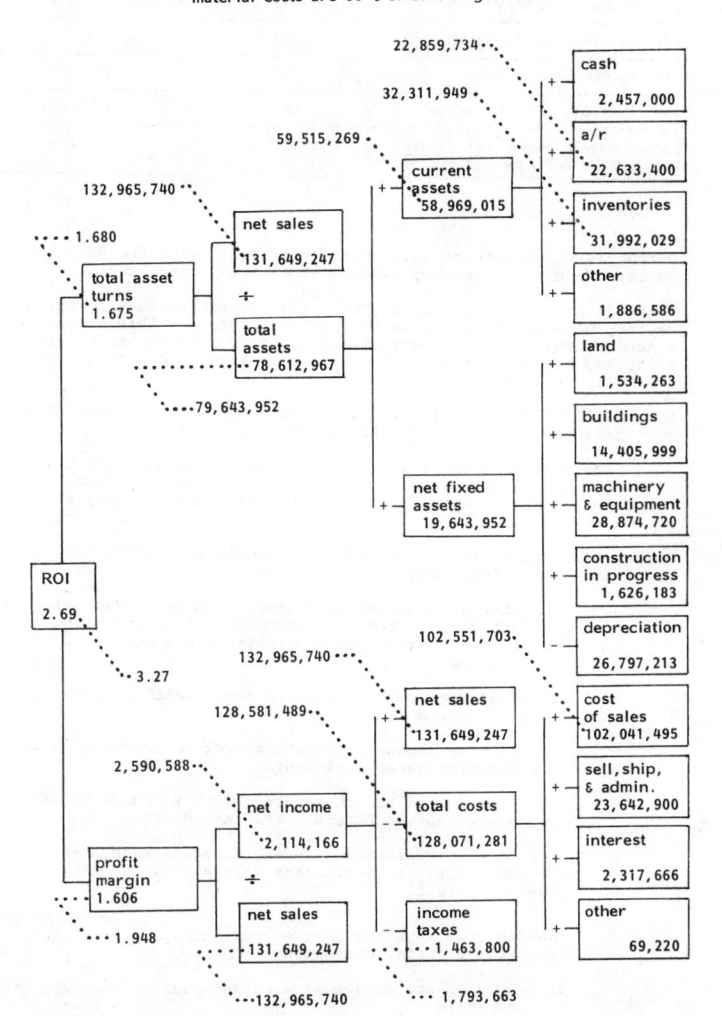

Figure 1.

ROI % plotted against % increase in output and % inventory reduction

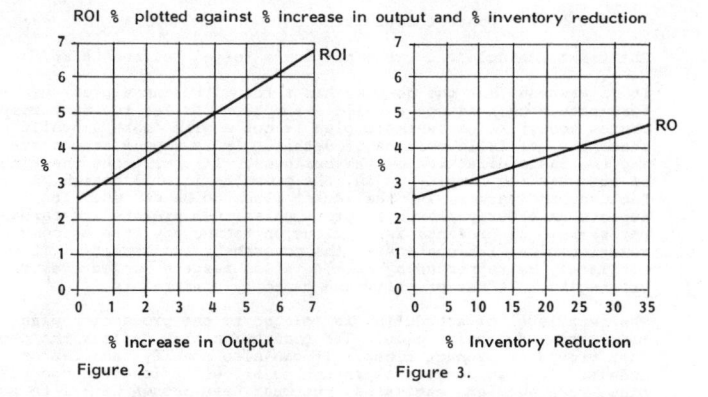

Figure 2.   % Increase in Output

Figure 3.   % Inventory Reduction

Other simulations were also conducted on purchased material cost reductions, reductions in selling, shipping and administrative costs, and a reduction in accounts receivable collection period (interest 10%).

A recap of these simulations presents some interesting comparisons in Figures 4. The financial impact on the company demonstrated by increases in output is truly dramatic.

CAPACITY MANAGEMENT REPRINTS—Revised Edition

	To increase earnings per share by 10 ¢	To gain an additional 1 % in ROI
Reduce inventory by	7.6 %	17.6 %
or..Decrease material costs by	2.6 %	8.9 %
or..Increase output by	.5 %	1.8 %
or..Decrease collection period by	10 days	24.3 days
or..Decrease ship., sell., and admin. costs by	1.6 %	5.6 %

Figure 4.

Output is related to capacity management, and hence the need for better capacity management systems is clearly emphasized.

There is also a legitimate argument that concludes that better inventory management will produce increased output. This emphasizes a need to relate both inventory and capacity management (or priority and capacity management) because in fact, one cannot successfully exist without the other.

B. CAPACITY MANAGEMENT . . . . A CLOSED LOOP SYSTEM, AND ITS RELATIONSHIP TO PRIORITY MANAGEMENT.

Figure 5. is a variation of the often illustrated and often discussed 'closed loop' manufacturing system. It forms the basis for any discussion of priority and capacity management.

The development of the discussion of capacity management systems is predicted by the following:

a. No matter now complex we attempt to make a discussion of manufacturing systems, a fundamental fact exists. The fact is that manufacturing systems are a series of scheduling systems.

b. All scheduling systems must be accompanied by some priority management system.

c. All priority management systems must be accompanied by some capacity management system.

d. Schedules change and therefore priority and capacity management systems change. They are dynamic.

e. There are multiple priority and capacity management systems. Their time horizons vary as well as their level of detail.

f. Manufacturing systems must support management in the following critical endeavors:

1. Develop and manage a valid and realistic master schedule
2. Plan priorities
3. Plan capacities
4. Control priorities
5. Control capacities

The first schedule . . . the company's formal business plan.

It is assumed that the company has a formal business plan. (Unfortunately this is not a valid assumption for far too many companies today). The business plan is not a glib 'make a profit' statement nor is it volumes of detail. It is a page or two stating the basic direction of the business. It spells out the kind of business the company is in, the products it will design, manufacture, and market, and the market place to be served. It depicts an orderly growth in gross sales, net profits and earnings per share. It presents assumptions on technology, the economy and relationships with customers, the government and society. It will ultimately be supported by more detailed targets, objectives and strategies. It has priority and capacity constraints.

The next level of scheduling is related to the production plan or long range production plan. The production plan defines the product groups or product lines. It can also specify families or models. It must be general enough to allow for longer range planning, forecasts and estimates, but must have enough detail to support the gross sales and net profit dollars of the business plan. It is often expressed in assembly rates per time period or units of build per time period.

The production plan horizon is coincident with the formal business planning horizon. It is typically around five years, but extends even further for some companies.

The master production schedule or master schedule is the scheduling system one level below the production plan. The master production schedule horizon varies by company, but it is common to see schedules covering from one to two and sometimes three years. It is completely supportive of the production plan but differs in its level of detail and the frequency of its re-evaluation and change. The level of detail includes specific identification of 'finished' goods or master scheduled items, and implies a unique

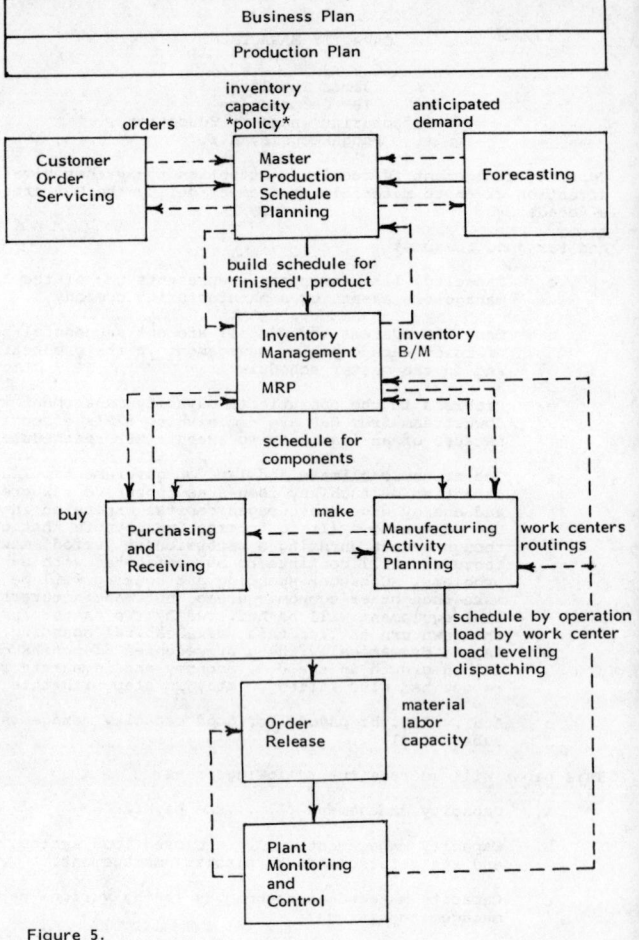

Figure 5.

manufacturing or planning bill of material for the item. ('Finished' items may be actual final assembled items, high level buildable options, modular-non buildable options, spare parts, etc.) Simply stated the master schedule is a schedule for 'finished' product: part number, quantity and due date.

The MRP system, or inventory management system, is downstream from the master schedule. MRP has been discussed and examined in detail for over a decade now. A review of the simple mechanics of MRP establishes that at a minimum the output of MRP is simply a part number, quantity and due date. It is a schedule for components. Dependent components are defined as demand items which support the building of the master scheduled items such as raw materials, purchased and fabricated parts, subassemblies, etc.

The recent emphasis on the priority planning and priority control aspects of MRP is evidence that MRP is finally being understood and accepted as a scheduling system.

The order schedule of MRP feeds both the 'make' system (Manufacturing Activity Planning) and the 'buy' system (Purchasing and Receiving). The Manufacturing Activity Planning system includes scheduling orders by operation, loading standard hours into work centers, load leveling and dispatching. These activities represent a major part of the operationsal level capacity management system.

Figures 6, 7 and 8 should assist in this review of scheduling systems.

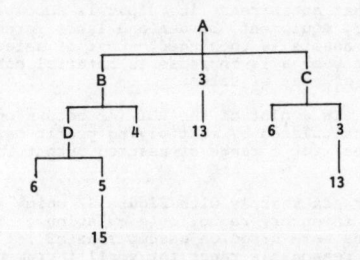

Figure 6.

```
                              WEEK
0  1  2  3  4  5  6  7  8  9 10 11 12 13 14 15 16 17 18 19 20 21
                    *————————6
                                      D
            *————————15————————5      B
                                  4
                  *————————13————————3————————A
                        *————————6
                                      C
                  *————————13————————3
```

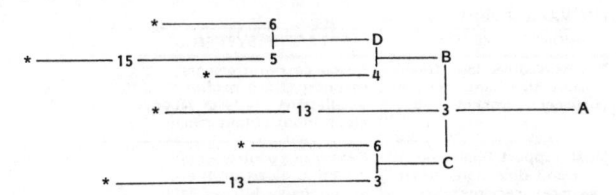

Figure 7.

1200 5 's due in week 11 (shop calendar day 450)
Lead time = 25 days
order release = day 425

ROUTING OPERATION	WORK CENTER	STANDARD HOURS	START DATE	DUE DATE
			ORDER RELEASE	425
10	A	3.4	428	429
20	B	1.6	432	434
30	C	2.7	437	438
40	D	5.8	441	442
50	E	6.5	445	446
60	F	7.6	449	450

For scheduling:

Assume 3 day queue and move between operations and round standard hours up to the nearest 8 hour day.

Figure 8.

All of these scheduling systems must be accompanied by priority management systems. Priorities in the business plan and production plan are typically related to the business direction, profitability and other major financial measurements such as return on assets, return on equity, earnings per share, etc. Business segments, major customers, markets and market share are among some additional considerations.

The master schedule priority system must reflect the business plan and production plan priorities. The master schedule by contrast though is the first schedule that defines specific products and it is the first schedule that is apt to be reflected in functional and operation level managements' performance plan objectives. It is an agreed to estimate of the build schedule by manufacturing. It represents in many cases, a compromise among the conflicting objectives of marketing, manufacturing and finance.

Company policy and practices in the business plan and production plan are often major determinants in priority setting in the master schedule. An example would be sequencing customer orders in the backlog, or sequencing allocation of finished goods inventory to customer orders. The master schedule also demands written, understood and abided by policy on who can change the master schedule, on what product and in what portion of the schedule horizon. This last item implies the establishment of time fences for products or product lines, and this may even vary by market or customer.

The resultant master schedule then becomes the driver for the operational level material planning and capacity planning systems.

Assuming that the master schedule is valid and realistic (reflects objectives and priorities of the production plan and is attainable) then MRP establishes a specific priority system. It is a natural due date (need date) driven priority system based on the comparison and ranking of valid order due dates. MRP establishes order priorities for both manufacturing and purchasing.

In short lead time manufacturing (for example, 5 days or less cumulative lead time) or manufacturing with very few operations, order due dates are adequate for priority management. Longer lead times with many manufacturing operations however, require one more level of detail in priority management.

This is provided by the operation scheduling system. Operation scheduling, as in Figure 8, provides the ability to establish and compare valid operation due dates. This is the basis for priorities by operation by work center. This operation priority overcomes the short comings of simply comparing order due dates by factoring in the work accomplished and work remaining on an order.

The operations scheduling system is divided into three subsystems: capacity requirements planning, completion time estimating and operation sequencing. These scheduling systems present a starting point for the development of priority and capacity management systems. This is summarized in Figure 10.

Priority management includes both priority planning and priority control. The initial flow through a manufacturing system is depicted by the solid lines in Figure 5. This establishes the priority plan. Changes originating in the business plan, production plan or customers orders and forecasting must be reflected down through the system. Changes originating from within the plant via plant monitoring and control such as scrap, machine down, worker absent, etc. and changes from vendors via Purchasing

and Receiving must also be fed back through the system. Engineering changes, inventory adjustments and other changes to the basic data of the business are also part of the feedback. Change and feedback are depicted by the dashed lines. All schedules must be kept valid and this then is the basis for priority control.

Priority control is particularly critical in the close-in portions of the horizon. Released orders dominate here and the operation priorities derived simply from due dates in capacity requirements planning must often be adjusted to reflect the unanticipated realities of the plant. User factors based on user judgement are therefore included in the completion time estimating and operation sequencing systems.

C. CAPACITY MANAGEMENT TECHNIQUES IN THE VARIOUS CAPACITY MANAGEMENT SYSTEMS

Capacity management is also represented by a series of systems varying in horizons, level of detail, and techniques. Various techniques are defined, but at a minimum, all capacity management systems should be supported by some type of input/output monitoring and control, even if it is a relatively simple manual system.

Capacity planning in the business plan, production plan, and master schedule is supported by resource requirements planning. The approach here is to identify a manageable number of typical products, groups of products or families. Products within groups or families should be related to similar resource utilization. The resources identified should also be a manageable number and should obviously be the critical resources. Critical resources cover a wide range of items such as cash, critical labor skill, long lead time components, expensive parts, engineering design time, warehouse cubeage, etc.

Resource requirements planning is often referred to by its techniques, such as load profile simulations, bills of labor, etc. Some advanced resource requirements systems include accommodation of learning curves (particularly appropriate in the integrated circuit business) and product life cycles. The business plan and production plan capacity systems can also be supported by econometric models.

The operational level capacity requirements planning system is fundamentally a scheduling by operation and loading by work center system. It is referred to as 'infinite' loading for the simple reason that capacity is not a constraint in the loading of work centers. The eventual load is however, compared to available capacity to pinpoint potential underload and overload problems. Important considerations in this system is the cumulative load to capacity measurement and the distribution of that load. If cumulative load is equal to or less than cumulative capacity, an evenly distributed load (no extensive periods of continuous overload) can probably be leveled.* If there are extensive periods of overload then the ability to level is minimized or eliminated all together. If these overloads are in the current periods of the horizon then an overloaded or front end loaded master schedule is often the cause.**

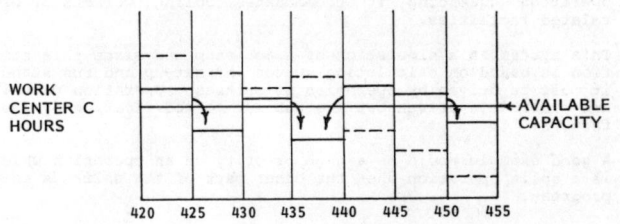

```
WORK
CENTER C                                    ← AVAILABLE
HOURS                                         CAPACITY

  420  425  430  435  440  445  450  455
```
Figure 9.

The capacity planning flow follows the same solid lines of the priority planning flow in Figure 5. The dashed lines of feedback are the basis for capacity control. If there is an unresolvable overload in the capacity requirements planning system then feedback to the MRP system and possibly to the master schedule is in order.

It is advantageous, of course, to solve problems within the bounds of the operational level system (MRP and CRP). This then insulates the master schedule from change. If, however, problems cannot be resolved in the operational system (and if no additional capacity is available) then the master schedule must absolutely be changed.

Completion time estimating operates in a much shorter horizon than all of the previous systems. It is the first system that is constrained by capacity in the scheduling operation. Since this syste is a finite loading system order priorities are a major consideration. (High priority orders are loaded first). The system gets its name from the fact that orders that are delayed because of capacity constraints are identified with their delay and anticipated completion time. Additionally, the overloaded work centers that contributed to the delay are identified.

The completion time estimating systems horizon is at least as long as the order lead time of released orders. Since it deals primarily with released orders it is particularly dependent on feedback and user priority factors. This is also true of the lowest level detail system, operation sequencing.

*This is illustrated by the solid lines and arrows in Figure 9.
**This is illustrated by the dashed lines in Figure 9.

SCHEDULING SYSTEMS/PRIORITY & CAPACITY MANAGEMENT

SCHEDULING SYSTEM	SCHEDULE FOR	HORIZON	DETAIL	PRIORITY SYSTEM	CAPACITY SYSTEM
Business plan	Business, business segments, major product lines	5 - 7 years	Varies monthly to quarterly into future, units & dollars	Business direction, financial measurements, major customers, markets, etc.	Resource requirements planning (load profile simulations, bills of labor, etc.) input/output mgmt.
Production plan	Product groups, models, families	5 - 7 years	Varies monthly to quarterly into future, units & dollars	Must support business plan and direction, financial measurements, key customers, markets, etc.	Resource requirements planning (load profile simulations, bills of labor, etc.) input/output mgmt.
Master schedule	Specific 'finished' products with specific B/M	1 - 3 years (product dependent)	Weekly units & dollars	Finished product date, priorities, backlog mgmt., customers, etc.	Resource requirements planning (load profile simulations, bills of labor, etc.) input/output mgmt.
MRP schedule	Specific components	1 - 3 years (product dependent)	Specific day date or week date by component part no.	Order priorities by specific day or week	MRP has no capacity calculation. It relies on the Master schedule and the operational capacity requirements planning system.
Operations schedule (Mfg. Activity Plng.) a. Capacity requirements planning	Specific operations/work center/component	1 - 3 years	Weekly bucket load hours	Operational priorities derived from order due	'Infinite' loading weekly bucket load vs. available capacity & cumulative load vs. cumulative available capacity, input/output mgmt.
b. Completion time estimating	Specific operations/work center/component	4 - 6 months & min. of released horizon	Weekly bucket load hours	Operation priorities derived from order due dates & user factors	'Finite' loading to weekly buckets with compl. time estimate in days
c. Operation sequencing	Specific operations/work center/component	5 - 10 days	Daily or shift load hours	Operation due dates and user factors	'Finite' facility loading (machine, tool, worker)

Figure 10.

Operation sequencing is very short term and ranges anywhere from two to five days or even up to 10 days. (Normally a few additional days beyond the MRP replanning interval). It, too is a 'finite' loader and in addition to the work center loading of operation sequencing, it accommodates tooling, workers or other related facilities.

This system is a simulation of a job shop and since this simulation is based on calculating queues and set-up and run standards, it must be driven by operation priorities. Operation priorities are order date driven but are subject to modification by user factors.

A good example would be a high priority on an operation which is a split operation when the other part of the split is in progress.

Solutions to capacity problems in this system which provides daily or shift work-to lists includes: operation splitting, grouping for set up, overlapping, alternate routings, alternate work centers, etc.

'Finite' loading systems tend to lead to much discussion and disagreement. The fact is that factories and work centers have 'finite' capacities and this is particularly apparent in the shorter range systems. The informal systems that have been effectively used over the years recognize this and therefore any formal systems we devise must also account for this fact.

SUMMARY

The details of the many systems defined here goes well beyond the scope of this paper. Fortunately today, more material is becoming available on the subject. The short list of references included is only a sample and by no means a complete list.

The reader is challenged to go well beyond this general overview that hopefully puts the many levels of priority and capacity management systems in perspective.

REFERENCES

'Master Production Schedule Planning Guide', IBM Publication GE20-0518.
'Capacity Planning and Operation Sequencing System-Extended', IBM Publication GH12-5119.
'Hot List', R. D. Garwood, Inc., January/February 1978, March-June 1978:
    'The Making and Remaking of a Master Schedule'.
'Hot List', R. D. Garwood, Inc., September-December 1978:
    'Capacity Planning'
'Communications Oriented Production Information and Control System-Master Production Schedule Planning', IBM Publication G320-1976.
'Communications Oriented Production Information and Control System-Manufacturing Activity Planning & Order Release', IBM Publication G320-1978

James T. Clark

Biography

Mr. Clark is a Senior Instructor in IBM's Manufacturing Industry Education Center in Poughkeepsie, New York. He has eight years of marketing experience and ten years of manufacturing education experience in IBM.

Mr. Clark teaches manufacturing courses and consults with IBM customer executives throughout the United States. He has taught in Europe, Japan and Canada. He is the co-author and co-producer of IBM's Material Requirements Planning (MRP) Video Course which is currently in use worldwide.

He has been presenting to APICS Chapters across the United States for the last six years. In the last two years alone, he participated in 35 APICS activities.

Reprinted from the APICS *1980 Conference Proceedings*.

CAPACITY MANAGEMENT
PART TWO

AN EXPANSION OF 'CAPACITY MANAGEMENT'
FROM THE 1979 APICS
ANNUAL CONFERENCE PROCEEDINGS

James T. Clark
IBM Corporation
Manufacturing Industry Education
Poughkeepsie, N.Y.

This paper is an expansion of the paper "Capacity Management" included in the APICS 22nd Annual Conference Proceedings (Page 191). If this paper is not available to the reader, one will be mailed by the author on request.

The initial paper addressed three capacity management topics: The financial payoff, a closed loop capacity management system and its relationship to priority management, and an outline of various capacity management techniques.

The major principle that was developed was that manufacturing companies are driven by a series of schedules ranging from the long range formal business plan to the detailed short range operation sequence or dispatch list. A derivation of this principle suggests there must be a series of priority systems and a series of capacity systems associated with each of the many scheduling systems.

This is recapped in figure 10 of the 1979 proceedings.

(Please note that the schedules listed and the corresponding diagram of a closed loop system in the 1979 Capacity Management paper imply that the final assembly schedule and master production schedule are synonymous. This is often the case in manufacturing build to order as well as make to stock products.

It is necessary however, in some manufacturing environments to separate the final assembly schedule from the master production schedule. The obvious example of this is assembled to order products that depend on a customer order dictating a mix of options for specific end-product configurations.

The scheduling system matrix would then include the final assembly schedule between the production plan and the master schedule. In the closed loop flow: customer order servicing would be input to the final assembly schedule, forcasting would be input to the master production schedule for option forecasts and there would be two way communication between the final assembly schedule and the master production schedule. The master production schedule would continue to feed MRP.)

The objective of this paper is to expand on the details of the series of capacity management systems.

The following topics will be addressed:

A. Resource Requirements Planning and Rough Cut Capacity Planning

B. Input/Output Monitoring and Control

C. Manufacturing Activity Planning

. Capacity Requirements Planning
. Completion Time Estimating
. Operation Sequencing

In the heirarchy of capacity management systems that support the heirarchy of scheduling systems a number of techniques and approaches have been employed.

It is impossible to identify a single specific technique with a specific level of schedule or level of planning and control for all manufacturers. One manufacturer for example, might use a detailed operations schedule and weekly bucket loading system for capacity management as it relates to the production plan. Another manufacturer might find this impractical because of the data and data processing volumes, and utilize resource load profile simulations. A consumer packaged goods manufacturer might use linear programming to optimize production schedules while this technique would be totally impractical in a job shop.

The definition of short, medium and long range vary by manufacturer and even by product as does the definition of the level of detail relative to the elements of time, product, capacity, etc.

In addition, the proliferation of terminology is overwhelming. Consider: Resource planning, load profile simulations, bills of resources, bills of labor, infinite loading, rough cut capacity planning, job shop simulations, etc.

To minimize this confusion, Figure 1 introduces the terminology of this paper as well as a relative placement of the capacity systems on the axes of planning horizon length and level of detail.

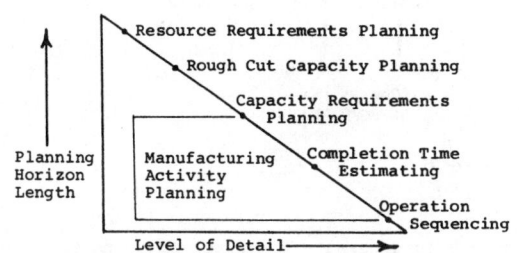

figure 1.

A. Resource Requirements Planning and Rough Cut Capacity Planning

Resource requirements planning, or simply resource planning, has been defined as the process of determining long range resource or capacity needs. The resource planning horizon is at least as long as the lead time to acquire the resource. The horizon should also include sufficient additional time to determine if the need will exist for a long enough period to justify capital commitments.

Rough cut capacity planning has been defined as an analysis of the master schedule to assist in evaluating capacity requirements for critical manufacturing facilities. It falls between resource requirements planning and detailed operational level capacity requirements planning (CRP). Rough cut capacity planning is by definition less detailed than capacity requirements planning and is generally done less frequently.

The major distinction between resource requirements planning and rough cut capacity planning is that the former is associated with the business plan and production plan while the latter is associated with the master production schedule. This implies differences in horizons, level of detail, frequency of evaluation, etc.

Capacity management approaches can vary from econometric models to load profile simulations to long range runs of CRP. The exact same technique might be used for both resource requirements planning and rough cut capacity planning, or the same technique but at different levels of detail, or entirely different techniques.

The technique of product load profile simulations is presented here. It presumes that the operational level CRP system involves too much detailed data, too detailed a forecast and too much data processing to be practical for long-range planning.

The steps involved in resource requirements planning include:
a. Defining a typical product structure.
b. Defining the resources that must be considered
c. Determining the "product load profile" for each typical product, that is, how much load is imposed on the resources by a single unit of an end product.

CAPACITY MANAGEMENT REPRINTS—Revised Edition

39

d. Extending these product load profiles by the quantity called for in the production plan or master schedule, and thus determining the total load or "resource requirement", on each of the production facilities and other resources.
e. Simulating the effect of different production plans or master schedules in order to make the best possible use of resources.

Figure 2. Depicts a typical product structure.

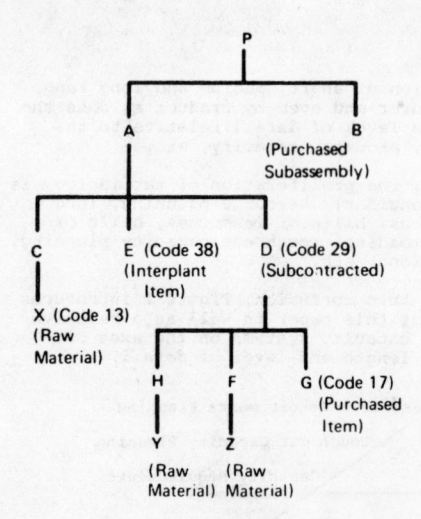

figure 2.

Product P is generally a product group to take advantage of the improved accuracy of aggregate forecasting. Product groups also decrease the amount of data to be considered and processed. The product group must be developed not only to allow aggregate forecasting but must group products that utilize similar resources.

Product P could be a group of machines including a statistical mix of options, it could be a single unique product or it could be an 'average' product that is never really built.

The next step is to identify critical resources consumed in the manufacture of P. Figure 2 specifies certain critical materials which are offset over lead time in Figure 3.

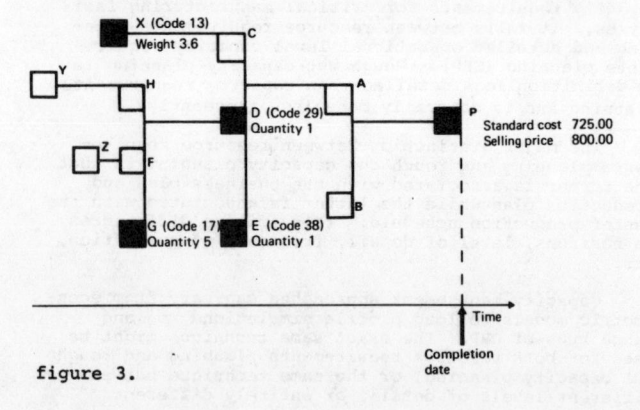

figure 3.

Critical labor is identified and offset over the lead time of product P in figure 4. This is often referred to as a bill of labor.

Other critical resources could include design engineering time, long lead time components, warehouse cubeage, cash, quality assurance, very expensive components, final assembly and test cells, etc. The objective is to include the truly critical resources but to keep the list to a manageable number.

Multiple individual resource profiles make up the product resource profile of Product P. This is depicted in Figure 5.

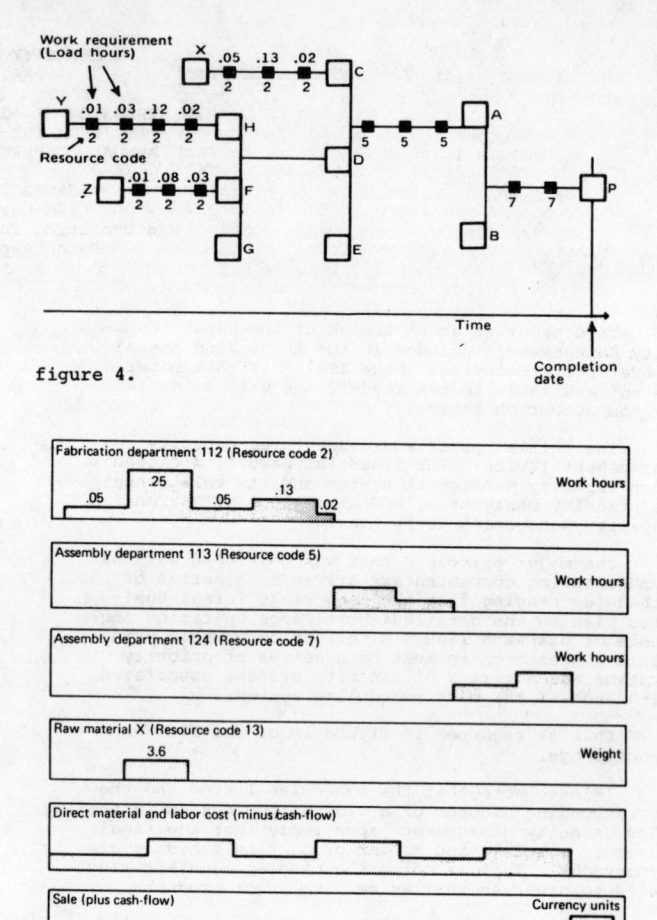

figure 4.

figure 5.

Figure 6. Demonstrates how the profiles are extended by the quantity in the production plan or the master schedule. The calculated total requirements profile could now be modified by other factors such as learning curves or be used to derive the profiles of related resources.

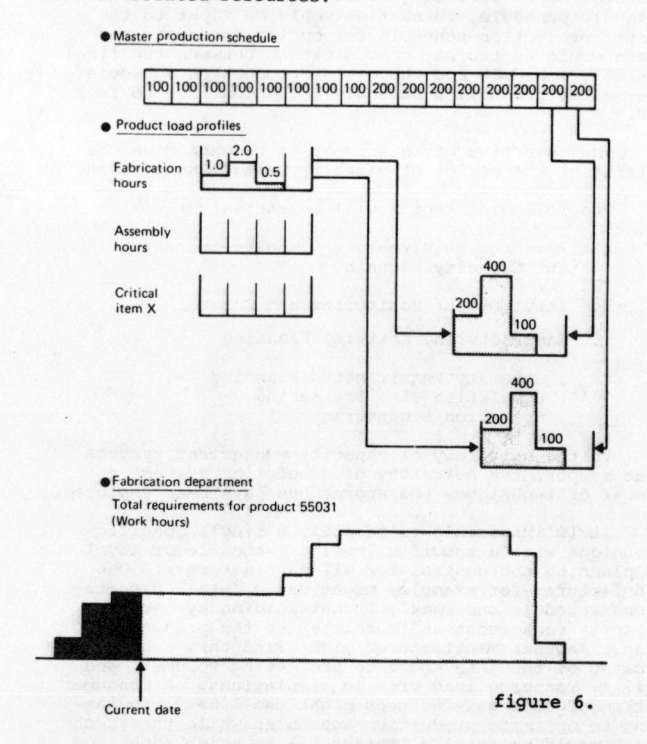

figure 6.

The advantages of the product load profile approach are:

a. It overcomes the data and data processing impracticalities often associated with using the CRP System for long range planning.
b. Its simplicity and speed of processing allows extensive simulation. The result is the ability to develop the probable results of many different possible courses of action. A simulation might indicate for example, that a product group forecast could vary by up to 15% before a major capital formation commitment was shifted into a different fiscal reporting period.
c. A completely computerized bill of material, MRP, routing and scheduling system is not necessary (although the availability of any of this data would obviously be helpful).
d. It allows for the identification of the specific "typical" finished product that created load problems (this may not be practical within the detailed CRP operational system).

The disadvantages include:

a. It is primarily a planning system and does not accomodate measurement and control.
b. The profiles are developed for the manufacture of one unit of the typical product so lot sizing assumptions must be made. A one for one lot sizing approach would usually produce a smoother load than the eventual load produced by the operational level MRP and CRP systems. This is not a serious deficiency for long range planning but could create some problems if the technique were employed in the nearer term. Capacity requirements for set-up would also have to be estimated. Another approach involves using current data from the operational level lot sizes and loads.
c. Available inventories and committed capacities are not considered. This problem is similar to the lot sizing problem and is of minimum consequence for long range planning. Utilizing the approach in the short range, again demands caution.
d. It is not exact. This is more a statement of fact than a disadvantage. The technique is not intended to be exact. If the user realizes this, then there should not be a problem.

B. Input/Output Monitoring and Control

Input/output monitoring and control can be utilized to support various levels of management in manufacturing. Input/output monitoring and control is as useful in production planning and master production scheduling as it is in supporting the management of individual work centers. The examples used here are oriented to a work center since this is the simplest form of input/output monitoring and control. As simple as it is, though, its use is ignored in far too many factories.

A sample input/output report is illustrated in Figure 7.

INPUT/OUTPUT

	PERIOD	1	2	3	4	5	6
INPUT	PLAN	500	500	500	550	550	550
	ACTUAL	450	520	580	540		
	DEVIATION	-50	+20	+80	-10		
	CUM. DEVIATION	-50	-30	+50	+40		

	PERIOD	1	2	3	4	5	6
OUTPUT	PLAN	500	500	500	550	550	550
	ACTUAL	470	480	530	550		
	DEVIATION	-30	-20	+30	-		
	CUM. DEVIATION	-30	-50	-20	-20		

figure 7.

It is important to inderstand the data elements in input/output monitoring and control.

a. Planned input is the most critical element and the most challenging to manage. Input must be managed. It is not simply taken blindly from a CRP computer report.
b. Actual input as well as actual output are measured values. Accurate and timely shop reporting is essential. Actual output establishes the true available capacity of a work center.
c. The planned output is an estimate into the near future from the work center foreman. It is based on his knowledge of machine and worker capability and availability, job characteristics and mix, and anticipated input.

Actual input and output will have some variability so the cumulative deviation is monitored as well as period deviations. This provides the first indication of whether a work center has an input or an output problem. Cumulative deviation is monitored relative to a specified band or tolerance. Action should be taken when the tolerance is exceeded.

Problems in input force the examination of upstream work centers or in the case of gateway or primary work centers the examination of the order release system and MRP system. The gateway work centers are easier to control in terms of input, particularly if a machine load report and MRP system are avialable. Order release dates must be managed to insure a steady and realistic flow into the gateway work centers. The order release system is extremely important because it provides a unique opportunity to manage gateway work center input. In fact, it also represents the last opportunity.

The input to secondary or intermediate work centers and to final assembly are more difficult to control because input load is coming from multiple sources. The availability of machine load reports and planned orders from MRP will also support this effort.

Some operation scheduling systems, utilizing combinations of forward and backward scheduling, have been used to accomodate bottleneck work centers, but the discussion of this is beyond the scope of this paper.

In some manufacturing environments the uncoupling of the final assembly schedule from the master schedule is a method of managing input to final assembly. Inventories of assemblies just below the final assembly are justified to maintain controlled input to a high volume final assembly line.

Problems in output are problems with capacity (unless of course they are the direct result of input problems) and the solution of the output problem is an effective capacity planning system. A realistic production plan and master schedule, should be developed with support from resource requirements planning and rough cut capacity planning. The master schedule is input to the MRP and CRP systems and the managed output of CRP develops capacity requirements. Capacity requirements essentially define output requirements. This obviously doesn't eliminate all output problems but hopefully it will minimize them. The short and intermediate range solutions to output problems such as alternate work centers, overtime, subcontract, buy vs. make, etc. will continue to support output management.

The monitoring portion of input/output monitoring and control is relatively simple to implement. It remains for management to provide the dimension of control. Input/output monitoring and control can be completely manual because computerized MRP and CRP is not a prerequisite. Readily available data from any current MRP and CRP systems, would of course, be helpful.

There is no legitimate reason why input/output monitoring and control is not a part of every factory's operation.

C. Manufacturing Activity Planning

Manufacturing Activity Planning, as depicted in the closed loop manufacturing system in the 1979 paper, is down stream from MRP and is the operational level or detail level capacity management system. This system is extremely critical to many interrupted flow manufacturers (job shop or discrete manufacturing) but of minimum importance in continuous flow manufacturing.

Manufacturing Activity Planning is subdivided into capacity requirements planning, completion time estimating and operation sequencing. Figure 8 below, as well as Figure 10 in the 1979 paper, put these systems in perspective.

MANUFACTURING ACTIVITY PLANNING			
	Level of Detail	Planning Horizon	Objective
Capacity Requirements Planning	Week	Months	Develop feasible capacity and material plans
Completion Time Estimating	Day	Weeks	Measure performance against due dates
Operation Sequencing	Hour	Days	Develop detail shop operating plan

figure 8.

It is essential to understand and accept the following premises before pursuing the details of these capacity management systems.

- a. Interrupted flow manufacturing is characterized by the presence of work in process inventory, or queues.
- b. The fundamental challenges of this type of manufacturing involve deciding on what in the queue to work on next and determining if capacity is available to work on it. (priority and capacity management).
- c. Capacity requirements planning and other shorter term detailed capacity management systems essentially involve scheduling by operation and loading by work center.
- d. The capacity requirements planning system can only be as good as the scheduling system.
- e. Scheduling orders and operations demands an understanding of manufacturing lead time.
- f. Manufacturing lead time in job shop or discrete manufacturing (interrupted flow) is made up of set-up and run and interoperation time.
- g. Interoperation time consists of queue for work, queue for move (wait time) and move time. In interrupted flow manufacturing this typically represents 80%-90% of manufacturing lead time.
- h. Queue time is the major ingredient in interoperation time and can easily represent 95% of interoperation time (or 75%-85% of manufacturing lead time).

Assuming that these premises are acceptable then a fundamental conclusion emerges that strongly suggests that capacity requirements planning demands the understanding of, the monitoring of, and the management of work in process inventories and queues.

The following details on capacity requirements planning, completion time estimating and operation sequencing develop progressively increasing refinements in the understanding of and the management of queues.

Capacity Requirements Planning

Capacity requirements planning consists of order scheduling and work center loading. This is often referred to as infinite loading since capacity is not considered in the scheduling or the loading.

Figure 9 is a simple example of scheduling an order by individual operations. The top portion of Figure 9 is input from MRP and includes the part number, quantity, due date and average lead time. The operation schedules are derived by backward scheduling from the due date using a simple scheduling algorithm.

1200 5's due in week 11 (shop calendar day 450)
Lead time = 25 days
order release = day 425

ROUTING OPERATION	WORK CENTER	STANDARD HOURS	START DATE	DUE DATE
			ORDER RELEASE	425
10	A	3.4	428	429
20	B	9.6	432	434
30	C	2.7	437	438
40	D	5.8	441	442
50	E	6.5	445	446
60	F	7.6	449	450

For scheduling:

Assume 3 day queue and move between operations and round standard hours up to the nearest 8 hour day.

figure 9.

A feasible schedule must be developed before the loading step can proceed. Figures 10 illustrate various scheduling situations.

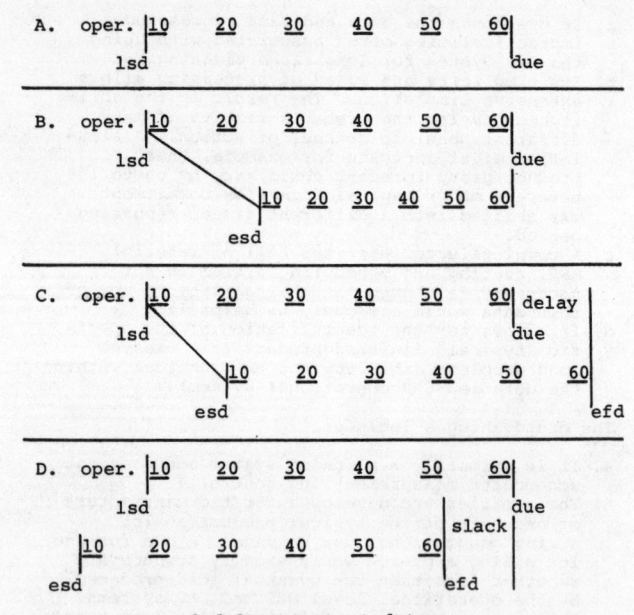

A. oper. |10 20 30 40 50 60|
         lsd   due

B. oper. |10 20 30 40 50 60|
         lsd   due
              |10 20 30 40 50 60|
              esd

C. oper. |10 20 30 40 50 60| delay
         lsd   due
              |10 20 30 40 50 60|
              esd   efd

D. oper. |10 20 30 40 50 60|
         lsd   due
                               slack
    |10 20 30 40 50 60|
    esd   efd

lsd=latest start date
esd=earliest start date
efd=earliest finish date
due=due date

figure 10.

Figure 10A is another way to view Figure 9 and it assumes the order can and will be started on the latest start date.

Figure 10B illustrates a situation where the earliest the order can be started is later than the latest start date. This could be caused by material availability for example. Since the available time is less than the lead time, the interoperation times have been compressed to meet the due date.

Figure 10C is a similar situation showing the delay that would result if interoperation times were not compressed. This decision may have been made in the initial schedule with the intent of compressing interoperation time after order release (expediting) or to simply be late on the order.

Figure 10D illustrates an early start date that is earlier in time than the latest start date and therefore slack is developed. This situation provides an option of starting on the earliest or latest start dates.

These many scheduling possibilities would obviously result in different work center loadings from a timing standpoint. Another key point is that a work center cannot be loaded in the past, so feasible start dates must be developed through logical scheduling.

Capacity requirements of all operations are accumulated for each work center in a given time period based on the results of order scheduling. Figure 11 displays the loads in weekly time buckets for work center C.

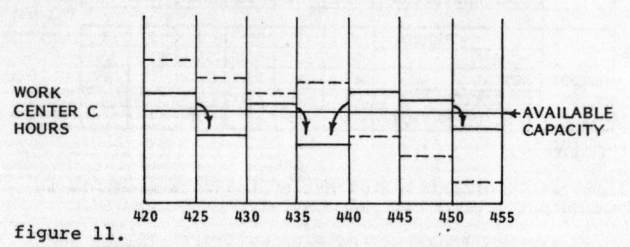

figure 11.

Load profiles can be developed for both early start dates and late start dates. In addition cumulative load should be presented and related to cumulative capacity over some specified horizon.

The load is compared to available capacity to pinpoint potential underload and overload problems. Another important consideration is the cumulative load to capacity measurement and the distribution of that load. If cumulative load is equal to or less than cumulative capacity, an evenly distributed load can probably be leveled. (Solid load lines and arrows in Figure 11). If there are extensive periods of overload or a "moving wave" of current period overloads (dashed load lines in Figure 11) then the ability to level is minimized or eliminated all together.

Capacity requirements planning has a quantity accuracy as good as the standards and a timing accuracy as good as the schedule. Industrial engineering techniques and data collection have long been utilized to define and adjust standards. Unfortunately not enough attention has been given to scheduling, and in particular queue times which is the largest time element in scheduling.

Figures 9 and 10A illustrates a schedule that assumes the same average interoperation time (primarily queue) for all operations and all work centers. This simplifying assumption can probably be tolerated in the longer range, but it can have serious consequences in the timing of load in the near term.

Another important point is that average lead time based on average queue time assumptions tend to be self fulfilling prophecies. (Assuming queues and lead time are not totally out of control). If MRP uses an average planning lead time then it will schedule order due dates and release dates with this average time. Since the planned lead time assumes queues and allows for them, execution to the planned schedule will develop the same queues. This is supported by one of the laws of queue, or backlog, which states that once a queue has been built it will tend to remain at a fixed level unless there are significant changes in personnel, equipment or the health of the business.

Breaking into this loop by reducing queues and lead times is a major challenge, and it also represents a very significant potential for overall improvement in a manufacturing business. The result can be a better competitive position via shorter lead times, less WIP inventory investment, more effective capacity utilizations, less scrap, fewer E.C. problems, etc.

A first step then toward improved capacity management is to evaluate queues by individual work center. This will support more accurate scheduling as well as pinpointing those work centers that have too little or too much queue.

The data gathered in input/output monitoring and control (Figure 7) can be utilized along with the value of the starting queue (prior to period 1) to develop a period by period measurement of queue. If the starting queue were 300 standard hours the queues for periods 1 through 4 would be as illustrated in Figure 12.

figure 12.

	QUEUE			
Period	1	2	3	4
Planned Q	300	300	300	300
Actual Q	280	320	370	360
Deviation	-20	+20	+70	+60

Figure 13 is a plot of the distribution of queue values in four different work centers.

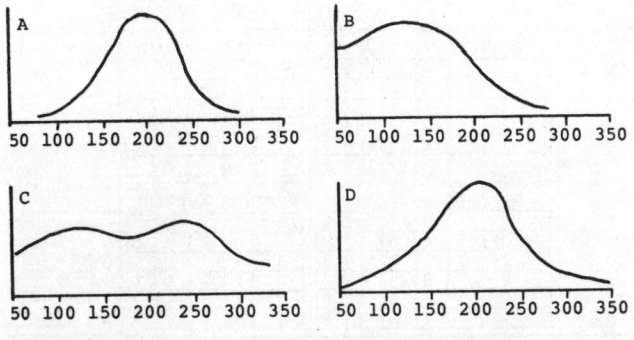

figure 13.   Queues in standard hours

Work center A has an average queue of about 200 hours and over the period of our data has never had a queue less than 80 hours. Clearly we could reduce the queue by almost 80 hours and still in all probability never run out of work in that work center.

Work center B however has a high incidence of idle time because of a frequent occurance of zero queue. Work center C shows a wide range of data and an indication that queues may be out of control

Work center D appears to represent the best situation, but even this distribution could be improved upon. Figure 14, progressing from a to b to c shows this improvement.

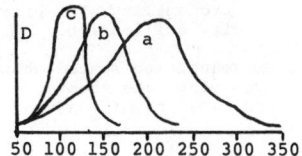

figure 14.

Queues can be viewed in a statistical sense like safety stock in finished goods inventory. The variability of input and output is similiar to the variability of demand (vs. forecast). The ability to manage and decrease this variability through input/output monitoring and control can result in more stable queues and decreased queues with all the associated benefits.

The evaluation of queues by work center will give the ability to introduce more accurate average queue times per work center in the scheduling algorithm. It will also draw managements' attention to work centers with queues that are too large or too small and to work centers with too great a variability in input and/or output.

Completion Time Estimating

Completion time estimating is the scheduling and loading system in the medium range. The previous level, capacity requirements planning, highlights potential capacity problems, while completion time estimating shows which individual orders are affected. This is the first system to consider finite capacity availability.

Each order is loaded considering latest start dates in priority sequence to the finite capacities of each time period for each work center. The order is loaded beginning with the first operation. If capacity is available, the operation is loaded. If capacity is not available, the operation is delayed until capacity is found. If an order is available, it can be pulled early to take advantage of any available capacity. In the event of delays interoperation time can be reduced.

The sequence of scheduling and loading of orders is dictated by order priorities initially determined in capacity requirements planning. These priorities can then be modified by other factors such as delay, slack, the amount of interoperation compression and external priorities.

Completion time estimating must also consider the results of operation sequencing which is the short range scheduling system

Completion time estimating develops an estimate of order completion time for orders based on the priority of the order and availability of capacity. Additionally, an individual order's contribution to any bottleneck conditions will be detailed.

Operation Sequencing

Operation sequencing is the short range scheduling and loading system and like completion time estimating, considers finite capacity availability. Completion time estimating and capacity requirements planning took into account only the total capacity within a time period without considering the sequence of operations. In contrast, operation sequencing considers the capacity and operation sequence each shift and computes a queue of operations for each machine.

Essentially, operation sequencing is a job shop simulation. It calculates a workable sequence of operations for each single machine considering the existing situation. This involves considering the capacity and the existing load of each individual machine, as well as operation due dates.

CAPACITY MANAGEMENT REPRINTS—Revised Edition

More advanced considerations could include alternate routings and operations, alternate work centers, operation splitting, overlapping, time critical operations and grouping related operations.

The objective of operation sequencing is to sequence the operations in a queue, therefore an operation priority must be established to determine the ranking of the operations. Some elements considered include operation in process, successive operations on the same order in the same work center, splits for this operation in process, operation belongs to high priority order and user specified priorities.

The scheduling techniques of developing a prioritized queue of operations for each machine significantly increases the probability of meeting schedules and maximizing capacity utilization.

The operation sequencing system should help manage release of orders into the shop and provide a priority controlled leveling of loads and a realistic dispatch list.

Supporting these three subsystems of Manufacturing Activity Planning is three levels of increasing refinement of queue management. This increased ability to manage queues was defined earlier as a critical prerequisite to better capacity management. This is detailed in Figure 15.

The capacity requirements planning system utilizes average queue time in its scheduling. This should be an average queue time by specific work center.

Standards, of course, are used for set-up and run times for all levels of manufacturing activity planning. An average move time is depicted for capacity requirements planning but the move time matrix shown for completion time estimating and operation sequencing could easily be used.

Completion time estimating introduces a logical refinement of queue times. It recognizes that some orders have longer than average queue times while others have shorter than average queue times in a given work center. The degree of "longer" and "shorter" is arbitrary and in our example there is four levels of detail. This approach demands rigorous record keeping and data collection because it is based on the measurement of actual queue time experienced by all orders and the relationship of the queue time to order priority. Completion time estimating is dependant on order priorities so the presence of priorities is assumed. The priority groups could be determined by simply stratifying the range of priorities.

The table indicates that orders in priority group 4 in work center B had an average queue time of 38 hours. This data from past intermediate range history will be used as projections for queue times for scheduling in the future intermediate range of completion time estimating. The single average queue time for this work center in capacity requirements planning could have been 22 hours.

This approach is identical for queue for move (wait) and the move time matrix is used for transit time.

The final refinement is the actual calculation of expected queue time in the operation sequencing function. Since a queue prioritized by operation exists for a work center, it is a simple matter to calculate specific operation and order queue times in a work center. The expected queue time for any operation is simply the total of the standard set-up and run times for all preceeding operations in the queue. The fourth operation in queue in the operation sequencing example will wait 15 hours, which is the sum of the standard set-up and run time of the preceding three operations. The estimate of queue for move is still a refined average because we assume no standards exist for transit time.

Summary

The capacity management systems defined here represent a wide range of systems to support a range of schedules from the formal business plan down to the dispatch list. These systems represent a natural sequence starting with gross and rough cut planning over long horizons and evolving down to very detailed job shop simulations over very short horizons. An essential element of this is the increasing levels of refinement in the understanding of and the management of work-in process inventories and queue times.

Clearly these approaches do not apply to all manufacturers. The systems described here, for example, would be more appropriate for interrupted flow manufacturing. Even within interrupted flow manufacturing, the classical build to order job shop might utilize some refined techniques that are beyond the needs of a build to forecast manufacturer. There is even a greater contrast in capacity management approaches when interrupted flow manufacturing is compared with process or continuous flow manufacturing.

Regardless of the industry, better capacity management should be a high priority for all manufacturers. The rewards are immense. Better capacity management will result in higher productivity, lower costs and shorter lead times, all of which are essential in an increasingly competitive world marketplace and in a U. S. economy that is plagued with productivity problems. Indeed, better capacity management may be the key to survival for many manufacturing enterprises.

	HORIZON	QUEUE (WORK)	SET-UP	RUN	QUEUE (MOVE)	MOVE
CAPACITY REQUIREMENTS PLANNING	'LONG' RANGE (MONTHS)	AVERAGE	STANDARDS		AVERAGE	AVERAGE
COMPLETION TIME ESTIMATING	INTERMEDIATE RANGE (WEEKS)	REFINED AVERAGE WORK CENTER PRIORITY / A / B / C / D 1 / 12 / 16 / 14 / 10 2 / 17 / 19 / 19 / 13 3 / 21 / 26 / 22 / 17 4 / 29 / 38 / 34 / 20	STANDARDS		REFINED AVERAGE WORK CENTER PRIORITY / A / B / C / D 1 / 1 / 5 / 3 / 2 2 / 3 / 8 / 6 / 3 3 / 4 / 10 / 8 / 6 4 / 7 / 12 / 11 / 8	REFINED AVERAGE FROM \ TO / A / B / C / D A / - / 2 / 1 / 4 B / 2 / - / 1 / 6 C / 1 / 3 / - / 2 D / 4 / 5 / 1 / -
OPERATION SEQUENCING	SHORT RANGE (HOURS)	CALCULATED OPERATION SEQUENCE / STANDARDS / QUEUE 1 / 6 / 0 2 / 4 / 6 3 / 5 / 10 4 / 3 / 15	STANDARDS		REFINED AVERAGE WORK CENTER PRIORITY / A / B / C / D 1 / 1 / 5 / 3 / 2 2 / 3 / 8 / 6 / 3 3 / 4 / 10 / 8 / 6 4 / 7 / 12 / 11 / 8	REFINED AVERAGE FROM \ TO / A / B / C / D A / - / 2 / 1 / 4 B / 2 / - / 1 / 6 C / 1 / 3 / - / 2 D / 4 / 5 / 1 / -

(Columns SET-UP, RUN, QUEUE (MOVE), MOVE span OPERATION LEAD TIME)

figure 15.

REFERENCES

'Master Production Schedule Planning Guide', IBM Publication GE20-0518

'Capacity Planning and Operation Sequencing System-Extended', IBM Publication GH12-5119

'Hot List', R. D. Garwood, Inc., January/February 1978, March-June 1978:
  'The making and Remaking of a Master Schedule'

'Hot List', R. D. Garwood, Inc., September-December 1978:
  'Capacity Planning'

'Communications Oriented Production Information and Control System-Master Production Schedule Planning', IBM Publication G320-1976.

'Communications Oriented Production Information and Control System-Manufacturing Activity Planning & Order Release', IBM Publication G320-1978

'Asset Management and Long Term Capacity Aquisition Planning', Frank O. Sunderland, 1979 APICS Annual Conference Proceedings.

'Manufacturing Scheduling', R. L. Lankford, A Paper presented at the University of Wisconsin, 1973.

'Short Term Planning of Manufacturing Capacity', R. L. Lankford, 1978 APICS Annual Conference Proceedings

'Master Production Scheduling-Principles and Practices', William L. Berry, Thomas E. Vollmann and D. Clay Whybark, APICS, 1979

Biography

Mr. Clark is a Senior Instructor in IBM's Manufacturing Industry Education Center in Poughkeepsie, New York. He has eight years of marketing experience and eleven years of manufacturing education experience in IBM.

Mr. Clark teaches manufacturing courses and consults with IBM customer executives throughout the United States. He has taught in Europe, Japan and Canada. He is the co-author and co-producer of IBM's Material Requirements Planning (MRP) Video Course which is currently in use worldwide.

He has been presenting to APICS Chapters across the United States for the last seven years. He was a topic coordinator and speaker in the 1977 and 1979 APICS Annual Conference and a speaker in the NCPDM National Conference in 1976 and 1980.

CAPACITY MANAGEMENT REPRINTS—Revised Edition

SCHEDULING THE JOB SHOP

R. L. Lankford
Otis Engineering Corporation

It is characteristic of the oil tool manufacturing business that customer requirements frequently impose rush conditions on the production facility. When the plant is producing to the limit of capacity--as it has been at Otis Engineering--the task of determining delivery dates and scheduling machine tools becomes especially crucial to productive and profitable operations.

Otis is a manufacturer of specialized production equipment for the oil industry. Some 980 people are employed in the Dallas plant, about 570 of them in the factory. This factory contains approximately 160 machine tools, divided into 53 work centers. Although a wide variety of manufacturing operations is represented, including machining, grinding, welding, painting, and assembly, heavy emphasis is placed on numerical control machining, with some 48 tape lathes and 13 three and four-axis milling machines in use.

Normally, there are about 7200 manufacturing jobs working in the plant at any given time, resulting in some 50,000 open operations to be scheduled. Because of the diversity of products furnished, lot sizes are small, averaging about 20 pieces per manufacturing job. The shop is oriented toward fast response, frequent changeovers, and an operational versatility ranging from hogging cuts on half-ton forgings to lapping a bubble-tight seal.

Otis is a job shop. The characteristics of a job shop are these:

1. The manufacturing facility is comprised of a group of discrete WORK CENTERS.

2. Each work center is composed of one or more MACHINES which, for practical purposes, have identical capabilities within the group.

3. Each JOB is a discrete batch of parts on which tasks are performed intermittently, and there are usually a large number of jobs relative to the facility size.

4. The work to be performed on a job consists of a sequence of OPERATIONS to be performed at specified work centers. Such a sequence is, of course, called a ROUTING.

5. The routing may theoretically direct a job from one work center to another in RANDOM order. Practically speaking, there is great variety in the routings of jobs in-process at a given time.

Other commonsense factors prevail, but these are the essentials by which a job shop is distinguished from the other logical extreme, a process flow or assembly line.

JOB SHOP	ASSEMBLY LINE
Discrete WORK CENTERS	Contiguous series of tasks
One OPERATION at a time	Simultaneous operations
BATCH processing	Continuity of work performance
RANDOM movement among work centers	Uniformity of routing

FIGURE 1

This combination of a large number of jobs, many work centers, complex routings, and random movement generates the overwhelming number of possibilities involved in job shop scheduling.

This plant manufactures both for stock and to order. About half of productive time is devoted to standard items for inventory replenishment, and about half to non-standard items made to customer order. All manufacturing jobs emerge from the computerized materials system.

Each industry has its own individuality insofar as ordering practices are concerned, and the oilwell drilling industry is no exception. It is frequently impossible for the customer to foresee exactly what configuration of equipment he will need, or just when his need will occur. Once a point is reached when a determination can be made, the customer's need is virtually immediate. For example, while an oil company is waiting for a packer, a $20 million offshore drilling rig may be idle, accumulating charges of thousands of dollars a day. The packer represents a relatively minor cost of drilling a well and is available from several competitors, so the customer's tolerance for manufacturing delays is minimal. It is a truism of the production control profession that every industry considers itself afflicted with unreasonable delivery requests. It is a fact, however, that in the oilfield, rush deliveries are an ingrained feature of daily operations, to an extent that few outside the industry can really understand.

A statistical measure of the difficulty of forecasting this type of business is shown in the following table:

MONTHS SOLD IN PAST TWELVE	NUMBER OF LINE ITEMS	CUMULATIVE PERCENT
1	6295	47
2	2280	64
3	1177	73
4	809	79
5	592	83
6	445	87
7	336	89
8	322	92
9	291	94
10	251	96
11	240	97
12	338	100
	13,376	

Almost three-fourths of the items sold during the year are sold no more than 3 months out of 12. Less than 5% of the items sell as many as 10 months out of 12.

In addition to the normal pressures of oilfield manufacturing, Otis has experienced a growth in business in recent years that has outstripped its capacity, in spite of remarkable increases in plant, machines, and trained personnel. These factors of make-to-order manufacturing, job shop structure, rush delivery demands, and capacity limitations cause the company to place heavy emphasis on the execution of orders on the shop floor, and hence to stress detailed operation scheduling in its manufacturing system development.

The Objectives of Scheduling

Different companies have different expectations of a scheduling system. In some firms, for example, marketing procedures permit quotation of calculated or historical lead times, placing few demands on the production control function. In other firms mass production of standard items lends itself to establishment of a master scheule with sufficient accuracy to allow scheduling to infinite capacity. It is only common sense that a scheduling system should be no more elaborate than absolutely necessary to support the sales philosophy of the company. At Otis that sales philosophy is very demanding, so the scheduling system seeks for relatively fine resolution in its forward vision.

When the system was designed, it was decided that this fine resolution could not be achieved by loading work centers to infinite capacity. Obviously, capacity is not infinite. Furthermore, the business at Otis is not solely one of manufacturing standard assemblies for inventory, like the manufacture of refrigerators, and so it would be very difficult, if not impossible, to manipulate a heterogeneous product mix by means of adjusting a master schedule to level the load on a job shop mix of work centers. It was decided that the easiest solution to establishing order on the shop floor was to schedule by finite loading.

In general terms, scheduling is an information system. Specifically, the information output is directed toward answering four practical questions which occur every day in the course of every business.

The most urgent of these questions is asked every time a salesman makes a sale: "When can we ship this customer's order?" At Otis the scheduling system is asked to acknowledge a realistic shipping date for each sales order and to report any deviation from that date. Sales orders entered in the late afternoon are scheduled before the opening of business the next morning. The delivery date promised is established after consideration of several complex factors:

1. the required completion sequence of all components and assemblies which must be manufactured or purchased;

2. the capacity constraints of all work centers required by all jobs supporting the subject sales order?

3. the urgency of each job compared to all other jobs contending for available plant capacity.

The second question answered by scheduling is that of the shop foreman: "What job goes on this machine next?" An effective scheduling system allocates currently available manufacturing capacity to those jobs which are most important to current company operations. It provides, each morning, a work list for each work center, enumerating the jobs in queue in the sequence of priority.

The third question answered by scheduling is frequent in production control: "How do we cope with all these changes?" An effective scheduling system will respond to change by rescheduling the entire backlog upon command. A customer insists he must have his equipment a week earlier than previously requested. The traffic manager reports a three week delay in the sailing date of a boat. These types of changes can be handled by MRP, insofar as dates are concerned. But what happens when our best customer doubles the size of an order that is already in trouble; the clutch goes out in one of our three radial drills; a new tape mill goes on line; and the flu epidemic has 17 people absent in various departments? These changes in load and capacity will impact many different jobs. Exactly which jobs and to what extent can be determined by scheduling.

The fourth question answered by scheduling is a management question: "Do we have enough capacity?" Although, capacity planning can be considered apart from machine loading, the two are really phases of the total process of scheduling. For example, it is generally recommended that capacity adjustments be made on the basis of infinite loading, or, if you prefer, capacity requirements planning. However, no intelligent adjustment of overtime for next week can be made until after finite loading has been accomplished, for only then is it known what amount of load will actually reach a work center in that period. So an effective scheduling system incorporates capacity requirements planning and machine loading working in unison.

The Limitations of Scheduling

It is important to recognize that scheduling is only part of the total manufacturing system. In particular, scheduling is not a substitute for inventory control, in that it does not plan to prevent emergency requirements for end items. It accepts the information it is given by the materials system and assumes (1) the item is really needed, and (2) the need is really for the date requested. For inventory replenishment jobs, date requirements are best determined by material requirements planning. On jobs made to customer order, the required date of an end item is specified by or negotiated with the customer. If the scheduling system has network planning capability—i.e., it schedules components before sub-assemblies and assemblies—the scheduling system will perform time—phasing in much the same manner as MRP. If date inputs are wrong, jobs will be scheduled wrong, with vital capacity being allocated to unnecessary recipients at the expense of jobs which are really needed to support customer expectations.

Unless shop floor operations are utter chaos, scheduling will not automatically increase a plant's output. Of course, an effective scheduling system may eliminate some of the confusion on the shop floor, and so make more productive use of people's time; it may improve the morale of foremen by telling them what jobs they should be working on, and so let them spend more time planning and supervising; and the capacity planning which is an essential preliminary to scheduling may make available more capacity when it is needed. But scheduling does not, of itself, increase throughput; it merely establishes the sequence in which jobs are worked. You cannot add a job or advance an existing job by human intervention and miraculously create the resources to do your "rush" job and all pre-existing jobs as well. Insertion of a high priority job will inevitably cause one or more other jobs to be retarded, unless capacity is adjusted by real-world methods, i.e., more machines, longer hours, or sub-contracting. If you play the tempting game of "priority shuffle", the computer will report back to you with speed and accuracy the effects of your wishful thinking. Whether you use a platoon of expediters with red tags or an intricate computer routine of finite loading, the name of the game is still "expediting" and it is a game with only one rule: Expediting is effective in inverse ratio to the number of jobs expedited.

Optimizing full scale job schedules by analytical methods has proved impossible. In an effort toward handling real-life situations, Operations Research has, in recent years, turned more and more to "heuristics". This term is generally taken to mean techniques depending on "rules of thumb". The schedules obtained from heuristic methods are conceded to be sub-optimal, but are alleged to be good enough for practical shop operations. Unfortunately, the heuristic methods disclosed in the literature have been as coldly received in the real world as were the analytical methods they try to surpass. The lesson to be learned from this is simple: OR should go further in the direction of empirical procedures yielding sub-optimal, but workable results. It is a fact of life that any optimum schedule, were it computed, would get hopelessly scrambled the first hour on the shop floor by normal, unpredictable dislocations of large scale manufacturing. All industry really wants is a computationally feasible method of scheduling which adapts to practical business usage and which will reduce job lateness to a tolerable level. Taking this view with respect to the usual job shop, the only thing to be optimized is the opportunity afforded the most important jobs to get done on time. A scheduling system which does this will perform so much better than any alternative approach that no responsible manager will lose sleep over real or imagined sub-optimality.

Persons looking at a computerized scheduling system from the outside often become preoccupied with the great amount of work that goes into its design and implementation. That is a dangerous fixation--first, because they may overestimate the initial task, and second, because they may ignore the very formidable effort required to keep the system operating properly. So, while other key aspects of system maintenance will be discussed later, a place among the limitations of scheduling should be given to the enormity of its dependence on facts. Scheduling, because its output permeates the organization and even extends to customer, is limited in its tolerance for bad input data. The most essential attribute of a scheduling system is believability; and yet it affords the user thousands of chances every day to lie to the system and be lied to in return.

At the basis of scheduling methodology is the capacity model, a mathematical model of the factory through which the flow of jobs will be simulated. In the course of constructing this model a company will learn a lot about itself. The definition of work centers must be done realistically, the manning table understood down to the last detail of employee mobility and machine interchangeability. Often, work plans--shifts, days, and hours--must be formalized, and two key factors must be investigated: utilization is the ratio of productive hours to scheduled hours, and accounts for losses due to downtime, absenteeism, and delays. Efficiency, of course, is the ratio of standard hours relieved to productive hours, and it, like utilization, must be continually observed and updated. Other events affecting capacity must be reported as they occur or before they occur, if they can be anticipated. Overtime plans, emergency breakdowns, preventive maintenance, vacation schedules-- all these inevitable departures from normal operations can be introduced into the model if a convenient access is provided. Timely recognition of such changes will permit expected capacity closely to match actual capacity at each point within the scheduling horizon.

It is no less important to know with accuracy the expected load competing with a job during its term. Standard times must be reasonably correct and they must be maintained. At Otis the computer is used to assist in the maintenance of time standards, so that each time a part is manufactured the computer "learns" from experience and uses this learning in scheduling the part on the next occasion.

CAPACITY MANAGEMENT REPRINTS—Revised Edition

Frequent rescheduling requires absolute knowledge of the status of a job at every point in its progress through the shop. If jobs are lost or mis-located through errors in data collection, false--and possibly alarming--reports will be sent to customers, credibility of the system will be compromised, and costly confusion will be generated on the shop floor. Plus and minus error in standards and/or capacities will tend to offset each other, but there is no automatic remedy for an error in reporting operation number or quantity complete. If data collection accuracy of 95% or better cannot be maintained in the plant, good schedules will not be produced.

The type of scheduling system adopted by a company must be based on real needs characteristic of the organization and the business it is in. If your business permits, for the most part, quotation of standard lead times and if you can externally analyze and manipulate the master schedule to conform reasonably well to the separate capacities of your work centers, then scheduling to finite capacity is an unnecessary exertion. Time-phased material requirements planning can generate your priorities; capacity requirements planning can probably help you adjust your capacities to a tolerable approximation of your needs; and critical ratio dispatching will sequence your jobs very well indeed. But if your total load is fragmented among a large quantity of small jobs, and if many of these are non-standard items with delivery requested in less than normal lead time, you will find human analysis of the master schedule terribly demanding and successful manipulation of that schedule virtually impossible. If your customers will not always accept canned average lead times, you may be asked to quote a specific day for shipment and to justify that date in terms of specific work center loads and specific contending jobs. And above all, if your circumstances change frequently, with many new jobs with varied priorities arriving each day and with old jobs subject to earlier or later replanning, then you might well benefit from a form of scheduling with finer resolution--and that means finite loading.

FINITE LOADING

Within the past several years, the feasibility of finite loading as a scheduling technique has been earnestly questioned by some of the best thinkers in the field of production control. This analysis has benefitted the profession by raising the admonition of caution, without which some companies might have attempted to use finite loading without understanding what is needed to make it work. Unfortunately, the force of negative pronouncements has raised a barrier to further thought and discussion, which--if continued--can only retard the development of more effective methods of manufacturing management.

It is not the purpose of this paper to argue the theoretical aspects of scheduling, although uninhibited discussion of a professional character is definitely needed on this subject. What is intended here, however, is to record the experience of one company using finite loading successfully under very demanding conditions. Other practitioners can judge for themselves whether this experience is significant. The Otis approach, to be sure, is not one in widespread use, but it is certainly not unique. It was formulated by studying the experience of others in this country, and it parallels an approach used successfully by commercial scheduling packages in Europe. If there is a lesson to be learned from our accumulation of experience, it is that earlier announcements of the death of finite loading may have been premature. We may recall that when asked to comment on newspaper reports of his death, Mark Twain referred to them as "greatly exaggerated".

One means of facilitating objective discussion of all production control methods is to clarify obscure terminology and to adopt a more standardized vocabulary--one readily understood by all professionals. A step in that direction was taken two years ago with the adoption of the term "capacity requirements planning" to replace "infinite loading". It has been suggested that a more meaningful expression should likewise be found to replace "finite loading". One of the terms which has been proposed is "detailed operation scheduling", which perhaps defines more exactly what is done when scheduling occurs at the detail level within the capacity constraints of the factory. And so, whenever the term "scheduling" is used in this discussion, it must be understood to mean detailed operation scheduling--that is, sequencing manufacturing jobs in priority order, loading machines in the factory so as not to exceed the capacity of any work center, and determining the completion date of each job from the simulated performance dates of its operations.

The Options

But how elaborate a system does your firm need? How many limitations can you accept and still do the job expected of scheduling? Or put another way, how many "bells and whistles" can you afford to pay for? Because pay for them you will, not only in system design cost, but also in the discipline required for ongoing operation and, not least, in computer run time. Here is a checklist of features which can be provided at greater lesser cost:

1. NETWORK OPTIMIZATION. It would certainly be ideal too have all parts going into a single assembly completed at the same time. Obviously, if one or more parts are delayed by capacity constraints, other parts for the same assembly could be rescheduled to later time periods, releasing that early capacity for other needed jobs. But, of course, shifting some load in this manner invalidates the previous schedule, leading to a succession of iterations that is both complicated and costly. Programs have been written to do this, but before you ask the cost in computer time, look at your business to see if you need this elegance.

    To let the computer automatically reschedule all parts to the same degree of lateness deprives the user of his opportunity to focus attention on the lagging part and correct the impediment in its schedule by alternate routing, subcontracting, multiple setups, flowing, or other corrective measures. Furthermore, the disparity among completion dates of related work does, greatly exceed the latitude consciously permitted in early and late start date options for scheduling flexibility. And finally, if all parts are scheduled to arrive at a common late date, exposure to unhappy surprises involving scrap and rework is very non-optimum. So, product structure networks should be optimized only if this elegance gives enough real improvement to be worth the cost.

2. MAKESPAN OPTIMIZATION. What is true of parts is also true of operations on the same part. If a later operation will be delayed in a long queue, why not reschedule preceding operations. This frees early capacity on upstream work centers, shortens queues, and reduces the active makespan of the subject job.

    The same considerations already cited argue against rescheduling operations. To exert maximum efforts toward corrective measures is preferable to the acquiescence of delaying properly scheduled early operations.

3. MULTIPLE SETUPS. Using two or more machines simulataneously to perform the same operation is sometimes a feasible way to reduce the makespan of a large job. An improved delivery date may be worth the extra setup costs. Such an option is easily added to a scheduling routine, either as an automatic feature or on a selective basis.

4. ALTERNATE ROUTING. Since alternate routing is the most frequently used corrective measure in job shop schedule improvement, it should be available to the production control planner, either selectively or automatically. As an automatic feature, it introduces a moderate degree of complexity into the system design, but it can greatly extend the computer run time. On balance, it is an option most users will probably want.

5. FLOWING. Particularly urgent jobs may be moved to the next work center before all parts have finished the current operation.

    Programs have been written which resort to flowing whenever a date cannot be met by other means, but whether this feature contributes much practical advantage is open to serious question. If the effect of flowing is desired, without being either automatic or complicated, an option can be provided for splitting a job on command into two or more parts which can be scheduled on separate work centers simultaneously.

6. PULL AHEAD. If a work center is temporarily low on work, the prudent production control manager will look into the future and try to reschedule some jobs into the deficient period. A finite loading program will usually do this automatically for all jobs which have completed their prior operations. A problem arises, however, when this is tried on jobs needing one or more prior operations, since those jobs will be forced out of priority sequence in the prior work center, a practice contrary to the whole rationale of scheduling. At Otis it is very easy for the production control planner to identify jobs for pull ahead, but it is practiced sparingly, almost entirely in gateway work centers.

None of the options enumerated here are entirely frivolous, and all will have their advocates. A scheduling system in which none of these features is automatic can still, in our experience, far excel alternative methods of scheduling. However, multiple machines and alternate routing are highly desirable features, with flowing a third choice if shop floor discipline and the data collection system will support it.

HOW SCHEDULING IS DONE

Scheduling is done by priorities; the mechanics are so much clockwork-- interesting as to function, but productive only insofar as the priority structure represents what the user really wants done. Material requirements planning will, of course, generate from a master schedule priorites expressed as need dates. If it were possible--which it is not--to adjust the master schedule perfectly to match the capacity of every work center, then little importance would attach to priority designation beyond a sort of tiebreaking function. However, when the need for capacity exceeds the availability in one or more work centers, a sound ordering of priority is of much greater importance. A simple list of due dates from MRP is quite insufficient.

The literature is, of course, abundant in the matter of priority or dispatching rules. Unfortunately, much of that abundance is useless sophistication. The needs of most manufacturers will be met by a relatively simple priority scheme embodying two principles:

1. It should be dynamic, i.e., it is computed frequently during the course of a job and so reflects changing conditions, and

2. It should be based, in one way or another, on slack, i.e., the difference between the work remaining to be done on a job and the time remaining in which to do that work.

When infinite loading is done, dispatching is normally based on Critical Ratio, which is both dynamic and slack-dependent. With its transparency of logic and simplicity of application, Critical Ratio will work well in many applications.

Otis uses a priority rule based on slack, with another dimension added to accomplish a specific objective. It is not uncommon for many independent demands to have the same required date and the resulting manufacturing jobs to have slack times within a very narrow range of values. Under such circumstances, many jobs would have nearly equal priorities. Consider three such jobs with equal slack:

JOBS WITH EQUAL SLACK

Job	Time Remaining	Work Remaining	Slack
A	16 days	6 days	10 days
B	21 days	11 days	10 days
C	11 days	1 day	10 days

FIGURE 2

Upon inquiry it may be found that these jobs are not equal in priority at all. Job A is a routine order to be shipped motor freight to a customer in Oklahoma. Job B is part of an exceptionally large export order and, if the boat sailing date is not met, that entire order will have to be shipped at our expense by chartered plane to Nigeria. Job C, on the other hand, is going to a drilling rig in the Gulf of Mexico, and, while we are making our product, that offshore rig is costing the customer $1000 an hour. No judicious manager would treat these three jobs as equivalent, nor would he give each an equal claim to the limited resource of, say, the one large boring mill in the plant.

So an inside salesman at Otis will pay particular attention to the circumstances of an incoming order, and he will use his judgement in assigning to that order a factor representing management's assessment of urgency. This management factor is applied objectively following certain guidelines which suggest how the management of the company intends for its resources to be allocated. The priority of the order, then, is composed of three elements: time remaining to due date, work remaining to be done, and the management factor, which assesses the consequences of failure. The distinctions among our three hypothetical jobs become dramatic:

EQUAL SLACK—DIFFERENT URGENCY

Job	Time Remaining	Work Remaining	Slack	Mgt. Factor	Priority
A	16 days	6 days	10 days	4	235
B	21 days	11 days	10 days	7	336
C	11 days	1 day	10 days	10	453

FIGURE 3

It will be noticed that priority is here expressed as an index number on a scale of 0 to 1000, because this has been found to be more readily understood in the shop than a Critical Ratio. A high number denotes a high priority job; a low number, a job of lesser urgency. One further refinement has been found helpful. A bias in favor of late jobs is introduced by increasing priority at a faster rate as slack decreases. It will be noted that this relationship is continuous for all values of slack. The "slack per operation remaining" rule, an otherwise useful expression of priority, suffers a reversal of logic as slack changes from positive to negative, and must be adjusted if continuity is desired.

Again it should be emphasized that it is easy to become enamored with the study of priority rules, when in reality costly sophistication is not justified by better results. The priority structure illustrated here is logical, easy to compute, and it implements the company's policy decisions regarding access to plant capacity. If a simpler approach will do the same for your company, by all means use it. What is important is that the priority system be credible, that it be beyond reproach in its objectivity, and that it be neither circumvented nor bent out of shape by subjective tensions.

We have seen that need dates form the basis of the priority system. Knowing the need date, we can calculate the date we must start the job by offsetting from the need date a span of time equal to the lead time of that part; and, of course, we all know the lead time of every part we build. We can read it off the Item Master File or look it up in the quotation manual our salesmen use to quote deliveries. If we use MRP, we know that lead time is the amount of time we offset from a required date to obtain planned order release. In any case, we conventionally carry some figure on the record as the lead time for a specific part. And yet, in many plants lead time is the one length of time that part almost never takes to manufacture! The part is built faster than lead time when the sales manager is pushing a job, and it invariably takes longer when the job moves without pressure. And if the president of the company wants the parts for his favored customer, a three-week job can be finished tomorrow night.

Then why do we honor that one number we call lead time for a manufactured part? Of course, it is because it represents average length of time it takes to build the part, or in some cases the length of time we wish it took. In either case, a make-to-order shop is deluding itself by attaching a canned lead time to all jobs indiscriminately.

At Otis we are regularly asked to build, in one week, a part which--if made for stock--would require five weeks to move through the plant. And so when we plan a job, as the first step in scheduling, we recognize the fact that lead times are flexible and vary according to job urgency.

We are all familiar with the elements of lead time:

> Operation Time - composed of setup and run time.
> Interoperation Time - composed of transit and queue time.

Lead time, of course, is usually composed predominately of queues, and so the queue element is extremely important in capacity planning. Average queues are usually determined by historical study of each work center. If historical values of queues are built into lead times, a capacity requirements plan will be produced which will mirror history.* At Otis, history has frequently been one of more work than the plant could do. So, on a part, we might show an historical use of mill time ten days after completion of lathe time. Both we and our customers might like for this milling to occur two days after lathe work is finished. What we want capacity requirements planning to do for us is to produce a model of the factory our customers want us to maintain. And so the values of queue in standard lead times should reflect a reasonable value for inventory replenishment jobs.

Then, in planning a job, lead time flexibility is recognized by the compression of interoperation time on urgent jobs. This is exactly what happens in the shop. Urgent jobs are identified and moved promptly to succeeding operations where they leap frog all or part of existing queues. Less urgent jobs, when completed, wait a longer period before subsequent activity. At the planning stage we know with some degree of accuracy the urgency (apart from due date) of each job. That relative urgency is signified by the management factor which is applied at the time of order entry. And so, the lead time of each job may be planned individually by squeezing Interoperation Time based on urgency, as shown in Figure 4.

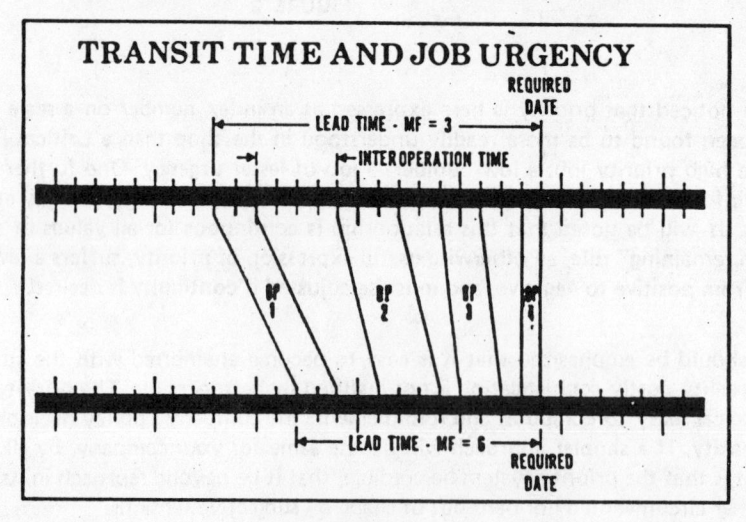

FIGURE 4

Using this principle, the start dates of each operation may be determined by backward planning (Figure 5), starting with the required date and ending with the planned start date of the job. So that planning will not be excessively disrupted by subsequent inability to fit the job into available time periods, some tolerance should be applied to operation dates. This may be accomplished by permitting a job to start somewhat earlier than the latest possible start date found through backward planning. This is a policy matter, which at Otis is related to job urgency.

Perhaps it is a small matter, but those who plan capacity entirely by infinite loading still put queues in their lead time estimates. If capacity were infinite there would be no queues. And if one agrees to recognize estimated queues in planned lead times for future capacity planning, does it not follow that current actual queues should be recognized in planning near term capacity?

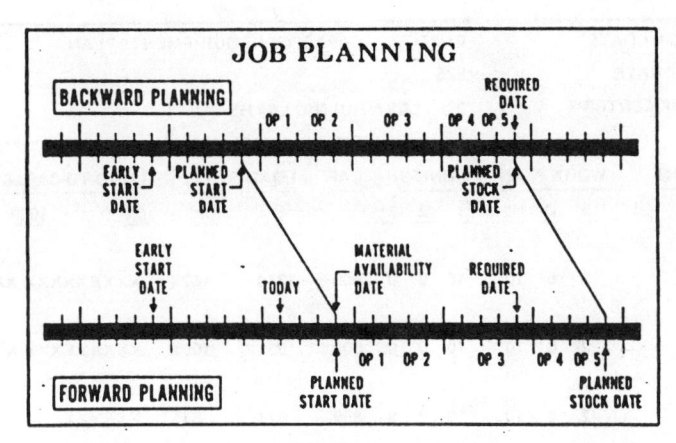

FIGURE 5

It is not uncommon for backward planning to yield a planned start date in the past, signifying insufficient time to complete the job before its due date. Furthermore, it does not make much sense to plan a job to start before its raw material is available. In point of fact, a job cannot realistically start until the latest of three alternative dates--Early Start Date, Today, or the Material Availability Date. Some jobs, therefore, must be replanned from the appropriate limiting start date as shown in the illustration.

This planning procedure must be carried from the end item level back through the bill of materials to all predecessor jobs which provide sub-assemblies and components (Figure 6). This is the time-phasing we are familiar with in MRP, which provides the required dates of components relative to the start date of their assembly. If any component start date will precede the current date or material date, all jobs in that branch of the product structure must be replanned in the normal manner.

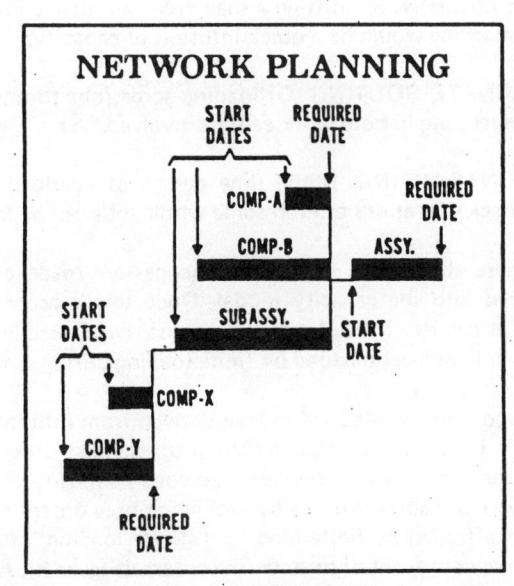

FIGURE 6

When all job planning has been completed, the capacity requirement of each job on each affected work center is known, based on the customer's expectations, modified only by a physical ability to start the job. If the machine hour content of each operation on each job is now loaded against prescribed work centers in the designated time periods, a load profile will be obtained for actual released jobs. If, then, this procedure is repeated for planned orders within the MRP system, a load profile will be obtained for all jobs within the planning horizon. The first 4 weeks of such a load profile is shown in Figure 7. This is the capacity requirements plan, one of the basic computer outputs of scheduling. We may look upon this as a model of the factory our customers are asking us to maintain. The first question we must answer is: Can we provide such a factory?

```
REPORT DATE        01/27/73   CAPACITY REQUIREMENTS PLAN
SHOP DATE          525
WORK CENTER        29   L&S NT-III N/C LATHE
                                ················· WEEK ·················
WEEK   START   WORK-PLAN   UNITS    CAP   LOAD   L/C    LOAD-TO-CAPACITY RATIO        OVER
               S  D   H   1  2  3                %     0%        100%      200%     (UNDER)

1      525     2  6  10   10 9  0   809   1310   162%   .XXXXXXXXX.XXXXXX            501

2      530     2  6  10   10 9  0   809   851    105%   .XXXXXXXXX.X                 42

3      535     2  6  10   10 9  0   809   523    64%    .XXXXXX                      (285)

4      540     2  5  10   10 9  0   675   898    133%   .XXXXXXXXX.XXX               223
```

FIGURE 7

The objective of capacity requirements planning is to determine required rates of output by work center and to adjust available capacity as closely as possible to the requirements of each time period. Obviously, in periods of overload such as those portrayed in Figure 7, the prudent production control planner will explore several methods of increasing capacity:

1. OVERTIME. In the example, the work plan already entails heavy overtime (2 shifts, 6 days, 10 hours in Week 1), but the situation might be critical enough to justify a 7 day week or 12 hour shifts.

2. MORE MACHINES. Shifting a man from another section on shift 2 so as to man the tenth machine would be a quick infusion of capacity.

3. ALTERNATE ROUTING. Offloading some jobs to underloaded machines contributes to load leveling in both work centers involved.

4. SUBCONTRACTING. If the time period of overload is far enough in the future the bottleneck operations or even some whole jobs can be farmed out.

If one or more of these alternatives is feasible, changes are made on the load file and changes in capacity are introduced into the capacity model. Once this is accomplished, capacity requirements planning has done all it can do. If overloads still persist, two possible courses of action are available: adjust the master schedule or level the load by finite loading during scheduling.

Insofar as capacity is concerned, the load profile derived from infinite loading is quite useful well out in the future where it is composed predominantly of planned orders out of MRP. But in the near term-- this week and the next few weeks--when load consists mostly of released orders, it is possible to get a more realistic view of capacity needs by looking at how orders will probably arrive at each work center. Such a view is afforded by finite loading. Infinite loading, of course neglects to consider the waxing and waning queues in front of prior work centers. (Figure 8). And so jobs will not arrive in the orderly fashion computed by infinite loading, and any plan for capacity requirements based on infinite loading alone will inevitably produce disappointment in the job shop. In a dynamic job shop operation these queues change dramatically even over the short term, and they are frequently different from the queue estimates--if any--carried in a firm's leadtime models. It has been suggested that the queue portion of leadtime be frequently altered to reflect current plant conditions. Inasmuch as finite loading recognizes queue conditions every time scheduling is done, it is simpler to consult the finite load report directly in making capacity adjustments in the near term, based on a knowledge of what jobs will arrive when. Then, after all management decisions responding to capacity needs have been made, capacity is fixed for purposes of scheduling.

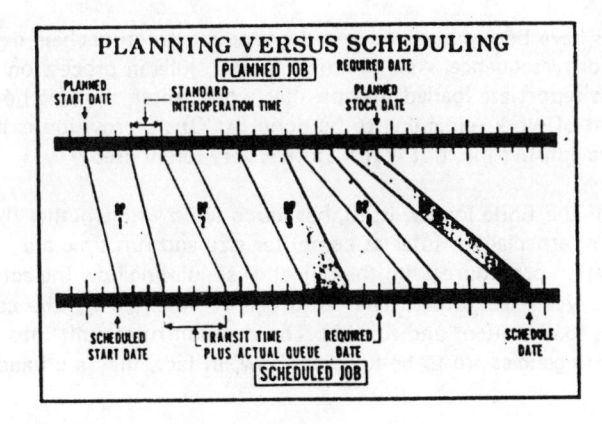

FIGURE 8

So, we may consider specific methods of doing finite loading--the daily process by which scheduling is actually accomplished.* All capacity decisions have been made, capacity is fixed for purposes of scheduling.

An effective scheduling system will begin with two objectives:

1. to optimize the opportunity afforded the most important jobs to get done on time; and

2. to observe product structure relationships, such that components are completed before their sub-assemblies, and sub-assemblies are completed before their assemblies.

The first objective is met by computing priorities each time scheduling is done, so the sequence of loading always reflects current conditions. To implement the second objective, jobs must be chained together according to product structure, forming a network in which predecessor jobs must be completed before their successors. Bear in mind that a single component for a sub-assembly may be derived in partial quantities from more than one predecessor job, while a single component job may furnish parts to several different successor jobs. An extremely simple diagram of this type of relationship is shown in Figure 9. The network of interdependences among, say, 7000 jobs is obviously complex, especially when it controls the dates on which parts will be available for higher level jobs and the priority relationships which must prevail between successors and their predecessors.

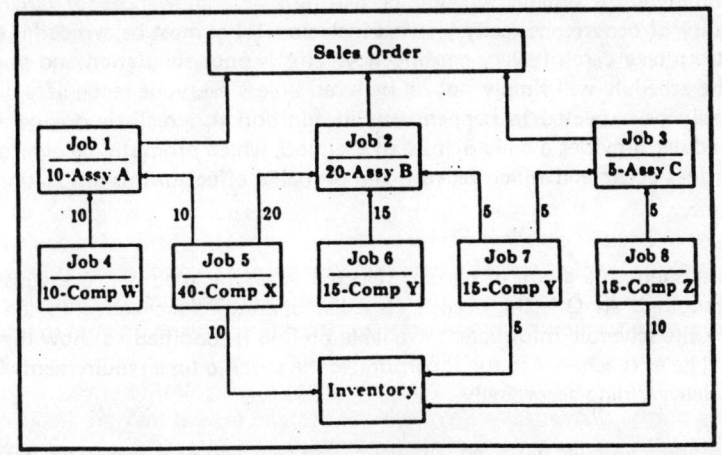

FIGURE 9

Obviously, scheduling can be done on any time cycle required, depending on the frequency with which significant changes in the backlog of open orders and the shop status of working jobs can be recognized by the total manufacturing system.

Once all priorities have been computed and the product structure chain developed, jobs can be sorted for loading in priority sequence. As a practical matter, jobs in process on a given work center at the time of last status report are loaded first on that work center, the load hours having been adjusted to reflect the amount of work remaining to be done. At Otis a provision exists for interrupting a job in progress with a pre-emptive job, but that feature is very rarely used.

The mechanism of the finite loader, itself, has much to do with whether the procedure is practical for a given application, especially insofar as computer size and run time are concerned. In essence, finite loading is a simulation procedure, with the object of simulating how the actual stream of jobs will flow through the factory in the future. The factory is represented by the capacity model; each job is represented by its load content and routing. The decision rules built into the finite loader govern the way in which contingencies are to be handled--how, in fact, they are handled when they arise on the shop floor.

During simulation the highest priority jobs encounter no queues at all, while descending priorities entail ever-increasing waiting periods on heavily loaded work centers. Queues are, therefore, related to priorities as shown in Figure 10. Transit time may also be squeezed according to priority, so that the total lead time compression which results will reasonably approximate not only what happens on the shop floor, but also the compression logic incorporated into job planning, from which the capacity requirements plan was derived.

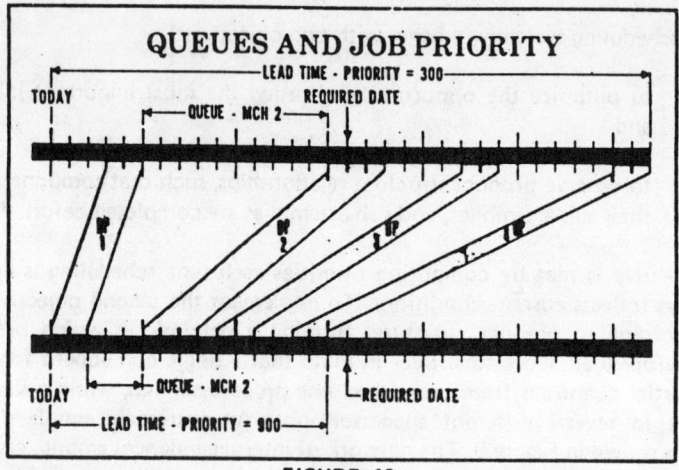

FIGURE 10

It must not be thought that every job can be simulated with infallible accuracy. Many dislocations do occur. In compiling the original schedule certain resonable allowances for variance can be included, if the probability of occurrence really justifies inclusion. What must be avoided is the temptation to pad the schedule to take care of every contingency. This is poor simulation and poor production control practice. The schedule will simply not be believed unless everyone recognizes that it is based on what can reasonably be expected to happen. But in addition to a realistic original delivery date, a finite loading scheduler provides a daily picture of each job, which promptly recognizes when an unforeseen dislocation does occur and which reckons the probable effect of this dislocation on the future course of the job.

For example, suppose a group of parts is rejected at a scheduled in-process inspection and extensive rework is required. At Otis the needed remedial operations are added to the routing via CRT and immediately the schedule information available on-line is modified to show that a change in schedule is required. The next scheduling run incorporates the specific time requirements for remedial work and adjusts the delivery date accordingly.

Some parts are scheduled with an allowance for rework provided after certain major in-process inspections, depending on the exposure to rejection. If no rework is required, the next scheduling run will predict an earlier completion for the job.

Some users may be bothered by the prospect of a formal system following the real world this closely--that is, moving dates as actual events occur. Some businesses do not demand that delivery dates be pinpointed to the best estimate current information can produce. Such users will be much more comfortable quoting canned lead times and avoiding frequent advisories which invite them to consider the consequences of what has already happened and to take action to correct whatever conditions prevent them from meeting their customer's expectations.

At Otis the scheduling system is expected to answer directly that first question of scheduling, "When can we ship this customer's order?" Delivery dates are acknowledged to field locations and directly to customers based on information derived from the nightly scheduling run.

When the Order Control Group arrives at the office each morning, sales order schedule (Figure 11) is waiting for them, providing up-to-date information on the delivery status of every order. This report is so arranged as to call attention to any significant changes since the previous day. If an order is ahead of schedule, that fact is noted. Or if delays have been encountered so that a previously promised delivery date is no longer realistic, a message appears on the report identifying that order for the analyst's attention. If an order is in trouble, that problem will not be solved unless some person takes appropriate action using human skill and experience with a determination to do everything possible to get the customer what he needs when he needs it.

```
SALES ORDER SCHEDULE         SO No. 69180

ORDER    REQUEST   PROMISE   SCHEDULE    MESSAGE
520      565       585       585         FIRST SCHEDULE

PART NO.  QTY      SOURCE    SCHEDULE

22DO30    3        171842    560

10XO78    3        171829    585

93WB40    2        PC 91852  570
```

FIGURE 11

Otis does not print out voluminous reports, but rather utilizes on-line files which provide via teleprocessing a wealth of information to the analyst concerning any order. Using the CRT terminal at his desk, he can obtain on his screen complete information on all items making up a particular order, on all components of each end item, and on the status of each manufacturing job or purchase order. Most important, he can in a short time identify the cause of a problem, even to the point of determining what machine in the shop might be causing a bottleneck.

Consider the example shown in Figure 11.

The message calls attention to the fact that this is the first schedule for Sales Order 69180. The planner gives this order particular scrutiny to see if all aspects are satisfactory. Obviously, the discrepancy between the customer's request date (565) and the promise date (585) shows that the order cannot, under current conditions, be shipped on time. The first line item (22DO30) will meet the request date and the third, a purchased part, will come close. But the second item, being manufactured on Job 171829 is going to be ready 20 days after the request date.

This Sales Order Schedule is printed by the computer only so that it may be scanned for action messages and so it can serve as a backup in case on-line files are temporarily unavailable. The same information is available at the terminal on the Order Control planner's desk. (Figure 12). Very quickly this order can be analyzed to determine the cause of any delays producing an unsatisfactory schedule.

```
SALES ORDER SCHEDULE      SO No 69180

      ORDER    REQUEST  PROMISE  SCHEDULE
      520      565      585      585

NO.   PART NO. QTY      SOURCE   SCHEDULE

1     22D030   3        171842   560

2     10X078   3        171829   585

3     93WB40   2        PC 91852 570
```

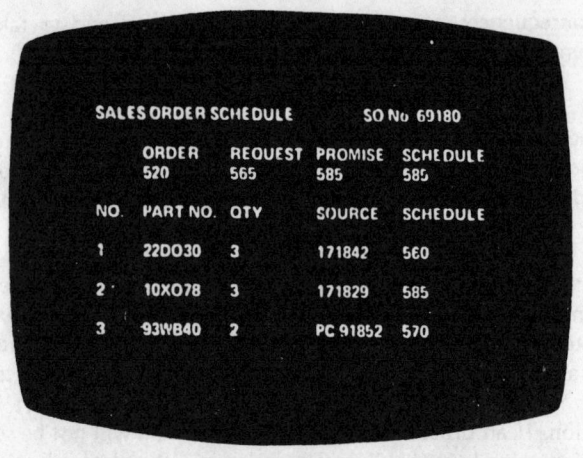

FIGURE 12

By entering '2' into the keyboard, the planner obtains a listing of all uncompleted components of the critical line item assembly. (Figure 13)

```
SALES ITEM STATUS         SO No 69180

PART 10X078      JOB 171829           SCH 585

PART    QTY      JOB        PTY       SCHED

10X435  3        775648     430       549

10X437  3        775649     511       556

10X438  3        775650     443       573
```

FIGURE 13

He determines that components 10X437 and 10X438 are delaying the critical line item. The first of these is being made on Job 775649 and by entering the job number (Figure 14) the planner sees that the start of this job is being delayed by lack of raw material, which is on order on Purchase Order 91420, but not expected until Day 547, over a month away. The planner will now confer with Purchasing to see if this material can be obtained when needed, and--if not--he will endeavor to secure an acceptable substitute so the job can be started earlier than it otherwise would.

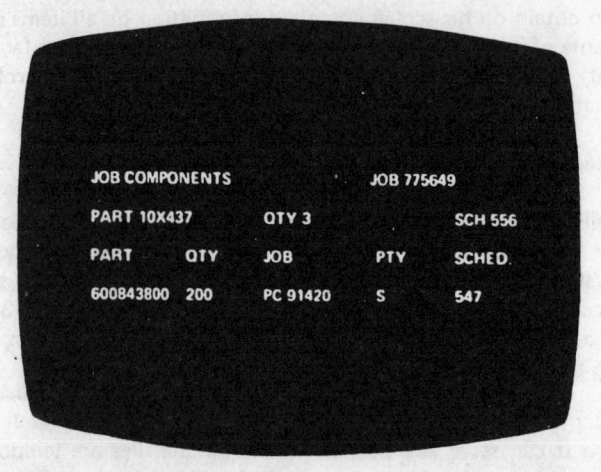

```
JOB COMPONENTS            JOB 775649

PART 10X437      QTY 3                SCH 556

PART       QTY   JOB        PTY       SCHED.

600843800  200   PC 91420   S         547
```

FIGURE 14

A similar check of Job 776650, the most critical component, discloses no raw material problem, but a look at its Job Status (Figure 15) shows a different kind of problem. This job, with a priority of 443, is not scheduled for completion until Day 573, well after its assembly has been requested by the customer. Job Status shows all operations and the work center they require, along with the day each operation will finish, according to the latest schedule. It is apparent from the 15 day delay between Operations 20 and 30, that this job--with its priority of 443 relative to other contending jobs--will lose 2 or 3 weeks in queue at Work Center 43 - the Milwaukeematic EA Tape Mills.

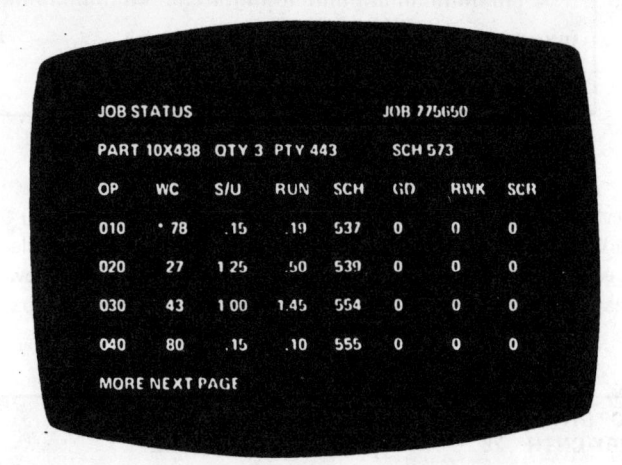

```
JOB STATUS                    JOB 775650
PART 10X438  QTY 3  PTY 443   SCH 573
OP    WC    S/U    RUN    SCH   GD   RWK   SCR
010   78    .15    .19    537   0    0     0
020   27    1.25   .50    539   0    0     0
030   43    1.00   1.45   554   0    0     0
040   80    .15    .10    555   0    0     0
MORE NEXT PAGE
```

FIGURE 15

Several corrective actions are possible, all of which require a detailed knowledge of queues. Very quickly the subject job can be found on the Queue list of Work Center 43 on Day 554. (Figure 16) It will be noted that this job shows an alternate routing for the critical operation. If Work Center 44, the Clereman Vertimatic Tape mills, has available capacity in an earlier time period, changing the routing of Job 775650 may improve its delivery substantially.

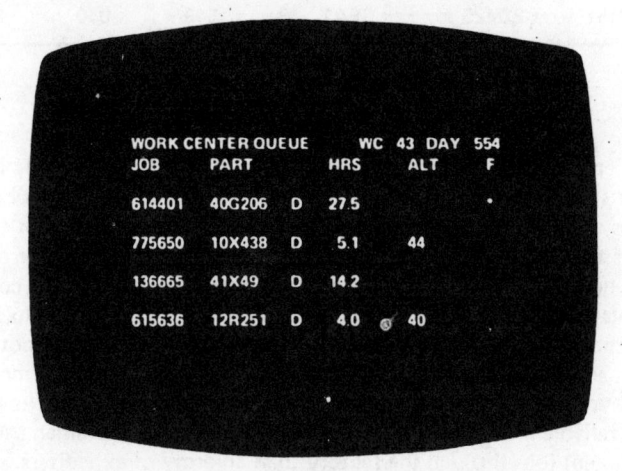

```
WORK CENTER QUEUE      WC 43 DAY 554
JOB      PART       HRS     ALT     F
614401   40G206  D  27.5                *
775650   10X438  D  5.1     44
136665   41X49   D  14.2
615636   12R251  D  4.0     40
```

FIGURE 16

In actual practice, the job of capacity planning is done before scheduling, using this queue information. All jobs which can be off-loaded to less crowded work centers are rerouted via CRT terminal. Note that Job 615636 may be transferred to Work Center 40. Job 614401, representing a substantial block of time, carries a flag indicating that Part No. 40G206 is approved for subcontract, a useful means of reducing load in peak periods.

In the case of Job 775650 the alternate work center was less loaded in the needed time period, and so this job could be completed earlier than the original routing permitted. After the next scheduling run, this fact is prominently visible on the Sales Order Schedule. (Figure 17) The delivery date of Sales Order 69180 is still not as early as the customer originally requested and the 10XO78 is still the critical item, but as the message indicates, a real improvement has resulted from experienced people taking decisive action based on reliable information. Of major importance is the fact that all this information is available within minutes, enabling people to solve problems and serve customers.

CAPACITY MANAGEMENT REPRINTS—Revised Edition

SALES ORDER SCHEDULE			SO No. 69180	
ORDER	REQUEST	PROMISE	SCHEDULE	MESSAGE
520	565	585	570	15 DAYS EARLIER
PART NO.	QTY	SOURCE	SCHEDULE	
22DO30	3	171842	563	
10XO78	3	171829	570	
93WB40	2	PC 91852	565	

FIGURE 17

The second question asked of a scheduling system is, "What job goes on this machine next?" It is the function of the Work List to assist the shop in carrying out the schedule which has been established. Every morning each foreman receives a computer-printed Work List showing which jobs require work in his section that day and the next two days. A portion of a Work List is shown in Figure 18.

SHOP DATE	534	WORK LIST				
WORK CNTR	28	J & L 4512 N/C LATHE				
JOB NO.	PART NO.	ITEM	PTY	OP	STATUS	HRS
779322	54076	END CONN	858	020	WORK	5.8
613522	10R48	PISTON	932	040	READY	4.3
780448	71B43	BODY	812	020	READY	1.2
779151	22M25	SEAT	543	030	DUE	7.5

FIGURE 18

It is, of course, arranged in priority sequence, except that any jobs already in process on a machine are listed first. The status of each job is given, so that the foreman knows whether a job is in queue with prior operations completed, or whether it is at some previous work center and due to arrive during the day. While it is not included in the illustration, a Work List shows for each job the previous work center and the next work center, so a foreman knows where the job is coming from and where it is going. Given this information, a foreman can plan his work ahead. If he has a machine coming open in a short while, and the next job on the list is an urgent job due from another section, he can contact the other foreman and find out when the previous operation will be concluded. Then he can decide whether to call up tools for the "due" job or for the next "ready" job he has in hand. Functioning in this way, using reliable information on priorities and job status, foremen can, if they are motivated, do more to move urgent jobs through the factory than an army of expediters.

If a job calls for the use of two machines simultaneously, that instruction is printed on the Work List. This feature is automatic in man-based work centers and manually selective in machine-based centers, where, among other factors, availability of duplicate tooling must be checked.

While the scheduling system as initially designed does some planning of tool requirements, much more could be done in this area. As a sub-routine of preparing the Work List, the next 10 work days are scanned to detect jobs which will start on operations requiring new NC tapes, tooling, or quality control fixtures. A Tooling Notification is provided each morning listing these jobs so that Manufacturing Engineering can complete their work in phase with shop requirements.

Two special Work List formats have been designed for specialized objectives. One is the Job Release List, in effect, a work list for Production Control. This report triggers the release of parts jobs to gateway work centers based on their start dates and of assembly jobs based on the arrival into stock of needed predecessor jobs.

The Work List for the Saw Shop, like other work lists, is arranged in priority sequence. In compiling it, however, the next several days are scanned and all jobs requiring the same raw material are grouped together for sawing at the same time. This feature eliminates the inefficiency of moving the same bar of steel in and out from the storage area several times a day to cut several different jobs.

Purchased items--both parts and raw materials--are included in the job planning procedure which precedes capacity requirements planning. It will be recalled that this procedure time-phases lower level items from the need date of the end item, much like MRP, except that manufacturing lead times are adjusted according to the management factor of the sales order which generated the requirement. Purchase contracts are then included in the chain of manufacturing jobs representing the product structure of the end item. As a part of scheduling, the need dates of purchase items are conveyed to the Purchasing Department. Figure 19 shows the type of information appropriate to purchase orders already outstanding with vendors. All of these purchase orders are designated sources of parts or raw materials for manufacturing jobs scheduled during the night. Only those items have been listed for which the currently prevailing arrival date of the order will not support the start date of the job. This action request will cause the status of each purchase order to be reviewed by the Purchasing Department in consultation, if necessary, with the vendor. During each day Purchasing enters via CRT revised dates on these orders, and the next scheduling run schedules affected parts or assemblies based on the up-to-date information. Similar information from scheduling is provided for purchase orders generated that same night by the computer but not yet sent to the vendors.

DATE 2/06/73   PURCHASED ITEM REQUIREMENTS

SHOP DAY 531

PURCHASE CONTRACT	QTY	PART NUMBER	PURCHASING DESCRIPTION	ALLOCATION REQMT	QTY	REQD. DATE	CURRENT DUE-IN
93414	180	91M191	EXTERNAL SEAL	172998	2	541	557
93431	50	91M166	END ELEMENT	136852	8	546	547
				127004	2	537	
93860	15	91M198	MALE ADAPTER	172942	2	547	569
94035	6	91M13	INTERNAL SEAL	172678	4	538	547

FIGURE 19

While the Purchasing Department follows accepted practices in monitoring outstanding orders, there remains the usual number of vendors who do not deliver on time and who do not notify us of that fact until the day their material is due on our dock. To minimize the impact of this kind of surprise on assembly work plans, the scheduling system looks ahead at jobs for parts and assemblies due to start three days hence, but requiring a purchased item not yet received. These jobs and their start dates are sent to Purchasing each morning for confirmation of the stipulated arrival dates. Often this final check prevents manufacturing plans from being made and then disrupted, when the time comes, by a vendor's failure to perform.

Again it should be emphasized that printed outputs ought to be kept to a minimum. Important files at Otis are disk-resident, on-line, accessed via CRT in all cases where access frequency justifies the expense of a terminal.

One of the most significant outputs from scheduling has been discussed previously. The Capacity Requirements Plan (Figure 7) contains both open orders and planned orders out of MRP for the next 52 weeks and is the appropriate source of information regarding capacity requirements in the future.

The Schedule Load/Capacity Report (Figure 20) is a load profile of the output from finite loading, showing for each work center the amount of capacity that will actually get used by arriving jobs for each period for the next 20 weeks. Obviously, the load coming out of finite loading will never exceed 100% of capacity. As has been stated previously, this load profile can be of greater use to the job shop manager than that produced by infinite loading. A comparison of Figures 7 and 20 shows a significant difference in the amount of load planned by infinite loading and the amount which will actually clear upstream work center and arrive at Work Center 29 in a given period. Capacity adjustment decisions based on these separate load profiles would be quite different, with that based on the Schedule Load/Capacity Report being more likely to succeed in matching near-term capacity to available work.

WEEK	START	WORK PLAN S D H	UNITS 1 2 3	CAP	LOAD	L/C %	LOAD TO CAPACITY RATIO 0% 100% 200%	OVER (UNDER)
	REPORT DATE	01/27/73	SCHEDULE LOAD/CAPACITY REPORT					
	SHOP DATE	525						
	WORK CENTER	29 L&S NT III N'C LATHE						
1	525	2 6 10	10 9 0	809	712	88%	XXXXXXXXX	97
2	530	2 6 10	10 9 0	809	655	81%	.XXXXXXXXX	154
3	535	2 6 10	10 9 0	809	807	100%	.XXXXXXXXX.	2
4	540	2 5 10	10 9 0	675	675	100%	.XXXXXXXXX.	0

FIGURE 20

The Load/Capacity Report provides relevant data to assist in capacity planning decisions. These figures show, among other things:

1. Current backlog compared to normal (i.e., historical) backlog

2. Capacity at the current operating level compared to nominal capacity and maximum available capacity

3. Current queue compared to normal queue

4. Queues encountered by jobs at various priority levels

Information pertaining to queues is used in queue control and is considered in lead time determination.

HOW TO MAKE IT WORK

For a company considering a finite loading scheduling system, the first prerequisite is a need. If you don't need it, don't try to do it just because it seems superficially appealing. There are other techniques of handling the problem of scheduling. If, for example, you are a production plant manufacturing to stock a reasonably homogeneous product mix with fairly consistent routings, then you can probably adjust capacity at the master schedule, load to infinite capacity, and dispatch by critical ratio. If, however, your business is mostly make to order, your product mix scattered among many orders with small lot sizes, and above all, if your routings follow a job shop random pattern then a more specific scheduling procedure will give you better control of your factory. But, first, reflect on the nature of your business, understand what your objectives are, before you decide how to manage what may be your largest capital investment--your plant-- and your most precious asset--your productive people. Then use the simplest system which will get effective results.

If you decide to undertake computerized scheduling, you should inventory some of your other capabilities.

These prerequisites ought to be well-established in any company before an effort is made to schedule to finite capacity:

1. A DATA BASE must exist to a degree compatible with the realism expected from scheduling. This includes--as a minimum-- bills of material, routings, and standards.

2. SYSTEMS EXPERIENCE at a reasonably sophisticated level is essential. * A large scheduling system is not recommended as a firm's first major effort. In the case of Otis, not only did several major systems precede scheduling, but also all had been designed and implemented totally within the company.

---

*In spite of corruptions in its usage relative to systems, "sophisticated" is a perfectly good word. The Random House Dictionary defines it as, "altered by education, experience, etc. so as to be worldly wise"—not a bad quality for a system. Those who prefer, may use the word "effective".

3. An adequate method of DATA COLLECTION is, of course, necessary to update job status. Usually there is a terminal based system, either batch or on-line.

4. Obviously, some HARDWARE is required. While it is conceivable to use time-sharing, most people, contemplating a scheduling system of any size will want operational control of their computer. The Otis system was initially implemented on an IBM 370 Model 145 with 256K under DOS. Within a short time it was switched to a remote computer without degrading effectiveness.

5. All of the foregoing essentials can be bought. The one requirement, however, that cannot be bought is DISCIPLINE. By this is meant, a spirit, a pride, a self-control existing in an organization which enables ordinary people to keep accurate records, perform exacting tasks, and work harmoniously together within the rules of a formal system. In a disciplined organization salesmen ask for delivery when the customer really needs the product; stockroom personnel count receipts and disbursements religiously; machinists count their production and report performance of the correct operations. Where discipline does not exist, scheduling cannot be done.

SUMMARY

The scheduling system which has been described here reflects, as it should, the business it is designed to serve. Half the products manufactured are made to a forecast; half are made to order. The shop has all the characteristics of the classic job shop: discrete work centers, small lot sizes, random routings. Growth has frequently made capacity a scarce resource. But at all times the business is first and foremost customer-oriented, committed to fast response, and willing to live in the dynamic environment characteristic of the oil industry. So the Otis manufacturing scheduling system may be summarized in these features:

1) It is designed to interface with materials requirements planning and to carry out the priority intentions of that system.

2) It is designed to determine actual delivery dates consistent with factory capacity and to report scheduled dates to the materials system and ultimately to the customer.

3) It preserves network relationships among assemblies and components.

4) It incorporates the concept of flexible lead times related to job urgency.

5) As implemented, it does not depend on an accurate master schedule. Because it incorporates indicators of management preference, the output of finite loading is accepted as the master schedule.

6) Conventional capacity requirements planning is employed for time periods beyond two months. In the near term, however, capacity is adjusted in accordance with the load profile derived from finite scheduling.

7) It operates with a minimum output of printed reports, but with implicit reliance on the motivation and discipline of the user.

BIOGRAPHY

R. L. Lankford is Manager of Production Control for Otis Engineering Corporation, with responsibility for capacity planning, scheduling, shop floor control, material handling, and purchasing of outside services. He is also involved in the design of manufacturing systems, including forecasting, material requirements planning, and scheduling.

Mr. Lankford received his Bachelor of Arts and Bachelor of Science degrees from Rice University. He is a member of the Advisory Committee on Materials Management at the University of Wisconsin and a frequent lecturer before professional societies. He is a member of APICS, a Registered Professional Engineer, and a Certified Manufacturing Engineer.

Reprinted from the APICS 1978 Conference Proceedings.

SHORT-TERM PLANNING OF MANUFACTURING CAPACITY

R. L. Lankford
McEvoy Oilfield Equipment Company

The two central concerns of manufacturing planning and control are quantity and timing, and these concerns are literally inseparable.

Capacity is, of course, "the quantity of work which can be performed . . . in a given period of time." In order to do capacity planning, the aspect of time must be mastered before the aspect of quantity can be registered in the calculation of load. That is to say, the concept of lead time must be understood and the task of controlling actual manufacturing lead times must be accepted as the fundamental mission of manufacturing control.

In view of the importance of lead time not only to the viability of manufacturing systems within a company, but also to the competitive strength of the firm in its markets, it is essential to understand the anatomy of lead time.

The Anatomy of Lead Time

As defined for production control, lead time is the elapsed time -- usually days, weeks, or months -- between the release of an order for manufacturing and the receipt of that order into stores.* (Figure 1)

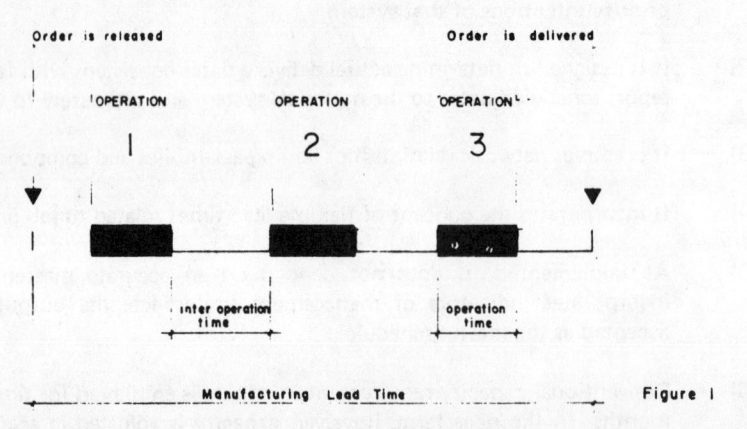

Figure 1

This is manufacturing lead time (MLT), the time required for production or processing activities, and is exclusive of pre-manufacturing activities, such as engineering design, manufacturing documentation and tooling, and material procurement. Each manufactured item in the bill of materials has its individual MLT and each purchased item has its procurement lead time.

The combined lead time of an assembly is obviously the total elapsed time between authorization of manufacturing and receipt of the assembly into stores -- this total constituting the critical path through the network of the bill of materials. (Figure 2) For the purpose of quoting a make-to-order product to a customer, a total lead time must be used, which is the total of pre-manufacturing activities, the combined lead time of the

---

* The COPICS manuals published by IBM present an excellent commentary on lead time. (1)

NETWORK PLANNING

FIGURE 2

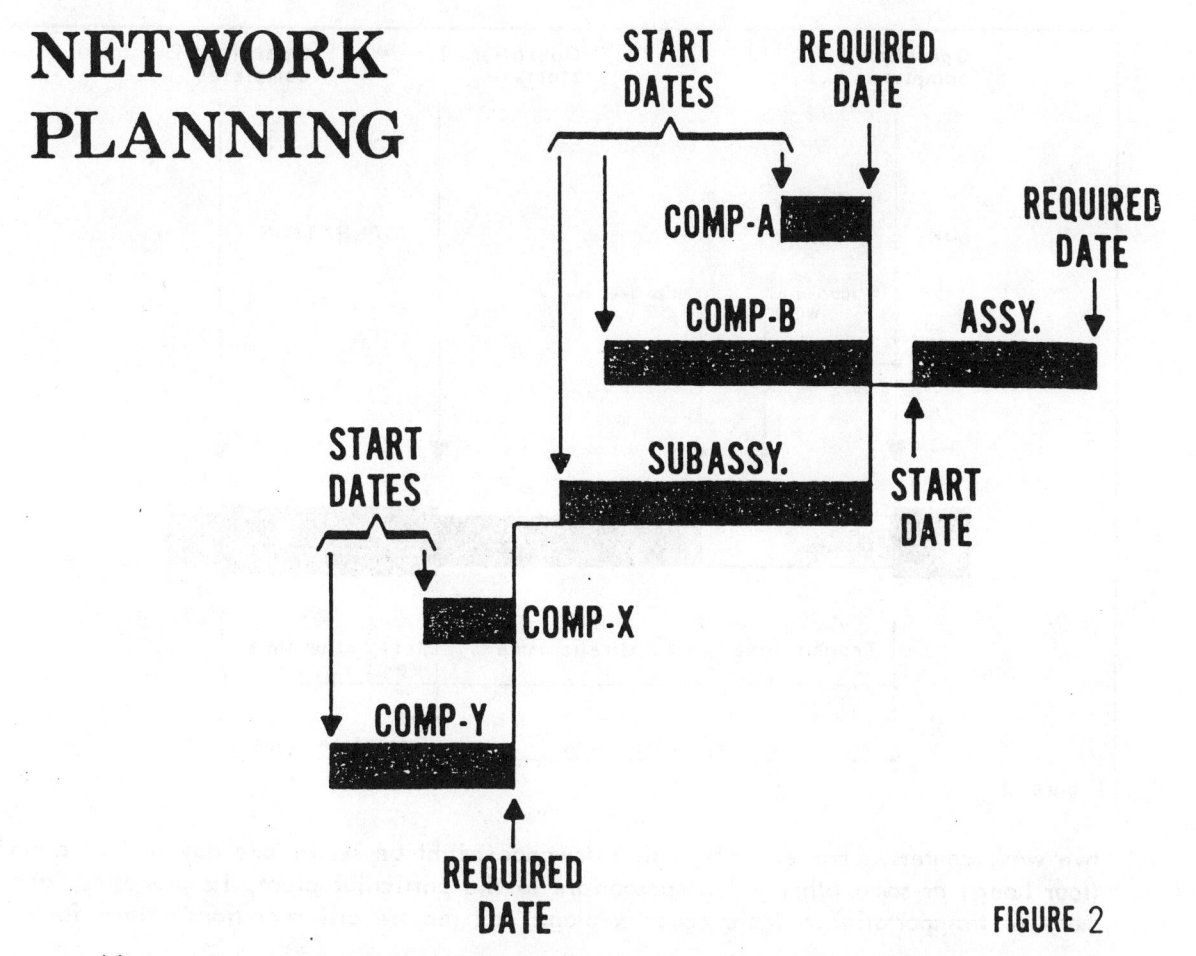

assembled product, and any post-manufacturing activities, such as crating, waiting for shipment, or other events preceding fulfillment of responsibilities under the terms and conditions of the order.

Manufacturing lead time consists of operation times and inter-operation times, as shown in Figure 1. Operation time is the duration of an element of the process. This is usually composed of setup, the time required to install tools, adjust, and otherwise prepare a machine for the forthcoming operation, and run, the time consumed in processing the quantity of product on the job. In some cases tear down time (to clean process equipment, for example) may be considered a separate element of operation time, although in metalworking plants this is usually treated as part of the ensuing setup.

It is not uncommon for the productive events of operation time to account for only ten to twenty percent of MLT, with the balance consumed in the non-productive events of inter-operation time. Operation time, moreover, is determined by the nature of the process and the efficiency of the worker, and so is a concern for industrial engineering rather than production control. On the other hand, interoperation time requires energetic and imaginative management by production control and offers a large target for improvement of manufacturing lead times.

The principal elements of interoperation time are waiting for move, transit time, and queue time. (Figure 3) In some processes, it may be useful to consider preparation time (layout, cleaning) and post-operation times (inspection, cooling) as separate elements, but these are usually regarded as part of direct operations or the wait element.

In order to simplify lead time determination in actual practice, it is common to merge "waiting for move" into "transit time" and then deal with a single value. Within most plants of average size the transit time allowance can be the same for movement between any

Figure 3

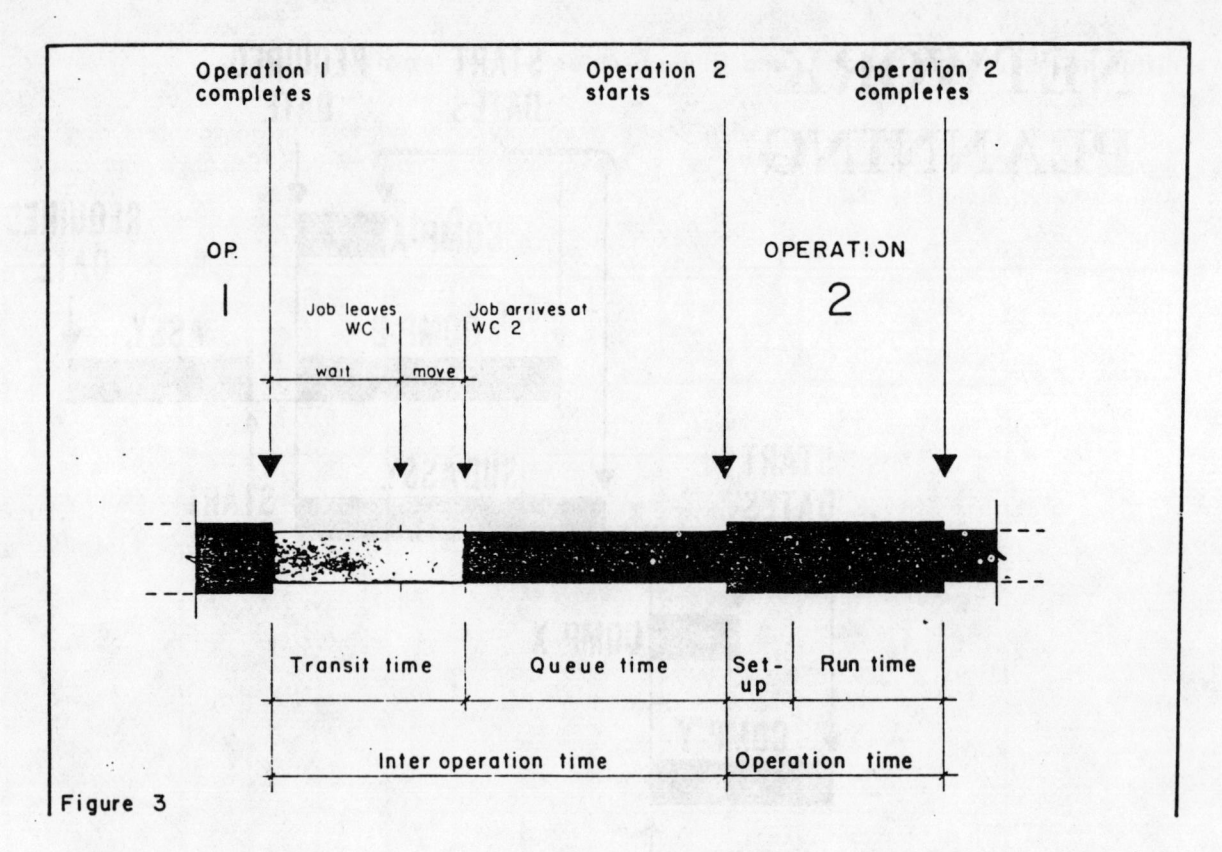

two work centers. For example, this allowance might be set at one day or half a shift (four hours) or some other value appropriate to the particular plant, its processes, and mode of transportation. More complex plants can require different transit times for

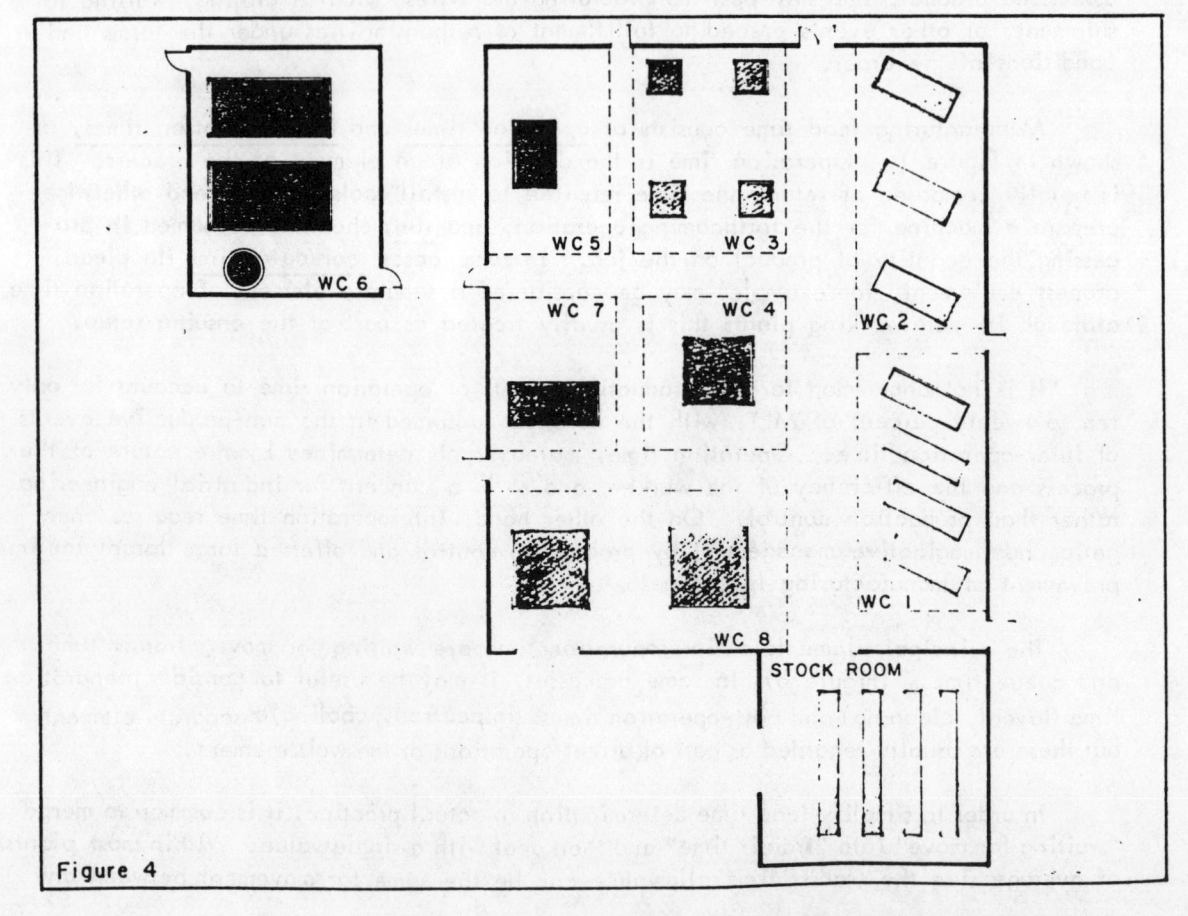

Figure 4

different move combinations, and in such cases a move matrix is useful.

Figure 4 portrays a plant with seven geographically adjacent work centers and a remote Heat Treat Department (WC 6). An appropriate move matrix for this compact plant might be that in Figure 5.

FROM WC \ TO WC	WC 1	WC 2	WC 3	WC 4	WC 5	WC 6	WC 7	WC 8	STOCK
WC 1	—	1	1	0	1	1	1	1	0
WC 2	1	—	1	0	1	1	1	1	1
WC 3	1	1	—	0	1	1	1	1	1
WC 4	0	0	0	—	0	1	0	0	0
WC 5	1	1	1	0	—	1	1	1	1
WC 6	1	1	1	1	1	—	1	1	2
WC 7	1	1	1	0	1	1	—	1	1
WC 8	1	1	1	0	1	1	1	—	0
STOCK	1	1	1	0	1	2	1	1	—

Figure 5

Transit times can be specified in accordance with distance, mode of transportation, or other variable. A company with two plant sites in the same general vicinity could use the move matrix for jobs moving both within a site and also back and forth between sites. A plant utilizing outside subcontractors for machining, plating, or heat treating would likewise find the move matrix useful.

Queue time is the most challenging element of lead time. Because it is the longest element, it is the one requiring the most control; but because it is affected by many diverse factors of plant operation, it is generally the most difficult element to control.

A queue, of course, is a group of items arranged in sequence waiting their turn to proceed. A queue of manufacturing jobs at a work center can be characterized by the amount of aggregate load they constitute, expressed usually in standard hours. Alternatively the load (standard hours) can be compared to the capacity of the work center (standard hours per day), and the queue can be expressed as the time (days) a newly arriving job will wait for service, assuming a first-come-first-served service rule.

A simple illustration of the dynamics of queues is the case of two single machines in a processing line performing sequential operations on the same workpiece. (Figure 6) If the processing time required for each operation is identical, one machine can feed the other machine directly and no queue will form in front of the second machine. No time will be lost by parts waiting in queue, but at the same time no buffer will exist to accommodate interruptions in the supply of parts from the feeding machine. If that machine, for example, goes down for maintenance, the fed machine must shut down. If material conditions are not optimum and the processing on the feeding machine slows down, the second machine will begin to experience idle time. In short, operating without a buffer or queue is not feasible even under the simplest of conditions involving a single machine feeding another. In the actual situation of a job shop work center receiving, at random arrival times, jobs having differing processing content from a variety of feeding work centers, the need for a buffer to insure the uninterrupted availability of work is evident.

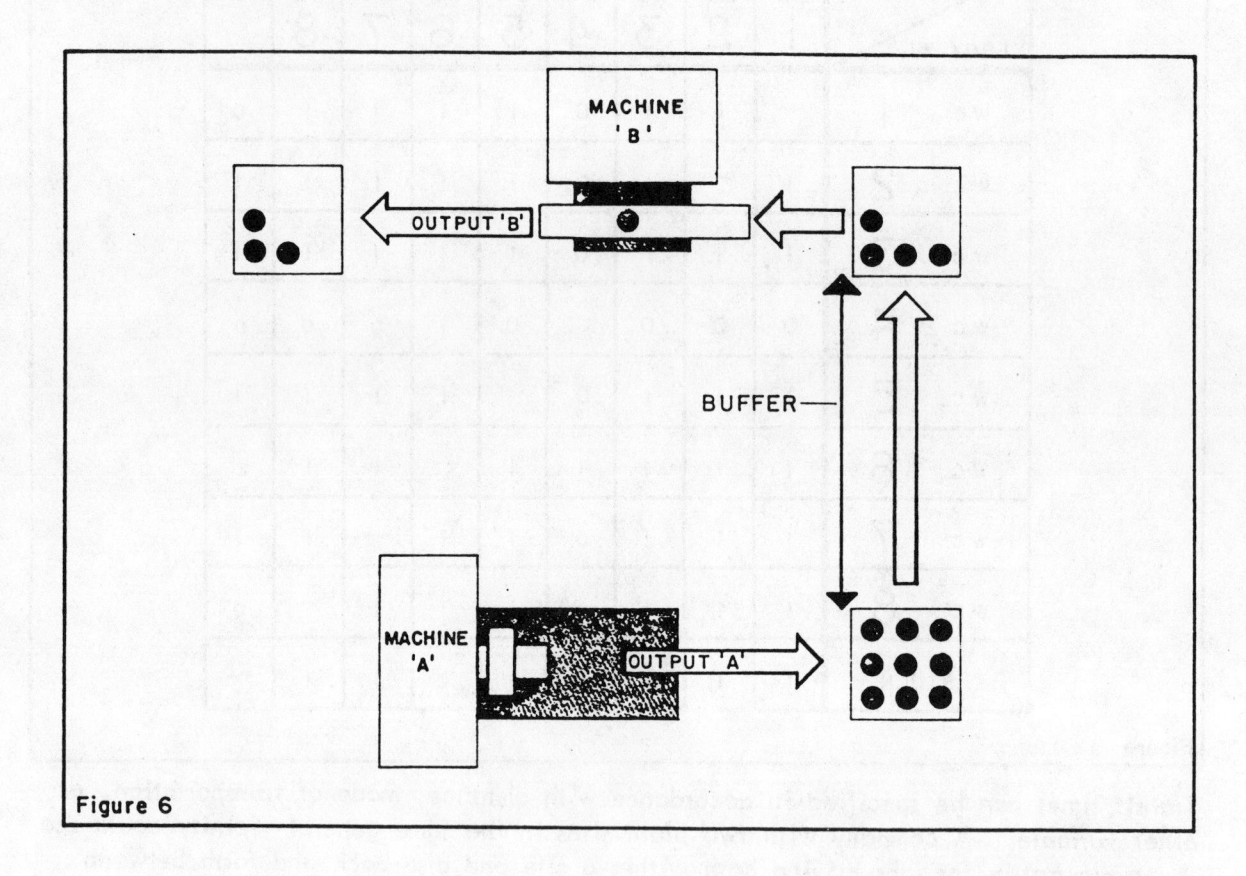

Figure 6

Queue, then, serves a useful purpose in addition to contributing a delay factor into all manufacturing lead times.

The question is, "How long should a queue be?" And when that is determined, "How can the shop be managed so that queues are maintained at the correct levels?"

The length of queue required for any facility to avoid idle time can be determined statistically. Suppose the amount of work in queue at the Horizontal Mills is found to be 427 standard hours. This is consistent with the foreman's experience that he needs about a week and a half of jobs on hand to keep from running out of work. Each week for 10 weeks the hour content of arriving jobs is recorded, with results as shown in Figure 7. The average arrival rate is 279 hours, so output is planned at that level. Assume that output is exactly as planned. The resulting queue can be computed for each week, and it will be seen that the average queue is 493. If output is constant and equal to the average input, as is the case here, the length of queue need only be long enough to cover variations in the arrival rate. That variation is measured by the standard deviation, 120. If it is desired to limit to a 5% probability the exposure to running out of work, this may be done by maintaining an average queue of 1.65 standard devistions, or 198 hours. Stated another way, 90% of the time the queue will be between 198 + (1.65 x 120) and 198 - (1.65 x 120), or between 396 and 0. (2)

The foreman, with usual conservatism, likes about 1.5 x 279, or 419 hours, ahead of the work center. Statistically speaking, there is only a 0.02% probability of this queue going to 0, based on the normal pattern of work flow. The price which is being paid for this excessive buffer or stabilization stock is 419-198 = 221 standard hours of work in process. If a similar reduction could be made throughout the plant, work in

Week	Arriving Jobs (Std. Hrs.)	Output (Std. Hrs.)	Queue (Std. Hrs.)
Beginning	-	-	427
1	164	279	312
2	195	279	228
3	420	279	369
4	481	279	571
5	244	279	536
6	424	279	681
7	208	279	610
8	293	279	624
9	222	279	567
10	142	279	430

Mean = 279
Standard Deviation = 120

Figure 7

process could be reduced 47% by accepting a 5% exposure to work centers running out of work. If this risk is unacceptable, a WIP reduction of 33% could be achieved with only a 1% exposure to running out of work.

The statistical nature of queues is illustrated in Figure 8. If a large number (say, 100) of randomly timed observations are made of the queues at four different work centers, the data might look like this:

Histograms of this data are shown in Figure 9.

Consider Work Center A. It is apparent that this queue is more or less normally distributed about a mean of approximately 140 hours, and if the average output of the work center is 24 standard hours per day (2 shifts x 8 hours x 2 machines x 75% realization), then, the average queue length is 5.8, say 6 days. This queue does not appear too small, since in only 1 observation out of 100 did the queue approach 0, whereas 99% of the time over 1.7 days of work resided at the work center.

QUEUE SIZE (STANDARD HOURS)	FREQUENCY OF OBSERVATION WORK CENTER			
	A	B	C	D
0-39	1	22	0	9
40-79	7	34	0	14
80-119	21	19	9	14
120-159	39	12	23	22
160-199	24	7	40	10
200-239	6	4	15	18
240-279	3	2	9	8
280-319	0	0	4	5

FIGURE 8

Work Center B, however, does have a queue too small for effective utilization. Frequently the queue approached 0, and examination of the actual values of the observations might reveal that often the actual queue was 0.

Returning to Work Center A, the queue does not appear too large either. There is no unnecessary buffer, i.e. a relatively large value of load below which the queue never drops. In the case of Work Center C, which has the same capacity as A, the queue is 9 days and at least 3 days of this is excessive, because it is not needed to prevent idle time. That excess represents capital tied up in work in process, it creates congestion on the shop floor, and it lengthens lead time unnecessarily.

Of course, some queues defy analysis because they are out of control. Work Center D is such a case. The queue is frequently high and frequently low. The average queue length, like Work Center A, is about 6 days, but unlike A, the flow of work is chaotic, with frequent occasions of massive overload and too many instances when there is no work to occupy the machines.

Queue Control

How can the length of queue allowance be determined for lead time calculation? A surprisingly large number of companies use historical queues derived from someone's memory without much modification by management judgment. This is an extremely risky approach. To understand why, consider the use of lead times in Capacity Requirements Planning (CRP).

In planning the need for capacity, CRP registers the need for machine time on Machine B, following completion on Machine A after an interval of time equal to transit time plus the queue in front of Machine B. Suppose that the historical queue at B is used. This says that Machine B is always needed just as long after Machine A as B has historically been available. But CRP is supposed to show when a machine is

Figure 9a

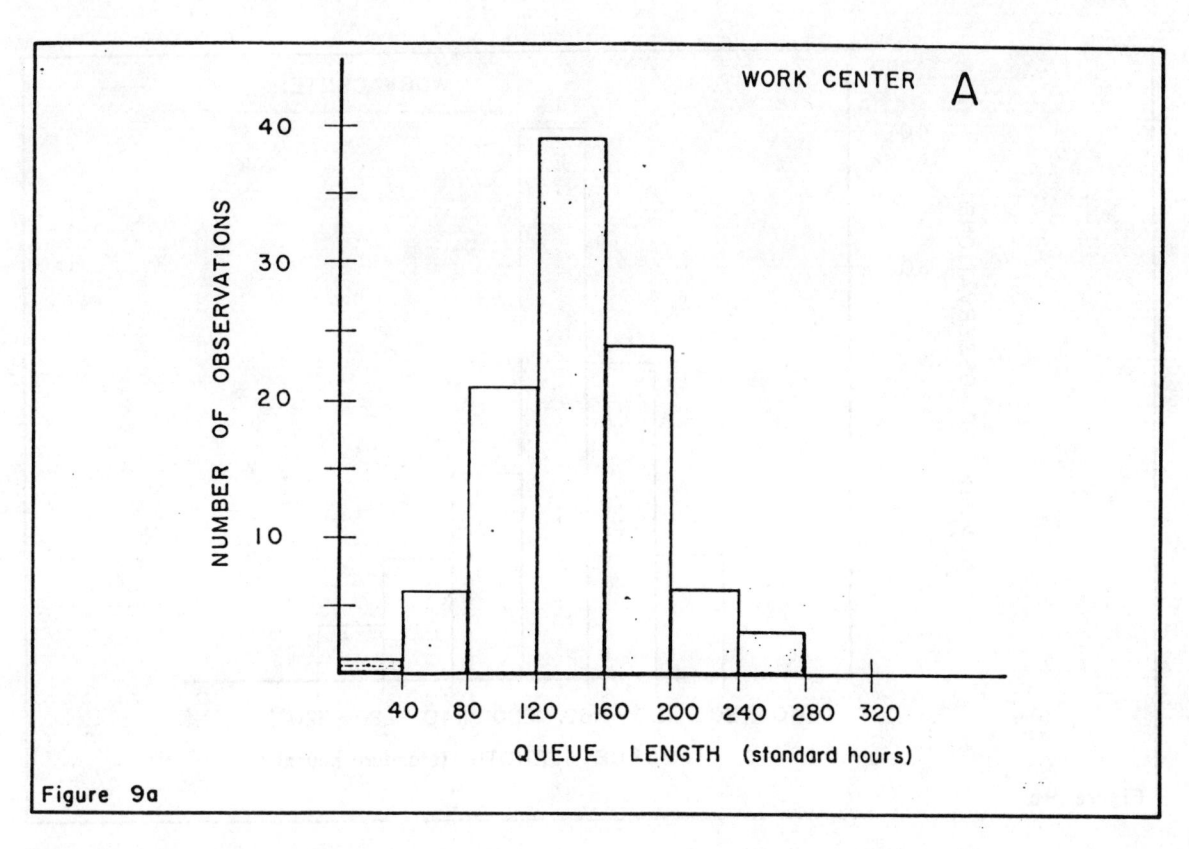

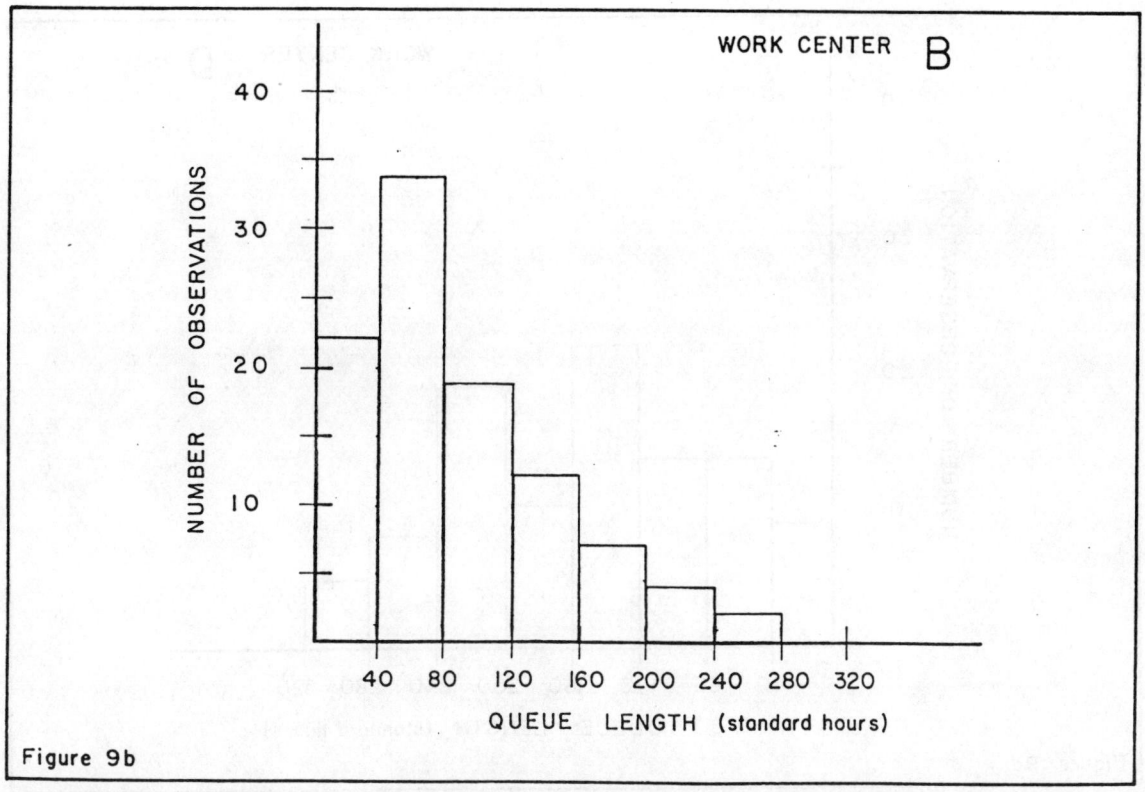

Figure 9b

required, not when it will be available. When a machine is required is determined by the delivery date required by the customer or by the lead time which management decides is appropriate to the business. Thus, lead time must be planned and controlled, meaning that queues must be planned and controlled. The queue in front of Machine B must be planned to be what management deems appropriate, not what has historically

Figure 9c

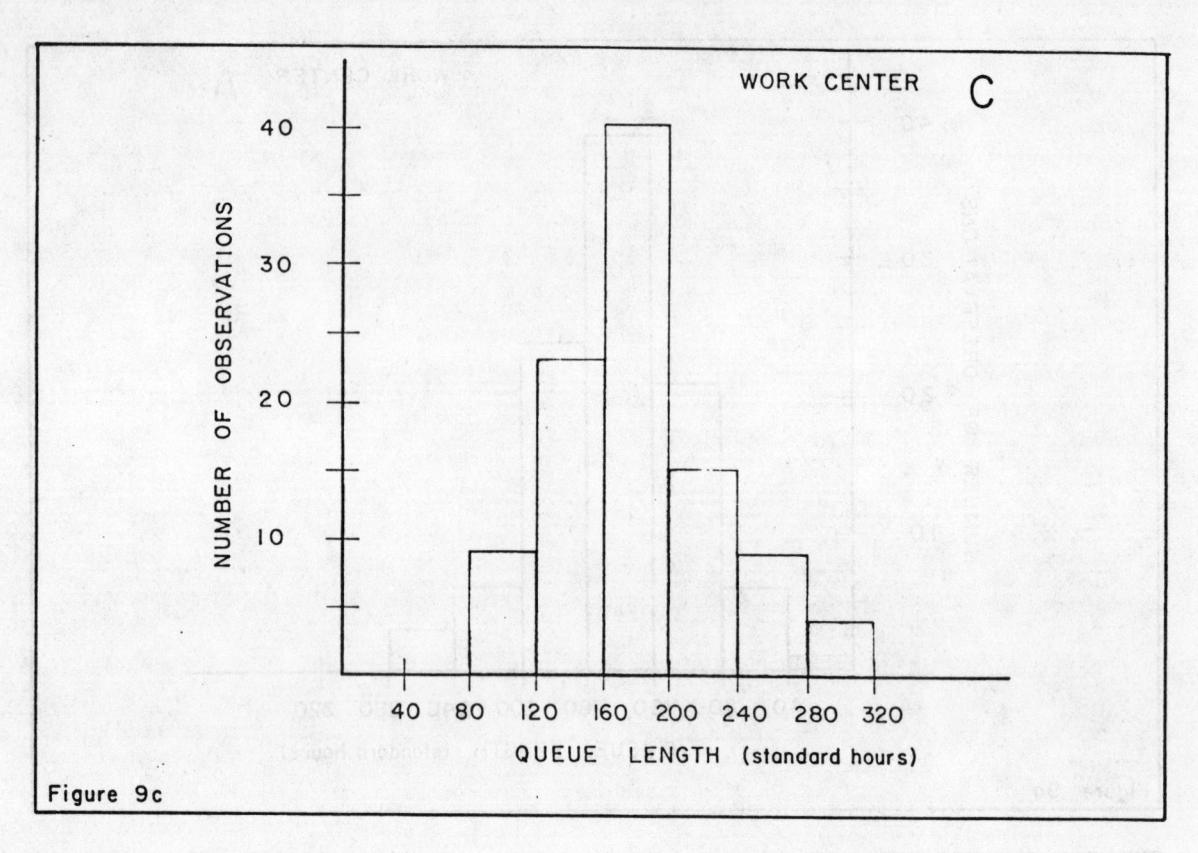

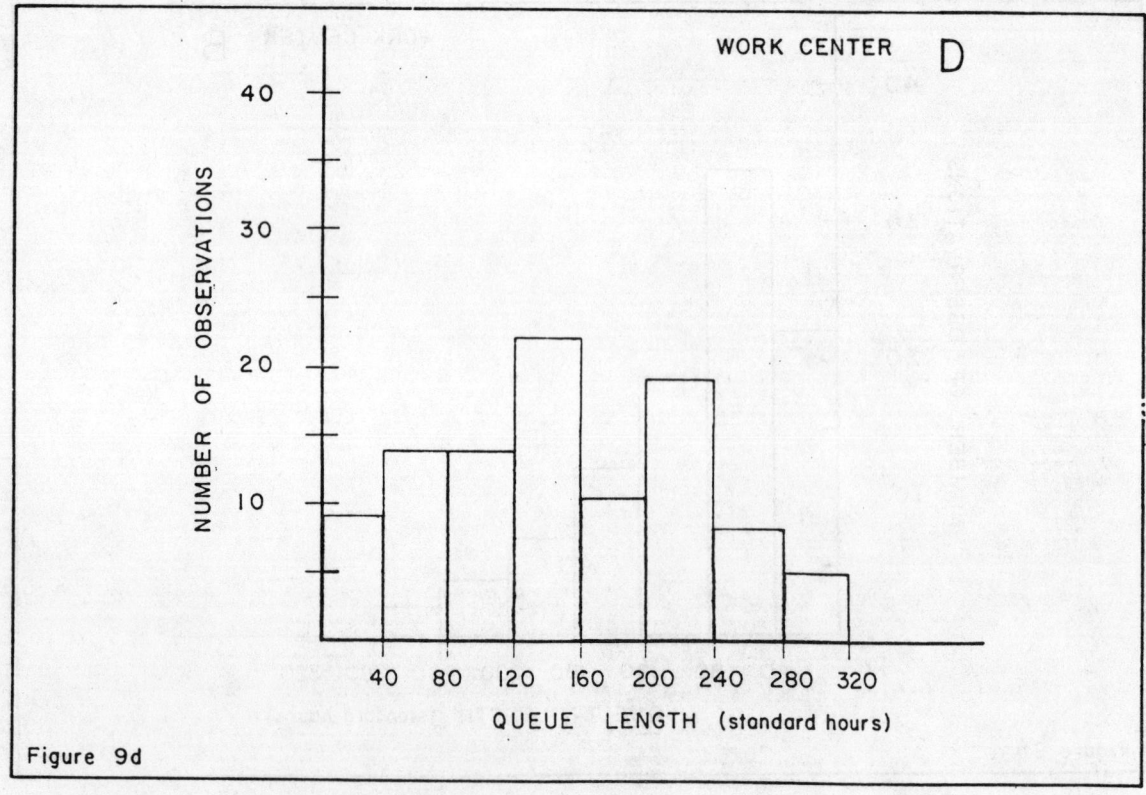

Figure 9d

prevailed, otherwise CRP will not show when capacity is required. The mission of production control is one of managing queues to the sizes prescribed by a rational plan of shop operation. Queues become an element of operations to be managed -- like efficiency, utilization, and material flow -- not a condition determined by events and passively accepted as a fact of life by supervision.

The planned queue allowance to use for capacity planning may be established in different ways, depending on the nature of the business and type of manufacturing environment. For example, a high production shop with line flow and constant time standards might decide to maintain in front of each machine or group of machines a specific queue calculated to provide the minimum buffer which will prevent idle time. On the other hand, a job shop making products with non-uniform routings and desiring to maintain competitive lead times might elect to put sufficient capacity in place such that the average job can obtain service at each work center in no more than a certain number of days -- say, three days.

Figure 10 is a computer output qued for queue control by a plant with this latter objective.* This data for each work center is used in conjunction with the correspond- approach. To understand why, consider the use of lead times in Capacity Requirements Planning (CRP).

In planning the need for capacity, CRP registers the need for machine time on Machine B, following completion on Machine A after an interval of time equal to transit time plus the queue in front of Machine B. Suppose that the historical queue at B is used. This says that Machine B is always needed just as long after Machine A as B has historically been available. But CRP is supposed to show when a machine is <u>required</u>, not when it will be <u>available</u>. When a machine is required is determined by the delivery date required by the customer or by the lead time which management decides is appropriate to the business. Thus, lead time must be planned and controlled, meaning that queues must be planned and controlled. The queue in front of Machine B must be planned to be what management deems appropriate, not what has historically prevailed, otherwise CRP will not show when capacity is required. The mission of production control is one of managing queues to the sizes prescribed by a rational plan of shop operation. Queues become an element of operations to be managed -- like efficiency, utilization, and material flow -- not a condition determined by events and passively accepted as a fact of life by supervision.

The planned queue allowance to use for capacity planning may be established in different ways, depending on the nature of the business and type of manufacturing environment. For example, a high production shop with line flow and constant time standards might decide to maintain in front of each machine or group of machines a specific queue calculated to provide the minimum buffer which will prevent idle time. On the other hand, a job shop making products with non-uniform routings and desiring to maintain competitive lead times might elect to put sufficient capacity in place such that the average job can obtain service at each work center in no more than a certain number of days -- say, three days.

Figure 10 is a computer output qued for queue control by a plant with this latter objective.* This data for each work center is used in conjunction with the corresponding CRP profile for the work center to determine what actions, if any, are necessary to maintain actual queues consistent with planned queues. The production control planner using this report is given current data on the load and capacity of this group of N/C lathes. The first thing he wants to know is the "Ready Load" -- the amount of work (in days) currently in queue at the work center -- so he can detect an excessive queue or an exposure to running out of work. Also important is "Current Queue" -- the length of queue currently being encountered by the average job arriving in the work center. This can be compared to the "Average Queue" -- the queue which has prevailed on average over the past three months. A detailed profile is displayed across the bottom of the report showing the queue encountered by jobs of different priorities. With job priorities expressed as a number between 0 and 999, the deciles of priority are

---

* The report shown is a product of the computer simulation of factory operations used to schedule manufacturing jobs.

8/27/73   WORK CENTER 29 - L&S M-III N/C LATHES

READY LOAD   4 DAYS AVAILABLE FOR WORK
CURRENT LOAD   5415 HOURS TODAY
AVERAGE LOAD   3706 HOURS PAST YEAR
SCHEDULED CAPACITY   792 CURRENT OPERATIONS
BASIC CAPACITY   634 HOURS SCHEDULED MACHINES - NO OT
FULL CAPACITY   634 HOURS ALL MACHINES - NO OT
CURRENT Q   3 DAYS TODAY
AVERAGE Q   1 DAYS PAST THREE MONTHS

PRIORITY	0–99	100–199	200–299	300–399	400–499	500–599	600–699	700–799	800–899	900–999
NR JOBS	19	36	70	101	109	105	84	48	14	73
QUEUE		2	4	3	2	2	1			
JOB HRS	246	353	601	775	747	788	644	304	157	795

FIGURE 10

designated in the column headings, with the number of jobs in each priority decile, the queue length encountered on average by this group of jobs, and the number of hours of load represented by the group. In this plant jobs are worked on in priority sequence. It can be seen that hishg priority jobs -- priority 700 and above -- obtain service the same day they arrive at the work center. Jobs in the 600's wait in queue an average of one day; the 500's wait two days; and so on. To reiterate, the average queue for <u>all</u> jobs is shown as "Current Queue."

This example demonstrates that queue time is variable with priority, which, of course, means that MLT is variable with priority at time of manufacture, a fact well known from observation of shop operations. Figure 11 shows the dramatic difference in MLT for the same product manufactured under low (300) and high (900) priority conditions. What queue allowance, then, should be used in lead time estimates for capacity planning?

The proper queue allowance is the one decided upon as appropriate by production management for the average job under normal operating conditions. Queues must then be maintained at or near planned levels as a routine part of production control, otherwise the execution of the manufacturing plan will bear little resemblance to the expectations of MRP and CRP. Queues are managed by regular attention to current conditions, as shown by a queue analysis such as Figure 10, and to future conditions, as shown by the Capacity Requirements Plan. Actions based on this information may either (a) regulate input and output, or (b) redistribute existing or anticipated load.

Input/Output Control seeks to control lead times by controlling queues, and to do so by metering input of load into the system based on measurement of output. Even when I/O cannot be used in a formal way, the controlled release of manufacturing jobs to the shop floor can be helpful in maintaining planned queues and avoiding excessive lead time through the manufacturing processes.

This, of course, does nothing for jobs being held in Production Control awaiting release. Whenever input is being regularly limited, output must be increased by over-

QUEUES AND JOB PRIORITY

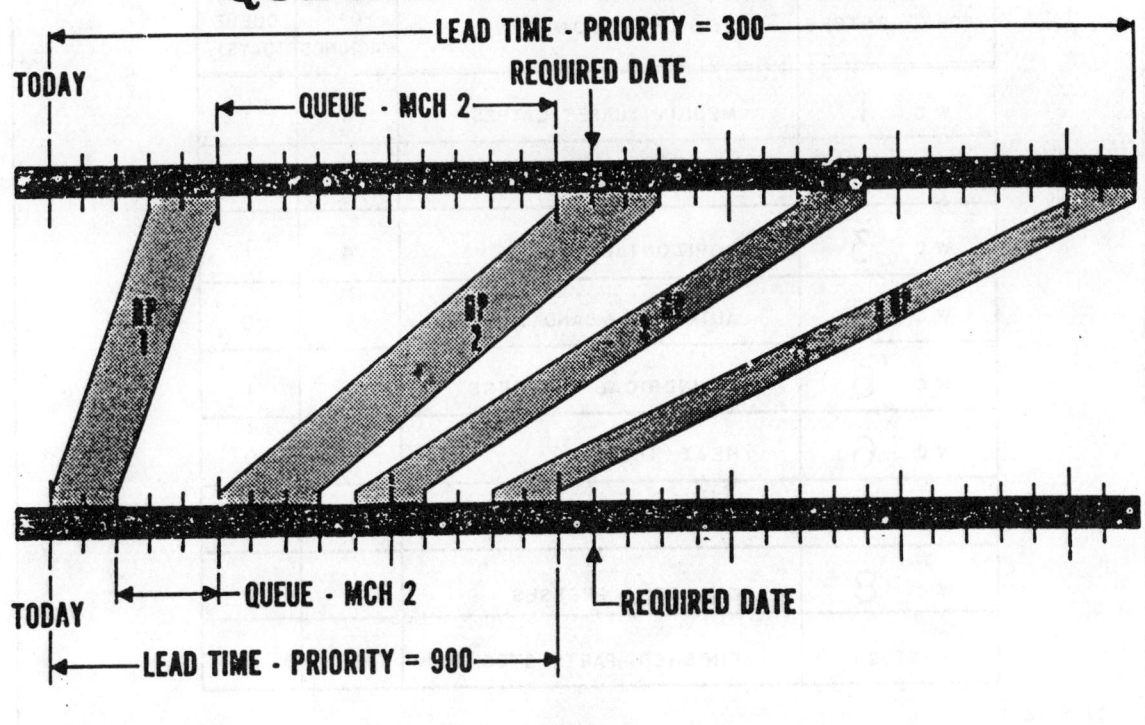

FIGURE 11

time, extra manning, or similar revision to the work plan, or else lead times will extend due to jobs waiting in the "paper queue."

Excessive queue lengths can be avoided on a selective basis by redistributing load -- routing jobs to less-loaded alternate work centers or removing work for sub-contracting. The usefulness of this approach is greatly enhanced by advance planning using CRP.

Lead Time Calculation

Consider again the plant shown in Figure 4. A study of normal operation discloses that queues are virtually never encountered at the saws, nor in heat treat -- i.e., jobs can obtain service in these departments on the same day they arrive. Based on the nature of the business, management recognizes that their customers expect short lead times and they decide to put sufficient capacity in place so that jobs will wait in queue at machining work centers an average of one day. These planned standard queue allowances are shown in Figure 12.

A move matrix was previously shown for this plant (Figure 5), giving the planned transit times between work centers.

With this information about the characteristics of the plant, it is possible to calculate the standard lead time for any product.

Consider a Main Shaft, which is normally produced in lot sizes of 60 pieces. The routing is given in Figure 13 and the step-by-step computation of lead time is outlined in Figure 14.

If a manufacturing job for 60 Main Shafts is released to the shop floor at the beginning of Day 1, it will go first to WC 4 for sawing. According to Figure 12, queue

WORK CENTERS	DESCRIPTION	QUANTITY OF MACHINES	PLANNED QUEUE (DAYS)
WC 1	MEDIUM TURRET LATHES	4	1
WC 2	N/C LATHES	3	1
WC 3	HORIZONTAL MILLS	4	1
WC 4	AUTOMATIC BAND SAWS	1	0
WC 5	CYLINDRICAL GRINDERS	1	1
WC 6	HEAT TREAT	—	0
WC 7	INTERNAL GRINDERS	1	1
WC 8	N/C DRILL PRESSES	2	2
STOCK	FINISHED PARTS STOCKROOM	—	0

Figure 12

time is 0, meaning that the sawing operation can start on Day 1 ($S_1 = 1$). The time required for sawing can be determined by:

$T = s + Qr$, where

T = Job Time, in standard hours
s = setup time
r = unit production time
Q = Quantity to be produced

FIGURE 13 - ROUTING

PART - MAIN SHAFT   AVERAGE LOT 60 PIECES

WC	OP.	DESCRIPTION	S/U	RUN
4	010	SAW	0.2	.05
1	020	ROUGH TURN	0.5	.25
6	030	HEAT TREAT (SPEC. 1.2)	---	---
2	040	FINISH MACHINE	1.0	.15
3	050	MILL	1.0	.20
5	060	GRIND	0.7	.30

For Operation 010,

$$T = 0.2 + (60)(.05) = 3.2 \text{ hours}$$

The date this operation will finish can be calculated by:

$$F = S = \frac{T}{C} \text{ (round down), where}$$

F = Finish date
S = Start date
T = job time
C = Capacity of work units employed

	M.F.	Part No. Main Shaft		Job No. 123		Quantity 60	Lead Time 4 weeks	
Queue Time	Start Date	Opr. No.	Work Center	Set Up	Run	Job Time	Finish Date	Transit Time
0	1	1	4	0.2	.05	3.2	1	0
1	3	2	1	0.5	.25	15.5	4	1
0	6	3	6	—	—	—	7	1
1	10	4	2	1.0	.15	10.0	10	1
1	13	5	3	1.0	.20	13.0	14	1
1	17	6	5	0.7	.30	18.7	18	1
0	20	STOCK						

Figure 14

Assume a work plan of 2 shifts, 8 hours per shift, 80% utilization and 90% efficiency on all work centers. The daily capacity of the saw is:

$$C = U E h d \sum ms, \text{ where}$$

U = Utilization
E = Efficiency
h = hours per shift
d = days in the period considered
$\sum ms$ = sum of the machine-shifts

For WC 4

$$C = (.8)(.9)(8)(1)(1 + 1) = 11.52 \text{ std. hrs./day}$$

CAPACITY MANAGEMENT REPRINTS—Revised Edition

Therefore, for Operation 10

$$F = 1 + \frac{3.2}{11.52} = 1.28 = 1 \text{ (rounded down)}$$

Referring to the move matrix (Figure 5), the time to move the job from WC 4 to WC 1 is negligible. The start date at the next work center can then be calculated from:

$$S_n = F_{n-1} + 1 + q + 1, \text{ where}$$

S = Start date
F = Finish date
n = number of operation
t = transit time from WC(n-1) to WC(n)
q = queue time at WC(n)

For Operation 020,

$$S_2 = 1 + 0 + 1 + 1 = 3$$

i.e., the job was sent to WC 1 on Day 1; it waited in queue all of Day 2; and work commenced on the turret lathes at the beginning of Day 3.

The job time on the turret lathes can be calculated as 15.5 hours. While the capacity of WC 1, consisting of 4 turret lathes, is 46.08 hours, not all this capacity will be dedicated to each job. Usually only one machine will be employed on a job to avoid the expense of multiple setups. Therefore,

$$F_2 = 3 + \frac{15.5}{11.52} = 4$$

So, all start and finish dates can be determined.

It will be noticed in the routing that there are no standard times for WC 6 Heat Treat. This is typical where work is not <u>piece dependent</u>. The time required to heat treat a batch of parts is determined by the requirements of the process, not by a time per piece. Therefore, a "block time" table is provided to specify the time allowance for all such processes (Figure 15). For Main Shafts, requiring a quench and temper heat treat cycle, 2 days (6 and 7) are allowed in the lead time.

Once planned start and finish dates have been determined for all operations, the lead time can be calculated from:

$$LT = \frac{S_s - S_1 + 1}{5} \text{ (in weeks), where}$$

S_s = the date of arrival in stock

For Main Shafts,

$$LT = \frac{20 - 1 + 1}{5} = 4 \text{ weeks}$$

It will be noticed that, even with the modest queue allowances of this simple example, only about 6 days of the 20 are spent actually working on the parts -- the remainder being spent in moving and waiting. In real situations, work will usually be an even lower proportion of lead time.

PROCESS	DESCRIPTION	BLOCK TIME (DAYS)
1.0	HEAT TREAT	
1.1	Normalize	1
1.2	Quench and temper	2
1.3	Carburize	3
2.0	COATING & PLATING	
2.1	Hard chrome - spec. 1	2
2.2	Hard chrome - spec. 2	3
2.3	Plastic coat (subcontract)	5

Figure 15

Alterations to Lead Times

The point has already been made that MLT varies with priority (Figure 11). When the need exists to manufacture an item in less than the normal lead time, one way to alter the actual lead time is to attach a high priority to the job, so that the time spent waiting in queue is reduced. This may be combined with expedited moves, so that

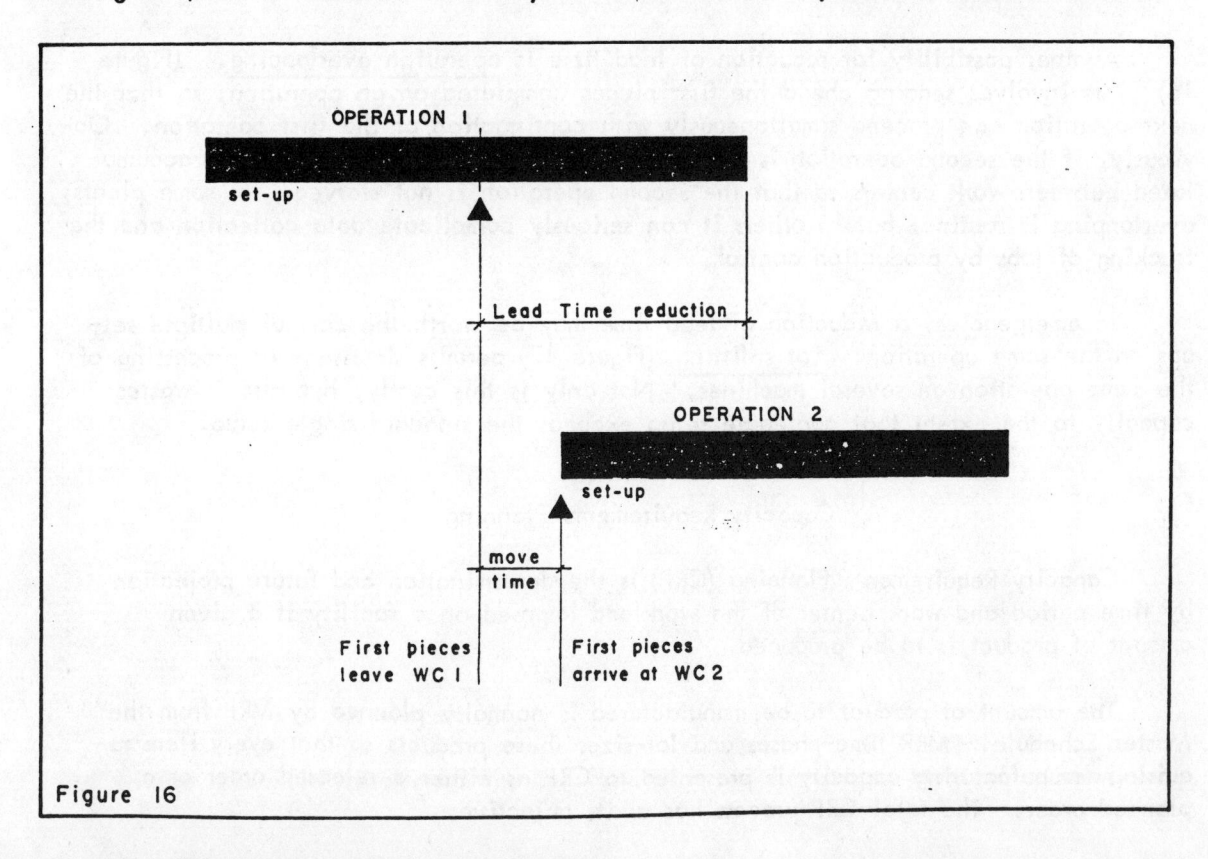

Figure 16

Figure 17

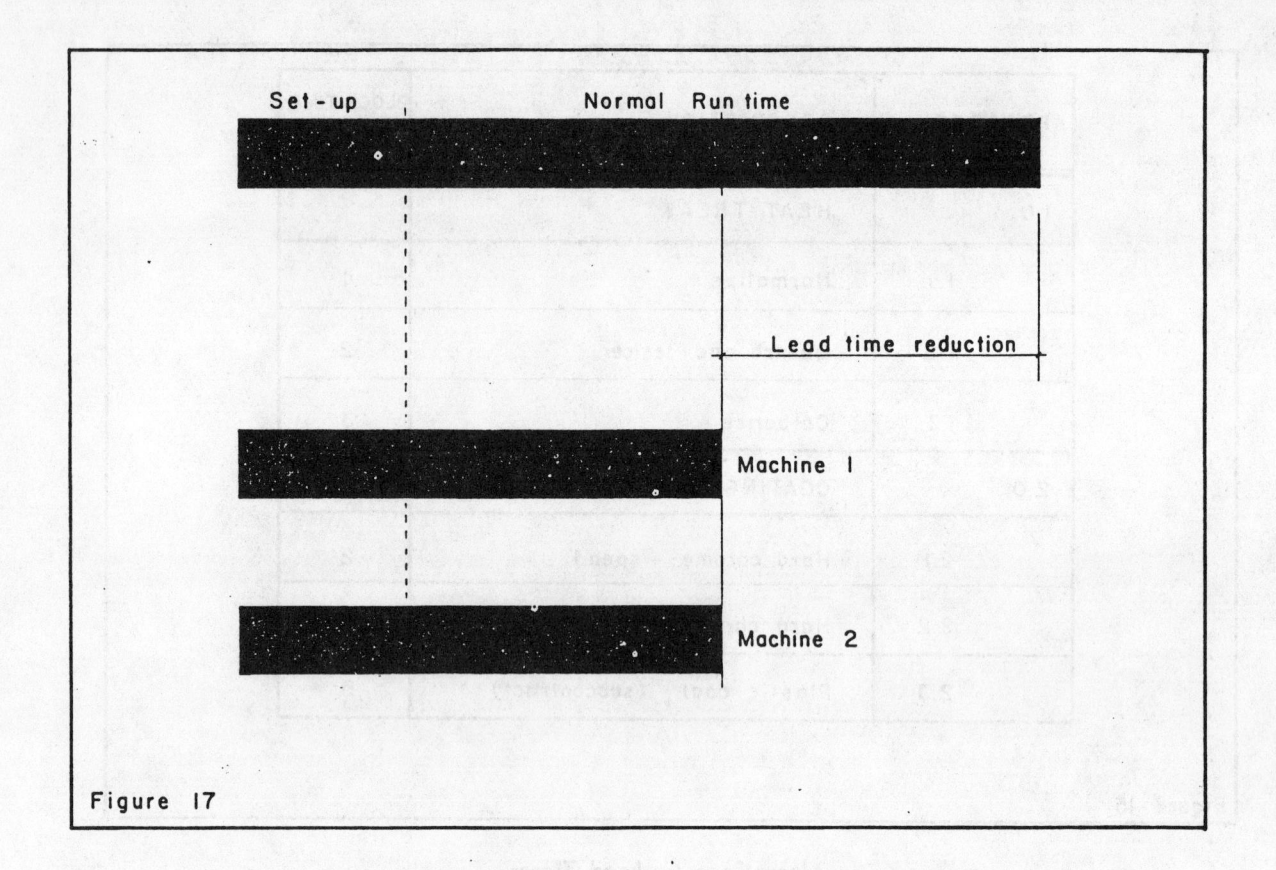

there is a total compression of interoperation time. Of course, the assignment of priorities to manufacturing jobs is a process which must receive the most careful thought in order to truly reflect the intentions of management, and once policies are established, the day-to-day application of those policies must be strictly and systematically enforced. No element of production control policy is more regularly prostituted than priorities.

Another possibility for reduction of lead time is operation overlapping. (Figure 16) This involves sending ahead the first pieces completed on an operation, so that the next operation can proceed simultaneously with continuation of the first operation. Obviously, if the second operation is faster than the first, enough parts must be accumulated between work centers so that the second operation is not starved. In some plants, overlapping is routine, but in others it can seriously complicate data collection and the tracking of jobs by production control.

In emergencies, a reduction of lead time may be worth the cost of multiple set-ups on the same operation. Lot splitting (Figure 17) permits simultaneous processing of the same operation on several machines. Not only is this costly, but also it wastes capacity to the extent that aggregate setup exceeds the standard single setup.

Capacity Requirements Planning

Capacity Requirements Planning (CRP) is the determination and future projection by time period and work center of the workload imposed on a facility if a given amount of product is to be produced.

The amount of product to be manufactured is normally planned by MRP from the Master Schedule. MRP time-phases and lot-sizes these products so that every item requiring manufacturing capacity is presented to CRP as either a released order or a planned order. The total CRP process has as its objectives:

CAPACITY MANAGEMENT REPRINTS—Revised Edition

JOB PLANNING

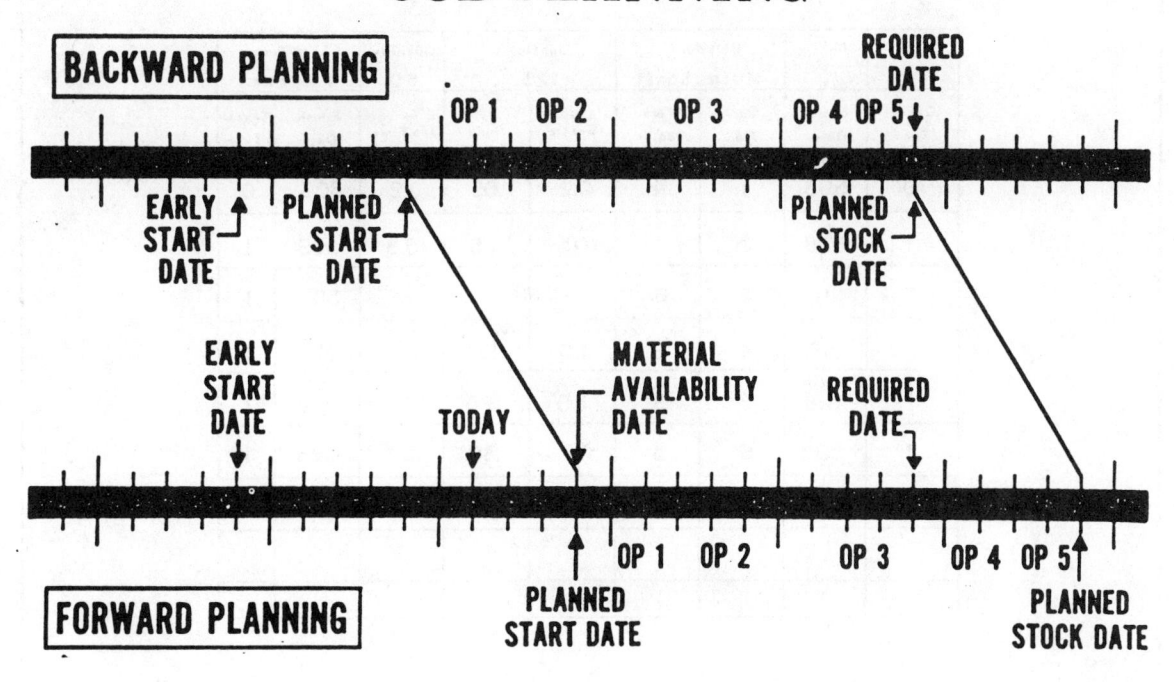

FIGURE 18

(1) determination of the manufacturing resources – men and/or machines, excluding materials -- needed to make the products in the Master Schedule;

(2) adjustment of work plans for effective use of capacity; and

(3) alteration, if required, of the Master Schedule for effective use of capacity and for accuracy of delivery commitments.

The Mechanics of CRP

The first step in CRP is backward planning. (Figure 18) This function is simply the reverse of lead time calculation. Each job is backward planned, starting at the required date dictated by MRP. If backward planning yields a start date in the past, the job plan must be shifted so as to start Today (or when material will be available), so that the demand for capacity impacts only the accessible planning horizon.

To see how backward planning is done, refer to Figure 14 containing the lead time calculation of a lot of 60 Main Shafts. Suppose the required date into stock is Day 525. Using queue and transit allowances, along with computed job times, the start and finish dates for every operation can be developed by a process the exact reverse of lead time development. The result is shown in Figure 19.

The second step of CRP is infinite loading, the classic illustration of which is Figure 20. (3) Normally, time buckets are selected to coincide with those in MRP; weekly buckets are typical. Increments of load are distributed to the various buckets without consideration of the capacity of work center. To accomplish this, an array of time buckets and work centers may be prepared, as shown in Figure 21.

Taking the first job from the job file, #123 for the Main Shafts, the first opera-

CAPACITY MANAGEMENT REPRINTS—Revised Edition

Queue Time	M.F. Start Date	Part No. Main Shaft Opr. No.	Job No. 123 Work Center	Quantity 60 Set Up	Run	Lead Time 4 weeks Job Time	Finish Date	Transit Time
0	506	1	4	0.2	.05	3.2	506	0
1	508	2	1	0.5	.25	15.5	509	1
0	511	3	6	—	—	—	512	1
1	515	4	2	1.0	.15	10.0	515	1
1	518	5	3	1.0	.20	13.0	519	1
1	522	6	5	0.7	.30	18.7	523	1
0	525	STOCK						

Figure 19

LOADING METHODS

INFINITE (WITHOUT REGARD FOR CAPACITY)

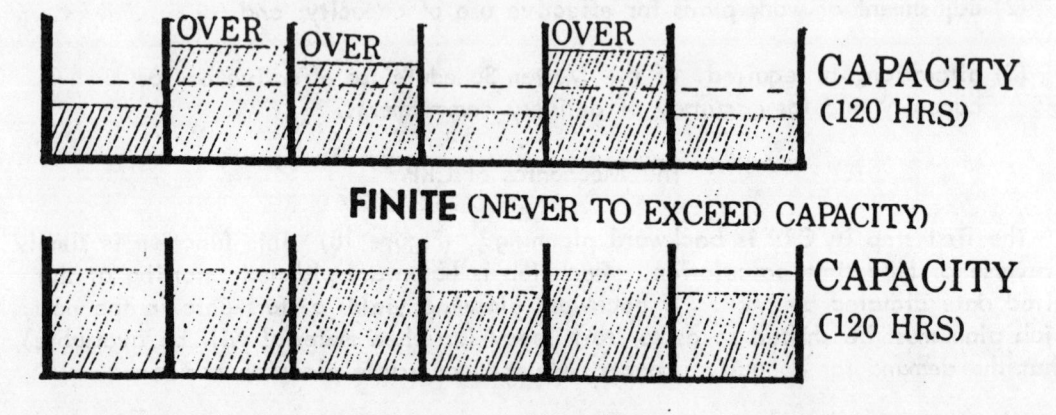

CAPACITY (120 HRS)

FINITE (NEVER TO EXCEED CAPACITY)

CAPACITY (120 HRS)

FIGURE 20
SOURCE: PLOSSL, G.W. AND WIGHT, O.W., "CAPACITY PLANNING AND CONTROL"
APICS INTERNATIONAL CONFERENCE, NOVEMBER 4, 1971

tion requires 3.2 hours at WC 4 on Day 506. This load is added to the appropriate bucket, and the process is repeated for all operations in the job. Then the next job in the file, #234 for 100 Housings, is selected (Figure 22) and loaded operation by operation.

After the entire job file -- both released and planned jobs -- has been processed, the weekly work center load accumulations are totaled. After only the two jobs of the

Week	Start End	WC 1	WC 2	WC 3	WC 4	WC 5	WC 8
1	501 505						
2	506 510	15.5			3.2		
3	511 515		10.0				
4	516 520			13.0 21.5 (34.5)	4.2		
5	521 525					18.7	10.5

Figure 21

	M.F.	Part No. Housing		Job No. 234		Quantity 100	Lead Time 2 weeks	
Queue Time	Start Date	Opr. No.	Work Center	Set Up	Run	Job Time	Finish Date	Transit Time
0	517	1	4	0.2	.04	4.2	517	0
1	519	2	3	1.5	.20	21.5	520	1
1	523	3	8	0.5	.10	10.5	523	1
0	525	STOCK						

Figure 22

example, the load accumulator for WC 3 in Week 4 would show 34.5 hours of load (Figure 21).

CAPACITY MANAGEMENT REPRINTS—Revised Edition

REPORT DATE   01/27/73   CAPACITY REQUIREMENTS PLAN
SHOP DATE   525
WORK CENTER   29   L&S NT-III N/C LATHE

•••••••••••••••••••••••••• WEEK ••••••••••••••••••••••••••

WEEK	START	WORK-PLAN S D H	UNITS 1 2 3	CAP	LOAD	L/C %	LOAD-TO-CAPACITY RATIO 0% 100% 200%	OVER (UNDER)
1	525	2 6 10	10 9 0	809	1310	162%	.XXXXXXXXX.XXXXXX	501
2	530	2 6 10	10 9 0	809	851	105%	.XXXXXXXXX.X	42
3	535	2 6 10	10 9 0	809	523	64%	.XXXXXX	(285)
4	540	2 5 10	10 9 0	675	898	133%	.XXXXXXXXX.XXX	223

Uses of CRP

When CRP is executed on a computer the resulting load profile may appear in a report like the one in Figure 23, which shows, by work center, the load and capacity by weeks over a 52 week planning horizon.

This report is a key control document in the management of queues, capacity, and delivery dates. The first task of production control is to adjust capacity to match to the maximum practical extent the specific loads imposed by the Master Schedule. In periods of overload, use of overtime to increase capacity and/or alternate routing to divert excess load will assist in balancing load and capacity. With foreknowledge of future problems provided by an adequate horizon, subcontracting may be arranged to handle abnormal loads. In periods of underload, work plans and manning levels can be reduced and load can in some cases be shifted from earlier or later periods to correct the deficit. And in those cases where all available means cannot correct foreseeable problems CRP provides guidance to the planner as to the extent of revision to the Master Schedule required to assure a realistic plan.

The Limitation of CRP

CRP is the basic capacity planning technique for medium-range planning. It can also be used for longer range planning, in lieu of simplified or short-cut methods, because once it is in place as a computer tool, it is easy to run and as accurate as the product specifications of the driving Master Schedule. In this mode it can be used for forecasting new machine tool needs or for capital investment planning for a complete new plant. There is, however, a major limitation of CRP -- it is usually ineffective and, indeed, frequently misleading in the short term.

To understand why CRP has this short-range limitation, it is necessary to re-examine its use of lead times.

Refer to Figure 19. CRP states that 18.7 hours of capacity is required on the cylindrical grinders (Wc 5) on Days 522 and 523. It is the job of production control to see that this capacity is available on the day that load arrives. The date of need has been approximated by estimating how long the job will wait in queue at WC 3, WC 2, and so on back to the job release date. Standard queue allowances have, of course, been used. If everything in the plant is normal -- product mix, load,

CAPACITY MANAGEMENT REPRINTS—Revised Edition

machine utilizations -- and if Production Control has been able to manage each queue to the planned level, the 18.7 hour increment of load will arrive at WC 5 on Day 520. But if variations away from a normal product mix has temporarily impacted WC 2 with abnormal load, so that the queue is actually 3 days, and if more-than-normal downtime in prior weeks has extended the queue at WC 3 also to 3 days -- in spite of Production Control's best efforts -- then, Job #123 will not arrive at WC 5 in time to be worked on in Week 5.

If CRP forecast a heavy load in Week 5, Saturday overtime was undoubtedly scheduled. But the fact that Job #123 will not arrive before Saturday negates entirely the value of that advance planning. That one job constitutes 1.6 days work on the grinder, so there could easily be a shortage of work to keep the machine utilized on Saturday.

This simplified example demonstrates the fact that the CRP is dependent on the reliability of the standard queue allowances used for lead times and that actual queues may vary planned levels due to a variety of events. The example dealt with just one job, however. In an actual plant, there will be thousands of jobs and dozens of work centers, and if it is a job shop, there will be a constantly changing product mix with an unpredictable routing flow. So, there is a compounding effect of the unknowable when it comes to estimating queues in the near term. This is not so much of a problem out in the mid-range -- say, from 2 to 12 months in the future -- because total load and total capacity overtime are accurately reflected by CRP and queues, while sometimes higher and sometimes lower than average, do tend over time to resemble the planned levels. Furthermore, the decisions of the medium-range plan are different from decisions of near-term.

In the medium-range, planning seeks to balance relatively large blocks of load and capacity -- to see, for example, that enough subcontracting is done so that the total load in a given month does not exceed total capacity in a work center. Two months hence, CRP may lead to a plan to schedule overtime 2 out of 4 Saturdays in the month. This Thursday, however, action must be taken to call people in this Saturday. That action is either right or wrong based on the specific jobs which will actually be in each work center on Saturday. CRP may show a demand for a lot of capacity in a work center, but very little ready work may be there right now. Will enough more load arrive to justify overtime? And should temporary transfers of manpower be initiated now for next week because the load shown in CRP will very likely arrive as planned? These are short-range decisions, and averages do not help very much in the short range. That is to say, CRP is very fallible for short-range planning.

Misleading Averages

Figure 24 is a Capacity Requirements Plan produced in a large job shop using the procedures outlined above.* It shows the near term, during which a number of practical decisions must be made. For example, there is an overload shown in Week 1, so a decision must be made whether to work overtime on Saturday. However, next week is underloaded, which obviously affects the overtime decision. But in Weeks 3 and 4 the overload condition returns in worse proportions. Beyond Week 4 there is a pattern of load equal to or greater than capacity. All in all, WC 24 seems to be a chronically overloaded work center, with a load 44% greater than capacity this month. Can anything be done?

---

* This example is based on actual conditions observed in normal operations at a plant of which the author was Manager of Production Control.

Figure 24 - CAPACITY REQUIREMENTS PLAN - ORIGINAL   WC 24

Week	Work Plan S	H	D	Week CAPY	LOAD	% L/C	Cumulative CAPY	LOAD	% L/C
1	1	8	5	31	37	119	31	37	119
2	1	8	5	31	16	52	62	53	85
3	1	8	5	31	47	152	93	100	108
4	1	8	5	31	78	252	124	178	144

Interestingly enough, it can be shown that by normal production control adjustments a perfect capacity plan can be developed in the short term.

Suppose that in Week 1, Saturday overtime is planned. In Week 2, because very little load is anticipated, a plan for utilization of the operator must be made. In actuality, this N/C turret lathe operator has experience on the N/C lathes in WC 30 and there is a machine open in Weeks 1 and 2 as a result of a WC 30 operator taking his vacation. So the WC 24 operator can be transferred to WC 30 for about half the time in Week 2. When the heavy load expected in Week 3 hits, the overtime can be scheduled by working 10 hours each day including Saturday. And then in Week 4 another operator on the Second Shift can be assigned to WC 24, so two 10 hour shifts can meet the demand for capacity. The result of all this would be a capacity plan as shown in Figure 25.

Obviously, there are other tactics which Production Control might adopt to deal with the WC 24 problem, but the key facts are that (a) CRP forecast a certain load, and (b) capacity can be readily adjusted to accommodate that load.

Figure 25 - CAPACITY REQUIREMENTS PLAN - REVISED   WC 24

Week	Work Plan S	H	D	Week CAPY	LOAD	% L/C	Cumulative CAPY	LOAD	% L/C
1	1	8	6	37	37	100	37	37	100
2	1	4	5	16	16	94	53	53	100
3	1	10	6	47	47	100	100	100	100
4	2	10	5	78	78	100	173	178	100

FIGURE 26 - LOAD PROFILE   WC 24

WEEK	WORK PLAN			WEEK			CUMULATIVE		
	S	H	D	CAPY	LOAD	% L/C	CAPY	LOAD	% L/C
1	1	8	5	31	14	45	31	14	45
2	1	8	5	31	32	103	62	46	74
3	1	8	5	31	35	113	93	81	87
4	1	8	5	31	59	190	124	140	113

And the result would be very <u>unsatisfactory</u>.

The actual load which is going to arrive in WC 24 is shown in Figure 26. It is a very different picture from Figure 24, and the reason is the one already explained: the actual queues being experienced by jobs upstream of WC 24 are significantly different from the standard queue allowances in their lead times. Instead of leading the planner to conclude that WC 24 is heavily overloaded this month, it shows that the work center is only moderately overloaded and the tactics required to manage capacity are very different from those suggested by CRP.

The Alternate Method

Of course, the big question is "How is it possible to know in advance what jobs will actually arrive each week at the work center?" The answer is that it is not possible to know with absolute certainty, but it is possible to predict job arrivals more accurately in the short term that CRP does. The way this can be done is with <u>simulation</u>. When simulation techniques are used as part of a computer-based production control system, the simulation module is called "Operation Sequencing."

Operation Sequencing

Simulation is "the imitative representation of the functioning of one system or process by means of the functioning of another ...."* In the computer, the stream of jobs flowing through the factory in the future is imitated. The factory is represented by a model consisting of the various work center capacities; each job is represented by its routing and time requirements. The rules of the computer simulation process duplicate as closely as possible the ways in which various contingencies are handled on the shop floor. For example, rules governing precedence, lot splitting and overlapping, transit times, and other functional and decision-making aspects of production control are built into the simulator.

Jobs -- i.e., operations -- are processed in priority sequence against available

---

* Webster's <u>New</u> <u>Collegiate</u> <u>Dictionary</u>, G. and C. Merriam Co., Springfield, Mass., 1976.

capacity in each work center. Using setup, run, and transit times, the start and finish time of each job is estimated. The highest priority available job is given first claim on open capacity, as would occur in the shop. Thus high priority jobs encounter short queues, while descending priorities experience ever-increasing waiting periods on heavily loaded work centers. In this way, queue lengths are simulated in advance and can be considered during planning. In the near term, these simulated queue lengths are more accurate than the average used in standard lead times, and so simulation will predict more reliably than CRP the arrival of jobs at work centers for the purpose of short-range capacity planning.

The following (Figure 27) is a comparison of the decisions which would have resulted from reliance on each of these two techniques:

FIGURE 27

	CRP	SIMULATION
WEEK 1	WORK OVERTIME ON SATURDAY	WORK HALF TIME IN WC 30
WEEK 2	WORK HALF TIME IN WC 30	FOLLOW NORMAL WORK PLAN
WEEK 3	GO TO 10 HOURS, 6 DAYS	FOLLOW NORMAL WORK PLAN
WEEK 4	GO TO 2 SHIFTS, 10 HOURS, 5 DAYS	GO TO 2 SHIFTS, 8 HOURS, 5 DAYS

The capacity plan based on simulation is shown in Figure 28, for comparison with Figure 25, based on CRP.

FIGURE 28 - SCHEDULED LOAD/CAPACITY REPORT   WC 24

WEEK	WORK PLAN			WEEK			CUMULATIVE		
	S	H	D	CAPY	LOAD	% L/C	CAPY	LOAD	% L/C
1	1	4	5	15	14	93	15	14	93
2	1	8	5	31	32	103	46	46	100
3	1	8	5	31	35	113	77	81	105
4	2	8	5	62	59	95	139	140	101

The Uses of Operation Sequencing

By far the greatest value of Operation Sequencing is its use as a scheduling method -- i.e., to predict delivery dates of manufacturing jobs. This application is described in the literature. (4) No other approach has a comparable accuracy.

A second use is for information with which to manage queues. The data in Figure 10, showing currently prevailing queues for various job priorities, was derived from simulation. It should be noted that simulation can predict queue lengths in the future, and it works as well for down-stream work centers as it does for gateway centers. In this respect it is more useful for queue management than Input/Output Control.

Operation Sequencing also facilitates preparation of a Work List for each work center. Jobs on the Work List are not only sequenced in priority order, but also with proper regard for the approximate time each will be available to commence production in a specific work center. In this respect, Work Lists derived from simulation display to the foreman only those jobs which have a reasonable probability of becoming available to him during the period covered by the Work List.

Finally, Operation Sequencing is the best way to plan and control capacity in the short-term. Obviously, CRP is the method of choice in the medium range -- say, 2 to 12 months in the future. In this range, load profiles derived from standard lead times permit planning and action to balance average capacity with the average load anticipated. But in the near term -- say, out 2 months -- when specific actions must be taken involving specific jobs, times, queues, and capacities, the more specific information obtained by simulation leads to more appropriate actions.

How Simulation is Done -- One Method

In 1967 Plossl and Wight predicted, "Simulation will undoubtedly become one of the most important tools for controlling shop operations efficiently." (2) Since then, however, many potential users of Operation Sequencing have been put off by apprehension over the complexity of simulation. In actuality, simulation need not be inordinately complicated, nor does it necessarily consume excessive computer time relative to its benefits. While there are various approaches to simulation -- some exceedingly sophisticated and difficult to understand -- two relatively simple approaches will be discussed here in order to permit a basic comprehension of the technique.

Consider a plant with 4 work centers and a list of jobs to be performed as shown in Figure 29. For simplicity in this example, suppose there are no jobs in process on Day 501, and let the transit rule provide that regardless of when an operation finishes in a work center, it cannot start in the next work center until the next day. All jobs are wanted on Day 505, but to define their relative priorities a number between 1 and 10 is assigned to each (with 10 being the highest).

A work center/time matrix may be constructed, as in Figure 30, with all buckets initialized at the capacity of that time interval. For example, the daily capacity of WC 1 is 23.04 standard hours (2 machines, 2 shifts, 8 hours, 5 days, 90% efficiency, and 80% utilization). By contrast, WC 3 has just one machine.

First, the highest priority job (B) is selected. It is accorded first claim on available priority. At the beginning of Day 501, the 6.71 hours of B-010 is consumed on WC 1 and the capacity register of that bucket is decremented to 16.22, the remaining capacity balance. The Start Date (501) and Finish Date (501) of the operation are recorded.

Figure 29

Job	Priority	UPN	WC	Job Time (Std. Hrs.)
A	6	010	2	4.78
		020	4	20.43
		030	1	9.74
B	9	010	1	6.71
		020	4	19.90
		030	3	24.27
C	4	010	4	16.10
		020	3	12.60
		030	2	7.76

ALL JOBS DUE ON DAY 505

PRIORITY #10 IS MOST URGENT; PRIORITY #1 IS LEAST URGENT

Next, B-020 is loaded on WC 4 starting on Day 502 as specified by the simple transit rule. It will be remembered that 23.04 represents the capacity of the 2 machines of WC 4. If only one machine is to be set up on a job -- to avoid the expense of multiple setups -- only 11.52 standard hours per day can be performed on one machine. The first 11.52 hours of B-020 is done on Day 502. The register is decremented to 11.52 hours remaining capacity and the Start Date is recorded. The balance of 8.38 hours of B-020 are performed on Day 503. The Finish date (503) is recorded and the register is decremented to 14.66.

Then, B-030 is loaded on WC 3, completing Job B. The resultant registers appear like Figure 31. Note that all the capacity of WC 3 has been consumed on Days 504 and 505.

Figure 30

		WC 1	WC 2	WC 3	WC 4
		23.04	23.04	11.52	23.04
1	501	23.04	23.04	11.52	23.04
	502	23.04	23.04	11.52	23.04
	503	23.04	23.04	11.52	23.04
	504	23.04	23.04	11.52	23.04
	505	23.04	23.04	11.52	23.04
2	506	23.04	23.04	11.52	23.04
	507	23.04	23.04	11.52	23.04
	508	23.04	23.04	11.52	23.04
	509	23.04	23.04	11.52	23.04
	510	23.04	23.04	11.52	23.04

Figure 31

		WC 1	WC 2	WC 3	WC 4
		23.04	23.04	11.52	23.04
1	501	16.33	23.04	11.52	23.04
	502	23.04	23.04	11.52	11.52
	503	23.04	23.04	11.52	14.66
	504	23.04	23.04	0	23.04
	505	23.04	23.04	0	23.04
2	506	23.04	23.04	10.29	23.04
	507	23.04	23.04	11.52	23.04
	508	23.04	23.04	11.52	23.04
	509	23.04	23.04	11.52	23.04
	510	23.04	23.04	11.52	23.04

Job A has the second highest priority. It is loaded uneventfully, after which the registers appear like Figure 32.

Job C has a relatively low priority, so it will not be unexpected if it has trouble finding capacity exactly when required. An effort to load C-010 on WC 4 on Day 501 is made. The first 11.52 hours can be done, but when continuation to Day 502 is attempted there is no remaining capacity (see Figure 32). It would not make sense to start the lowest priority job, if it were known that it would seriously delay

Figure 32

		WC 1	WC 2	WC 3	WC 4
		23.04	23.04	11.52	23.04
1	501	16.33	18.26	11.52	23.04
	502	23.04	23.04	11.52	0
	503	23.04	23.04	11.52	5.75
	504	13.30	23.04	0	23.04
	505	23.04	23.04	0	23.04
2	506	23.04	23.04	10.29	23.04
	507	23.04	23.04	11.52	23.04
	508	23.04	23.04	11.52	23.04
	509	23.04	23.04	11.52	23.04
	510	23.04	23.04	11.52	23.04

the highest priority job. Nor would it be reasonable to start C-010 and tear down the setup the next day with the job uncompleted. The simulation, therefore, should do what would be done in actual practice -- i.e., endeavor to load the entire operation in contiguous time periods. So, Register 4-501 is reset to 23.04 and the Start Date erased. On Day 503, 5.75 hours can be performed, with completion on Day 504.

When C-020 arrives at WC 3, B-030 is occupying the machine. Thus, the time C will spend waiting in queue is simulated. At the end of Job C, the registers look like Figure 33.

Figure 33

		WC 1	WC 2	WC 3	WC 4
		23.04	23.04	11.52	23.04
1	501	16.33	18.26	11.52	23.04
	502	23.04	23.04	11.52	0
	503	23.04	23.04	11.52	0
	504	13.30	23.04	0	12.69
	505	23.04	23.04	0	23.04
2	506	23.04	23.04	0	23.04
	507	23.04	23.04	9.21	23.04
	508	23.04	15.28	11.52	23.04
	509	23.04	23.04	11.52	23.04
	510	23.04	23.04	11.52	23.04

At the conclusion of the simulation, the delivery date of each job has been estimated as a consequence of determining the individual operation start and finish dates. These are shown in Figure 34. It will be noted in the simple example that the highest priority job (b) will not complete until a day later than its due date, despite its first claim on all resources. The work requirements exceed the time allowed (given the particular rules of this over-simplified example). Job A will not encounter any bottlenecks and will deliver on time. Job B, with its low priority will wait in queue at 2 of its 3 operations and will be late due to competing higher priority jobs.

In this highly simplified example, a logical problem is apparent. When A-020 consumed the 5.75 hours of capacity in 4-503, that 5.75 was composed of 3.14 on Machine 1 and 2.61 on Machine 2. The job would not occupy both machines. While this difficulty can be eliminated by scheduling on a machine basis rather than on a total work center basis, in actual practice this need not be done to achieve reasonable accuracy in completion time estimating, as long as there is a good mixture of short duration jobs in the job mix. Consequently, some very successful applications simplify their computer processing by loading by work center instead of by machine.

FIGURE 34

JOB	PRIORITY	UPN	WC	JOB TIME (STD. HRS.)	SCHEDULE DATES START	FINISH
A	6	010	2	4.78	501	501
		020	4	20.43	502	503
		030	1	9.74	504	504
B	9	010	1	6.71	501	501
		020	4	19.90	502	503
		030	3	24.27	504	506
C	4	010	4	16.10	503	504
		020	3	12.60	506	507
		030	2	7.76	508	508

ALL JOBS DUE ON DAY 505

PRIORITY #10 IS MOST URGENT; PRIORITY #1 IS LEAST URGENT

Obviously a workable simulator is vastly more complex than our rudimentary exercise, and includes provisions for closely approximating the many contingencies that occur in manufacturing. Jobs in progress on a machine at the time of simulation must, of course, be handled before others in the queue. Intricate transit rules are devised, sometimes with provision for accelerating movement according to priority. The degree of resolution will be matched to the plant's needs, but will usually range from a half-shift down to a hundredth of an hour. And each capacity register will have a discrete value to reflect vacations, machine down-time, and other real world events. When the degree of thoroughness of simulator design is matched to the facility portrayed, the accuracy of emulation can exceed any other method of foreseeing the specifics of plant operations.

Simulation exemplifies the technique of finite loading (Figure 20), in that the load accepted by a work center in a given period is limited to the understood capacity of the center. The specific technique illustrated by the previous example is sometimes referred to as "horizontal loading." Its definitive characteristic is that it loads all operations of an individual job to completion before proceeding to the next lowest priority job. In this way, the maximum opportunity is given to high priority jobs to claim capacity everywhere needed, and hence to finish early.

Other Methods of Simulation

A more sophisticated simulation technique is one which is sometimes referred to as "vertical loading." This approach considers all operations of all jobs and moves from job to job loading the highest priority operation which is available at each encounter of available capacity. There are several ways this can be accomplished by the computer.

In one method, all operations of all jobs are separated by work center and arranged in queues in priority sequence. A master clock advances by increments of time and at each advance all work centers (usually individual machines) are polled for available capacity. If open capacity is found, the queue of the available center is scanned for a job which is ready at master clock time. That job is assigned to a machine, the machine clock is set to the finish time, and the next operation of that job is tagged with its ready time (previous finish time plus transit).

An alternative method sequences all jobs and their operations in priority sequence and constructs an event chain, which is maintained in chronological order. An event (job completion) is selected, the clock is advanced to that time and the finish time recorded. The succeeding operation of that job is then placed in queue at its work center (ready at previous finish time plus transit). The next operation in queue at the work center just unloaded is selected and loaded. Its finish time is calculated and it is placed in the event chain in its chronological position.

A vertical loader will load the next ready job to a spot of available capacity. It may happen that a higher priority job arrives at the machine to find it occupied by a long-running operation of significantly lower priority. So the high priority job is delayed by waiting on the lower priority job. This potential result of vertical loading may be tolerated in the interest of full utilization of machines. In the horizontal loader the high priority job would have reserved the contested capacity and the low priority job would have been deferred.

If a dynamic slack-time priority rule is being used with a vertical loader, the priority of each operation is usually recalculated after completion of the preceding operation of the same job, thus simulating the priority it will have in the future when it is competing for service with other occupants of the queue.

The added complexity of simulation in the vertical mode requires much more computer time than the horizontal mode. For this reason the time horizon is usually limited to about five days of operation sequencing for Work List preparation. Completion date estimating over, say, a six month horizon will be accomplished by horizontal loading.

In the interest of accuracy in imitating factory operations, a simulator may include such refinements as alternative sequencing of operations within a job, operation overlapping, composite people/machine limitations, and reiteration to improve the degree of schedule optimization. All of these refinements increase the computer resources required. They are never justified unless the discipline throughout a company -- and especially in the shop -- is exceptional, so that operations are regularly executed with a predictability commensurate with the design of the simulator.

Summary

Operation Sequencing is regularly thought of in connection with estimating delivery dates and preparing work lists for shop operations. However, this technique is also extremely useful for planning capacity in the short-term, when a reasonably accurate foresight as to job arrivals helps in making better decisions.

REFERENCES

1. Communications Oriented Production Information and Control System, White Plains, N.Y., IBM Corporation, 1972, Volume V.

2. Plossl, G. W. and Wight, O. W., Production and Inventory Control, Prentice-Hall, Inc., Englewood Cliffs, N. J., 1967.

3. Plossl, G. W. and Wight, O. W., "Capacity Planning and Control," APICS International Conference, 1971.

4. Lankford, R. L., "Scheduling the Job Shop," Proceedings of Sixteenth International Conference, American Production and Inventory Control Society, Washington, D.C., 1973.

Reprinted from the APICS 1982 Conference Proceedings.

JOB-SHOP SCHEDULING: A CASE STUDY

Ray Lankford - Plossl & Lankford
Tom Moore - Remmele Engineering, Inc.

Even though Remmele Engineering, Inc. had virtually no prior experience with computer-based manufacturing systems, they recognized that better management of capacity could help them achieve a significant competitive advantage. In this case study, the Vice President of Operations of Remmele describes their implementation of a capacity management system with exceptional capabilities, and he assesses the performance improvements they achieved. To provide a perspective on capacity management systems, the consultant on the Remmele project evaluates developments of the last decade in an effort to define what is the "state-of-the-art" today.

CAPACITY SYSTEMS IN PERSPECTIVE (Ray Lankford)

Ten years ago, in the early 1970's, the revolution in systems of manufacturing planning and control had just begun. Not only did the innovators of those years bring to the attention of the world the power of MRP and the importance of master scheduling, but they also stimulated thought and development in major aspects of capacity management. The formative paper on Input/Output Control appeared in 1970 (1); a redefinition of what was thereafter called Capacity Requirements Planning occurred at APICS Conference of 1971 (2); and at the Conference of 1973, I spoke about the feasibility of what we now call Operation Sequencing (3).

Interestingly enough those three papers are still in the reprints offered by APICS for study for the certification examination. They represent pioneering thought and are still useful for the study of basic concepts, but they come from an early period in the "systems revolution" of the 1970's and 1980's. As chairman of the APICS Certification Committee on Capacity Management, I am involved now in the search for and examination of new papers which will replace the earlier ones for our study - new works which portray what we have learned and what we have developed in the intervening decade.

There have been significant developments in recent years, which I will describe and evaluate. At the same time, there is a tremendous gap today between what we know about capacity management and how we apply the techniques available to us. This "proficiency gap" between what we know and what we accomplish in capacity management is one of the most serious problems of manufacturing control today. It is the root of failure of many firms to derive benefits from their installation of MRP. It is a major impediment to increasing productivity in countless manufacturing companies. Without a doubt, improving the management of capacity offers for most companies the greatest single opportunity for improving performance of any sector of manufacturing planning and control. And because of this common "proficiency gap", the fact that a company relatively inexperienced with systems implemented and is successfully using an advanced capacity management system makes the Remmele story interesting and significant.

Remmele's capacity management system consists of Capacity Requirements Planning and Operation Sequencing. They elected not to use Input/Output Control because of characteristics of the production environment which Tom Moore will explain. In this perspective on capacity management, I will not focus on Input/Output Control, since that was done in a paper at the 1980 Conference (4). We will look, however, at the "state-of-the-art" today in CRP and Operation Sequencing.

In 1971, George Plossl and Oliver Wight wisely proposed the term "Capacity Requirements Planning" to replace what was previously called "infinite loading" or "loading to infinite capacity". They pointed to two weaknesses of traditional machine loading:
1. a typically high past-due load; and
2. a misleading decay of load derived from released orders only.

A solution was proposed for each of these defects:
1. improve priority planning with MRP, so as to reschedule late but unneeded jobs to their time of actual need; and
2. use planned orders from MRP to portray future loads over the entire CRP horizon.

Thus Capacity Requirements Planning took its place as a major module of the integrated manufacturing system.

Despite the demonstrated effectiveness of the technique, however, a "proficiency gap" still exists today. A minority of companies are using CRP effectively - not unlike the situation ten years ago when a relatively few companies had mastered MRP. Moreover, the capacity planning modules of commercial software are usually the weakest part of the packages, making CRP unnecessarily difficult to use effectively. Finally there are some extraordinary misconceptions regarding CRP which may cause confusion to potential users. One such misconception is that CRP is expensive. One consultant has written, "It probably consumes more computer capacity than any other single step within MRP". Leaving aside the semantic confusion of this reference to MRP, this commentator is simply misinformed.

In a plant handling 6,420 manufacturing jobs using the same software as Remmele, total processing time for MRP, CRP, and Operation Sequencing (with networking) is about four hours, with CRP requiring about 60% of the time of MRP. In terms of actual CPU time, excluding file manipulation and printing time, CRP loading requires about one minute.

Certainly, when compared to the benefits of having advance visibility of capacity overloads and underloads, the cost of CRP is acceptable and should not deter anyone from using it.

Some other misconceptions about CRP will be dispelled in a later section.

When the manufacturing people at Remmele Engineering decided to improve their ability to schedule their shop, the specific technique they wanted was Operation Sequencing. As Tom will explain later, they arrived at this conclusion independently, without the advice of any so-called "expert" advisor. This was probably fortunate, because no technique in manufacturing control is more misunderstood by consultants and practitioners alike than Operation Sequencing.

Operation Sequencing is sometimes thought of as "finite loading" because it loads work centers only to their known capacity - i.e., to "finite" capacity. Just, however, as the term "infinite" loading was a disservice to the perfectly valid technique we now call Capacity Requirements Planning, so the term "finite loading" bestows confusion and even animosity on what is really an extremely powerful and useful technique of capacity control.

Correctly understood, Operation Sequencing is a technique of <u>simulation</u>. It simulates in advance, inside the computer, the sequence in which manufacturing jobs will flow through the various work centers of the plant. Unlike some of the more complex mathematical methods sometimes applied to real-world problems, computer simulation has proven effective in many applications. In their classic book of 1967, Plossl and Wight devoted a section to Job Shop Simulation, which concluded, "Simulation will undoubtedly become one of the most important tools for controlling shop operations efficiently."(5) Indeed, at that time a number of companies, especially in Europe, were already using simulation successfully. One of my clients in Scandinavia has had the technique in continual use with good results since 1968.

The development of manufacturing systems in Europe has been very different from that in the United States. Because of the damage sustained by manufacturing plants during World War II, European industry in the post-war years concentrated on the management of critical capacity. In the United States, by contrast, capacity was plentiful and readily expandable, but materials were frequently critical in a booming economy. It is not surprising that the thrust of systems development was toward materials planning and inventory control. Of course, the eventual development of MRP improved priority planning for both purchased and manufactured items. Nevertheless, capacity management received far less emphasis in the United States than in Europe.

Recently, a group of manufacturing system specialists came from Europe to review several major U.S. software packages for potential purchase. Their conclusions were that the U.S. uses bills of materials far more expertly than they do, and that Master Scheduling and MRP software are highly developed here. They were, however, appalled at the crudity of the capacity management modules which they examined and, in particular, they were shocked at the infrequent use of Operation Sequencing, which they regard as commonplace.

That Operation Sequencing became both misunderstood and controversial in the United States is one of the major

misfortunes of the generally productive past decade of system evolution. Several factors contributed to the confusion:
1. the "infinite" versus "finite" debate carried over from prior years tended to polarize opinions before real analysis could begin;
2. the development of MRP concentrated thought and effort, and rightly so, on priority planning methodology;
3. companies implementing MRP were so totally occupied with the demands of data integrity, master scheduling, rough-cut capacity planning, and MRP utilization that they were slow to develop beyond MRP to capacity management; and
4. some of the major opinionmakers in the field, for a variety of reasons, quickly denounced Operation Sequencing as unworkable.

It is both interesting and useful to examine this last factor and ask whether some of these early denunciations were valid then or remain valid now. Certainly Remmele Engineering went into their implementation of Operation Sequencing fully aware of the reasons given by some "experts" as to why the technique will not work. Remmele simply concluded that the objections of a decade ago are no longer valid today.

Criticism of Operation Sequencing derives from that fundamental misconception referred to earlier, that <u>it is the same as finite loading</u>. Let's look at the facts.

Oliver Wight has described finite loading in this way: "It automatically revises the need priorities - that is, the priorities developed by MRP, for example, in order to level the load." (6)

Does Operation Sequencing do this? Absolutely not! It uses the required dates developed by MRP to prioritize all jobs and <u>does not revise them</u>.

The definition of Operation Sequencing is: "...a simulation of what is likely to happen on the shop floor, given the <u>current production plan</u> and existing man power and machine availability." (7)(Underlining emphasis was added by the author.)

By "current production plan" is meant the Master Schedule converted into manufacturing jobs with required dates developed by MRP. As will be seen later, Operation Sequencing at Remmele uses the required date of each job to state its priority and always endeavors to schedule to that date.

Although Operation Sequencing loads work centers to finite capacity, it clearly is something different from "finite loading".

As a result of the confusion over finite loading, some of the defects of that limited technique have been linked to Operation Sequencing.

In the early 1970's, four specific problems were attributed to any system using "finite" loading:
o <u>Assumes predictable job arrival</u>.
This alleged defect of simulation is ironic, in that the prediction of job arrivals by simulation is far more accurate than it is with backward planning, upon which CRP and conventional Dispatch Lists are based. Some early ultra-sophisticated simulators pretended to predict events to fractions of an hour, which deserved the ridicule of practical manufacturing people. The objective of Remmele's system is to do better - much better - than backward planning which uses "planned" queue allowances, which frequently do not prevail in the plant. This will be illustrated in the section on the mechanics of Operation Sequencing.
o <u>Component priorities are usually dependent</u>.
Here the objection was that getting all components of an assembly scheduled to complete at the same time required endless reiterations of the loading process. This is really a "paper tiger" in that the purpose of simulation is not to schedule all components equally late, but rather to identify those which will probably be late so that early action can be taken to solve the problem.
o <u>Automatic master scheduling is risky</u>.
Nothing could be more true! However, no practical proponent of simulation ever advocated letting the computer have the final say in determining the schedule. All simulation purports to do is to make a reasonable estimate of completion dates, to highlight potential problems in advance, and to allow production controllers and master schedulers to decide if problems can be solved or if the Master Schedule must be revised. Again, this will be demonstrated in a later section.

o <u>There are easier, better ways to do the job</u>.
In some production environments, this is unquestionably true. But for the complex network of thousands of manufacturing jobs competing for capacity at hundreds of work centers in a job shop with non-uniform routings, the alternatives of CRP, Input/Output Control, and conventional MRP pegging are grossly inefficient in the solution of the enormous number of daily problems confronting the production controller.

In addition to these alleged problems, there are two other misconceptions which often perplex critics of Operation Sequencing:
o <u>One must use either Capacity Requirements Planning or Operation Sequencing</u>.
In reality, of course, these techniques are used together, as was recognized by Plossl and Wight fifteen years ago when they advised, "Orders are first...loaded to infinite capacity to see where overloads will occur, then orders are rescheduled ...based on available capacity after corrective actions have been taken..." (5)
o <u>It requires enormous amounts of computer time</u>.
Here, two things have happened in the last ten years: simulators have become simpler and computer power has become cheaper. Tom Moore will address this issue in his remarks.

Where, then, does the "state-of-the-art" stand today?

On this matter Oliver Wight has proposed: "Since we've abolished infinite loading, if we're going to continue with our progress, in my opinion, we should abolish finite loading, and if necessary replace it with some kind of a shop simulator that tells the planner what he might want to do in order to do some load leveling on the vital few, rather than having the computer automatically do the load leveling on everything." (6)

This is sound advice. "Finite loading" is a dead issue. But what about simulation? Wight goes on: "I would have no objection to somebody using the basic logic of finite loading in simulation mode, where they showed the planner what would happen if jobs flowed through different work centers at the current production rate." (6)

Remmele Engineering is doing <u>exactly that</u>. They call it Operation Sequencing, and Tom Moore is here to tell you how they got started.

THE MANUFACTURING ENVIRONMENT (Tom Moore)

Remmele is in three basic businesses: 1. contract machining, 2. fabrication, and 3. designing and building special machines. Manufacturing operations are located in five plants comprising a total of 271,000 square feet. Each plant is individually designed and equipped to offer a specialized type of precision machining or machine building and fabrication service.

Each of these basic businesses presents a somewhat different manufacturing environment.
<u>Contract machining</u> - Remmele's contract machining or general machining activities encompass a broad spectrum of part sizes and lot quantities. At the top end of the size range are a number of large boring mills. The largest is capable of machining a work piece 100 feet long by 14 feet high and weighing up to 75 tons. At the lower end, equipment such as small jig bores handles very small precision work to tolerances of .0001" on a production basis. Lot sizes vary from single piece parts to quantities of 1,000 per week in continuous runs.
<u>Fabrication</u> - Fabrication activities are targeted at jobs requiring both machining and fabrication. These jobs have ranged from the complete fabrication of large paper-making machinery on a one-of-a-kind basis to producing pumps used in the oil fields in quantities of several a month.
<u>Special machinery</u> - The special machines activity consists of designing and building special purpose equipment ranging from individual units to complete production lines. Applications have included the automation of: assembly, fabrication, packaging, testing, processing, machining, and web-handling functions. Although these machines are primarily one-of-a-kind, there are occasional repeat orders for a previously-built machine. In addition to designing machines, this activity also includes building machines to a customer's design.

It should be evident from the above description that the manufacturing process in all three product areas meets a number of the criteria of a classic job shop. These criteria can be grouped generally into demand and processing characteristics as follows:

Demand characteristics - Production is initiated with a customer's order. There is no production to a forecast and no inventory is kept at any level.

Demand is predominantly independent demand. Because of the non-repetitive nature of the special-machine business, the bill of materials is approached as a simple, minimum-level bill without emphasizing assemblies and subassemblies and their relationships. Further, since materials and purchased components are bought to order, there is no need to net against inventory levels to determine required production quantities. These demand characteristics led to the conclusion that Materials Requirements Planning was not essential at the present time.

Unexpected demands and the rapidly changing nature of the product mix require frequent and rapid rescheduling.

The one-of-a-kind or low-volume, nonrepetitive production may result in more frequent changes to the process and to estimated run times than would be the case with repeat production.

Repair orders, which may be time-and-materials, and other types of emergencies are part of the business.

Process characteristics - Batch-mode processing with complex routings across a variety of general purpose machine tools characterizes the small lot or one-of-a-kind production. Overlapping operations are the rule in high-volume parts production.

Machine assembly operations, such as mechanical, hydraulic, and electrical, are seldom sequential but tend to be in parallel.

The plant load at the outset of the project consisted of 3,000 manufacturing jobs requiring 15,000 operations. This load was spread over approximately 150 work centers, including outside processes.

In the contract machining and fabrication business, there are three major features of the service that are being sold: 1. quality or conformity to the customer's specifications; 2. the timeliness and predictability of deliveries; and 3. the cost. In the special-machine design business, the added dimensions of engineering and a solution to the customer's problem are present. However, timely production of machine parts, which are competing with all other parts in the shop, is also essential to satisfactory performance.

With all of the above characteristics of the manufacturing process to deal with, two primary business objectives need to be accomplished:

1. improve the ability to set accurate delivery dates; and
2. once these delivery dates are set, improve the on-time delivery performance.

To accomplish these objectives, it was imperative to deal with capacity as a finite resource. Infinite loading did not seem to be a complete solution.

What was needed was the ability to simulate the manufacturing process on each of the jobs to give a realistic delivery estimate. This simulation needed to deal with the complexities of the routings and the diversity of the work centers. It also needed to recognize the finite capacity that existed in all the work centers. This led us to Operation Sequencing.

CAPACITY REQUIREMENTS PLANNING (Ray Lankford)

The five segments of an integrated manufacturing system are:
o Demand Management
o Priority Planning
o Capacity Management
o Production Activity Control
o Inventory Management

These correspond to the five subdivisions of the body of knowledge defined by APICS. An idea of the relationship among these segments may be gained by reference to Figure 1.

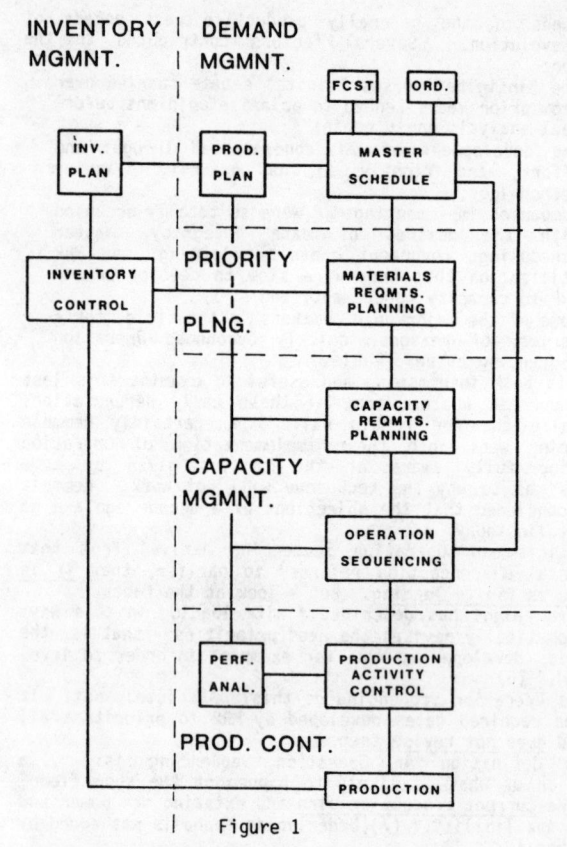

Figure 1

The software installed by Remmele is designed to do all the necessary functions of the Capacity Management segment of the integrated system. In addition, it provides some of the most important outputs needed for Production Activity Control, the most notable of which is the prioritized Dispatch List.

The purpose of Capacity Requirements Planning is to disclose the amount of work which must be performed by each work center in each time period in order to produce the products in the Master Schedule.

Master Scheduled items are normally exploded through MRP into time-phased requirements for subassemblies and components. The need for future capacity is then derived from two sources:
1. released manufacturing jobs resident in the open job file; and
2. jobs planned by MRP, but not yet released.

Because the great majority of Remmele's work consists of single piece parts, with customer stipulated required dates, they do not use MRP; because they do not forecast, their Master Schedule is their backlog of customer orders. Thus, there are no "planned jobs", and the only constituent of future load is the open job file.

The process of CRP has been described in the literature (8), but will be summarized here to illustrate technical features of the Remmele system.

The first step in CRP is backward planning, in which each job has operation start and finish dates calculated using planned values for move and queue times. Remmele utilizes a Move Time Matrix to specify transit time. Planned values of queue are specified for each work center in the Work Center Master file.

The second step in CRP is infinite loading, in which each future demand for capacity is registered on each work center for each future time period. These demands are totaled and a report is produced showing the overloads and underloads. Let's examine the information contained in a CRP report and be certain we understand the significance of the numbers.

An extremely useful feature of the Remmele CRP report is that it shows the action plan from which the work center's output will be derived. This action plan, which portrays how we intend to operate the work center in the weeks ahead, consists of two parts:
1. the Work Schedule in shifts per day, days per week, and hours per shift; and

2. the number of productive units (machines or people) which will be operational each shift.

The CRP report can thus be used as a working document to plan adjustments to schedules or to staffing and at all times shows the planner such things as planned overtime, personnel shifts, and scheduled holidays. It is apparent to the planner where the capacity is coming from to meet the requirements of the Master Schedule.

It is sometimes said that the "capacity" to be used for CRP must be "demonstrated" capacity. This is provided in the case of Remmele by using the demonstrated productivity of the work center during the recent past. The reason for calculating capacity from the productivity ratio, instead of using some "normal" capacity in standard hours, is so that planned outputs for different operating schedules can be readily obtained. For example, there is a capacity of 809 standard hours in a week when six days are scheduled, but only 675 standard hours in a five-day week.

It is important to recognize this fact that capacity is not static, but rather adjustable. What is contained in the "Capacity" field of a CRP report is the planned output based on a demonstrated capability from actual output tracking in the recent past.

The "Load", on the other hand, is the required output, which must be achieved if the Master Schedule is to be accomplished.

When "output needed" is compared to "output planned", it may be necessary to adjust the capacity plan. Remmele's software will accept this adjustment to the Work Schedule and/or the Units in any period and will calculate and display the expected capacity.

Another important, but poorly understood, fact is that the required output in any period will, in fact, be required only if the jobs comprising it arrive in time to be worked on that period. That will occur only if these jobs wait in queues in various preceding work centers a total time equal to the planned queues at those work centers. If queues are longer or shorter than planned, the timing of required capacity may be quite different from that shown by CRP.

A CRP load profile by itself is of limited usefulness. Also required is a Detailed Load Report listing the jobs which comprise the load in each period. With this information, jobs may be routed to alternate work centers, shifted to other time periods, or pegged to end items which are to be rescheduled in the Master Schedule.

When Remmele first implemented CRP, they found some surprising maldistributions of load. Separate salespeople had sold the same machine time, causing unsuspected problems with promised delivery dates. Changes to personnel assignments would clearly be required in the future, but had not been foreseen. And perhaps most important of all, the amount of unsold capacity on each machine could be quantified for focusing the sales engineer's efforts on machine time that could be converted to revenues.

Tom Moore will tell you about how they applied the system, but first he will review how they got the company prepared for a new way of operating.

PREPARATIONS FOR CAPACITY MANAGEMENT (Tom Moore)

Focusing on operation sequencing as the major system feature, an extensive software search was undertaken including:
o Visits to a number of companies around the country
o Contacts with all major computer vendors either for references or their own software
o Independent software firms
o Custom development programs were discussed with several systems consultants and software firms

The overriding conclusion was that Operation Sequencing applications were relatively few in number and none were found in a business similar to Remmele's.

Most manufacturing systems were MRP oriented and involved a master schedule. One commercially-available system that was found was judged to be too complex. A "black box" solution complete with dedicated stand-alone hardware was discarded because we couldn't find out, to our satisfaction, the logical basis of the programs and how they worked. We were unwilling to turn our manufacturing process over to this type of systems solution.

With the findings above and the lack of alternatives, a program to develop in-house software was begun. Working with two mathematics professors from the University of Minnesota, the development of a prioritizing algorithm for use in operation sequencing was started. Although a workable program was ultimately completed and tested, the question arose as to whether Remmele had the experience or the resources to design or even manage the design of a total system by ourselves.

An article on job shop scheduling, written by Ray Lankford when he was responsible for production control for an oil-field equipment manufacturer, ultimately led us to our consultant.

At the time we discovered the article, Ray was in the consulting business. Contact with him led to a visit by Remmele's top management group to the company featured in his article. In addition, the management group attended a Plossl and Lankford seminar on top management's role in manufacturing.

Seeing the complexities of an actual systems application and drawing on this seminar for background, we concluded that the assistance of a consultant would be very valuable, even necessary to implement a system in a reasonable period of time.

After a visit by Ray and a review of Remmele's operations, we agreed to work together on the implementation of a capacity management system.

Although the search for software had not produced any solutions considered acceptable, we continued our efforts, and ultimately became aware of a new capacity management package that had been successfully implemented, but was not, as yet, commercially released. This package, developed by Manufacturing Management Systems, Inc., incorporated both Capacity Requirements Planning and Operation Sequencing. We judged it to be suitable to our needs.

During implementation, the final documentation was completed and we had the opportunity to incorporate some features that were required to suit our operation.

The software, as it had been developed, did not operate on the computer we had selected. However, the vendor agreed to make the required conversion.

At the time this project began, the Data Processing Department consisted of a manager and two data entry people. Remmele had outgrown its small, punched card batch-processing computer and faced the need to expand due to needs for improved financial and general management systems, as well as manufacturing systems requirements.

No major manufacturing systems existed, except for a job-status reporting system that was driven by time cards. In the financial area, payroll and cost accounting were the major systems in place.

The first objective in the selection process was to select a computer that would meet the company's needs for the next five years. There were a number of key issues that emerged in this selection process:
o The computational requirements of the scheduling system required a certain minimum capability.
o As we examined the upper end of computing capability that we thought we might need, the cost and perceived complexity of large main frames pushed us in the direction of large mini-computers with 32-bit architecture.
o Except for the question of our scheduling requirements, other system needs could have been met by a comfortable, more evolutionary step to an interactive 16-bit mini-computer.
o Substantial differences of opinion existed within our management group over which course to take since there was no commercially-available software to benchmark; however, some tests run on the Operation Sequencing programs developed by the university professors led to a decision in favor of the larger computer.
o As it turned out, the purchased software was more computer efficient than we anticipated, but initially it had not been converted to the type of computer under consideration.

The conversion process was accomplished via a remote terminal tied into the new computer. The process went very smoothly and approximated the following timetable:

New computer fully operational   January, 1981
Software conversion completed   May, 1981
CRP in production   July, 1981
Operation Sequencing in production August, 1981

A project team was established with the Plant Manager of the largest plant designated as the project manager. Also assigned to this team were the Plant Superintendents from two other plants, the Production Control people from each of the plants, the Data Processing Manager, and a representative from the Sales Department. As Vice President of Operations, I worked in a dual capacity: working with the consultant and the project manager, and also working on individual tasks as a team member.

To get the initial direction for the project and to bring the tasks into focus, we concentrated on the major files that we needed to build to get the scheduling system working.

<u>Work center master file</u> - This file contains all the capacity and schedule data for each work center.

<u>Open job file</u> - This consists of both the job master file (information about the job) and the job detail file (specific routing information).

<u>Job chaining file</u> - This file links the bill of materials of an assembly by job numbers.

For each of these files, it was necessary to determine the who, when, and how for all the pieces of information that were required. Certain general task groupings emerged:

<u>Numbering system</u> - After considering a change to a non-significant six-digit job number, we decided to retain our significant job numbering system. In retrospect, this was a good decision because the added complications of introducing this change along with the new system implementation would have outweighed the benefits. It was necessary, however, to establish a common definition of terms for the complete numbering system including sales orders, manufacturing jobs, part numbers, and detail numbers.

<u>Purchasing system interface</u> - Reliable material availability dates are essential to effective scheduling. In our situation, this meant the availability dates of raw materials, purchased components, or customer-supplied materials, such as castings or forgings, are necessary. Some consideration was given to finding a commercially-available purchasing system, but the idea was dismissed when a quick solution was not available. Instead, Remmele developed its own material-control system, which focused narrowly on meeting the needs of the scheduling process and left the implementation of an expanded purchasing system for a future date.

<u>Labor reporting</u> - The existing procedures for labor reporting had to be expanded substantially and formalized to support the requirements of the scheduling system. This was a lengthy process as the requirements of the system led to the development of new procedures to permit accurate execution on the shop floor. The approach we selected involved the use of three individual time cards: on-line operations, off-line operations, and attendance. Although we expect to streamline this process in the future, it was functional and met the necessary requirements of our scheduling and cost accounting systems.

<u>Routings</u> - When the system was first implemented, the quality and thoroughness of the routings varied widely, dependent largely upon the individual writing them. To meet the needs of an accurate scheduling system, it was necessary to include more detail in many cases. The existing route sheets were essentially complete, but it was necessary to make revisions to include additional information. Although the changes were not substantial, this represented a major educational effort given the large number of people involved in writing route sheets.

<u>Networking</u> - This task consisted of developing simple procedures for linking the bill of materials together at the time a special machine or any form of assembly was released to the shop. The goal here was to collect and present in meaningful form all the relevant scheduling information on a project, as well as to take advantage of the feature in the system that relates priorities to the relationship of jobs in the network.

<u>Data integrity</u> - The initial task was to measure the accuracy of the information collected off the shop floor. The target was set at a 95% accuracy level; Remmele was initially confident that it would be close to this figure. The issue was interpreted too narrowly, however, and the initial results were much worse than expected. The more detailed information requirements of the scheduler, the lack of consistent procedures, and poor file maintenance were major problems. With the aid of some very comprehensive audit programs generating time-card error messages, the target level has been achieved for information going into the system. Work is continuing on the reduction of errors and the resulting time-card rejections. Substantial improvement, primarily through education, has been made.

<u>Data processing operating routine</u> - The new computer, followed shortly by this new scheduling system, necessitated a dramatic change in data processing operations. The change in hardware from the batch-processed punched cards to a more interactive environment with the new system changed the whole data processing mentality. Before the scheduling system implementation, a job status run was made on Wednesdays with the previous Friday's time cards. Now, the new system is run at night with the day shift's time cards, and the foremen's work lists are ready at 6:30 AM the following morning.

<u>Interface programming</u> - This task consisted of formatting the data files which the Capacity Management System needed from our work-in-process master files. This was done on a part-time basis over a period of two months by the Data Processing Manager. In addition, a number of custom reports were created that would integrate the Capacity Management System results with the work-in-process data. On-line access has also been provided to display results generated by the system.

<u>System documentation</u> - Our response to this task was slow in spite of the consultant's continual stressing of the need to fully document policies and procedures. In addition to the uncertainties of feeling our way, our team, almost to the man, did not like to write nor had we much experience at it. After solving a couple of the same problems twice, however, we did begin to write down our conclusions with the objective of developing a Production Control Manual. With the focus on procedures, policy issues emerged for resolution, and this manual evolved into what would more appropriately be called a "business guide".

<u>Project planning</u> - As the project began, the breadth of these tasks was not apparent in all cases, nor was the interdependence of these tasks. The plan started using a simple, milestone-planning technique. As progress was made and learning occurred, the milestone chart was updated. This proved to be a very valuable tool to help manage the project.

<u>Education</u> - Implementation of systems of this magnitude are difficult because they introduce new concepts, and they involve almost everyone in the organization. A substantial amount was invested in education and communication to help overcome these difficulties. The major efforts were:

o <u>Company newsletter</u> - Even before a system was found to implement, the President of the company began to talk about the need for a system and its importance to the company. He continued to comment at various points throughout the implementation process and left no question as to his commitment to the project.

o <u>Top management briefing</u> - All members of the top management group attended an appropriate seminar.

o <u>Capacity management seminar</u> - After the project team was selected, all team members attended.

o <u>System newsletter</u> - The project team wrote a series of newsletters to all employees on different aspects of the system and its impact on them.

o <u>Consultant</u> - Ray Lankford conducted a number of educational sessions for the top management group, foremen, sales engineers, design engineers, and office people. In addition, his periodic visits during the implementation process provided necessary education and problem-solving aids for the project team.

o <u>Production control meetings</u> - Ray Lankford also attended these in all of the plants after the system was running. Focus then began on the effective utilization of the system output - actual on-the-job training.

o <u>Employee meetings</u> - Departmental meetings for all employees were conducted by the project team to explain portions of the system and introduce new procedures.

In addition to the above, there has been a lot of one-on-one training and small group sessions with all users and project team members.

OPERATION SEQUENCING (Ray Lankford)

Let's review the capacity planning process which has taken place before Operation Sequencing:
- o The Master Schedule has been tested against a rough-cut capacity plan on critical work centers, so there are no gross errors in Master Schedule content.
- o MRP has planned the quantity and timing of manufacturing jobs; some jobs have been released, while others are still at the "planned" stage.
- o Capacity Requirements Planning has, for all work centers, displayed the "output needed" in each time period to accomplish the Master Schedule.
- o An aggressive and resourceful Production Control Department has taken a myriad of actions to match the "output planned" for each work center to the "output needed", overtime has been scheduled, subcontracting has been arranged, personnel have been shifted, and jobs have been re-routed.

At this point, one thing is certain: A lot of problems still remain!
- o Some work centers are still overloaded in some time periods and underloaded in others.
- o Because each job takes a different route through the plant, it is impossible to predict the size of queues at all work centers in the future; hence, lead times are uncertain.
- o Since queues at some work centers will undoubtedly differ from the "planned" levels assumed by CRP, the load profiles may contain significant errors.
- o We are working to averages, but specifics are killing us!
- o As each "problem" work center is recognized, the planners start trying to work their way up through the pegs to the end items to communicate with Master Scheduling. But there are hundreds of problems and several thousand jobs to deal with.
- o The changes keep coming!

In short, as one knowledgeable realist recently observed, "No matter how carefully Master Scheduling has been executed (rough-cut cycles included), the planner cannot possibly foresee all manufactured-part shortages generated by standard lead time offsets." (9)

Before we conclude that the quality of life in Production Control is not likely to improve, let's look at what we have to work with.

The action plans for altering capacity devised by our energetic planner have been entered into the computer, so as to portray planned output for comparison with required output. In actuality, this data, derived from practical planning work, constitutes a mathematical model of the factory.

Moreover, we have a file of all current and future jobs with their priorities expressed by their required dates.

We also know from production labor reporting those jobs currently working in the plan, with their status of completion.

Common sense might tell us that we could see how our jobs, sequenced according to priority, might fit the capacity produced by our action plans. However, conventional wisdom in this body of knowledge says, "Don't do it! Ignore what you know about capacity and priorities."

The common-sense approach of simulating the processing of jobs in order of priority using replanned capacity is, of course, Operation Sequencing. This is what Remmele uses to schedule their shop.

The particular software at Remmele is significantly different from other simulation-mode scheduling routines. While it has some very powerful capabilities, it is much simpler and, hence, more practical than some of the elegant, highly-sophisticated simulators which have been used in the past. For example:
1. Time resolution is a half-shift, not a fraction of an hour.
2. It does not try to solve problems automatically. Instead, it reports problems to the human scheduler so that judgement and experience may be applied to the solution.

Because of these and other simplifications, the simulation program requires only a modest amount of computer time, meaning it can be run frequently enough to recognize changed conditions.

The second of the simplifications cited is quite significant! The point was made emphatically in an earlier section that the computer does not "automatically reschedule". What Operation Sequencing does is to produce a manufacturing job schedule which shows for each job the following information:
1. Required Date - from MRP or MPS
2. Planned Start and Finish Date - the standard lead time using planned move and queue times
3. Scheduled Start and Finish Dates - the probable, actual lead time, recognizing available capacity and the job's relative priority

Thus, the planner can see these jobs which will probably be late. From detailed operation dating, bottleneck operations are evident. Using this information, the planner can go to work solving the problems. The computer did not change the required date, nor did it automatically change the plan. It merely reported the degree to which reality will probably deviate from the plan. It is entirely up to the planner whether to solve the problem or to re-promise.

In cases of dependent demand in which a number of components are required at the same time for assembly, the software used by Remmele will simulate component job completion and the subsequent start and completion of subassembly and assembly jobs. This process is called "networking". It identifies any component jobs which will not be completed in time to support the Master Schedule, but it does not automatically reschedule all other component jobs equally late. It allows the planner to solve the problems causing lateness or to decide that rescheduling is, indeed, required.

Most make-to-order plants like Remmele require the ability to identify the manufacturing jobs which are providing components to the final assembly. Unfortunately, much MRP software provides only single-level pegging, whereby a demand for an item is linked to the next higher level part causing that demand. This linking is part number to part number. When a component job is going to be late, it is necessary to trace upwards through the pegs to identify all other jobs at all levels which will be affected. This is a time-consuming and laborious process.

The networking option in Remmele's software utilizes "job chaining", a form of multi-level pegging, which links requirements to sources by job number. Thus, for every sales order, Remmele can, at any time, see each job which is producing parts, subassemblies, and assemblies for that specific sales order; this is an enormously useful capability when answering customer inquiries or considering revision of the Master Schedule.

Since a simulation-mode scheduling system utilizes priorities to sequence operations at work centers, the manner in which priorities are designated is of some interest. Remmele's software offers a choice of two alternatives, each based on slack time: Critical Ratio and Index Number. The former is well-known, and the latter is described elsewhere in the literature. (3)

Tom Moore will now discuss this point and some other special requirements of Remmele's scheduling system.

APPLYING THE SYSTEM (Tom Moore)

Given the nature of Remmele's organization and it's business, we recognized a number of special problems that would require us to evolve our own particular solutions.

Remmele's decentralized organization had implications in two areas. First, there were three separate plants, each with an individual Plant Manager. The plants differed in size and somewhat in mission. The need for a "better" way was recognized in the largest plant, but was less apparent in the two smaller plants. We resisted the temptation to implement in the larger plant first and, instead, brought everyone through the process together. The result was a smoother implementation and broader acceptance in all plants when the switch was turned.

A second concern centered on the widely dispersed responsibilities for process engineering and production control. The routings for many of the jobs are the responsibility of the Sales Engineers, as is the responsibility for establishing required dates with the customers. These Sales Engineers, as well as the Design Engineers, function as project managers for their jobs, and in doing so, performed much of the production control function, working closely with the foremen. This "decentralization" or dispersion of responsibility required the involvement of many people in the process of changing our procedures and, to some degree, even the changing of key roles as a more concentrated production control function evolved.

In addition to the dynamic characteristic of demands, the one-of-a-kind or non-repetitive nature of much of the manufacturing means a minimum of up-front investment in process, design, and standard setting. While striving to constantly improve this, estimates and processes that change when the job reaches the shop floor are always present. Added operations and revised routings and estimates are a way of life on many of our jobs, and we had to find a convenient way of making these changes as well as getting the people involved to recognize the need to change our computer files.

We promoted the adage "You don't have to do things differently because of the system, just tell someone when you make a change." Most of the changes involved the route sheet file, so on-line file maintenance procedures were developed for use by the Production Control Department to make this task easier.

Operation overlapping - or as we call it "flowing" - was not in the software as we purchased it initially, but we knew this to be a requirement for effectively scheduling any of the volume-production jobs. This practice was also found useful with our small-lot production to reduce lead times in emergencies or to get work to open downstream work centers.

Working with the consultant and software vendor, this capability was brought on-line six months after the initial implementation.

Two options for expressing job priorities are available in the software: Critical Ratio and Index Number. Index Number was chosen. Based on the required date, a number between "0" and "999" is derived from the time remaining and the work remaining. An external priority or management factor can also be applied to intensify the priority in an emergency.

Initially, the idea of structuring or formalizing the decision of which job to work on first was a difficult concept to become comfortable with. However, experience has shown that it has a sound basis in logic and, while not perfection, it does satisfactorily handle the vast majority of jobs.

The quantity and quality of information received from this system far exceeded what existed in the past. Initially there was more information than we could digest, and we had to learn how to efficiently use the system output to pinpoint problems and take the necessary actions.

Lacking the ability to accurately "benchmark" the system in advance, estimates of the computer resources required were made. Processing time remained a concern until the actual operation began, however, the results turned out to be fairly close to the estimates.

At shop workload peaks, the CRP and Operation Sequencing phases were both run within an hour. Report printing was a large time-consumer, but we are printing less and using the CRT's more. Currently our total cycle from building the work files to printing the reports takes less than three hours at night.

THE USER'S APPRAISAL (Tom Moore)

The value of this system to Remmele and the primary results achieved to date can be summarized as follows:
1. In terms of the primary objective of improving on-time deliveries, steady progress has been made. The system has contributed to this, but it can't take sole credit. With the impact of the recession and the resulting reduced work load, contention for scarce capacity hasn't been as pronounced as in normal times. It is expected, however, that when the demand for absolutely full capacity resumes, the system will make possible much more reliable delivery promising.
2. We have achieved the required level of accuracy in work-in-process reporting. Jobs don't get lost and the information as to their status is realistic. In addition to benefiting the scheduling process, this has paid dividends in cost accounting as well.
3. Capacity bottlenecks are visible, and the response to them is more timely.

The system has proven to be very well designed and a highly-effective tool. It has contributed substantially to Remmele's ability to manage its capacity.

IMPLICATIONS OF THIS CASE STUDY (Ray Lankford)

Ten years ago, the type of capacity management system being used today by Remmele was considered very sophisticated. Simulation-mode scheduling, what we now call Operation Sequencing, was regarded as extremely complex. Software was of limited availability, computer requirements were large and expensive, and applications were confined to relatively large companies.

Today, Tom Moore has described how his company, a relatively small firm with limited systems experience, is successfully using Operation Sequencing. Software, while not abundant, is more readily available; computer power is no longer the obstacle it once was. There are a number of other companies of various sizes using similar systems. Two examples are especially interesting. One large, aircraft-equipment manufacturer has been so impressed by the results of Operation Sequencing that for some years after its installation in 1973, no publicity about the system was permitted because management regarded it as a major competitive advantage. Only recently one of my clients, smaller than Remmele, programmed in-house for a mini-computer a simulator which is producing schedules enthusiastically endorsed by shop foremen, production controllers, and salespeople alike.

Another major improvement of the past ten years is the increase in knowledge about capacity management systems. And with knowledge has come understanding that some of the controversies of the formative years are behind us. Infinite loading and finite loading are obsolete concepts. True to the prediction of Plossl and Wight in 1967, simulation has developed into a technique of genuine usefulness. Today, it is the "sleeping giant" of manufacturing control.

Using simulation - Operation Sequencing, as we now call it - companies like Remmele are closing the "proficiency gap", applying with skill and enthusiasm the "state-of-the-art" in capacity management.

REFERENCES

(1) Wight, Oliver, "Input/Output Control: A Real Handle On Lead Time", Production & Inventory Management, Volume II, Number 3, Third Quarter, 1970

(2) Plossl, George W. and Oliver W. Wight, "Capacity Planning and Control", Proceedings of the Fourteenth Annual Conference of the American Production and Inventory Control Society, 1971

(3) Lankford, Ray, "Scheduling the Job Shop", Proceedings of the Sixteenth Annual Conference of the American Production and Inventory Control Society, 1973

(4) Lankford, Ray, "Input/Output Control: Making It Work", Proceedings of the Twenty-third Annual Conference of the American Production and Inventory Control Society, 1980

(5) Plossl, George W. and Oliver W. Wight, Production and Inventory Control, Prentice-Hall, Inc., Englewood Cliffs, New Jersey, 1967

(6) Wight, Oliver, "Finite Loading", Managing Inventories and Production, Oliver Wight Video Productions, Inc., Audio Tape Number 9, Copyright 1976 ASI

(7) Communications Oriented Production Information and Control System, Volume V, IBM Corporation, White Plains, New York, 1972

(8) Lankford, Ray, "Short-Term Planning of Manufacturing Capacity", Proceedings of the Twenty-first Annual Conference of the American Production and Inventory Control Society, 1978

(9) Thomas, Gene, "Real-Time, Behind Schedule Replanning", Production & Inventory Management Review, April, 1982

RAY LANKFORD

Ray Lankford is a principal in Plossl & Lankford, a firm engaged in management counseling and education. He has over twenty years of experience in manufacturing management. He was Vice President of Operations for McEvoy Oilfield Equipment Company, with responsibility for four plants around the world. Prior to that, he was Vice President of Manufacturing for Reed Tool Company. His experience includes management of production control, systems design, and plant supervision. He holds a Bachelor of Arts and a Bachelor of Science Degree in mechanical engineering from Rice University. He has served as Chairman of the APICS Certification Committee on Master Scheduling and Capacity Planning, and he has written several major articles on plant scheduling and capacity planning.

TOM MOORE

Tom Moore is Vice President of Operations for Remmele Engineering, Inc., a manufacturer specializing in contract machining and the designing and building of special machines. In addition to heading all manufacturing operations, he has responsibility for Remmele's financial, personnel, and data processing functions. Prior to joining Remmele in early 1979, his experience was primarily in the areas of general management, sales, and marketing. He began his career in international sales for Graco Inc., a major manufacturer of fluid-handling equipment. He progressed to general management positions in Japan and in Europe before becoming Vice President of International Operations. He has a Bachelor of Science Degree in Civil Engineering and a Master of Business Administration, both from the University of Minnesota.

PRIORITY FIXATION VERSUS THROUGHPUT PLANNING

Presented at the APICS International Conference, 1977

Hal Mather & George Plossl
Mather & Plossl, Inc.   Atlanta, GA

Hal Mather:

INTRODUCTION

There are two essential elements in every manufacturing control system. These are priority (what to make, when) and capacity, (volume flowing per time period). Most people in manufacturing control concentrate on priorities to the exclusion of capacity. In many plants, capacity desired and available are reviewed annually, plans made to solve any mismatches, and once that is over, concentration switches to getting the right things made at the right time. This is a natural approach as pressures are hourly or daily for information on customers' orders, checking whether vendors' deliveries will be on time, reacting to line shortages, etc. But these two sides of a manufacturing control program are interrelated and one cannot be successful when disregarding the other.

The performance of formal priority systems to date (material requirements planning and shop floor control) is proof of this. So far these techniques are not approaching anywhere near their potential in the bulk of applications. The major reason is that capacity is not getting its share of attention. They must *both* be managed for a successful manufacturing control program.

There are five basic functions in all manufacturing control programs, shown in Figure 1. The first of these is the need for a master production schedule, specifying the total amount of product that is needed to be made over a given time period. It is called a game plan; it is a set of numbers formulating the strategy that the whole plant will be trying to achieve.

The next two functions, capacity planning and control, answer the question "Is the volume of material flowing adequate to support the master production schedule?" Visualize a manufacturing plant as a refinery. These two techniques together are planning and controlling the diameter of pipelines feeding product through work centers and from

---
FIGURE 1

BASIC FUNCTIONS

    MASTER SCHEDULING   —   GAME PLAN

    CAPACITY PLANNING
    AND CONTROL   —   GET ENOUGH

    PRIORITY PLANNING
    AND CONTROL   —   GET RIGHT THINGS

---

vendors. They ensure the diameters are adequate to handle the volume of product to be made in the plant, defined as the master production schedule.

The next two functions, priority planning and control, answer the question, "Are we getting the right items?" Here is where the flow of product through work centers or from vendors must be sequenced correctly to get the first items first, second items second, etc. Here is where manufacturing control people concentrate their attention, on the sequencing or priority problem. However, if capacity is inadequate in any of the pipelines in a plant or at vendors, it is impossible to get the right priority on jobs.

"Are we getting the right stuff?" is the wrong question to ask unless we are sure we are getting enough. Few of us are getting enough! That means fewer still are getting the right ones!

PRIORITY FIXATION

The oldest technique in manufacturing control systems is expediting. It is still running the bulk of industry to ensure parts get made when needed. An expediter's role is to go out and locate missing or late parts and prioritize these through the plant. Even with the new techniques of material requirements planning and shop floor control, expediting is not out of favor. Recently I saw some new advertising for "Hot stickers", in beautiful colors, shaped like flames, containing special wording, etc. However, these hot stickers have been made more modern. Now they get stuck on computer generated paper instead of being stuck on handwritten paper.

The interest in material requirements planning and its emphasis in industry to the exclusion of most other techniques is relatively understandable. It was only logical that the expediter's process, our most successful technique, would be formalized first. MRP identifies shortages systematically and provides a better "when" system. In the early days of MRP, weekly time buckets were used and the system usually replanned weekly. This seemed adequate for a while, but then concern started to grow over priority changes within the week. Hence a lot of interest has developed in the technique called "Net Change MRP". Its great contribution to the field is that many times it requires less computer time to perform the same job as a regenerative program because it only processes exceptions. The practitioner's interest, however, was not in saving the computer resource, but freeing up enough of that resource to be able to prioritize his jobs more often; hence daily net change or at least twice a week net change. This provided more priority information, more up-to-date.

But now concern has switched from running the process more often to looking at the time increment that is being used. The early net change programs still used weekly time buckets; hence the priority system was relatively coarse providing information only in five day increments. But what if the demand was on Monday and replenishment on Friday of the same week. (We all know that early in the week to purchasing means any time up until noon on Friday.) This obviously was untenable and a more definitive time increment was needed.

This has caused bucketless MRP, or one day bucketing systems, to be in vogue to provide priority information to the day of the week. The only question now is, "Is the demand in the morning or the afternoon?" I expect the next generation of MRP programs to be not only date responsive but also time of the day. And the real big question is "How well do we know what we intend doing in the future to the day, and how good is much of the data we are using, eg. lead times, shrinkage factors, lot-sizes, etc. to support this level of precision?"

And heard like a voice in the wilderness from the users is the plea to reduce the amount of information they are getting. "MRP means More Reams of Paper" is heard fairly often and users have difficulty reacting to all the exceptions on a timely basis. Hence a suggestion has been made to allow the computer to reschedule open orders automatically. Another suggestion has been to apply dampening rules to the exception messages. For example, if the expedite is two days or less don't report that, and if the delay is five days or less don't print that either. So from weekly regeneration of weekly buckets has evolved daily net change with daily buckets and, applying these over-rides, changes either get made automatically without full cognizance of the effects these changes are making or dampening rules blunt the precision of these techniques to provide information on weekly changes only. Is this progress?

And in the bulk of cases, making changes to priorities more often will not improve the situation at the plant. Priority is not the major problem in most situations.

From this level of expertise interest is now swinging to the need to execute priorities in the plant, hence shop floor control. This is a series of techniques to provide a list to the foreman showing the sequence in which work should be performed to make the master schedule happen. Here, people are choosing up sides. One group says, "The foreman should be constrained and must follow the lists exactly the way they are shown", and the other side says, "Don't do that, let him be flexible, let him cherry pick". But the major problem at the moment is the list *cannot* be followed. The production control man goes out to the foreman and says, "Work on the top job for me would you Joe," and Joe says, "Where is it? When you get it here I'll work on it." Obviously the P.C. man recovers quickly and says, "O.K. Joe, if you can't do that one, how about working on the second one?" And Joe says, "Where have you been, I finished that job three days ago." But maybe the most important problem of all is that there are too many urgent priorities and too many changes to these priorities for anybody in a plant to consider the list a valid plan. How about vendors; can they, or are they, willing to react to changes on a daily basis? If they are not, what good is changing the plan daily if materials will not be received in matched sets to make products?

WHERE DO PRIORITIES COME FROM?

The priority system starts from a set of numbers defined as a master production schedule. This is a statement of what, how much, and when something will be made, relatively high up in a bill of materials. A master schedule typically has a one-year horizon, although many companies have much longer horizons than this, and a few have shorter. The definition of products put into the master production schedule is usually for specific items, either finished goods or an intermediate level lower down in the bill of material. MRP takes this information and converts the overall plan into detail plans. A typical example is shown in Figure 2. The master production schedule explodes through bills of material, calculates requirements at the first level, and nets against inventory, both on-hand and on order. Lot-sizes are calculated or applied where justified and lead times offset to generate the next level requirements, etc. MRP's role is to provide exception reporting wherever a mismatch of timing between demand and supply exists. It is a priority system and typical messages are "expedite, delay, launch a new order, cancel an existing order, etc." MRP provides what is called order priority.

To get order priority into operational priority at the foreman level, these orders must be broken down finer. MRP or order priority provides the need date to the scheduling system. Scheduling rules take the total

FIGURE 2

MASTER PRODUCTION SCHEDULE

WEEK NO.	40	41	42	43	44	45	46	47
WILL MAKE		20		30		25		35

MAJOR ASSEMBLY

REQUIRE		20		30		25		35
HAVE NOW 10								
WILL GET		10						
NEED				30		25		35
START			30		25		35	

SUB ASSEMBLY

REQUIRE			30		25		35	
HAVE NOW								
WILL GET			30					
NEED					25		35	
START		60						

lead time for an order and break it into smaller segments, as shown in Figure 3. Using the setup and run times for a job, move and queue times for work centers, etc., due dates can be calculated for each operation.

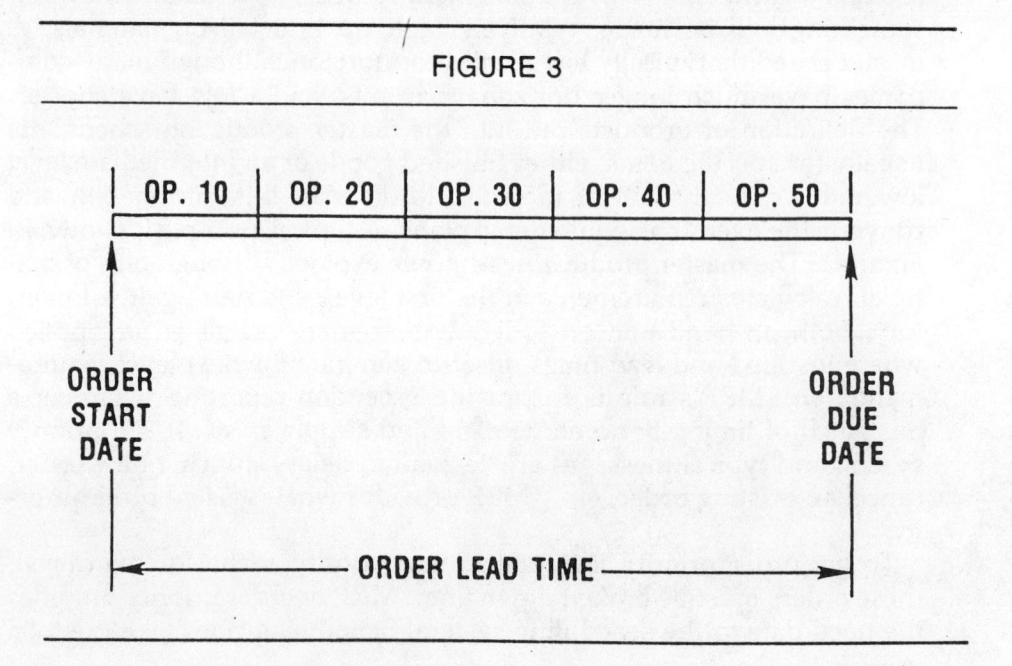

FIGURE 3

| OP. 10 | OP. 20 | OP. 30 | OP. 40 | OP. 50 |

ORDER START DATE ← → ORDER DUE DATE

←———— ORDER LEAD TIME ————→

110   CAPACITY MANAGEMENT REPRINTS—Revised Edition

These estimated operation dates are now used to create a priority list for each foreman, as shown in Figure 4. Priorities can be calculated using techniques such as critical ratio, queue ratio, etc., to rank jobs in their desired sequence. As changes occur to the master production schedule, engineering changes are implemented to the bills of material, inventory adjustments are made to the on-hand inventories, scrap or late delivery occurs to the open orders, etc., then these priorities are up-dated, first of all through MRP and then through the scheduling system into a priority change at the foreman or vendor level. The priority system is a date driven system.

FIGURE 4

DAILY DISPATCH LIST
WORK CENTER 103

DATE: 10-3　　　　　　　　　　　　　　　　　　　　CAPACITY: 298

PART NUMBER	DESCRIPTION	ORDER NO.	QUANT	HRS	PRIOR RANK	GOES TO
117175	SLEEVE	841A	1500	22	1	106-1
276112	GEAR	920E	300	13	2	110-2
523153	HOUSING	663B	120	8	3	106-4
319181	FRAME	717C	165	10	26	108-2

TOTAL HRS IN 103 = 287

If these data are analyzed in more detail, estimates, forecasts, guesses, and averages are found throughout the system, which obviously affect the quality of information generated. The master production schedule is the starting set of numbers for the planning system. The detailed priority list that a foreman gets is the execution phase of that plan linked to the master schedule through bills of material and MRP, and through scheduling rules to operational priorities.

There are some problems with this flow of information. The first of these is the tendency within industry to make the master production schedule anything but a realistic plan. It is usually well over-stated and hence provides far too many priorities to foremen for them to execute. Another problem with the master production schedule is that it is often too dynamic. Dynamic changes at the top of bills of material obviously ripple throughout the whole planning system and result in rather dramatic changes in priority on the plant floor which may or may not be achievable. A master production schedule often contains elements of forecast. These are frequently placed in arbitrary time buckets, especially if the forecast is for monthly quantities and the master schedule is in weekly time increments.

The bills of material used in the plan are usually today's bills of materials. Future changes to existing products and new products engineers are designing are not in this planning program and will affect today's decisions as these changes get implemented. The system uses lot-sizes at each level in the BoM to cover net requirements and explodes these lot-sizes to calculate requirements at the next lower level. Frequently these lot-sizes are over-ridden when releasing work for short term reasons. This means that the priorities used for lower level materials that are already made were wrong, even though calculated precisely. Many other factors such as scrap, rework, inventory adjustments, unplanned requirements from sales or engineering, etc. are all going to impact and affect the priority system to a greater or lesser degree. Hence precision of planning in the priority system has to be balanced against the quality of information available.

THROUGHPUT PLANNING'S ROLE

Another critical parameter for timing is the one labeled "Lead time". The lead time for a part is the length of time from knowing it is required until it is ready, complete for use at the next level of manufacture. However, it is not the lead time for individual parts that is important to the priority system but the stacked lead time from initiating procurement of materials all the way through the various processing steps up to the master production schedule. This stacked lead time has a major effect on the priority system. The longer this lead time is, the more time there is for change, either with the master production schedule or with the other sets of data used in the system. As these changes are made, the system will attempt to reflect these changes in priorities but maybe it will be too late to react. The earlier comments about bills of material that change obviously are more severe the longer the stacked lead time. It provides the engineers more time to change their minds on the product design. Lead times are critical to the priority system but very little is being done to control and manage lead times to a minimum.

A company several years ago was a classic example of the problems of long lead times. I gave a presentation to the shop foremen and schedulers in this plant regarding inventories, customer service, productivity and their roles in improving these. Just a few minutes after my presentation started a foreman stood up and wondered why I was wasting his time. When I explained that I thought he had something to do with getting products made on time, efficiently, with low inventories, he agreed that was true, but suggested I go and talk to the purchasing department. He said the purchasing people were the ones who had all the wrong material in the plant and hence he could not make what customers needed. They were the ones that were causing most of the problems.

This is a typical feeling among many plant people. They have the opinion "give me the materials and I can make anything the customer wants". They also feel victims of purchasing departments not having needed materials. They feel they can react with materials on hand to provide a given customer what he needs, but if the materials are not available they cannot get a customer out of trouble. A little analysis and digging on my part found the following conditions in this company's planning system. Their bill of materials was relatively simple with few levels in it; however, their stacked lead time was as shown on Figure 5. They procured castings with 13 weeks lead time which at that period in the economic cycle was far better than most other people buying castings. Their purchasing department was doing an *excellent* job of getting reasonably short lead times for product. These castings were then machined with very tight tolerances and a significant number of operations. 16 weeks was the lead time in the planning system for machining castings. After the machining was done the castings were sent to a secondary department where they were welded together and subsequent machining performed. The tolerances again were very tight and several operations were necessary to make sure these castings were perfectly balanced. This again took 16 weeks of processing time, or at least that was in the system. The last stage of making the product was assembly and test, and the system was told this took 4 weeks because everything had to be 100% tested under some rather stringent conditions.

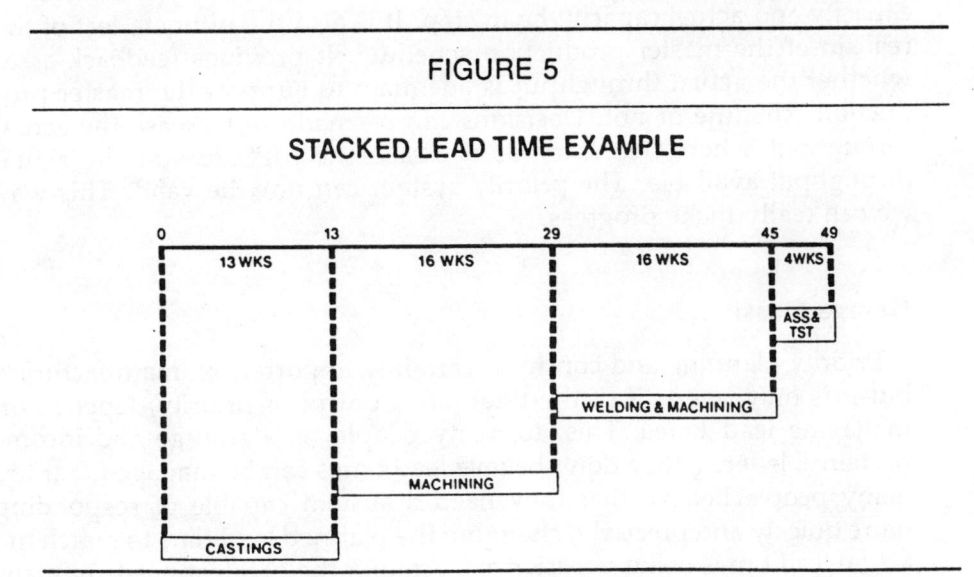

FIGURE 5

STACKED LEAD TIME EXAMPLE

```
0           13              29              45  49
|  13 WKS   |    16 WKS     |    16 WKS     |4WKS|
|           |               |               |ASS&|
|           |               |               |TST |
|           |               |WELDING & MACHINING |
|           |    MACHINING  |
|  CASTINGS |
```

As you can see, this put the quantity in the master production schedule 49 weeks in the future, triggering purchasing people to order castings now. There is no chance of getting the right material procured with a master production schedule quantity that far out. No matter how precisely the priorities are calculated they will be invalid, both for vendors and the plant, as changes occur when that number gets closer to the current time period. In this plant there was plenty of material around, including castings, but they were all the wrong ones. Inventories of material were high at the same time as customer service was low. And with priorities shifting fast, the efficiency in the plant was poor because of broken set ups, confusion, expediting and the rest of the activities that occur when a plant goes out of control.

Capacity control was the missing link. Their actual capacity was adequate to make all the product customers required. However, their effective capacity, making what was needed in matched sets to suit a customer order, was inadequate. They were making many things not required because of the invalid priority system.

This tendency of lead times to cause effective capacity to be well below actual capacity must be solved. Many plants have multi-level bills of material with cumulative lead times that are very long. It is not valid to plan priorities this way. Replanning more often won't solve the problem, neither will doing it with more precision. The only way to attack this problem is to cut lead times down to a bare minimum.

The technique of throughput planning (input/output control) can reduce them dramatically. The emphasis in plants must be changed to volumes flowing, making sure the pipeline diameters are large enough. When volumes are planned and controlled adequately then lead times can be reduced to provide valid priorities. Only this way will effective capacity and actual capacity be in step. It is also the ultimate test of the realism of the master production schedule. It provides feedback as to whether the actual throughput is adequate to support the master production schedule or not. Decisions can be made to increase the actual throughput where necessary or decrease the MPS to suit the actual throughput available. The priority system can now be valid. This way we can really make progress.

George Plossl:

Priority planning and control is certainly important in manufacturing but it is only one-half of the total job. Control of priority depends on managing lead times. This, to many people, is a strange and incomprehensible term; they don't believe lead times can be managed. Far too many people believe that they need a system capable of responding more quickly and precisely, changing the planned lead time to match the actual lead times being experienced. Among the greatest needs in manufacturing control today is a better understanding of lead time—its management and its true role in manufacturing control.

Lead time is viewed differently by the two material ordering techniques. The order point approach assumes some average lead time required for replenishment of the item. It recognizes that demand will often exceed the planned average over this lead time and that the lead time itself might be longer; hence, it needs safety stock to compensate. In effect it uses excess inventory to cover the likelihood that actual demand over the real lead time may be in excess of the planned quantity. It depends on expediting when the safety stock is not available or when the quantity required over the actual lead time exceeds the planned maximum.

Material requirements planning, on the other hand, assumes controlled lead times. It makes a rigorous calculation of requirements and plans a replenishment, scheduling an item as needed to support its parent's schedules. It plans the release of the item at the beginning of some average lead time. During this lead time, however, it recognizes that requirements will change, machines will break down and other failures will interrupt the flow of replenishment orders. MRP assumes that actual lead times can be managed (i.e., compressed or extended) as needed to meet the latest and best due date assigned by the MRP program.

Unfortunately, too few managers and practitioners recognize that managing lead time requires sound planning and effective control of capacity. The missing link in most modern systems is capacity planning and input/output control.

FIGURE 6

---

2 LEAD TIMES

- WORK CENTER LEAD TIME
  PLANNED-AVERAGE
  ACTUAL-AVERAGE

- ORDER LEAD TIME
  PLANNED-AVERAGE
  ACTUAL-SPECIFIC

Figure 6 identifies two types of lead time. Each work center, because of its work-in-process queues, requires some average lead time to complete a new order arriving at the work center; this depends on how many other orders are there ahead of it, in other words, on the level of work-in-process. This work-center-average lead time can be controlled only when the input of work to the work center matches its output so that backlogs are kept constant. Managing this average lead time, then, requires managing capacity. To run a sound system, the objective must be to have the actual average lead time to get work through the work center match as closely as possible the planned average lead time.

Each order in the queue at a work center has a priority which determines its position in the queue and sets the length of time it remains there. Orders can experience literally no queue, for example, when the general manager issues an edict that he wants some order out as soon as possible. On the other hand, all other orders with lower priority will then spend more time sitting in the work-in-process queue.

To plan priorities in an MRP program, we need a planned average order lead time which will be the sum of the setup time, running time, move time and queue time in each of the work centers through which it is processed, as shown in Figure 7. Subtracting this average order lead time from the due date, MRP sets a start date suggesting when the order should be released. In operation, however, the objective *is not* to get the actual order lead times to match the planned average. Actual lead time must be "managed" to complete the order on the adjusted due date; the position or ranking of each order in the queue is based on the latest and best priority requirements.

FIGURE 7

ELEMENTS OF LEAD TIME

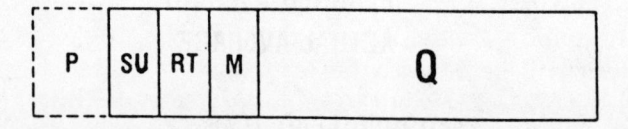

| P | SU | RT | M | Q |

Figure 7 also includes an element of paperwork time or preparation time. This would include, for example, writing requisitions, having the purchasing department solicit bids from vendors, review their quotations and place a firm order; it normally is thought to include all work necessary preparatory to releasing the order to the vendor. In manufacturing in-house, this would include preparing shop packets, getting tools ready and otherwise completing all work needed prior to release of the order. In well-designed ordering techniques, however, the "forward visibility" of the release date for the order provides adequate time in which to accomplish this paperwork. It is, therefore, unnecessary to build allowances for paperwork time into planned lead times. The real advantage of this is in reducing the total manufacturing cycle time within which material is being committed and capacity being assigned to specific items associated with some end product. Two weeks of paperwork time at each of nine levels of a bill of material will lengthen the horizon of the master schedule, directing that some material and capacity be committed to specific items, up to eighteen weeks farther out into the future than is necessary. The validity of the whole manufacturing plan can be improved by shortening the cumulative or stacked lead times; eliminating the paperwork element makes a significant contribution to this.

Obviously, since the queue time represents 90–95% of the total lead time of most manufactured and purchased items, this is the element which must be controlled. It is absolutely ridiculous that castings, bearings, forgings, chain, steel, chemicals and most products made from these are thought to require lead times of many weeks when the time actually required to process a normal batch of any of these is a few hours.

Only a very few items made in industry require more than a few manufacturing hours to produce a normal quantity; why is it that most lead times are expressed in weeks and many stated in months? The reason is a basic misunderstanding of the truth about lead time. Most people think that planned lead times must be adjusted to match the actual time experienced. They believe the system is then told "the truth about lead time". Nothing could be further from the real truth.

To understand the truth about lead time and how it can be managed, we must identify the basic problems to be solved. The first problem is inadequate capacity. Obviously, if the capacity of a work center is not able to handle the volume of work flowing to it, backlogs ahead of such work centers will grow and the lead times required for orders to get through the work center will become increasingly long and more variable. In the past, we attempted to use machine loading to determine whether or not the capacity of a work center was adequate. Figure 8 shows a typical machine load diagram. Most material control people would concentrate on the load during the first few weeks and would

FIGURE 8

TYPICAL WORK CENTER LOAD REPORT

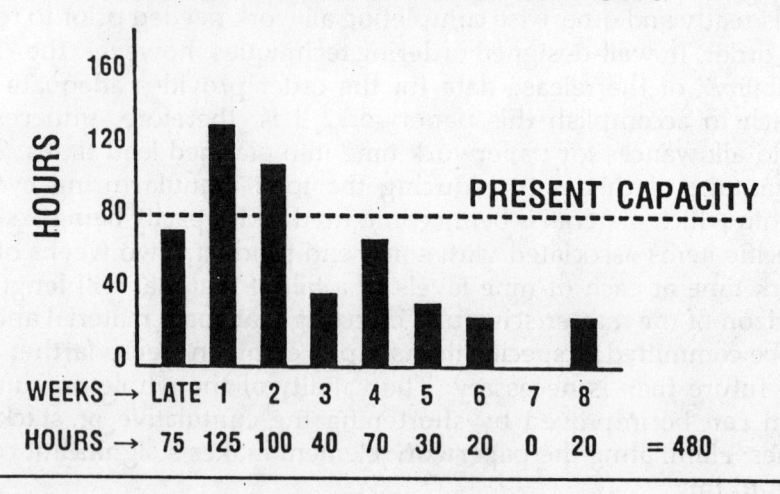

WEEKS →	LATE	1	2	3	4	5	6	7	8	
HOURS →	75	125	100	40	70	30	20	0	20	= 480

conclude that the capacity of the work center was inadequate, pointing to the late orders together with the heavy load in the first two weeks. They would bring pressure to bear on manufacturing foremen and superintendents to increase the output of the work center to "get back on schedule".

Line operations people, however, looking at the total load over the eight weeks illustrated, would be most reluctant to increase capacity "to run out of work sooner" seeing that the total load over the eight weeks is not sufficient to keep the work center busy at its present output rate of eighty standard hours per week. Material control people have an answer to this objection, of course. They point out that the total load shown over the eight-week horizon is *based only on released orders* and that more orders will be released in this period. Those with MRP programs developing a planned order profile well out into the future and with computerized scheduling and loading techniques can calculate this planned load in addition to the released load as indicated by the open bars in Figure 9. This is the classical capacity requirements planning technique.

Now it would seem clear that the work center capacity is truly inadequate; the 800 total standard hours in the load is far in excess of the 640 hours the center is capable of handling. However, two factors must not be overlooked. First, if all of the orders in the load were to be completed, the work center would be out of work at the end of Week 8. The erratic flow of work to this work center, indicated by the varying lengths of the bars, makes it imperative to have a substantial queue

FIGURE 9

CAPACITY REQUIREMENTS PLAN

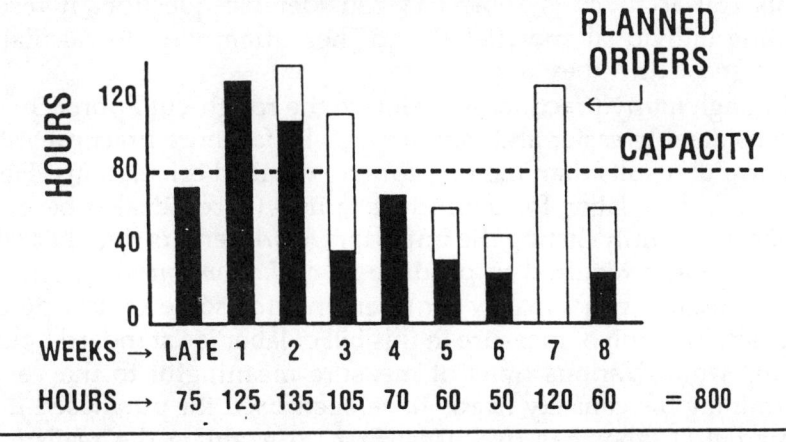

WEEKS →	LATE	1	2	3	4	5	6	7	8	
HOURS →	75	125	135	105	70	60	50	120	60	= 800

ahead of the center at all times to avoid down time which would really cut into its effective capacity. If this "standard queue" is set at two weeks' work (160 hours), the net load to be handled will be only 640 hours, matching the available capacity of the work center. Load and capacity are different as illustrated in Figure 10. Machine loading and the classical capacity requirements planning techniques assume that they are the same. They are not!

FIGURE 10

LOAD vs. CAPACITY

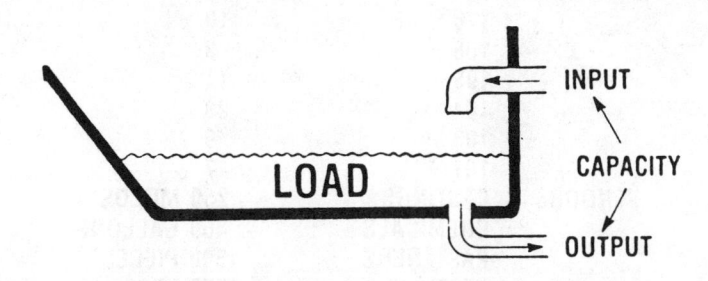

CAPACITY MANAGEMENT REPRINTS—Revised Edition

The second factor to be considered is that unplanned occurrences will place additional requirements on capacity above those shown in the formal plan represented in Figure 9. These include scrap, rework, methods changes, design changes, new product introductions and record errors, all of which require capacity. These are not in the present formal plan. Classical capacity requirements planning is highly precise but its real accuracy is subject to considerable question. It resembles counting individual snowflakes and then attempting to calculate how deep a snow drift they might form.

Although many practitioners criticize the rough-cut approaches, they are considerably easier and may, in fact, be far more practical and yield more useful results than the full, formal, detailed calculations. Figure 11 shows a bill of labor for a product family (it could also be a typical product in a family) listing the important work centers together with the standard hours required to produce *all of the components in the product family* together with capacity requirements for some critical purchased materials. The unit of measure in this bill of labor is "standard hours" for internal work. Various units of measure meaningful to the vendor in determining his capacity needs have been used for purchased items.

This bill of labor has two uses: first, to evaluate the realism of the master production schedule and, second, to develop planned levels of capacity required to support the master schedule in specific and critical work centers. Figure 12 shows a rough-cut plan developed for one month for all of the product families in the master schedule. Figure 13

FIGURE 11

BILL OF LABOR

PRODUCT FAMILY #1

WORK CENTER	STD. HRS PER 1000 UNITS
110	10
108	8
105	14
104	28
103	9
101	17
VENDORS — CASTINGS	250 MOLDS
CHEMICALS	400 GALLONS
FASTENERS	4500 PIECES
STEEL	520 LBS

FIGURE 12

ROUGH-CUT CAPACITY PLAN

WORK CTRS	FAMILIES						TOTAL MONTH #1
	#1	#2	#3	#4	#5	#6	
MPS UNITS	5570	3120	830	6120	2220	4610	
110	56	⌇		⌇			330
108	45						200
106							150
105	78				⌇	⌇	650
104	156	⌇					1,450
103	50						290
102							460
101	95			⌇			1,010
100			⌇				370
CASTINGS	1,395						6,200
CHEMICALS	2,230						8,320
FASTENERS	25,100	⌇			⌇	⌇	97,960
STEEL	2,900						15,520

FIGURE 13

SUMMARY ROUGH-CUT CAPACITY PLAN

WORK CTRS	PRESENT CAPACITY	REQUIRED CAPACITY — STD. HRS.			
		MO. #1	MO. #2	MO. #3	MO. #4
110	320	330			⌇
108	230	200			
106	170	150		⌇	
105	500	650		⌇	
104	1,500	1,450	⌇		⌇
103	310	290			
102	440	460	⌇	⌇	
101	960	1,010			⌇
100	370	370	⌇		
CASTINGS	5,900	6,200	⌇	⌇	
CHEMICALS	8,450	8,320	⌇		
FASTENERS	98,000	97,960			
STEEL	12,000	15,520			

CAPACITY MANAGEMENT REPRINTS—Revised Edition

summarizes the results for all products in the master schedule over the full planning horizon. Even when the master schedule is expressed in weeks, rough-cut capacity plans are frequently set up in months.

People who are detail-minded have several criticisms of this approach. First, there is no time-phasing; the hours required to make the product are assumed to be needed in the same time frame in which the product appears in the master schedule. This obviously will not be the case; work in a given bill of labor may extend over several weeks. However, the purpose is to develop an estimate over a long time period of the *average capacity needed;* offsetting work to recognize lead times is an unnecessary refinement. A second criticism is that there is no "netting" out of quantities of components already in inventory. This factor, like lead time offsetting, is usually negligible unless a significant reduction is planned for component inventories. Then it may be necessary to reduce the summarized capacity figures to allow the master schedule to "draw capacity out of the inventory" instead of supplying it in the work centers. A third criticism of the rough-cut approach is that it neglects the effects of changes in the mix of products within and among the families. Again, this is usually not a significant factor but, if it should be, adjustments can be made to recognize it. The ease of developing and modifying the data more than makes up for these deficiencies in most companies.

The basic purpose of the summary rough-cut plan is to evaluate whether or not the master schedule is realistic. This requires a comparison of needed and available capacity, shown in the column headed "Present Capacity". These data are best obtained by using *actual production rates of good pieces in the recent past.* Last week's output is your plant capacity whether you think it should be more or not. Some companies average output over the last four weeks to compensate for factors like holidays, serious production problems of a temporary nature and other intermittent effects.

Viewing the rough-cut approaches in proper perspective, it is obvious that there is no excuse for delaying capacity planning and control. Even companies which do not yet have full routings and well-engineered standards can utilize simple bills of labor and input/output control to insure that backlogs on the plant floor are well-managed and that lead times are kept under control.

The second major problem in controlling lead time is that good ordering techniques do not release work at a level rate. Figure 14 shows the erratic way in which work can come out of a sound MRP program. The ordering technique is following its own rules regarding due dates, lead times and release times. In one time-period, several orders will be suggested for issue and will total a very significant load. In another, there may be hardly any work released by the system. This tendency must be overcome if work-in-process levels are to be controlled. There are so few work centers that can handle a very erratic load that it is useless to talk about them. Every effort must be made in the starting or gateway centers as well as in secondary centers to level or smooth the flow of work into and through these operations.

The proper approach in starting operations uses MRP or time-phased order points to rank the items in a priority sequence. A scheduler then selects items from the top of the ranked list until the total of work released equals or is close to the planned input rate to his work centers. He thus smooths out the release of work. In some periods he withholds issuing orders which would exceed the planned input rate; in others he "reaches ahead" into the system and draws out early orders which would otherwise not yet be released in order to feed his work center at a level rate. There is only one alternative to doing this—accepting erratic backlogs and erratic lead times in critical work centers.

For secondary or downstream work centers it is not so easy to smooth out the flow. Simply measuring the input, however, and keeping track of cumulative deviations from the planned average will indicate whether or not a work center is being overloaded or is starving. In some cases a careful adjustment of the mix of orders into starting operations will help to get work to flow better through downstream work centers. This is relatively easy for "semi-process" flow operations such as the production of pharmaceuticals, chemicals and many hard goods products where materials follow the same operation sequences.

FIGURE 14

WORK PROJECTION

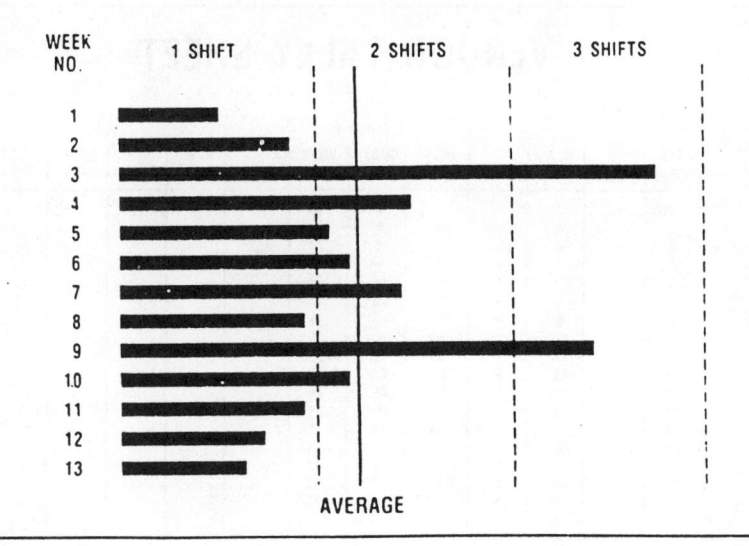

The basic principle of input/output control, known for a long time, is that the input should be less than or equal to the output—never more! The prime objective is to keep backlogs in work centers under control and not let them grow or become highly erratic.

The third major problem is one of a basic understanding of the nature of lead time and its influence in ordering techniques. We have called it the Lead Time Syndrome. To illustrate this, we have developed a game which can be played by four teams of people representing companies buying a variety of materials from a game leader representing one of their suppliers.

Orders are placed via small cards; the color indicates the customer company and the number of the card indicates the week delivery is desired. Each card represents a batch of material. The vendor could be supplying any one of a wide variety of commodities such as castings, forgings, glass bottles, chemicals, etc. sold in a number of different items to each customer.

There are two basic rules: the vendor must quote honest lead times based on his capacity and total backlog of orders, and customers must place orders covering their requirements over the vendor's quoted lead times. Each customer's real requirements are one order per period over the duration of the game. The vendor has capacity as the game begins to produce four orders per week, which is adequate to cover his customers' total needs. The vendor has been quoting three weeks lead time; as a result he has twelve orders in his backlog, three from each customer. A typical run of the game is illustrated on the attached tabulation entitled "Vendor Tally Sheet", Figure 15. In Week 1, with three weeks quoted

---

FIGURE 15

VENDOR TALLY SHEET

WEEK NO	CAPAC	NEW ORD	SHPD	BACK LOG	QUOT L.T	WEEK NO	CAPAC	NEW ORD	SHPD	BACK LOG	QUOT L.T.
START	4	-	-	12	3	18					
1	4	4	4	12	3	19					
2	4	4	4	12	3	20					
3	4	5	4	13	4	21					
4	4	8	4	17	5	22					
5	4	8	4	21	8	23					
6	4	16	4	33	12	24					
7	4	20	4	49	16	25					
8	4	20	4	65	20	26					
9	4	20	4	81	25	27					
10	5	24	5	100	25	28					
11	5	4	5	99	25	29					
12	5	4	5	98	20	30					
13	5	-16	5	77	15	31					
14	5	-16	5	56	11	32					
15	5	-12	5	39	7	33					
16	5	-12	5	22	4	34					
17	3	-8	3	11		35					

lead-time, the vendor receives four orders, ships four orders, maintains his backlog of twelve orders and continues to quote three weeks lead-time. In Week 2 the same things happen again. In Week 3, however, we introduce *one additional order* from one customer allowing the normal three weeks delivery. The vendor receives five new orders, ships four, sees his backlog increase to thirteen orders and, therefore, "to be honest", quotes four weeks lead time.

In Week 4, each customer must now cover his normal week's needs *plus an additional week's requirements*. The vendor receives eight new orders, ships only four and sees his backlog increase to seventeen which is still beyond his capacity to handle. He, therefore, quotes five weeks lead time.

Because of the increase in lead time, each customer must again release one additional order to cover requirements. The vendor again receives eight orders, ships four, sees his backlog rise to twenty-one and still has more orders than he can deliver in the quoted lead time. Seeing how the incoming order rate has increased and, faced with the continuing overload in the backlog, the vendor tries to "get ahead of it" by jumping his lead time to eight weeks.

Just to cover real requirements of one order per week over the longer lead time, each customer must now issue four orders, three to cover the increased lead time and one for the regular week's business. The vendor's incoming order rate jumps to sixteen, he ships his usual four and his backlog is now at thirty-three orders, still one excess! (Whether he knows it or not the vendor will never catch up to this one extra order simply by increasing his lead times since the customers respond with additional orders).

Following the same logic the vendor goes through successive lead time increases to sixteen, twenty and twenty-five weeks by Week 9. His order backlog now has increased to eighty-one orders and he has seen a remarkable increase in incoming new orders. He is now confident he can justify investing in additional capacity so he plans to add twenty-five percent in Week 10 and raise his output to five orders per week.

Believing the "good business" he's enjoying will continue to bring in a heavy flow of new orders, he decides to hold twenty-five weeks lead time in Week 10, although his capacity now is adequate to clean up his backlog of one hundred orders in twenty weeks. The excess backlog has finally disappeared! Since the vendor has not increased his lead time, each customer needs to place only one order, a normal week's requirement, so the vendor receives only four orders. He ships five and his backlog drops (for the first time) to ninety-nine orders. Thinking that this one week drop-off in orders is purely a temporary situation, the vendor holds his twenty-five week quoted lead time in Week 11.

Each customer again places only one order, he ships five and his backlog drops to ninety-eight. Becoming somewhat concerned that he is "losing his share of the market", the vendor decides to "offer his customers better service" and drops his lead time to twenty weeks in Week 12.

Each customer now recognizes that he has orders placed with the vendor too far out into the future and cancels orders for the excess. With his shipments for Week 13, the vendor sees his backlog slump to seventy-seven total orders, panics and cuts his lead time to fifteen weeks. Again the cut in lead time shuts off new orders and cancels more; with his shipments his order backlog is reduced by another twenty-one orders to a total of fifty-six. In Week 14, the vendor reduces his quoted lead time to eleven weeks.

It takes only three weeks more for the vendor's backlog to be reduced close to the original total, permitting him to quote in Week 16 an "honest" three-week lead time. By now the new order rate over the last few weeks indicates that a "depression" has hit his business. The obvious action indicated is to reduce capacity dramatically so the vendor now cuts capacity to three orders per week. In a very few weeks, this will start the cycle all over again.

This game shows clearly the fallacy of assuming that a gap between planned and actual lead times can be closed by changing the planned numbers. What is not so evident is that this approach, so commonly used in industry throughout the world, leads inevitably to the vicious cycle illustrated in Figure 16. When delivery dates are missed, orders are not received on time and it is too easy to assume that the basic problem

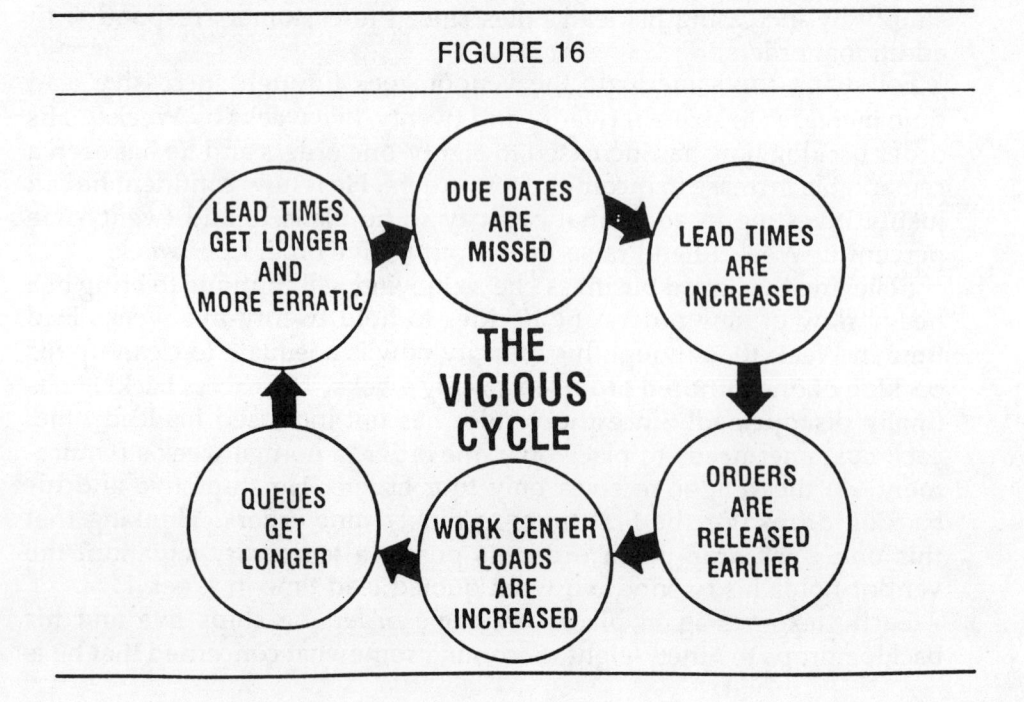

FIGURE 16

THE VICIOUS CYCLE

- DUE DATES ARE MISSED
- LEAD TIMES ARE INCREASED
- ORDERS ARE RELEASED EARLIER
- WORK CENTER LOADS ARE INCREASED
- QUEUES GET LONGER
- LEAD TIMES GET LONGER AND MORE ERRATIC

is that lead times are too short and must be lengthened. Increasing the lead times, of course, only generates more orders to go into the plant to increase the queues, lengthen the lead times and make them more erratic. The true result is aggravating the basic disease.

We must learn to recognize the truth about lead time — it will be what you say it is, occasionally plus a little more. When actual lead times do exceed the planned figures because of an increase in input or because of a lack of capacity caused by machine breakdowns, interrupted production or any other reason, it must be recognized that this difference between planned and actual can be removed only by changing the capacity. Lead time management is capacity management not simply priority planning and control.

It is time that practitioners recognized that lead times have several roles in controlling manufacturing. Most people know that lead time is a vital parameter in ordering techniques like MRP and order point. Many see clearly that it determines the level of work-in-process and the resultant capital investment. This is shown clearly in Figure 17. With shorter lead times, materials are held in process for less time and the investment is lowered proportionately.

Figure 17, however, illustrates clearly another role of lead time, not well understood. The primary strategy of manufacturing control is,

FIGURE 17

WORK IN PROCESS vs. LEAD TIME

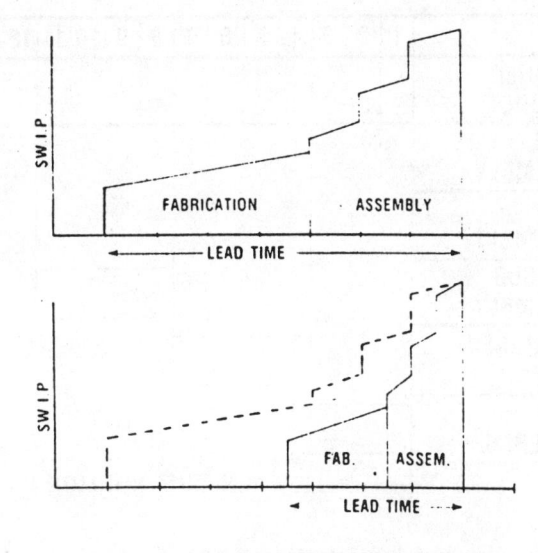

"Never commit materials or capacity to a specific item until the last possible moment". Stated simply, "Keep it moving!" This is possible, of course, only if lead times are short and work doesn't wait long periods in queues.

Another important role of lead time, also not clear to most people in manufacturing or to those who view its activities, is its influence on the validity of the whole manufacturing plan. One of the most ridiculous statements ever made in our field was that a company could live with infinite queues if they had a sound priority planning and control system. We're not just referring to the choice of the word "infinite" either. As is clearly shown in Figure 18, the longer the lead times (based upon longer queues) the earlier materials will have to be committed and capacity assigned to individual items. As queues grow and lead times lengthen, this commitment will have to be made far in advance to satisfy some quantity in a future master schedule time period. How can a priority plan be valid when based on long lead times? The only thing known for certain is that changes will be made many times before the actual completion date arrives and material and capacity will have been assigned to more wrong items. A company can live with changing demands on its facilities and with the upsets that it will inevitably experience only if lead times are short. Only then will a priority plan have any validity. Control of lead times requires planning and controlling capacity, not simply planning and controlling priorities.

FIGURE 18

MASTER PRODUCTION SCHEDULE

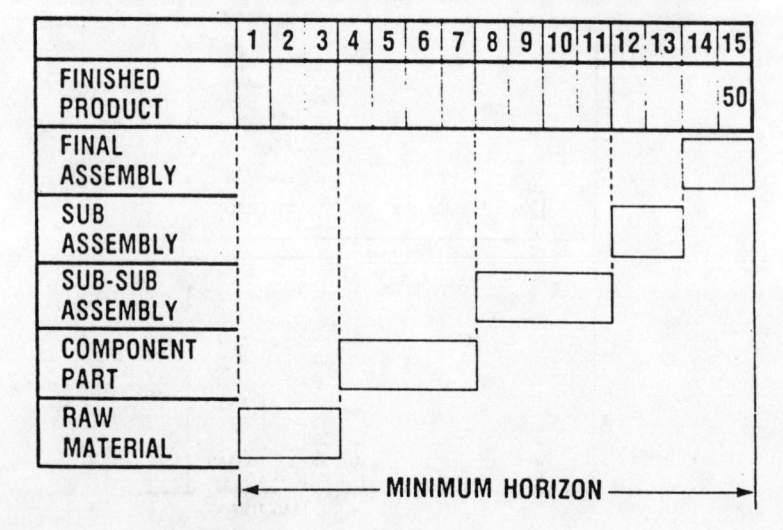

	1	2	3	4	5	6	7	8	9	10	11	12	13	14	15
FINISHED PRODUCT															50
FINAL ASSEMBLY															
SUB ASSEMBLY															
SUB-SUB ASSEMBLY															
COMPONENT PART															
RAW MATERIAL															

←—————— MINIMUM HORIZON ——————→

The need for education in these concepts is enormous. Not only do we have to get understanding among practitioners in material control and manufacturing line people, we must also convince marketing and purchasing people that long lead times are not better but, in fact, are much worse if their objectives are to be met. We must also convince top management that lead time is one of their primary "handles" on the whole operation and that extending lead times or tolerating long lead times is sure to develop inefficiency, upset and extra cost. Add to this the need for educating editors of technical journals and newspapers, economists, college professors and government analysts so that these people understand fully the effects of the lead time syndrome on the basic statistics relating to manufacturing. The two most common sets of data used to analyze the health of a business or of our overall economy are Incoming Order Rates and Order Backlogs or Bookings Totals. Both figures, as shown by our lead time syndrome game, are distorted immensely by changes in lead times introduced by "amateurs" who do not understand their full influence. The benefits in manufacturing and improved control from a clear understanding of lead time and sound management of this important variable are literally enormous.

About the Authors—

HAL MATHER is currently President, Mather & Plossl, Inc., Management Counselors and Educators in the area of Manufacturing Control. Prior to this he was Materials Manager at Gilbarco, Inc., manufacturers of gasoline pumps and related service station equipment. His formal education was in mechanical engineering, and he has held positions of Project Engineer, Quality Control Manager, Production and Inventory Control Manager and Administrator of Manufacturing Systems.

Hal is a frequent speaker at professional society meetings, seminars and universities. He is co-author of a booklet, "The Master Production Schedule", as well as the author of several articles in the field of manufacturing control.

He has been certified at the Fellow level by the American Production and Inventory Control Society and is a member of that Society's National Advisory Planning Council.

MR. PLOSSL is Chairman of the Board of Mather & Plossl, Inc., a Management Education and Counseling firm with clients throughout the United States and in Europe and Africa. Formerly he was Plant Manager of the Stanley Strapping Systems Division of the Stanley Works with plants in New Britain, Connecticut, and Pittsburg, California. Prior to that he held the position of Materials Manager of its Stanley Tools Division.

He received AB, BS and MS Degrees in Mechanical Engineering from Columbia University. He is a Registered Professional Engineer in Massachusetts. Mr. Plossl has taught production control and industrial management college courses and is a frequent speaker at meetings of APICS, other technical societies and leading universities.

He has written many articles on production and inventory management. With O. W. Wight, he is co-author of "PRODUCTION AND INVENTORY CONTROL: Principles and Techniques", Prentice-Hall, 1967. He is author of "MANUFACTURING CONTROL: The Last Frontier for Profits", Reston Publishing Company, 1973. He was Chapter Editor of the APICS Production and Inventory Control Handbook and editor of the 3rd edition of the APICS Bibliography. His latest book, co-authored with H. F. Mather, is "THE MASTER PRODUCTION SCHEDULE; Managements' Handle on the Business", 1975.

Listed in Who's Who in the Southeast, Mr. Plossl has been active in professional organizations, holding offices and directorships in APICS, AIIE and other technical societies. He has been certified at the Fellow level with the American Production and Inventory Control Society. He was Chairman of APICS Curriculum and Certification Program Council and a member of the National Advisory Planning Council.

Reprinted from *Production and Inventory Management,* Third Quarter, 1973.

CAPACITY PLANNING AND CONTROL*

George W. Plossl and Oliver W. Wight

George W. Plossl

When we were invited in 1971 to address the APICS International Conference in St. Louis, Oliver Wight and I selected as our topic, capacity planning and control, with the focus on machine loading. We recognized the need to prepare ourselves more fully to handle this interesting aspect of production control. While it has been around a long time, machine loading has not been well understood and is rarely, if ever, well done. During the year, we visited many companies and talked with many people who had experience using this technique. This research culminated in a two-day conference in September at Lake Sunapee to which we invited a small group to review our conclusions.

We regret that this work was not completed in time to have our presentation included in the Conference Proceedings, but we believed it more important to verify our conclusions and present the latest thinking on the subject rather than to meet a publishing deadline. We wish to thank the people who gave so freely of their time and experience to help us assimilate their knowledge gained from actually using scheduling and loading techniques. While emphasizing that we assume full responsibility for the conclusions presented, we want particularly to express our appreciation to the following men: James Burlingame, Twin Disc Incorporated; Dr. Joseph A. Orlicky, IBM Corporation; Thomas Putnam, Markem Corporation; Alex Willis, IBM Corporation; and, of course, our associates, Walt Goddard and Ernie Theisen.

There is a great deal of confusion in the meaning of the terms "Capacity" and "Load." While both are simple in concept, successful application appears to be extremely difficult in the real world; part of the problem is confusion in meaning. Figure 1 uses a bathtub to illustrate the difference. The

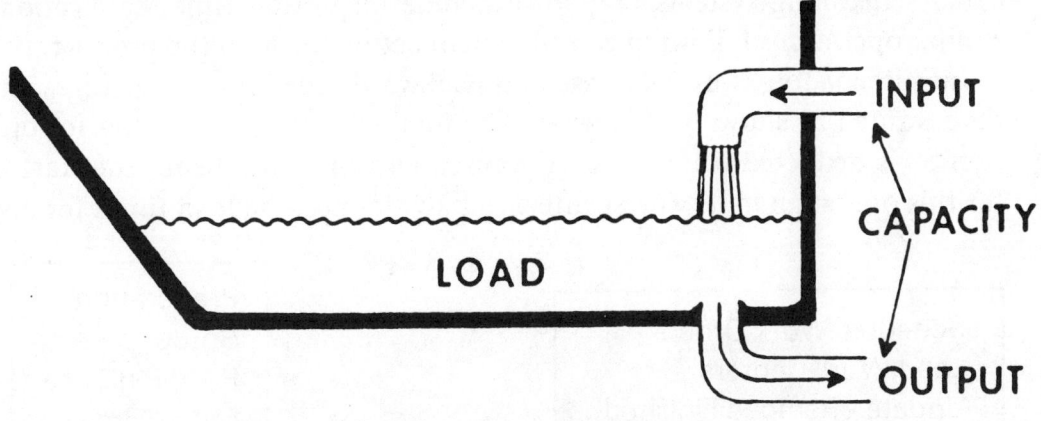

Figure 1. Load vs. Capacity

*This article was presented at the APICS International Conference in St. Louis, Missouri on November 4, 1971.

"Load" is the level of water in the tub; the "Capacity" (input or output) is the rate at which the water is flowing. These are closely related concepts but quite different in meaning.

Almost every company has tried machine loading but few succeed in really making it work. Production control people are about equally divided between the "haves" and the "have nots" and both groups appear to be equally dissatisfied. Often, in speaking to APICS and other groups, we will ask the group, "How many of you have a machine load program?" and usually between 40 and 50 percent raise their hands. Our next question is, "How many of the rest of you would like to have one?" This brings the balance of the hands up. Our third question is, "Of those having such a program, how many find that it is really being used?" and usually one or two will raise their hands. The obvious question, then, is, "Well, what do the rest of you want it for?" While it is the second oldest production control technique (only expediting has been around longer) available since Henry Gantt showed us how to make bar charts about 1903, it has had little effective use.

On the other hand, not too many companies have really tried capacity planning. Recently, however, because of the availability of computer programs, there has been a rapid growth in interest in capacity planning and more companies are attempting it now. This will be covered in more detail later.

Let's review some definitions starting with "Infinite Loading." This is really "loading to infinite capacity" and, shown in Figure 2, begins with a schedule of work orders.

The schedule is based on calculations or estimates of the elements of lead time shown in Figure 3.

Setup and running time are frequently covered by labor standards; preparation and move times can be estimated along with want-to-move times, but some rule of thumb is generally used to provide queue times. Some sophisticated scheduling systems may also include inspection time, calibration, or similar operations following completion of actual work on the product.

Infinite loading is usually based on backward scheduling, starting with the date wanted as shown in Figure 4. The total lead time calculated for operation 50 is deducted from the date wanted and this establishes the start time for this operation in its work center. In like manner, the lead times for opera-

```
Schedule Work Orders
Load Work Centers
Update - Remove Finished
Add New
```

Figure 2. Infinite Loading

```
Preparation
Setup
Running Time
Move Time
Queue Time
```

Figure 3. Elements of Lead Time

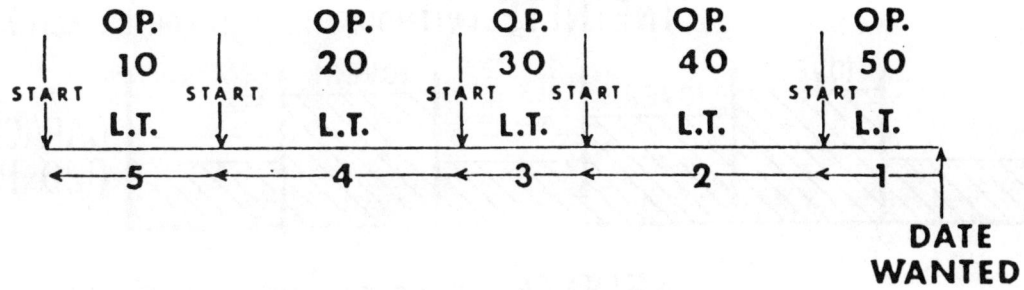

```
    OP.        OP.        OP.        OP.        OP.
     10         20         30         40         50
  START      START      START      START      START
     L.T.       L.T.       L.T.       L.T.       L.T.
  ←———5———→←———4———→←———3———→←———2———→←———1———→|
                                                DATE
                                                WANTED
```

Figure 4. Backward Scheduling

tions 40, 30, 20, and 10 are deducted successively to set start dates in the work centers involved. These starting dates determine the time periods in which it is assumed the load will hit the individual work centers. As shown in Figure 2, the second step in infinite loading is to total up the load from all jobs in each time period for the individual work centers. Updating an infinite load is simple; completed jobs are removed and new jobs added as they are released.

Finite Loading, really "loading to finite capacity," is not simple and requires considerably more work. As shown in Figure 5, it also starts with a schedule of work orders determined in the same way as for infinite loading.

> Schedule Work Orders
> Set Priorities - Components
> Set Work Center Capacities
> Load Work Centers - in
>   priority sequence
> Reschedule overloads
> Update - Start Over

Figure 5. Finite Loading

Before finite loading can begin, however, priorities must be set on individual orders. Obviously, the highest priority orders should get first claim on available capacity in each work center. The next step is to set limiting capacities for each work center. This is usually done with two values: "standard" capacity and "maximum" capacity, the latter including overtime or an added shift. The jobs are then loaded into the individual work centers in priority sequence. As soon as a work center is filled to its limiting capacity, additional jobs are rescheduled either earlier or later until they find available capacity. Because of the requirement to load based on priority, a finite load cannot be updated using the same add-and-deduct approach as an infinite load. The only way to revise a finite load is to start over, rearranging jobs in the new priority sequence and reloading.

INFINITE (WITHOUT REGARD FOR CAPACITY)

CAPACITY (120 HRS)

FINITE (NEVER TO EXCEED CAPACITY)

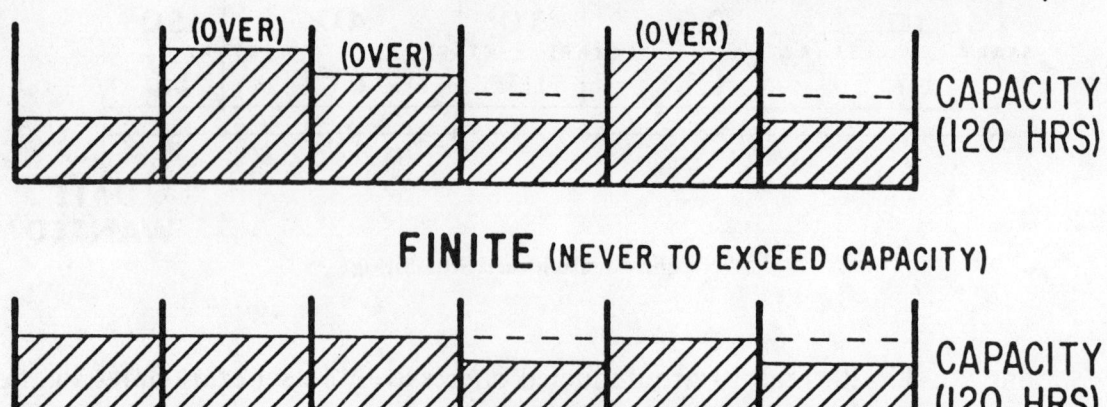

CAPACITY (120 HRS)

Figure 6. Loading Methods

Figure 6 illustrates the difference between finite and infinite loads. The infinite load shows both overloads and underloads because the jobs were loaded in without regard to capacity limitations. It identifies and measures these overloads in addition to showing the time periods in which they will occur. The detailed load information gives the specific jobs involved so that overloads can be analyzed. The finite load, in contrast, does not permit overloads; it reschedules jobs to earlier or later time periods. It will show underloads, however, when the full nominal capacity is not utilized.

Finite loading is supposed to develop realistic schedule dates based on priorities assigned and the capacity limitations assumed for the various work centers. It is interesting to note that if the Master Schedule covering the finished products to be assembled could be handled properly, the infinite load picture in Figure 6 would look like the finite load. In effect, then, infinite loading measures the inability to schedule properly at the end product level.

Capacity planning answers the question, "How much is enough?" showing the output required to meet the total demand forecast and also bring the total inventory to planned levels. Obviously, if the inventory is to be reduced, the factory must produce less than is shipped and vice versa. The equation in

$$I_S + P - S = I_E$$

Where: I_S = total inventory at start of planning period
I_E = total inventory at end of planning period
P = total production
S = total shipments

Figure 7.

INPUT	w1	w2	w3	w4
plan	270	270	270	270
actual	270	265	250	
dev.		-5	-25	
OUTPUT				
plan	300	300	300	270
actual	305	260	280	
dev.	+5	-35	-55	

Figure 8. Input/Output

Figure 7 is used to calculate capacity needed.

A form of capacity plan more useful for individual work centers is shown in Figure 8. Here, planned rates of both input and output are shown for future weekly periods. In this particular example, output is planned to exceed input by 30 hours each week and for three weeks to reduce the level of work-in-process inventory now in this work center. Actual data for both input and output rates are posted to the plan as they develop. Deviations are calculated for input and output and these are most useful figures. Applying these simple concepts, though, has given many people serious problems.

Oliver W. Wight

Last year, in an attempt to solve some of the problems with standard scheduling and loading techniques, I wrote a paper on a technique we've had great success with called "Input/Output Control." The concept is simple: First, for a given work center, you plan your capacity requirements; then you average these to give the foreman a level, realistic production rate; then actual production in standard hours is measured against this planned rate. This planned rate, of course, would be the "output" required. Output is simply the number of standard hours completed by the work center.

I suggested also that we should plan the input rate to a work center and measure that also; that is, measure the standard hours of work coming into that work center as well as going out. Now the reasoning behind planning both the input and the output was very simple: lead time in practically any company is a function of backlog. Backlog, obviously, is a function of the input/output relationship. If output is higher than input, the backlog will drop and the lead time will be reduced. If input is higher than output, the backlog will increase and the lead time will increase. Input/Output Control was designed to focus attention on this vital relationship.

In my article on Input/Output Control, I mentioned that, particularly for starting work centers, there is no reason—and we have done this in practice many times—why the actual input from the inventory system or the scheduling system couldn't be smoothed out. If, for example, a production rate of a screw machine work center is planned at 240 hours per week, there's no reason why planners can't smooth out the release of work rather than releasing 600 hours one week and 150 the next. If the input isn't smoothed out, larger backlogs or queues will be needed in the work center to absorb the fluctuation. I also mentioned that if backlogs started to build up in the shop, it would be better to hold work back rather than keep feeding it in. I probably should have mentioned that this would be a temporary expedient since the real cure for a backlog problem is to get the output or capacity and, if you can't get it, ultimately you will have to change the Master Schedule. So the idea behind the input/output concept was to focus our attention on the *production rates that caused backlogs and lead time problems* when they get out of control as opposed to focusing on the backlogs themselves. The I/O technique in application has proven to be very satisfactory. In retrospect, however, I do wish I had put a little less attention on leveling input to a starting work center because I think this diverted many people's attention from the real significance of Input/Output Control.

There has been a great deal of confusion in the minds of practitioners about all three of the "Capacity Planning" techniques we've discussed. The debate over infinite loading vs. finite loading has raged for years with the "infinite loaders" claiming finite loading wasn't a valid technique and vice versa. In practice, both sides have been proven partially correct; *neither technique* has been used very satisfactorily! Recognizing, then, that there has been some misunderstanding, let's look at the *apparent problems* with these three techniques:

1. **Infinite Capacity Is Not Infinite**
   The opponents of the infinite loading concept have objected to it because they recognize that you simply can't load work into a plant without regard for its capacity and assume that the plant is going to respond. In fact, if production control simply accepts orders and actually loads the plant to infinite capacity, they are doing little more than passing the buck. On the other hand, proponents of infinite loading have hastened to point out some serious problems involved with finite loading. Their most vehement objection has been:

2. **Finite: Deliveries Will Be Extended**
   Obviously, if each order comes along and is fit into the capacity avail-

able and nothing is ever done to increase capacity when an increase is required, customer service is likely to be very poor indeed. Many people have pointed out a problem with the third technique:

3. I/O Control: Difficult to Control Input

It takes quite a bit of effort to identify all of the items the inventory system is likely to feed into a given starting work center and then to smooth out this flow. Beyond that, of course, the problems involved in smoothing out the flow of input to downstream work centers are virtually insurmountable.

Before discussing these *apparent* problems any further, let's go back to infinite loading and try to understand some of the real problems that have existed with this technique in practice a little better.

Even where practitioners using the infinite loading technique have tried not to abuse it and have tried to load their shop as realistically as possible, they have run into serious difficulties. The typical machine load report almost always shows a large backlog in the past due period. It is not only large, but it's almost always *unbelievable.* In one company, for example, 60 percent of the entire load is past due in the fabrication department, yet the plant superintendent points out that the factory is really "on schedule" since assemblies are going out the door on time.

What causes this situation? Obviously, if the machine load report says that most of the work is past due and it really isn't, little credibility will be given to this report. Its value as a capacity plan will be seriously impaired.

Really, what we see here is due to a breakdown in the "priority planning" system. By priority planning, we mean the system that puts "due dates" on orders. It tells us what material we want and when. Usually the inventory system, in most companies, does the "priority planning." This problem of establishing *and maintaining* proper priorities is a very serious one. As a matter of fact, in most companies, the "formal system" simply doesn't do it well. Nevertheless, the priority problems vary from company to company. Let us think of companies in four general categories from the point of view of *priority complexity:*

1. One Piece. Make to Order Shop

This could be a shop that makes and sells forgings. The customer sends in an order and *he* establishes the order priority. Production control tries to fit it into the load somewhere and then acknowledges a delivery date. This becomes the priority. In this kind of company, the date due is the customer promise date. This isn't to say that the customer doesn't sometimes change this due date by requesting a reschedule. But even when he does, *it's easy to see that the due date is changed!* In the more complex types of businesses, from a priority point of view, one of the great difficulties is knowing that the priority really has changed.

In the second type of company, the priority problem becomes much more complex:

2. Assembled Product, Made to Order

In this type of company, *priorities are dependent*. Any change in the assembly schedule will mean changing the required dates for all components. Another type of rescheduling must take place when any one of the components going into a sub-assembly or assembly must be rescheduled because the original lot was scrapped, for example. There is no sense in bringing through all of the other parts when the assembly can't be put together. This is what we meant about the difficulty of recognizing a priority change. In most companies, if one part is scrapped, the original due dates remain on all other parts even though it's obvious that it would be far better to use available capacity to make some parts that could be put together into an assembly and shipped.

The third type of company has a comewhat different priority problem:

3. One Piece Product, Made to Stock

Here the problem is to update priorities, *after* shop and purchase orders have been released. A stock replenishment order, for example, is released when a reorder point is tripped. This reorder point has built into it some kind of estimate of future demand over lead time. Obviously, the due date placed on this replenishment order will be determined based on that lead time. Whenever the forecast of demand over lead time isn't exactly right — and it's not likely to be very often — the due date on the replenishment order should be updated. In practice, particularly with manual systems, this was very difficult to do and, as a consequence, most companies tried to pretend that the original due date they put on the order was going to be valid throughout the entire lead time. The natural result was that many items went out of stock *and then* the expediting started! And many other orders were "late" but not needed.

The fourth type of company combines the problems of companies 2 and 3:

4. Assembled Product: Made to Stock

Obviously, the stock replenishment due dates have to be kept up to date and this has to be related to the components going into the assembly. Once again, if any one of the components is scrapped and can't possibly be completed by the required due date, the other components going into the assembly should be rescheduled to give them valid priorities.

With the manual system that companies had for years, keeping priorities valid was virtually impossible in all but the one piece, make to order type of company. The amount of calculation and recalculation simply wasn't practical. So the *Formal System* usually didn't attempt it. But somehow someone had to find out about at least some of the changed priorities in order to keep the factory operating and the bulk of the shipments going out the door. This became the expediter's main task. Even though priorities weren't officially updated, he found out about some of the material that was *really* needed when the items showed up on shortage lists and backorder lists.

The expediters in a company making an assembled product, for example, usually pulled the parts required to make an assembly out of the stockroom; "staged" (or "accumulated") them; made up shortage lists; and expedited the missing parts. Of course, this *Informal System* always found the shortages too late to do anything about them without generating chaos in the factory, in the purchasing department, and with vendors. As a result, expediting is a dirty word in most companies. But it's also a necessity when the formal priority planning system simply doesn't work.

The four categories of companies listed above are intended to be representative rather than all inclusive. There are companies that don't make assembled products, for example, that do have the dependent priority problem. Consider a company making mechanic's hand tools. They make a forging, process it through some preliminary operations, and then put it into semi-finished inventory. When they wish to make a given size of box wrench, for example, they will draw the proper forging out of inventory and run it through the finishing operation. One semi-finished forging could make a number of different wrench sizes. Note that while this isn't a classical assembled product, the demand on the semi-finished forging *is dependent*.

In fact, a "bill of material" for this particular type of product would look "upside down" as compared with a normal bill of material for an assembled product. An assembled product is made up of a number of parts. The semi-finished item can be finished to make a number of different items.

The practitioner should recognize that even though he doesn't have an assembled product, he may very well have the dependent priority type of problem. The breakdown of the formal priority planning system is indicated when expediters must spend a large part of their time trying to find out *what the real priorities are*.

The inability of most formal priority planning systems to keep priorities properly updated has been one of the most significant causes of machine load reports that simply aren't credible to shop people. One of the reliable features of the informal priority system is that it *expedites and never unexpedites!* Figure 9 attempts to show this graphically. The vertical line represents the original due date put on eight different shop or purchase orders. The expediter has discovered that four of these shop orders are needed sooner than originally planned. But he has not been able to determine that a number of these orders should be rescheduled to a later date. After all, expediting takes a lot of time and effort. There is none left over for unexpediting.

The result is a system that says, "Work on all the orders to meet the original dates unless they're needed sooner." Of course, this means plenty of late orders that aren't really needed. *The consequence is a machine load report that's badly overstated in the early time periods!* It usually shows a

```
        X------X
               X
        X---X
               X
               X
               X
               X
           X--X
         X---X
```
EARLIER | LATER
ORIGINAL DUE DATE

Figure 9.

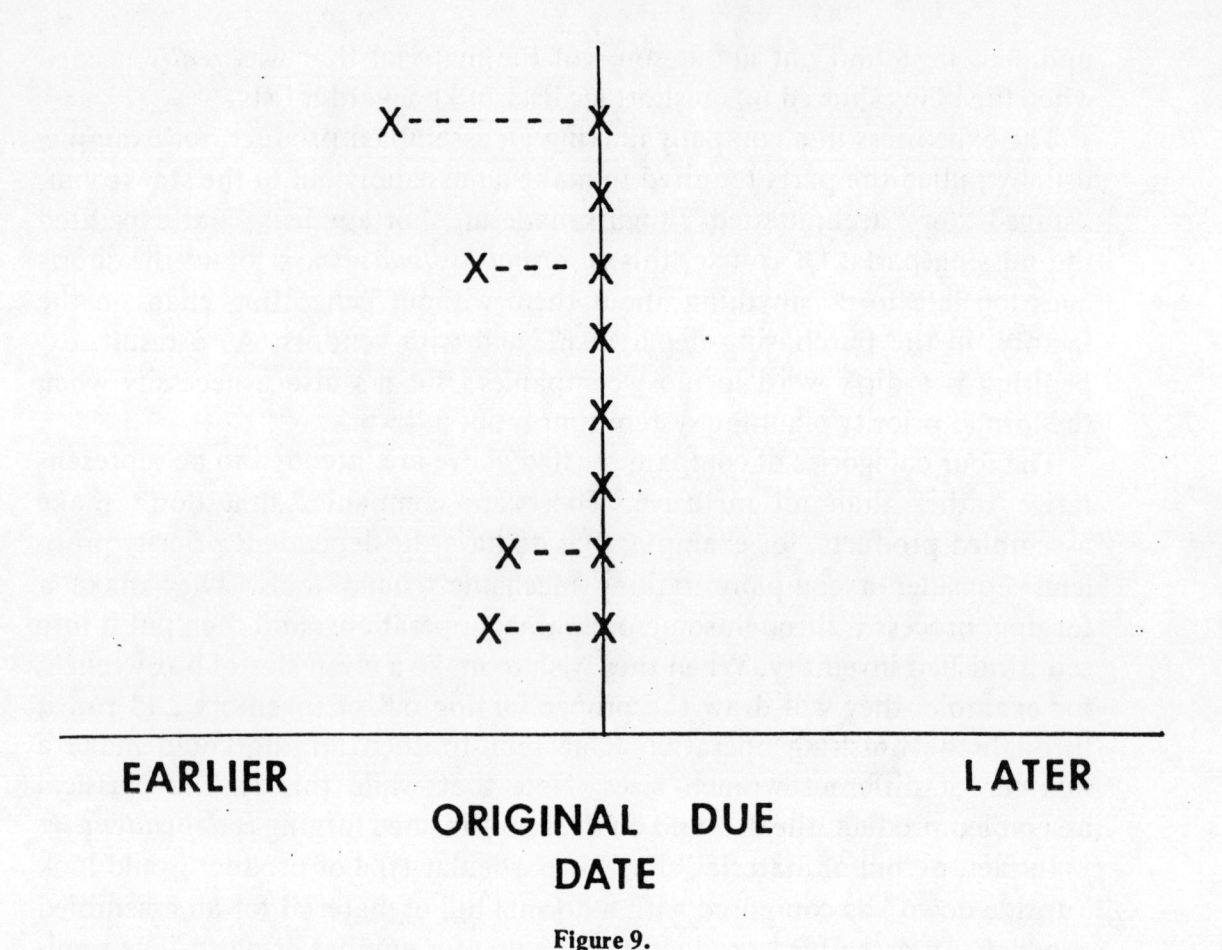

large past due load because jobs that are not needed have not been rescheduled. The result: Nobody believes the machine load report.

We can conclude, then, that capacity planning is not going to be very effective until priority planning is effective. If there are many "late" jobs around that are not really needed, capacity plans will always be overstated and they won't be credible to the users. *A prerequisite to an effective capacity planning system is an effective priority planning system.*

The function of the priority planning system is to put the proper due dates on orders and to maintain those due dates so that they are correct. Until this can be done successfully, capacity planning will not be able to generate credible information.

George W. Plossl

Successful scheduling and loading requires accurate priorities for individual jobs; these priorities are set by the ordering system. There are two basic systems: the Order Point/Order Quantity System and Material Requirements Planning. Figure 10 illustrates how the order point system works to set priorities. Item Y2L has a forecast of 200 per period with an order point set at 300, a lot size of 600, and a lead time of 1 period. There are 700 on

O.P. = 300   O.Q. = 600   L.T. = 1

Y2L		1	2	3	4	5	6	7	8
PROJECTED REQUIREMENTS		200	200	200	200	200	200	200	200
SCHEDULED RECEIPTS			600				600		
ON HAND	700	500	900	700	500	300	700	500	300
PLANNED ORDER RELEASE						600			600

Figure 10.

hand at the start of the planning period and a quantity of 600 is on order, due in period 2. If the 200 forecast for period 1 are actually used, the projected balance on hand will then be 500. Using another 200 and receiving 600 would give a balance on hand at the end of period 2 of 900. Using 200 per period, the available balance on hand would drop to the order point of 300 in period 5 and the system would then trigger a new order to be released to replenish the inventory. With a lead time of 1 period, the order would be scheduled to come in in period 6. This would establish its priority relative to other orders in the system; those due in earlier weeks would have higher priority and those due later would be lower.

Figure 11 shows how Material Requirements Planning sets priorities. Here the data shows rather lumpy demand in the 8 periods because the Y3L is required in a variety of assemblies at higher levels. The quantities shown are calculated from the Master Production Schedules to make the end product assemblies. The order quantity is 350 and the lead time is 2 periods with a quantity of 400 pieces on hand to start the planning period. Using the projected requirements, the on hand figure would drop to 300 in period 1, 150 in period 2, and would show a negative balance of 120 in period 4. In require-

O.Q. = 350   L.T. = 2

Y3L		1	2	3	4	5	6	7	8
PROJECTED REQUIREMENTS		100	150	120	150	100	90	110	120
SCHEDULED RECEIPTS					350			350	
ON HAND	400	300	150	30	-120 / 230	130	40	-70 / 280	160
PLANNED ORDER RELEASE			350			350			

Figure 11.

ments planning, this is the period in which we need more material and 350 would be scheduled to be received in period 4. This would establish priority on this item relative to other items also on order. The release date would be indicated by backing off 2 periods (lead time); the first order should be released in period 2.

Because of basic differences between the two systems, significantly different priorities can be developed. At the 1970 APICS International Conference in Cincinnati, Dr. J.A. Orlicky used an example to illustrate how uniform demand for finished products results in very lumpy demand for components. His data are shown in Figure 12. The demand for each of the four end products is uniform in each week. Their inventories are replenished by running the lot sizes indicated on the "Production" line. The sub-assemblies then have demands for 14 and 35 in alternate time periods as shown in the center section. The part common to both sub-assemblies has extremely lumpy demand; although its average demand is 17, individual period demands vary from 65 maximum to 0 minimum.

The order point system would plan replenishment of this item as shown in the upper section of Figure 13. The demand would be forecast at the average of 17 and actual demand would reduce the available balance week by week until it had dropped below the order point of 85. The system would then say, "Start a new order and schedule it in at the end of its planned lead time of four weeks."

Contrasted to this, the bottom section of Figure 13 shows how requirements planning would handle this. The requirements would be calculated as shown and the available figure projected into the future indicating that the inventory on hand would be used up in the last week shown. This would then

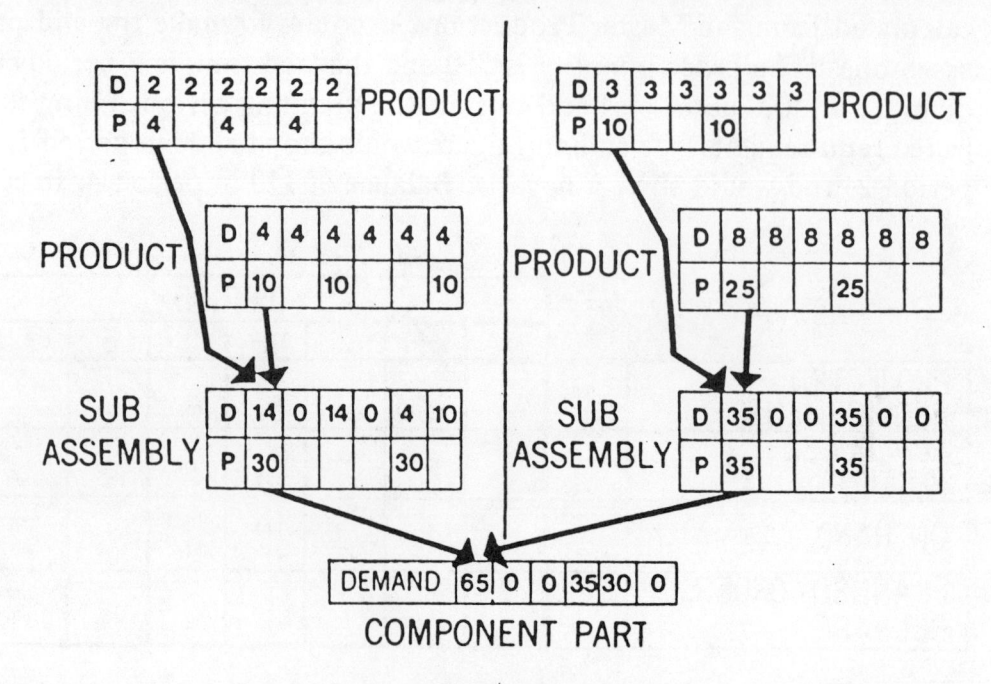

Figure 12.

ORDER POINT

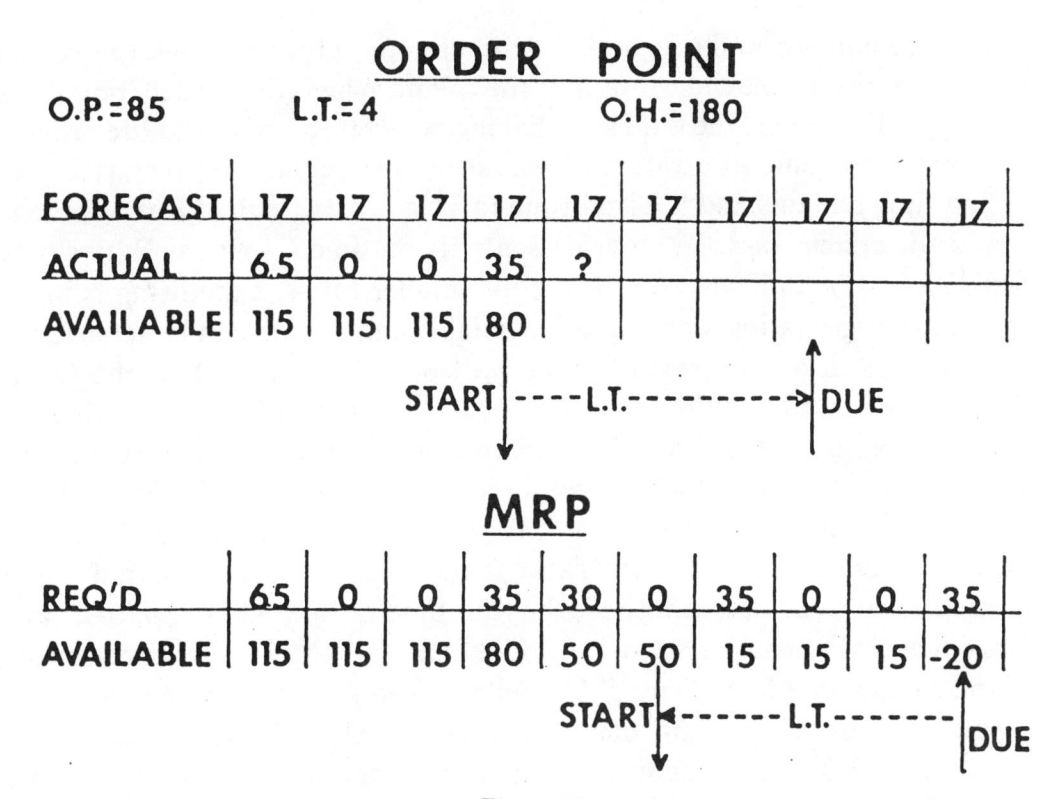

O.P.=85   L.T.=4   O.H.=180

FORECAST	17	17	17	17	17	17	17	17	17	17
ACTUAL	65	0	0	35	?					
AVAILABLE	115	115	115	80						

START |----L.T.---------→| DUE

MRP

REQ'D	65	0	0	35	30	0	35	0	0	35
AVAILABLE	115	115	115	80	50	50	15	15	15	-20

START ←------L.T.-------| DUE

Figure 13.

be the due date for a new order which would be scheduled to start the lead time of four weeks earlier. Notice the two weeks difference in priorities for this item between the two systems.

Many practitioners feel they can overcome this problem by installing a dynamic priority system such as Critical Ratio. Let's examine how Critical Ratio would work under these conditions. Figure 14 illustrates the basic formula for Critical Ratio with a numerator based on the balance on hand of

$$CR = \frac{OH/OP}{LTR/LT}$$

O.P.=85
L.T.= 4

WEEK	1	2	3	4	5
OH	80	50	50	15	15
OH/OP	.94	.59	.59	.18	.18
LTR/LT	1.0	.75	.50	.25	.12
CR	.94	.79	1.2	.72	1.5

Figure 14. Critical Ratio

CAPACITY MANAGEMENT REPRINTS—Revised Edition

parts remaining in stock and a denominator reflecting how the replenishment order is moving through the plant. When the order point system triggered an order, the On Hand balance was 80 compared to the order point of 85 so the numerator ratio is 0.94. Since work had not been started, the full lead time remains and the lead time ratio is 1. The Critical Ratio is then 0.94 and the system says: "You are essentially on time." Critical Ratios between 0.95 and 1.05 indicate "on time"; for smaller ratios, expediting is indicated and for larger ratios, slack time is available and the job can be set aside.

In week 2, an additional quantity of 30 has been used so the On Hand figure is now 50 and the On Hand/Order Point ratio 0.59. Assuming the job progressed normally through the plant (since it was not being expedited), the lead time remaining is three weeks and this ratio is 0.75. The Critical Ratio is 0.79 which says, "Expedite, you are behind schedule." In week 3, no more parts were used so the numerator remains 0.59. Assuming that a normal week's work was accomplished, the lead time ratio would drop to 0.5 and the Critical Ratio would rise to 1.2, indicating that the job is no longer critical and saying, in effect, "You did it, fellows, you got back on schedule. In fact, you are now ahead and can relax." In week 4, however, an additional quantity of 35 was issued, dropping the numerator to 0.18. Since no extra effort was being put on the job, perhaps only one week's work was finished and the lead time ratio would be 0.25, indicating a Critical Ratio of 0.72. This says in effect, "Get on the ball again because this job is now urgently needed." At the end of week 5, with no more parts being used, the numerator remains unchanged. Whatever work is done to reduce the remaining lead time might drop the denominator to 0.12 and the system could easily again indicate slack time available. In this kind of environment with lumpy demand, Critical Ratio behaves like a yo-yo.

Obviously, there is no way to cope with use of the wrong ordering system through fancy scheduling, priority systems, loading, or any other technique. Using the wrong ordering system, the wrong due dates will be established. With incorrect dates, the schedule, the priorities, and the projection of when the load will hit individual work centers will be fiction.

In such an environment, the informal system usually takes over and the real priorities are set by the "hot list" based upon known shortages at assembly. The number of jobs *apparently* past due invariably rises, but the factory people know most of these are not really needed and pay attention only to the informal system priorities. The credibility gap widens until the formal system is ignored or discarded. I know one company with 93 full-time expediters working to five different priority systems—one indicates jobs needed 10 days hence, one 5 days hence, one tomorrow, and one (called the "drop dead" list) covers items without which the assembly line will shut down within the hour. Guess what the fifth priority system is? That's right—when there are no higher priority jobs to do, work to the "date wanted" on the order. Only 8 percent of the orders come through on the original wanted date. No wonder the credibility gap exists.

Effective scheduling and loading requires the elements shown in Figure 15.

Plan	*Control*
Priorities	Capacity
Capacity	Priorities

Figure 15.

There must be a priority planning system that works; this means using the proper ordering system for independent and dependent demand items. There must be a capacity plan to insure that adequate capacity is available to handle the work. There must be a control system to see that capacity is adjusted to meet changes in both customer requirements and in the factory's output. And there must be a priority control system to respond to changes, adjusting priorities to bring the proper jobs through in the right sequence. No machine load or scheduling system will work when based on the wrong priorities. Let's now take a closer look at infinite loading and how it works.

Oliver W. Wight

Remember that there are two fundamental ways to go about loading; one is to show the load in the time period when it's scheduled *regardless* of the available capacity (infinite capacity loading), and the other is to load to "finite capacity" which means, of course, that even though the load may be scheduled in a given time period, if capacity isn't available in this time period, the load will be moved to another time period.

Whoever coined the term "loading to infinite capacity" really did the field of production and inventory control a disservice. When you think about it, it's pretty obvious that a company *should start* by doing some kind of "infinite loading." Certainly finite loading doesn't even show them the capacity they *need!* It just assumes that this capacity is absolutely inflexible. The first step is to find out what capacity is needed. You must start with "infinite loading" rather than "finite loading."

Let's review the steps in scheduling and loading. Figure 16 shows a typical shop order. Note that this shop order is due on calendar day 412. We're working with a shop calendar that shows only the working days to facilitate scheduling. Note that the standard hours for each operation have been calculated based on the quantity on the shop order; in this case, 300 pieces. Assume also that we're working with some scheduling rules. In this case, our scheduling rules allow two days for inspection and two days "transit time" between operations in different departments. The job is due to be completed on day 412; it has to be out of the polishing operation on day 410. This company works on eight-hour shift so two days will have to be allowed for the polishing operation. Since two days are allowed between operatons in different departments, the job must be completed out of grinding on day 406. In this manner, the job can be "Back Scheduled" to determine when each operation must be finished (and/or started) and a "schedule date" can be assigned to each operation.

Part No. B-4848	Shop Order No. 50043 Quant. 300 Due: 412			
Oper.	Dept.	Mach.	Description	Setup	Per Piece
10	08	1322	Cut off	.5	.010
20	32	1600	Rough turn	1.5	.030
30	17	8660	Heat treat		
40	32	1204	Finish turn	3.3	.048
50	32	1204	Drill, ream	1.2	.035
60	12	1466	Mill slots	1.8	.025
70	03	1742	Grind	.6	.010
80	22	1003	Polish	.3	.029
90	11		Inspect		

Release		
Std. Hrs.	Start	Finish
3.5		
10.5		
17.7		
11.7		
9.3		
3.6		
9.0		
65.3		

Figure 16.

		WEEKLY LOAD IN STANDARD HOURS						
DEPT.	MACH.	376 380	381 385	386 390	391 395	396 400	401 405	406 410
03	1742							
08	1322							
12	1466							
22	1003							9
32	1204							
	1600							

Figure 17.

Note that nine standard hours of polishing work will then be required in work center 1003 and must be completed by day 410. Figure 17 shows the weekly load report in standard hours. The nine hours have been loaded in the proper work center in the proper week. By doing this with all of the shop orders, an "infinite capacity load" would be developed.

As we've pointed out, *it's essential that we know what capacity is needed* and only this kind of approach will do that. We frankly think that *the biggest problem with infinite capacity loading is the name!* If we had been astute enough to give it a name that properly described the function, this technique would have had far better acceptability and more intelligent use. My nomination for a more descriptive term is CAPACITY REQUIREMENTS PLANNING.

We have Material Requirements Planning (MRP) that tells us what material we need and when we need it. Capacity Requirements Planning should tell us what capacity we need and when we need it. How is Capacity Requirements Planning different from infinite loading? Since I have coined the term, allow me to define it. Capacity Requirements Planning uses exactly the same logic as the old "infinite loading" with one minor difference. In addition to picking up the released orders or "load," it also picks up the *planned orders* from MRP. These planned orders *are not real shop orders*. MRP simply generates a part number, a quantity, and a time period when an order is to be released. MRP uses these planned orders to generate lower level material requirements. But they can also be run against the routing file, each planned order can be back-scheduled and a forecast of capacity requirements can thus be developed.

Capacity Requirements Planning is certainly an essential function in any production and inventory control system. But let's stop using that emotion-laden word "Infinite" right now! Nobody can really load a plant to infinite capacity! But certainly we do need to have an idea of capacity requirements before we start trying to load the plant to a given capacity.

Remember Figure 15 that showed the four basic elements in a production and inventory control system:

Plan Priorities / Plan Capacities / Control Capacities / Control Priorities

The inventory control system (usually MRP) is the priority planning function. Capacity Requirements Planning is the capacity planning function. Dispatching is the priority control function in the shop. But how about *capacity control?*

We frankly don't believe that the typical machine load report was ever designed to be a "control system." A control system has four fundamental elements to it:

A NORM / TOLERANCE / FEEDBACK / ACTION

The wall thermostat is our favorite example of a control system. The temperature is set to the desired level, then the actual temperature is monitored via a feedback system. Whenever the actual has deviated from the norm—or "Plan"—by a predetermined amount (tolerance), action is taken to get the temperature restored to the norm.

Think of the typical machine load report. Is there a norm? Where is there a plan that's practical? A plan that you can hold people responsible for executing. Certainly when you have tremendous variations in the amount of load in a work center each week, *there's no way* you can hold the foreman responsible for working to that production level. It simply isn't practical in most factories to have dramatic fluctuations in capacity. Manpower and machine capacity are limited and it is most economical to hold them as stable as possible from one week to the next.

By the same token, where is the comparison of "actual" with "plan" in the typical machine load report? Very seldom does the load report show the output from the work center involved and if output is shown, it's usually only shown for one week. Obviously, output for one week is hardly representative of the ability of that work center to meet the capacity plan. Actual output should be compared with planned output for a number of weeks.

Certainly two essentials that ought to be involved in any kind of "capacity control" or "output control" system are:

A practical plan

Feedback to compare "actual" with the plan.

1.	284	6.	286
2.	61	7.	50
3.	321	8.	147
4.	139	9.	695
5.	531	10.	176

Figure 18. Capacity Requirements

Let's look briefly at a Capacity Requirements Plan. When all of the hours by work center, by time period, are accumulated, the result would look something like Figure 18. This shows capacity requirements for 10 weeks for a given work center in standard hours. Note that there is a random variation from week to week.

How can this random variation be smoothed out? The most practical way is simply to *add it up and average it out*. The minute you get a week out into the future, your prediction of how many hours are going to be at what work center at what time is an approximation at best. The average weekly capacity requirement from Figure 18 would be 270 hours per week.

	W1	W2	W3	W4	W5
PLANNED	270	270	270	270	270
ACTUAL	250	220	190		
DEVIATION	-20	-70	-150		

Figure 19. Output Control

could be set up in an "Output Control" report. Remember that we're trying to show a "norm"—a realistic attainable plan that people can be held responsible for attaining. Below the *plan*, the *actual* standard hours of output are shown. Below that, of course, we show the deviation.

It would be a good idea, in practice, to determine a tolerance. How far away from the planned can the actual be allowed to drift? We've seen companies use this kind of report. By pre-determining what the tolerance was, the foreman coming into the weekly production meeting knew whether or not they were going to be required to work overtime or do something else to increase capacity. They were told, for example, "If the cumulative deviation is more than 50 hours off the plan, the burden is on *you* to get extra capacity—quick!" Setting the tolerance *in advance* saved a lot of debates in production meetings.

Infinite loading is dead; it has been replaced by *Capacity Requirements Planning*. There is nothing wrong with the technique *if it used properly!* We certainly need to plan capacity well out into the future. The term Capacity Requirements Planning—by definition—implies that we are using planned orders out of MRP as well as actual released orders. Then the leveled planned production rate is just the average of the weekly capacity requirements usually planned out three to four months in advance. This sets the production rate against which the actual output will be measured. Many people spend a lot of time trying to figure out what their capacity is when the actual current capacity is very easy to determine by looking at labor variance reports and other already existing reports that show the number of standard hours worth of work produced.

Note that the report I showed you, the Output Report, is really part of the technique that we called Input/Output Control. Let's think a little more about the real significance of this technique.

George W. Plossl

The traditional approach to developing a production and inventory control system has been to first design and install an ordering system—a set of procedures to trigger orders for both purchased and manufactured parts. This has been generally called "Inventory Control." The next step is to release immediately to vendors or to the factory the orders triggered by this system. Next comes an attempt to control the sequence in which these orders are worked on by activities in the plant under the general heading of "Production Control."

A popular technique among manufacturing people is to watch the backlogs in a machine load and attempt to use them as a tool for adjusting capacity. Unfortunately, this rarely works. Increasingly popular are shop floor control systems using dynamic priority techniques and data collection equipment. The basic idea seems to be that if we know where each job is, we can get it through when we need it. This, unfortunately, doesn't seem to be very effective either. In fact, both approaches are nothing but a massive assult on the symptoms while the basic diseases of poor priority information and/or inadequate capacity go unchecked.

We now have two fine ordering systems and a basic principle to tell us when to use each of them. The independent/dependent demand principle clearly identifies where the order point/order quantity system should be applied and where to use Material Requirements Planning. With both systems, however, we still need dependable lead times and this means that queues or backlogs of work-in-process must be under control.

There are three reasons why queues (and lead times) are out of control:

1. Inadequate Capacity—if you are not making enough in total, then something must wait, queues grow and lead times get longer and more erratic.
2. Erratic Input—no ordering system releases work at a level rate matching the capacity of the plant. When the lumps and bunches of work triggered by either of the basic ordering systems hit the shop, it is obvious that all cannot move steadily through the plant. Backlogs and queues will increase and lead time will get longer and more erratic.
3. Inflated Lead Times—it is now well recognized that we can't "make it easy" for the plant or for the ordering system by simply allowing more time to get jobs finished. Increasing planned lead times triggers more orders and dumps more load into the plant without regard to its ability to hadle it. Longer queues and erratic lead times result.

Lead times will never be controlled and a plant will never be on schedule unless it controls capacity. The Input/Output approach is the first available tool which has been successfully used in controlling capacity. Unlike the typical machine load shown in Figure 20, Input/Output measures and

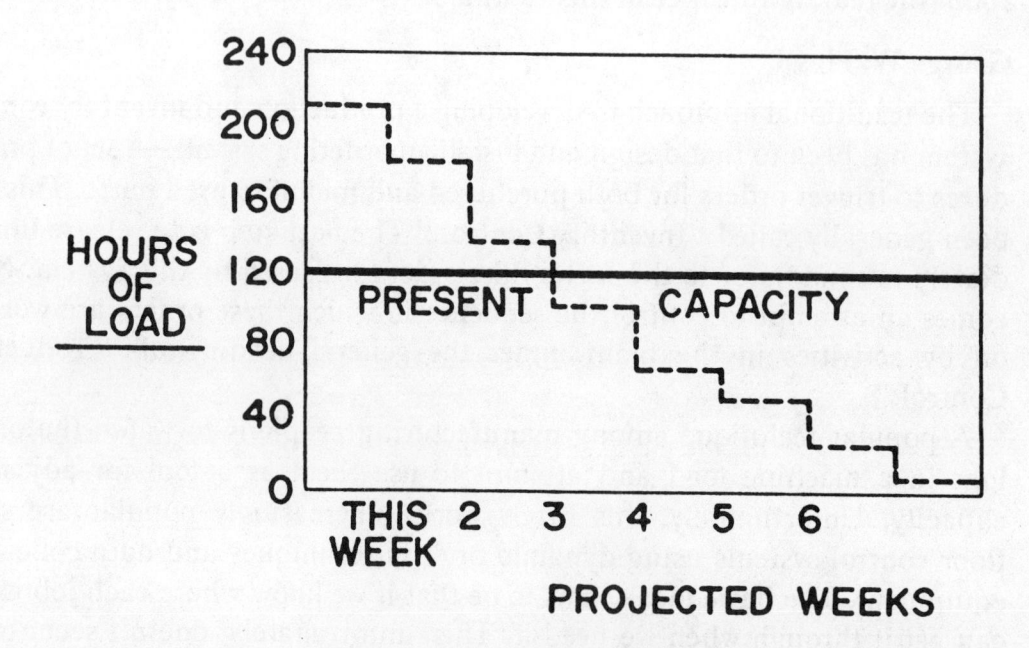

Figure 20. Typical Machine Load Pattern

attempts to control the *through-put*, the flow in and out, rather than the backlogs. Production control people look at the present overloads on the machine load in **Figure** 20 and tell the foreman, "You're in trouble." The foreman looks at the future underloads on the machine load and says, "You better believe it." They're thinking of something entirely different.

Recently, I sat with a plant manager, his manufacturing superintendent, and his production control manager looking at a report issued weekly for each major work center in the plant. This report showed standard machine hours of actual input, actual output, total backlogs and the past due portion of the backlog in each work center. The manufacturing superintendent said his people looked only at the backlog figures. I asked why they didn't use the actual output information and he said, "Notice how steady and level these figures are. They don't tell us much." I also asked why they did not use the input figures and he said, "Look how they jump up and down. What does that really tell you? We've run out of work before and there is no indication in these input figures we won't run out again. We use the backlog figures which are the only data giving us any *forward visibility at work* in the plant." Could you argue with him? With future *planned* capacity data lacking, what else could he do?

The biggest hangup on applying the Input/Output Control approach seems to be the difficulty of seeing how to control input in secondary work centers. Input can really be controlled only at starting operations and at assembly or sub-assembly areas where we have control of the orders released from the planning system to the plant. However, *average rates* of work input can be planned and *actual rates measured* at all work centers. This gives very valuable information as illustrated in Figure 21. Against a planned average rate of 210 standard hours per week, actual output has fallen short by a cumulative total of 300 standard hours. Looking at the output figures only, a logical conclusion would be that this department needs more capacity. However, the input figures make it obvious that the real problem must lie in the departments feeding this work center. Its input total is more than 300 hours behind the plan. Measuring input focuses attention on the real capacity problem areas.

Extending the planned figures into the future as shown in Figure 21 gives manufacturing people that forward visibility which is so vital to them in controlling capacity. Another company decided to apply Input/Output Controls and immediately ran into difficulty in getting sufficient data to plan input and output rates and to measure input at major work centers. They decided to go ahead, however, with the data they had. They ranked all new orders released by the inventory planning system in priority sequence. They completed the routings on all orders, estimating time standards in major work centers where they were missing. Using an infinite capacity machine load program they had running on their computer, they tested what load these orders would place on each work center. Since they had no formal scheduling system, they ignored the time delay from starting an operation in one work center and

(ALL FIGURES IN STANDARD HOURS)

WEEK ENDING	505	512	519	526
PLANNED INPUT	210	210	210	210
ACTUAL INPUT	110	150	140	130
CUMULATIVE DEVIATION	-100	-160	-230	-310

PLANNED OUTPUT	210	210	210	210
ACTUAL OUTPUT	140	120	160	120
CUMULATIVE DEVIATION	-70	-160	-210	-300

Figure 21. Input/Output Control

having it reach a subsequent work center some days or weeks later. They assumed each job hit each work center immediately when it was released, just as if all were starting operations.

From payroll data, they logged the actual hours of output in each of the major work centers and carried a weighted running average. When the scheduled orders to be released exceeded this average actual output in any work center, they rescheduled some orders to minimize such overloads. Their objective was to *put into each work center less work than it was turning out*. In a period of six weeks, the work-in-process was reduced almost 40 percent, lead times came down proportionately and their ability to get needed jobs through the plant increased rather dramatically.

The real use of Input/Output Control techniques is, of course, to measure actual versus planned data as a basis for control. Control of all priorities and inventory levels depends on controlling capacity. Among the elements of the effective production control system shown in Figure 15, the key is controlling capacity. With adequate capacity, even if you can't level out the input, you can manage long queues of work and long average lead times *if you have a priority planning system that works*. Without adequate capacity, you can only hope to minimize the pain or isolate it.

```
            MASTER SCHEDULE ──→ ROUGH CUT
                    │            CAPACITY
                    ▼
               MATERIAL
             REQUIREMENTS
                PLAN
                    │
                    ▼
               CAPACITY
             REQUIREMENTS
                PLAN
                    │
                    ▼
         NO   ╱ CAPACITY ╲
        ◄────      ?
              ╲         ╱
                  YES
                    ▼
             INPUT/OUTPUT
                CONTROL
                    │
                    ▼
               DISPATCH
                 LIST
```

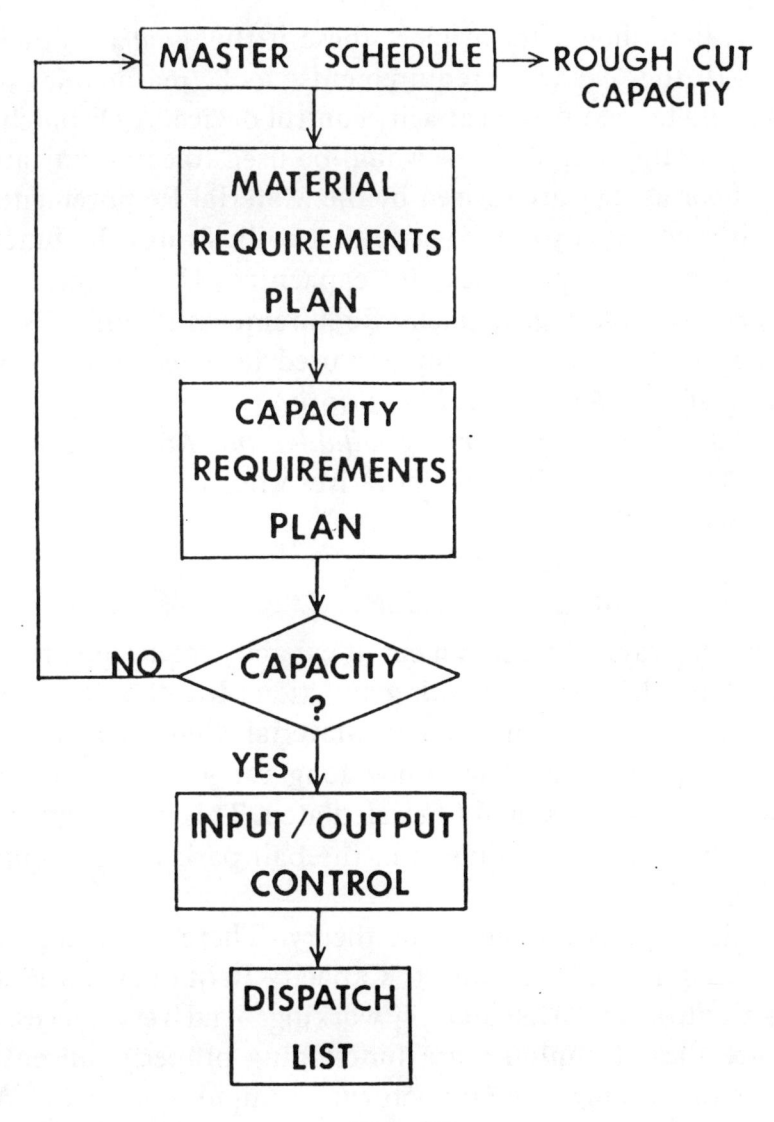

Figure 22.

Oliver W. Wight

We've talked about planning and controlling priorities and capacities. Let's see how the techniques we have discussed fit into this overall format.

    Priority planning — the *Material Requirements Planning* technique will be used in most companies.

    Capacity planning — this is where we need to use *Capacity Requirements Planning*.

    Capacity control — Input/Output Control.

    Priority control — Dispatching in the shop, follow-up in Purchasing.

Figure 22 shows the overall relationship of the elements in a production and inventory control system. Starting with a Master Production Schedule, it goes into a Material Requirements Plan; the Capacity Requirements Plan can then be developed from both released orders and planned orders. Then a decision is indicated. Can the plant meet the capacity requirements?

CAPACITY MANAGEMENT REPRINTS—Revised Edition

Obviously, they should try to meet these if this is at all practical and economical. If the capacity requirements look reasonable, Input/Output Control could be set up as a capacity control device. A Dispatch List — probably issued to the shop daily — would be used to communicate priorities to the shop floor as they are revised by the Material Requirements Plan. Looking at this schematic, you recognize that it illustrates the functions of planning and controlling priorities and capacities. The Material Requirements Plan is *priority planning*. Capacity Requirements Planning is *capacity planning*. The Input/Output technique is used for *controlling capacity* and the Dispatch List is used for *controlling priorities*.

Note that if capacity is not available, the Master Schedule *must be changed!* There are really two alternatives when capacity requirements are in excess of actual capacity:

        Change capacity.
        Change the schedule.

Note by the way, that a rough cut at capacity requirements might be made as part of the Master Scheduling function. In other words, before going through the detail of the actual Material Requirements Plan and the Capacity Requirements Plan, some long range determination of requirements against resources might be calculated. This is a rough cut just to make sure that the Master Schedule is in the ball park before going through the detailed calculations.

This schematic is anything but theory. There are companies that have Material Requirements Planning, Capacity Requirements Planning, Input/Output Control, and Dispatching working. And very successfully, I might add. Once these techniques are functioning properly, an entirely different approach to running a manufacturing company emerges. With a formal system like this *that works*, decisions are put into their proper perspective ahead of time. Let me give you an example.

One company that I've worked with has all of the techniques mentioned above working successfully. The results from using these techniques have impressed me. But the thing that's impressed *them* more than anything else is their ability to spot problems ahead of time and make good, strategic decisions.

The Director of Manufacturing for this company told me some years ago that he'd be pleased the day he could answer some of the questions put to him honestly. For example, when the President says, "We've got to get a new product out the door in much less than the standard lead time, *can we really do it?*" Without the kind of system that will generate this kind of information, the only course open is to say, "Yes," and try.

Let me show you how this company handles this type of problem today. This past September, the President said he wanted a particular product introduced into the schedule immediately and available for shipment

November 1st. The Director of Manufacturing had the load profile for this new product calculated on the computer and superimposed on top of his current Capacity Requirements Plan. He could see immediately that an impossible backlog would have resulted in front of one of his numerically controlled work centers. There wasn't any chance of getting this work subcontracted for a great many reasons including lack of available capacity in the immediate geographical area. The detailed backup report for the capacity plan showed the actual parts that were causing the capacity requirements. Looking at some of these parts, he traced these to the assemblies they went into. Then he went to the President and showed him that if one of the products that was declining in sales could be removed from the Master Schedule for November, there would be enough capacity available to make the new product. The President readily agreed and this plan was implemented. I might also add that the new product was introduced in November on schedule and everyone was very pleased.

In the past, this Director of Manufacturing pointed out to me that he would have added the new product without being able to determine ahead of time what some of the alternate plans were. And he probably would have been criticized severely if the product that had the declining sales had experienced longer delivery times! Since he had the information available to call it to the attention of the President ahead of time, this was anticipated, and when it materialized, people understood that this was the cost of launching a new product in considerably less than standard lead time.

One manufacturing executive made a very astute observation on this. He said, "You know, a manufacturing executive without the proper information can never say 'No.' All he can do is say 'Yes' and try to meet impossible plans and then be criticized afterwards because something else suffered!" But what a new ball game. The ability to point out ahead of time what the alternatives are, what the consequences are, and to pick out ahead of time what will suffer and recognize why this choice was made. In the next five years, I hope to see the emphasis change from developing systems to learning to use systems to manage. Many managements are going to have an entirely new world to work in when they have the alternatives in front of them *ahead of time*.

Let's come back to our overall schematic of production and inventory control. One point should come through loud and clear:

> Lesson #1: WORK LOAD ON A PLANT WILL BE LEVELED VIA THE MASTER SCHEDULE.

The first job is to *get* the needed capacity, if possible and practical. When capacity is not available, the Master Schedule must be revised. Large lumps of capacity requirements will be smoothed out in the Master Schedule.

We have talked a lot about the Master Schedule. Perhaps a couple of words about the types of Master Schedule that different companies might use would be in order. In a company operating strictly off backlog, the Master

Schedule would be primarily customer orders. Most companies don't have the luxury of having enough backlog to work from. They need to forecast what orders they're going to have to manufacture. Under these circumstances, the forecast must be "bled out" constantly as actual demand materializes. The short term Master Schedule consists of actual customer orders, the middle term Master Schedule is a combination of forecast and actual, and the long term consists of forecast only.

The Master Schedule in different types of companies can take many different forms. In a company manufacturing stocked finished goods, the Master Schedule would be the production plan that tells the total number of units that they're going to make for a particular type of product. This could then be allocated for various part numbers as a production forecast and that would be used to create a Material Requirements Plan and Capacity Requirements Plan. In a foundry, the Master Schedule might be expressed in very general terms showing the number of molds to be made per day per work center.

Every company has one or more Master Schedules, even though they may not explicitly recognize this! The Master Schedule drives MRP which drives the rest of the production and inventory management system. It is also the key to better management strategy.

Lesson #2: THE MASTER SCHEDULE CAN BE USED TO SIMULATE AND SHOW THE CONSEQUENCES AND IMPLICATIONS OF VARIOUS POLICY DECISIONS.

When a new product is to be introduced, when production is to be increased or decreased, the Master Schedule will be the point of entry to show the consequences of this change in plan. It's the very guts of production and inventory control. Therefore, if the company doesn't explicitly recognize that they have to have a Master Schedule, their chances of being able to control the production and inventory function are very slim indeed. Back in the days of the informal system, few companies had a recognizable Master Schedule. In the days of formal systems, every company should.

But as we look back at our schematic in Figure 22 again, there's something disturbing. *What became of Finite Loading?* We seem to have handled the four fundamental functions of production and inventory control without even touching on Finite Loading!

George W. Plossl

Let's take a more detailed look at finite loading. As discussed earlier, jobs must be loaded in priority sequence, since we want the highest priority jobs to have first claim on available capacity. When priorities change, we must rerun the whole finite loading program. The problem is further complicated by "dependent priorities." Components going into an assembly should have a priority dependent upon the status of other components. It is obvious that there is no need to rush one part through if it will just wait for others before the assembly can be completed.

Load data is really a forecast of when work will hit the work center involved and, like all forecasts, will be less accurate for periods farther out in the future; in other words, for longer lead times. It's certainly optimistic, at the least, to say, "Job 123 will hit this work center 15 weeks from now," and really believe it. With all these problems, few companies have attempted finite loading. It is a good question *if any of them has succeeded*.

The two best known computer programs for finite loading are the PICS Capacity Planning and the CLASS program, both put out by IBM. In Business English, the PICS program says, "If you know all the products you are going to manufacture in the next year, if you have a complete bill of material for each of them, if you have routings and standards for each manufactured item in this bill of material and if you have accurate stock status and open order files, then the computer can calculate for you the load on each work center in each time period over the planning horizon and, in addition, can rearrange this load to meet capacity limitations. Figure 23 shows the steps in the PICS Capacity Planning program. Using the Material Requirements Planning program (RPS), the computer translates a Master Production Schedule into planned orders for components; it then schedules both planned and released orders and develops an infinite load profile for each work center. If the user elects to do finite loading, the computer will then reschedule orders with low priority which hit work centers having inadequate capacity. The program will show which orders were rescheduled, how many hours of load are involved and the specific work centers affected. The user must then analyze the rescheduled orders to determine the effects on the end product Master Schedule and decide whether he can live with these or if he must make other changes. The user can assign job priorities or the system will use the Earliest Start Dates or the Latest Start Dates developed by the

<u>CAPACITY   PLANNING</u>

MASTER   PRODUCTION   SCHEDULE

PLANNED   ORDERS   -   COMPONENTS

SCHEDULE   ALL   ORDERS

INFINITE   LOAD

    OR

FINITE   LOAD

ANALYZE   ORDERS   RESCHEDULED

REVISE   MASTER   SCHEDULE

REPEAT

Figure 23. PICS

scheduling portion of the package. The user must define capacity available in each work center; he has an option of putting in a table showing a planned level and a maximum level of capacity. The difference might be working Saturdays or other overtime periods or transferring a number of men between work centers. The program does not handle unplanned loads such as scrap and rework, machine breakdowns, operator training, and other capacity-wasting activities.

There has been considerable publicity given to another IBM program called called CLASS. CLASS stands for Capacity Loading And Scheduling System, a classic finite loading program developed by Werner Kraus for IBM in Germany. The sequence of activities followed is shown in Figure 24. Unlike PICS capacity planning, CLASS starts with individual work orders and does not require a Material Requirements Planning program to generate them. It does need to know how these orders relate in a product structure since it uses this information to tie the priorities of components to that of the final assembly. The first step is to schedule the work orders and the next to develop an infinite load showing how each work center would be affected if the schedule were followed. The user then adjusts work center capacities as best he can to meet the loads.

Based on user-established priorities on the assemblies, the system develops a finite load attempting to schedule the parts in assembly priority sequence to match available capacity in each work center. The user must then analyze how assemblies were rescheduled to see if he can live with this. If he cannot, he must make other decisions about capacity or priorities and start over. CLASS has an interesting feature in that it simulates the progress of each job through the plant to see if it will be affected by *future overloads*. If jobs #1 and #2 are competing for capacity in one work center, but #1 will be delayed at a subsequent work center, job #2 is given first claim on capacity. Both PICS Capacity Planning and CLASS are truly elegant computer programs and are beautifully designed. They both require massive amounts of computer time because of the tremendous number of calculations involved.

The basic requirements for success with finite loading would appear to be

SCHEDULE WORK ORDERS

INFINITE LOAD

ADJUST WORK CENTER CAPACITIES

SET PRIORITIES - ASSEMBLIES

FINITE LOAD

RESCHEDULE ASSEMBLIES

UP-DATE - START OVER

Figure 24. CLASS

a well-ordered environment, few Master Schedule changes, tight discipline on data accuracy *and a priority plan that is valid*. It is hard to imagine an operation where the work of finite loading programs would be justified by improved results over simpler, more effective techniques. Oliver Wight and I have wondered for a long time if finite loading will ever be a practical technique.

Oliver W. Wight

Finite loading is certainly an excellent example of "barking up the wrong tree." When a company finite loads the individual shop orders, there's bound to be one predictable result. Some orders won't be able to be completed on time. Obviously, if these orders can't be completed on time, the Master Schedule must be changed. But, as we pointed out before, Capacity Requirements Planning will quickly identify a capacity requirement that can't be met and that the Master Schedule must be changed. Why bother with all the sophistication of finite loading? If ever a technique fell in the general category of "using 300 horsepower to blow the horn," finite loading is it.

Beyond being an over-sophisticated technique, it simply isn't valid. If finite loading were to be done correctly, it would result in endless iteration. Consider a company where they have dependent priorities—parts that go into assemblies, for example. If one part can't be fit into the capacity and its due date has to be extended, then the Master Schedule should be changed for the assemblies using this part. *But when this Master Schedule is changed, the finite load that caused the schedule change is no longer valid.* Some of the load that kept the part in question from being made on time was probably being generated by other parts going into the same assemblies. The minute the Master Schedule is pushed out, some of this load will be pushed out. Now we must finite load again, but, once again, something probably won't be completed on time. Back to the Master Schedule! This, again, will generate the need to recalculate the finite load. If done properly, finite loading would be an endless iteration. One of the companies, using the IBM CLASS program on an IBM 360 Model 40 (certainly not a small computer!) requires *35 hours* to make their computation. When we called to their attention the fact that it's important in most companies to have a daily dispatch list, they pointed out that while they were anxious to do this, they had yet to figure out how to squeeze 35 hours of computer time into a 24-hour day!

But what if we don't change the Master Schedule? Suppose we don't reschedule all of the other parts that go into the assembly. Well, this is certainly a waste of capacity. If any one item can't be made, it's usually necessary to make some other item, particularly if it's important to meet a monthly shipping budget of some kind. When this is true, it's essential to change the Master Schedule and thus reschedule all the parts that aren't needed so that capacity will be available to make the parts that are needed.

One point comes through very clearly: *Overloads will be resolved via the*

Master Schedule. Load leveling is going to take place in the Master Schedule. The only load leveling left to be handled will be minor weekly variations in load that are usually not very significant or controllable!

Finite loading, then, was a great way to attack the symptoms, but, in practice, it doesn't work very well. Let's look at the *problems with finite loading:*

1. **Assumes Predictable Job Arrival.**
Going through the precise detail of determining when each job will be at each work center and leveling out this work load assumes that we can predict when jobs will arrive at work centers in the future. The folly of this is obvious to anybody who has ever worked in a factory.

2. **Component Priorities Are Usually Dependent.**
The literature of production and inventory control, be it the order point/order quantity literature or the literature on scheduling has been obsessed with methods for handling individual independent items. In the real world, most items simply aren't independent. They are parts that go into assemblies, they are raw materials that go into a product. These priorities cannot be looked at independently as so many people have tried to do with order point type systems which apply only to independent priority items. By the same token, *they cannot be scheduled independently.* A new revision in the schedule of any of these items will affect all of the other items that are related to it. This gets to be a complex problem and we have to focus our attention on what's important and what isn't important. In a company that makes an assembled product, for example, optimizing the schedule of any one component is an exercise in triviality. The important thing is to get all of the components together at the right time to make the product. Having any one of them without the rest of them is valueless. And, as we pointed out above, the computations involved in a genuine finite loading exercise where there are dependent demand components would result in endless iteration.

One of the difficulties, of course, is that at the end of each one of these iterations, the Master Schedule would have to be revised. This would require human intervention before the program could continue in its operation. This probably wouldn't be practical. Therefore, some people have suggested that the Master Schedule should be revised automatically by the computer. *Don't do it!* There is a major problem with finite loading:

3. **Automatic Master Scheduling Is Risky.**
As was pointed out, the Master Schedule drives the entire production and inventory control system. A lot of considerations go into the Master Schedule. It's attempting to deal with the real world where some large customers of a company may get preferential treatment in practice, where things like a dock strike may cause an export order to have a

higher priority than it normally has and where an order for a new customer who was sold based on the company's ability to give service might have to be given preference. These are the normal day-to-day things that have to be addressed in the real world factory. To try to capture all of that logic in a computer program may intrigue the theoretician. The practitioner recognizes how futile—and silly—it is.

The name of the game is to plan capacity requirements and see if we have this capacity. If we don't, get the capacity or change the Master Schedule. Probably the greatest reason for not using finite loading in most situations is:

4. There Are Easier, Better Ways To Do The Job.
Finite loading assumes a very stable environment where a lot of logic can be captured in a computer program and executed. It is filled with pretentious precision as it tries to predict which jobs will arrive at what time at what operation in a factory. Yet, in practice, the company that does finite loading only learns what they could have learned by way of much simpler techniques: when there is a capacity requirement in excess of available capacity, it must be met — or the Master Schedule must be changed.

If this is true, why has finite loading even gained credence? To be sure, it is not something that *most practitioners* view as logical. But a few do.

Well, let's take a look at one prime example. It has often been stated that there are "200 users of the IBM CLASS program in Europe." First, we have to define users. What this really means is that there are 200 people who have accepted a free program from IBM. Then we are likely to hear that there are 30 companies that are actually "running" it, but this usually means that these 30 companies have the program running on the computer. Whether or not anybody uses the output is questionable. As we tried to pin it down further, we find that there are a few companies who are actually supposed to be running their factories this way. The only one that has had much written about it actually makes magnets. Fundamentally, a one-piece product without many dependent priorities and a very simple manufacturing environment. Questionable that they really need finite loading. The fact that is worked under these circumstances is interesting, but not particularly signifiant.

We also hear that there are "a number of companies" using it in the United States. We've tried to track this down and have learned some very interesting things. At one company, for example, the Manufacturing Vice President and Data Processing people speak very highly of finite loading. They are located in a corporate office in Chicago. It works there. Unfortunately, when you get down to the plant in Moline, you find that it does not work.

How can we determine whether finite loading works or doesn't work? First, we've got to understand what the function of finite loading really is. It isn't a capacity planning technique; it certainly isn't a capacity control technique; it isn't a priority control technique either. *It's really a priority planning technique.* It takes the priorities generated by the Material Requirements Plan and attempts to revise them in order to level out the work load. Perhaps a more appropriate name for it would be something like "Order Release Planning," since it addresses the problem of releasing orders into starting work centers in an attempt to level work load.

How do you determine if finite loading is actually working, then? The test is simple: *Does the company using it actually run to the priority list generated by the finite loading system?* This is the only way you can determine if finite loading is working. If they are not running to this priority list, *finite loading does not work.*

I went to a company recently, for example, where they were using the IBM PICS Infinite Loading and Finite Loading packages. They claimed great results from the finite loading system. I was skeptical. Looking at the priority list generated by the finite loading reports confirmed my skepticism. They certainly were not following it. In fact, they worked to a hot list and then crossed the jobs off the weekly computer generated priority list as they were done in the sequence dictated by the hot list.

They did get some lead time reductions, however. They mistakenly attributed this to finite loading! In calculating the infinite load—a prerequisite to finite loading in the IBM package—they had to develop some scheduling rules. The result of using these scheduling rules was to come up with shorter planning lead times than they had been using. Shortening the lead times reduced the input to the factory. Reducing the input dropped the backlogs. Dropping the backlogs cut the lead time. Now normally this would result in a *temporary reduction in lead time* because, in most companies, since they're used to working with the informal capacity planning system, the minute visual backlogs decrease, the output tends to drop off. But this company's production control manager, who is a pretty clever guy, had come up with a capacity control device very similar to Input/Output Control. He took the infinite load report, *discounted 40 percent of the backlog in the current period,* and then averaged that load out over the next 12 weeks. He then set this as a production plan and got the foremen working to this plan. The result: Having reduced input and controlled output, backlogs stayed down, lead time decreased. Finite loading had nothing whatsoever to do with the excellent results these people attained.

People often ask us how IBM could have presented the Finite Loading package in PICS if it isn't a legitimate technique. The answer is—it was an honest mistake. Finite loading looked good. We've got to remember that a lot of the computer people tend to favor the sophisticated. As Townsend said, "These people are complicators—not simplifiers." While blanket indictments like that are never fair, it certainly is true that data processing and systems people generally have favored the sophisticated approaches. The people who develop application programs for computer companies are usually systems people, not practitioners. It's hardly surprising that they would pick up something like finite loading, especially since the reaction of most practitioners to "Infinite Loading" was negative!

Our research this year, our discussions with a lot of people, indicates to us that *not one responsible professional we have talked with believes that finite loading is a valid scheduling and loading technique in a machine shop!*

I hasten to add that George and I both are very much in favor of the IBM PICS package. We favor standardization rather than reinventing the wheel. We applaud IBM for their outstanding contributions with these packages, such as the RPS or Material Requirements Planning portion of PICS. We have a number of clients who have used it and used it successfully. We are very much in favor of the infinite loading or "Capacity Requirements Planning" part of their capacity planning module in PICS, but we feel obligated to tell other practitioners that we simply cannot endorse finite loading as a valid production and inventory control technique.

Does that mean that finite loading will die? Hardly. There is a latent appeal to finite loading and the chances are that it will be with us for some time to come. There are three basic reasons for its appeal:

1. **It's the Apparent Alternative to Infinite Loading.**

    Probably the biggest reason that finite loading was ever invented is because of that inappropriate term, "Infinite Loading." If the two choices are infinite loading and finite loading, obviously any man in his right mind is going to take the alternative of finite loading because infinite loading, by definition, just doesn't make sense. When we understand how a production and inventory control system fits together, we recognize that the actual "Finite Loading" is going to take place via the Master Schedule, not by some sophisticated detailed scheduling and loading algorithm.

    Perhaps a more insidious reason for wanting to use finite loading was the basic misunderstanding of the relationship of the elements of production and inventory control because finite loading was an:

2. **Apparent Way to Reschedule the Backlog.**

    Where there is a large amount of past due work in a machine load report, it's apparent that there's a need to reschedule. So it often looks to top people like the way to handle this is finite loading. Rescheduling that load will get that backlog out of there and put the load out in a realistic time frame. Unfortunately, they don't see how the pieces of the system fit together. Rescheduling the load in front of screw machine, for example, will only result in having to change the Master Schedule because screw machine parts won't be coming out as scheduled. They should have determined ahead of time what the capacity requirements were, and if they couldn't meet these capacity requirements, then the Master Schedule should have been changed ahead of time rather than after a large backlog had built up. So, finite loading seems like a way to reschedule the backlog when, in fact, that backlog is only really going to be rescheduled by changing the Master Schedule. Why not do it directly? Why go through all the nonsense of finite loading?

In the company I mentioned above where they were supposed to have finite loading working, they had to discount the infinite load report by a substantial amount in order to set up their actual capacity plan. Why did they have these large backlogs in the infinite load report? For a very simple reason —they had a Master Schedule that was feeding the Material Requirements Planning system and this Master Schedule was no longer valid. There was a lot of work in there that was late and had never been rescheduled, never put out in the time periods when it was really going to be produced. The result— a large past due backlog. *Finite loading for them was a mirage; it was an attempt to reschedule that backlog.* What a great way to assault the symptoms. The real disease was in the Master Schedule.

Of course, in the twilight of the age of naive sophistication, as I have chosen to call the early years of computer application, we cannot fail to recognize that finite loading has an appeal:

3. It Is Sophisticated.

You must remember that many people believe that the more sophisticated approach is the better one. This, of course, is nonsense. It usually results in getting systems so complicated that no flesh and blood mortals can use them intelligently and these systems soon crash down around the designer's ears. They never seem to recognize that if people don't understand systems, they won't use them intelligently.

Many of you know how I have been on the warpath against sophistication. How strongly I feel that this is one of the biggest single reasons for systems failure in most companies. *Sophistication as an end in itself is an immature preoccupation.* So often the man who develops a sophisticated technique doesn't really understand the problem. To express this, I have formulated "Wight's 7th Law: *WHENEVER PEOPLE DO NOT UNDERSTAND FUNDAMENTAL RELATIONSHIPS, THEIR SOLUTIONS TO BASIC PROBLEMS WILL BE OVER-SOPHISTICATED.*"

Certainly finite loading falls into that category!

Finite loading violates another principle that is fundamental in designing systems: *SYSTEMS ARE TO SUPPORT PEOPLE, NOT TO SUPPLANT THEM.*

Finite loading attempts to build too much logic into the computer system. Most of it is trivial logic that doesn't really matter in the real world. Thus, the natural result is for people to throw up their hands and either obey it blindly or ignore it completely. People can understand the *intent* of systems; if the systems are "transparent," they can use them quite intelligently. The systems designer who feels that he is doing something smart by sophisticating the system has a lot to learn—the hard way! This is not to say that Capacity Requirements Planning and Input/Output Control give us precise control over a factory. It's very questionable that we ever will have precise scheduling and loading in the real world of factories. The objective is to come up with a system that's better than what we've got today. Many people tend to take the attitude that until they can solve all of the problems, they aren't very interested in solving any of them. It's well to remember:

BEST IS THE ENEMY OF BETTER.

We suspect that finite loading will be around for a long time. Many people will try to do it just to prove that it can be done. There's no question that it can be done, the question is whether it's a worthwhile, practical technique. Everest is there—must we, therefore, climb Everest? It certainly is not a responsible business attitude to want to try to do things just for the sake of doing them when they have no practical value and there are better ways, simpler ways, of doing the same thing.

Let's review then, the apparent problems with the three techniques we've talked about:

1. **Infinite: Capacity Is Not Infinite.**
   Of course, it isn't, but the purpose of Infinite Loading—or better, Capacity Requirements Planning—is to determine what capacity is really needed.

2. **Finite: Extending Deliveries.**
   That's right. Loading to finite capacity will extend deliveries. As a result, the Master Schedule will have to be changed. But we don't need to go through all the gyrations of the sophisticated finite loading computation to determine that.

3. **Input/Output Control: Difficult to Control Input.**
   Controlling input is fine. But *controlling output* is the real important thing. Undoubtedly, too much emphasis was put on the subject of controlling input in some of the things that have been written on Input/Output Control. Perhaps a better name for it would have been Output/Input Control since *it is the only practical tool that we have seen for controlling capacity.* Planning what the input level should be and monitoring the total number of hours going into the downstream work center can give us valuable information. But the prime function of Input/Output Control is *capacity control.* It serves a purpose that no standard

production control technique really addressed.

Let's evaluate, then, the opinions we've arrived at about scheduling and loading techniques:

1. Infinite: Function Is "Capacity Requirements Planning."

The technique we used to call Infinite Loading should be called Capacity Requirements Planning and it should pick up the *planned orders* out of Material Requirements Planning to extend the planning horizon rather than just try to measure backlog. Obviously, no plant can be loaded to infinite capacity. This is a planning technique, not a loading technique.

2. Finite:
   A. WORKS FOR ONE WORK CENTER.
   B. MISGUIDED SOPHISTICATION IN A MACHINE SHOP.
   C. LOAD LEVELED BY MASTER SCHEDULE.

There's no question but that one starting work center—or, as I've called them before, "gateway work centers" (indicating the first *significant* work center in the sequence) can be finite loaded. Work can't be precisely controlled going into all the subsequent work centers. There are too many other things that affect the flow of work into downstream work centers. A detailed finite load can be planned on paper. It certainly isn't going to work out that way in a factory.

Finite loading will tell us that certain items aren't going to be finished on time. The result: The Master Schedule must be changed. Actually, if the Capacity Requirements Plan is used, it can show us where capacity requirements exceed available capacity and where the Master Schedule needs to be changed without going through all the details and sophisticated calculation of finite loading. Remember that the load eventually will have to be leveled by changing the Master Schedule.

3. Input/Output: Function Is Capacity Control.

Input/Output Control is an excellent technique. People have used it and had very good results. The fact that it focuses attention on backlog and, consequently, lead time, is one of its greatest attributes. But, in essence, it's a capacity control device. It's a way to monitor the capacity plan to see if the production rates required to meet the Master Schedule are actually being attained.

We've spent a good deal of time in the past year gathering information, visiting companies, learning more about Finite Loading. We went into this with an open mind. Certainly the last thing we want to do is tell people that a technique isn't practical and later have it proved to be practical. We hate to take a negative stand on anything. It's much easier to just ignore it and make believe it doesn't exist, but we felt a responsibility. A lot of people have asked us about Finite Loading. A lot of people have asked us to take a stand to help them to understand it better. We have done our homework, in our opinion, and we have taken our stand. We don't believe that Finite Loading is a valid technique for scheduling and loading a machine shop. Certainly this doesn't say that any company that wishes to support pure research shouldn't pursue Finite Loading. For companies that cannot indulge in this luxury, the mirage of Finite Loading should be avoided.

George W. Plossl

To summarize, we've been discussing Input/Output Control, Infinite and Finite Loading. We have concluded that Input/Output might more accurately be called Output/Input Control and that Infinite Loading is really Capacity Requirements Planning. We seriously question that finite loading is a valid technique. The best that can be said for it is that it may be a fine-tuning device for very special applications.

We have worked hard to dispel some of the fog surrounding this important area of production management. Production and inventory control is obviously no longer a collection of loosely related techniques. There are underlying principles and sound techniques for applying these principles. It is now possible to see how a plant can be kept on schedule with a priority planning system that works. Capacity Requirements Planning, control of output and a dynamic priority control system to respond to real world changes.

Keeping on schedule requires three basic actions:

1. Load leveling via the Master Schedule. You must smooth out the peaks and valleys as much as possible and scheduling only what you're capable of producing.
2. Some jobs must be started early. You must reach ahead either through the Master Schedule or by individual starting operations and release some jobs *before* the planning system says it is necessary. The plant must be fed at a level rate with a balanced mix of work.
3. You need a two-way priority system which recognizes jobs needed later as well as those needed earlier. Tom Putnam of Marken Corporation at our Sunapee conference stated this very clearly. He said, "You must push out the orders you don't need."

Jim Burlingame of Twin Disc in his article, "Finite Capacity:" in the 2nd Quarter, 1970 issue of the APICS Journal, *Production and Inventory Management*, stated the basic fact as well as it can be said, "The answer to a capacity problem is not to retard the job but to find a way to do it." The vital need is for adequate capacity, not sophisticated computer finite loading and scheduling programs.

RESOURCE REQUIREMENTS PLANNING AND CAPACITY REQUIREMENTS PLANNING -- THE CASE FOR EACH AND BOTH

F. John Sari
Richard C. Ling, Inc.

Introduction

The need for effective computer-supported capacity planning and control tools has existed since the earliest implementations of Material Requirements Planning (mrp*). In fact, one of the basic tools now in use - Capacity Requirements Planning (CRP) - has been in use (unfortunately, in very few firms) just as long as mrp.

> *Mrp or mrp will be used throughout to distinguish Material Requirements Planning (mrp) from Manufacturing Resource Planning (MRP).

There has been a natural evolution of these capacity tools which roughly parallels our 1970's progress in basic top-down manufacturing planning. Using the 1980 APICS Dictionary definitions, this top-down hierarchy of capacity oriented tools proceeds as follows:

LONG-RANGE RESOURCE PLANNING-A planning activity for long term capacity decisions, based on the production plan and perhaps on even more gross data (e.g., sales per year) beyond the time horizon for the production plan. This activity is to plan long term capacity needs out to the time period necessary to acquire gross capacity additions such as a major factory expansion.

RESOURCE REQUIREMENTS PLANNING-The process of converting the production plan and/or the master production schedule into the impact on key resources, such as man hours, machine hours, storage, standard cost dollars, shipping dollars, inventory levels, etc. Product load profiles or bills of resources could be used to accomplish this. The purpose of this is to evaluate the plan prior to attempting to implement it. Sometimes referred to as a rough-cut check on capacity. Capacity requirements planning is a detailed review of capacity requirements. Syn: rough-cut capacity planning, rough-cut resource planning. (cf. closed-loop MRP).

CAPACITY REQUIREMENTS PLANNING (CRP)-The function of establishing, measuring, and adjusting limits or levels of capacity that are consistent with a production plan. The term capacity requirements planning in this context is the process of determining how much labor and machine resources are required to accomplish the tasks of production. Open shop orders, and planned orders in the MRP system, are input to CRP which "translates" these orders into hours of work by work center by time period. (cf. resource requirements planning, infinite loading, closed-loop MRP).

INPUT/OUTPUT CONTROL-A technique for capacity control where actual output from a work center is compared with the planned output developed by CRP. The input is also monitored to see if it corresponds with plans so that work centers will not be expected to generate output when jobs are not available to work on. (cf. capacity control, closed-loop MRP).

RRP is the more recently formalized capacity planning tool. The need for RRP came, and good RRP mechanics came into use, in the late 70's as the APICS community and P & I/C professionals formalized the front-end processed to mrp - Production Planning and the MPS. In terms of acceptance and use in practice, our experience shows the use of RRP to be growing faster than CRP.

We frequently see confusion on the uses of RRP and CRP because a certain amount of overlap exists in practice. This article will discuss environments in which RRP and CRP work well, factors influencing your choice(s), and their respective strengths and weaknesses.

RRP is a gross, pre-mrp analysis. It is a means to evaluate a proposed Production Plan and/or a MPS prior to plan acceptance. RRP is accomplished by extending (exploding) load profiles or bills of labor by these plans. The load profiles typically define only critical capacities required. This minimizes computational requirements yet is effective because overall factory output is usually dictated by the performance of a very few work centers or critical resourses.

Figure 1 is a summary comparison of RRP vs. CRP.

RRP vs. CRP

	RESOURCE RQMTS. PLANNING	CAPACITY RQMTS. PLANNING
WHAT?	PROJECT GROSS CAPACITY RQMTS FOR CRITICAL CAPACITIES OR KEY RESOURCES	PROJECT NET CAPACITY RQMTS FOR EACH WORK CENTER
HOW?	EXPLODE PROD. PLAN OR MPS THROUGH LOAD PROFILES	EXPLODE MRP PLANNED ORDER RECEIPTS THROUGH DETAILED ROUTINGS; COMBINE WITH CURRENT WIP STATUS FROM SHOP FLOOR CONTROL
WHEN?	AS REQUIRED FOR SIMULATION	ANNUAL & QTRLY. BUDGET DEVELOPMENT; WEEKLY
WHY?	1) PRE-MRP EVALUATION OF PRODUCTION PLAN &/OR MPS 2) INTERMEDIATE TO LONG-RANGE PLANNING	1) POST-MRP DETAILED ANALYSES; SHORT TERM VIEWS 2) PERIODIC CHECK OF ALL WORK CENTERS
PRECISION?	AGGREGATE OR GROSS - KEY RESOURCES ONLY	DETAILED - CONSIDERS ON-HAND, LOT SIZING, WIP COMPLETIONS. VOLUMINOUS DATA.
COST?	MUCH LESS THAN CRP	USUALLY EXCEEDS MRP
PLANNING HORIZON?	NO PRACTICAL LIMIT	MRP HORIZON LESS LEAD TIME OFFSETTING
IMPLEMENTATION TIME?	SHORT	REQUIRES MPS, MRP, AND WIP STATUS OF SFC
WHO USES?	VIRTUALLY ALL MANUFACTURERS MANY MANUALLY	10% OF MANUFACTURERS

Figure 1

RRP is a _gross_ hours analysis for two basic reasons:

1. In constructing load profiles, all hours or capacities required per Production Plan or MPS unit are included.

2. Since RRP is a pre-mrp analysis, its load projections do not reflect on-hand component balances or completed work-in-process.

CRP, on the other hand, is a net, post-mrp analysis. Essentially, it takes the plans projected by MPS and mrp at all levels, extends and back-schedules them through the standard routings and accumulates this _planned_ load for each active work center. The current _actual_ or scheduled load from the WIP status information of Shop Floor Control is then included. These two sets of information are consolidated into the total projected load by work-center.

CRP is a _net_ hours analysis since mrp does net available on-hand and on-order inventory and CRP includes only the remaining portion of work-in-process. For example, if only the last operation is required to complete a given shop order, that is all CRP includes.

This understanding of the mechanics of RRP and CRP helps to explain their respective strengths and weaknesses.

RRP Strengths

1. Since Material Requirements Planning assumes capacity is available and CRP is a post-mrp analysis, RRP is the only available tool which permits advance testing of the Production Plan and the MPS. This reasonability of gross hours leads to a certain level of assurance that the rest of the down-stream planning process makes sense.

2. Since RRP utilizes load profiles which identify only a few key resources, it doesn't require massive supporting data. Many firms effectively rough-cut plan manually. Others implement simple, computer-aided solutions which don't require heavy integration or interface with existing systems.

3. The computational ease of RRP makes it much simpler to quickly evaluate a wide variety of "what if" situations.

4. RRP's planning horizon is unlimited.

RRP Weaknesses

1. RRP cannot be used to evaluate the short-term. As a gross analysis insensitive to both available inventories and WIP, its close-in projections will always overstate the load.

2. RRP profiles assume standard lot sizing will always be used in the factory. On balance that's correct, but day-by-day practices will vary.

3. Because RRP is somewhat imprecise, it can lack credibility.

CRP Strengths

1. CRP is a valid short-term capacity planning tool. Since CRP does factor in on-hand, on-order and WIP inventories, its short-term loads can accurately depict current factory status. Thus, it can identify the need for overtime, alternate routings, etc., in the weeks just ahead.

2. CRP projects loads on all active work centers. Periodically, it must be used to insure that today's minor work center doesn't become tomorrow's bottleneck.

3. CRP can be useful in developing RRP load profiles. The mrp/CRP process, assuming no on-hand and on-order inventory, can be used to project gross hours required by work center. This data can then be summarized and used to update the critical resource and load profile data of RRP.

CRP Weaknesses

1. CRP is expensive. It probably consumes more computer capacity than any other single step within MRP. In order to calculate projected hours, it must extend the complete planned order projection for each active mrp component through every routing step.

2. CRP outputs are voluminous. It's normal outputs are hard to use as effective management tools unless good exception oriented analyses have been incorporated.

3. CRP requires current, accurate standard routings and work center standards. A large, accurate data base must exist in order for CRP to work.

4. CRP's 5-decimal precision appears so precise that it can also lack credibility, particularly in the intermediate-to-long term. It suffers from the same weakness as a statistical forecast -- the farther out one goes, the less comfortable one gets.

5. CRP's planning horizon is limited to mrp's planning horizon less cumulative lead time offset.

As one reviews these respective strengths and weaknesses of RRP and CRP, it's interesting to note how one is strong where the other is weak. The two tools very much complement each other in many important respects.

Factors Favoring RRP or CRP

Certain characteristics of the manufacturing environment or product tend to favor one tool or the other. Some considerations:

1. *Type of manufacturer and facility*.

Flow-like manufacturers frequently rely exclusively on RRP. Examples would include integrated manufacturing processes, process industries, or many assembly line situations. Because there is a defined flow, that which starts will flow to the finish. Very little beyond loading to process capacity is needed. RRP profiles accomodate this very well.

Discrete manufacturers, particularly those with common use equipment and facilities, usually don't rely exclusively on RRP. The actual lead time for a manufactured item can vary substantially because of queuing and contention. The load profiles of RRP do assume a manufacturing flow and do not depict well the effects of this contention for common work centers, particularly for lower-level component items. Even though CRP, particularly infinite loading CRP, suffers from the same problem, it does provide additional visibility into the situation.

2. *Levels of manufacture in the product*.

The shallower the bill of material for the product, the less one is exposed to the lead time and standard lot sizing assumptions built into RRP profiles.

3. *Lower-level independent demand*.

Manufacturers with significant spare parts businesses, direct sales of lower-level items, interplant component supply situations, etc., may utilize CRP to reflect this lower level demand. Typically, these items are forecast individually and the forecast becomes an input to mrp. Mrp then projects a replenishment plan for the item which covers these independent requirements as well as dependent requirements calculated from upper-level build plans. CRP load projections thus include capacities required to cover both requirement streams.

Unless these segments of the business are substantial, many firms do not routinely include such items in their Production Plan and MPS. If they are not included, RRP load projections cannot reflect the required capacities. When there is significant lower-level demand, companies do identify these segments of their business for Production Planning and RRP purposes. This is especially true with service parts due to the high margins they generate.

4. *Part Number Precision*

The following excerpt from REPORT, Richard C. Ling, Inc., September, 1980, discussed this issue.

"Recently, we encountered Firm A which manufactured long-lived, major capital equipment. Depending on the unit, the equipment was either engineered-to-order with many custom components or primarily assembled-to-order from standard components. Over the years, Firm A had also developed a very significant spare or service parts business. Significant amounts of productive capacity (30-50%) were used to manufacture service parts. The company had been utilizing MRP and CRP for years. Unfortunately CRP did a decent job of projecting only about 60% of the capacities required!"

"CRP did a good job for standard master scheduled options (and their components) which were forecast and planned. It also did a good job for volume service parts which were forecast, planned, and stocked. CRP did no job at all, however, for the camshaft which didn't get engineered until 3 months into a 4 month specification process. CRP also blew it on the flywheel just ordered for service which wasn't too surprising since the item was last made 18 years ago! CRP requires the following to work:

1. A replenishment plan by part number, quantity and date due created by mrp because of MPS planning, service forecast, etc.

2. A current standard routing.

3. Current work center standards."

"If you, like Firm A, cannot accurately forecast and plan for most or all of your business by part number, quantity and date, don't bet all your marbles on CRP. Firm A knew that the new equipment ordered would require a camshaft and could effectively profile the capacity required in RRP. They could not through CRP, however, plan enough in advance for the specific capacity required until engineering specs were complete and they had a part number, routing and associated work center data. Firm A was reasonably sure that 100 fly wheels would be ordered as spare parts per year and could profile that general capacity in RRP also. There was absolutely no way Firm A could forecast specific service part requirements by part number for CRP with any acceptable degree of accuracy."

"CRP was effective for Firm A only out through the firm order horizon. Beyond that, RRP was the preferred tool since it could comprehend more of that 40% of capacity which could not be forecast and planned by specific part number."

Other RRP Considerations

1. *Computerization Requirements*

Data volume and planning frequency will ultimately dictate the amount of computer support required for RRP. If there are a lot of MPS items to profile, many critical capacities or frequent requirements to evaluate "what if" situations computer help becomes a must.

Because of the relatively small amount of data required for RRP, however, this planning can frequently be accomplished without large-scale computer support. Personal computers and time-sharing implementations have been successful for several firms.

The amount of data manipulation is frequently reduced by development of typical product or average product load profiles. This simplification is very helpful when the need is to evaluate loads at the Production Plan family level. These families usually are composed of many specific, but similar, MPS items. When used, the technique does require periodic reviews of the mix of items used to construct the average or typical profile.

2. RRP Profile Capabilities

The degree of precision of RRP is a frequent issue, part of which will dictate the sophistication required in the load profile itself. For example, manufacturers with long manufacturing lead times usually demand the ability to time-phase RRP loads with some form of lead time offset facility. Forms of lead time offsets can also be used to project simultaneous loads on different critical capacities. This may be important to discrete manufacturers with common use facilities.

Often, it is necessary to project loads both forward and backward in time. For example, companies which MPS at levels below the end item may choose to project forward loads for final assembly.

Simpler RRP implementations don't utilize time-phased loads. Gross hours are merely projected in the Production Plan or MPS period. This is most valid when lead times are short. It may also be a legitimate assumption because loads will tend to wash over time in a reasonably balanced factory.

3. Degree of RRP Precision

The following excerpt from REPORT, September, 1980, further expands the degree of precision issue mentioned above:

"Frequently, it is necessary to determine both the planning level at which you must perform RRP as well as the degree of precision you require. In many firms, profiles by Production Planning families get it done. If the products within the family are similar and require like processes, profile and evaluate RRP at family levels. What you really want to evaluate is the impact of the overall rates of production by family on critical resources. If, however, specific item mix within the family can hurt you, consider profiling a level below the product family for MPS items."

"Recently we've seen interesting RRP approaches in-use by manufacturers who master schedule product at levels below the salable end item. This is, of course, common amongst firms who produce a wide variety of end item configurations from a smaller number of options, features, attachments, etc."

"For RRP analytical purposes, some master scheduled items can be assumed to flow through manufacturing on a fairly steady basis. This might be true, for instance, for common parts sets on a volume product. Other MPS items, like stocked manufactured or purchased subassemblies and components will be built or procured periodically as stock lots and not on a steady basis. Because of this difference in replenishment _timing_ (steady versus sporadic), you might have to profile these items separately and develop RRP projections from the MPS."

"Similarly, load profiles must be prepared with some lot size assumption in order to reflect setup properly. One lot size assumption may be necessary for steady, repetitive MPS options. Another, very different assumption would be appropriate for a truly "sold-to-order" option which is manufactured one-for-one upon receipt of customer order."

"Under such circumstances, we now see firms 'disentangling' or modularizing load profiles in order to better reflect timing of loads and/or varying lot size practices."

"The level of profile precision required is, again, a function of your product and processes. More often than not, it's a good idea to provide for profile capabilities at both Production Plan and MPS levels. A flexible RRP facility can easily provide both."

4. Consider RRP Early in an MRP Implementation

It is difficult to demonstrate tangible results during the early stages of an mrp implementation. There usually are long duration efforts to educate, improve records accuracy, audit bills of material, etc. Because CRP can't come on stream before MPS/mrp, this capacity planning tool is a long way off.

RRP, however, because it's simpler forms do not require substantial computer development or heavy interfaces, can be addressed early. In conjunction with Production Planning, RRP can be used to demonstrate some very substantial, early improvements.

5. RRP and Lower-Level Demand

As mentioned above, it may be absolutely required to include service parts and other lower-level demands in RRP planning. Techniques such as grouping like parts into families associated with typical load profiles can be used. This reduces the data volume and still provides a gross measure of capacities required.

An alternative approach is to relate critical capacities required to dollar volumes of these lower-level demands. Although subject to mix variation, this does provide a gross capacity allocation which must be considered.

6. RRP and Capacity Booking

RRP is frequently used by make and assemble-to-order firms as an aid when customer promising. If the MPS/mrp process has provided the materials required, RRP can be used to determine the availability of capacity required to convert the product to shippable form.

One client company of ours fabricates primary metals. Their MPS/mrp process provides stocks of an intermediate product. When customers order finished material, the task is to determine availability of the needed finishing capacities. This normal 6-8 week finishing process will vary with backlog. By converting incoming orders to hours required in critical capacities, an up-to-date hours 'available-to-promise' is maintained.

RRP and CRP Assist Each Other

RRP profiles have proven to be of real use to many confirmed CRP users, particularly in heavy job shop environments. With many levels in the bill of material and common use machinery, it is cumbersome to analyze an under/over load and know which MPS items could be changed to resolve it. RRP profiles automatically provide this needed visibility.

As noted previously, a periodic, non-netted mrp/CRP is an excellent tool for two purposes:

1. to monitor and maintain RRP profile and critical resource data
2. to monitor all work centers, not just critical ones.

Even though the CRP process is used, gross hours are generated very much like the normal RRP process.

Conclusion

All manufacturers, regardless of product or process, require an appropriate RRP mechanism. Many, but not all, also require more detailed CRP capabilities. Those with both RRP and CRP in their bag of tools are well equipped to plan capacity.

ABOUT THE AUTHOR

F. John Sari is Executive Vice-President of Richard C. Ling, Inc.

Formerly, John was Vice-President, Consulting Services for Arista Manufacturing Systems, A Xerox Company, and was responsible for the consulting and project activities of the firm. In this capacity, he also conducted many training courses for the public as well as Arista clients.

John is a Mathematics graduate of Wayne State University in Detroit. Upon graduation, he joined General Electric Co. and participated in GE's three-year rotational Manufacturing Management Training Program. Mr. Sari accepted a GE position as Supervisor-Production and Inventory Control upon completion of the MMP program.

John is an active speaker at APICS seminars and events. He holds a Fellow certification in inventory management. He is a Past-President of the Piedmont Triad Chapter of APICS.

WHY THE PROCESS INDUSTRIES ARE DIFFERENT

Sam G. Taylor
University of Wyoming   *Laramie, WY*

Samuel M. Seward
University of Wyoming   *Cheyenne, WY*

Steven F. Bolander
Colorado State University   *Fort Collins, CO*

Much of the literature of production and inventory management has been devoted to the fabrication and assembly industries. In the past few years APICS has sponsored seminars, workshops, and research projects for the process industries. This has resulted in the development of a planning framework for process industries [3] and the exchange of many ideas. There seems to be a growing consensus within some process industry groups that they are fundamentally different from fabrication and assembly industries. In this article, we will compare the marketing, manufacturing, and financial environments of process industry groups with fabrication and assembly industry groups. These comparisons will then be used to show why many process industry groups require a production and inventory management system with a much different emphasis than the closed loop MRP systems used in fabrication and assembly industries.

MARKETING ENVIRONMENT

One of the most important factors in developing a business strategy is differentiating a firm's products and services from its competitors'. The amount of product differentiation can be viewed as a continuum from custom products at one end of the spectrum to commodity products at the other end. Examples of commodity products are soda ash, methyl alcohol, cement, beef, lumber and steel. Industry groups and individual companies may have products at several different points along the product differentiation spectrum.

The process industries tend to have less product differentiation than fabrication and assembly industries. Accordingly, the process industries tend to be associated with products at the commodity end of the product differentiation spectrum and products from fabrication and assembly industries are found nearer the custom product end of the spectrum. However, it should be recognized that some fabricated products such as containers and fasteners tend toward the commodity end of the spectrum while some process industry products, such as drugs and specialty chemicals, tend toward custom products. In order to compare the marketing environments of process industries with that of fabrication and assembly industries, we will contrast characteristics of commodity products and markets with custom products and markets.

Table 1 summarizes differences in custom and commodity products and markets. Commodity marketing emphasizes product availability and price while product features are emphasized in marketing custom products. Commodities are often sold from stock while custom products are made to order. Commodity products generally have a limited number of products within a product family (product grades), while custom product families may have an unlimited number of products. Commodity products have few, if any, changes in product specifications while custom products are designed to order. A commodity is generally sold in large volumes to several customers. On the other hand a custom product is committed to a particular customer for a particular use. Commodities frequently have a relatively low value-to-weight ratio which results in transportation costs contributing a higher portion of the cost of goods sold than for custom products.

TABLE 1
Comparison of Product and Market Environments

CUSTOM PRODUCTS	COMMODITY PRODUCTS
• Marketing Emphasis on Product Features	• Marketing Emphasis on Product Availability and Price
• Many Products	• Few Products
• Many Product Design Changes	• Few Product Design Changes
• Consumer Demand	• Derived Demand
• Low Sales Volume	• High Sales Volume
• High Unit Volume	• Low Unit Value
• Relatively Low Transportation Costs	• Relatively High Transportation Costs
• Discrete Units	• Nondiscrete Units

Custom products are produced and sold in discrete units. Serial numbers or lot numbers are assigned to each unit. In contrast, commodity products are produced in nondiscrete units and production, sales and inventory records are in pounds, gallons, tons, barrels or similar units of measure.

MANUFACTURING ENVIRONMENT

Manufacturing facilities can be classified along a spectrum with job shops at one end of the spectrum and flow shops at the other end. A job shop is a manufacturing facility in which materials flow through the shop with routings dependent on each job. A flow shop is a manufacturing facility in which materials flow through the plant with a fixed routing. Most manufacturing facilities fall somewhere in between a pure job shop (random routings where jobs could start and finish in any work center) and a pure flow shop.

Process industries tend more toward the flow shop end of the spectrum than fabrication and assembly industries. In order to compare the manufacturing environment of process industries with fabrication and assembly industries, we will first contrast characteristics of flow shops and job shops and then examine some additional characteristics of process industries.

Comparison of Job Shops and Flow Shops

Table 2 summarizes differences in job shop and flow shop manufacturing environments. By definition, a flow shop has fixed routings and can use fixed path material handling equipment, such as conveyors and pipes. In contrast, a job shop has variable material routings and must use variable path material handling equipment, such as fork lift trucks and tote bins.

Job shops and flow shops have different plant layouts. The layout of a job shop is by manufacturing process. For example, a job shop may have one work center where all grinding is done and another work center for all welding. If a job required grinding, welding, and then grinding, it would first go to the grinding work station, then to welding, and finally back to grinding. However, the layout of a flow shop is determined by the product. If a product requires grinding, welding, and then grinding, a production line would be designed with two grinding work stations, separated by a welding work station. Accordingly, the production line is laid out according to the processing requirements of the product it is designed to produce.

Job shops and flow shops differ significantly in their capabilities. A job shop has flexible, general purpose equipment which can be used to produce a wide variety of products. In contrast, flow shops have specialized equipment which can be used to produce a group of closely related products.

Flow shops generally have longer lead times for increasing capacity than job shops. In order to efficiently use their relatively high capital investment in facilities, flow shops tend to operate more shifts per day and more days per week than job shops. Thus flow shops have less flexibility to increase capacity by adding shifts or working overtime.

TABLE 2
Comparison of Manufacturing Environments

JOB SHOP	FLOW SHOP
• Variable Routings	• Fixed Routings
• Variable Path Material Handling Equipment	• Fixed Path Material Handling Equipment
• Process Layout	• Product Layout
• Flexible Equipment	• Specialized Equipment
• Low Volume	• High Volume
• Shorter Lead Time to Increase Capacity	• Longer Lead Time to Increase Capacity
• Capacity Is Difficult to Define	• Capacity Is Well Defined
• Labor Intensive	• Capital Intensive
• Strikes Shut Down Plant	• Strikes Have Lower Impact
• Skilled Craftsmen Who Build the Product	• Highly Specialized, Trained Operators Who Monitor and Control Process Equipment
• Significant Work In Process Inventories	• Low Work In Process Inventories
• Often Warehouse Work In Process	• No Warehousing of Work In Process
• Jobs Not Overlapped Between Work Centers	• Job Overlapping
• Equipment Failure Shuts Down a Machine	• Equipment Failure Shuts Down the Plant
• Late Receipt of a Purchased Part Delays a Customer Order	• Raw Material Shortage for a Basic Raw Material Shuts Down the Plant

Since flow shops are production lines designed for a group of closely related products, the line capacity can be determined by examining the bottleneck process. In contrast, a job shop is designed to produce a wide variety of products. In a job shop, the load created by different products in each work center often varies widely. The capacity of each work center can be specified in man hours and machine hours; however, the aggregate capacity of the plant depends on the particular mix of products being manufactured at a point in time. Since the product mix changes frequently in a job shop, the aggregate capacity is difficult to define.

The work force requirements are significantly different for job shops and flow shops. Job shops are generally labor intensive and use skilled craftsmen to build the product. A strike in a job shop will shut down the plant. Some flow shops, such as assembly lines, are also labor intensive and will also be shut down by strikes. However, in many other flow shops, such as oil refineries, the number of operators is low enough so that management personnel can run the plant during a strike.

Job shops and flow shops differ in the relative amount of work in process inventory. Job shops require work in process to buffer variations in work center loads which are caused by variations in product mix. This permits better utilization of work center capacities. In contrast, processes and operations in a flow shop production line are balanced for the limited group of products which can be produced by the line. Thus, work in process is not required to help smooth work loads, although some work in process may be used in a flow shop to buffer sequential operations from short range variations in processing rates. In a flow shop, the amount of work in process inventory is relatively small compared to the throughputs; accordingly, storage facilities for work in process inventories are provided for in the process flow.

Another result of the low work in process inventories in flow shops is the need for reliable equipment. If a particular piece of equipment in a production line breaks down, the entire line must stop production after downstream work in process is consumed or upstream storage capacity is filled. Job shops have more work in process, variable routings, and more flexibility to increase capacity through extra shifts and overtime to speed recovery from an equipment failure. Accordingly, job shops are not as dependent on reliable equipment as flow shops.

The effect of late material is different in job shops and flow shops. In a job shop, the late receipt of a purchased part may delay a customer order and increase inventories of other parts used in the item being made unless these parts are rescheduled. In a flow shop, shortage of a basic raw material can shut down the entire plant.

Process Industry Manufacturing Environment

Several characteristics of the manufacturing environment of both job shops and flow shops within the process industries are summarized in Table 3. The process industries often obtain their raw materials from mining or agricultural industries. These raw materials have natural variations in quality. For example, crude oils from different oil fields have different sulfur contents and different proportions of naphthas, distillates, and fuel oils. Oil refinery designs, production plans, and operating schedules must account for this variability in crude oil qualities.

Variations in raw material quality often lead to variations in bills of material. For example, variations in the moisture content, acidity, color, viscosity or concentration of active ingredient in raw materials may cause variations in the ingredient proportions required to make finished product quality specifications.

TABLE 3
Process Industry Manufacturing Environment

- Variability in Raw Material Quality
- Variability in Bill of Material
- Product Yields May Vary Widely
- May Have Large Demands for Intermediate Products
- Coproduct Demands Must be Balanced
- Products or Raw Materials May Have a Shelf Life

Another factor which causes variations in bills of materials is the price of alternate ingredients. For example, a pet food may have specifications for the minimum amount of proteins, carbohydrates, and fats per pound of pet food; however, the proportions of various ingredients may be varied depending on their current price and availability.

An additional source of variability in a process industry manufacturing environment is product yield. A number of process industries have processes which are difficult to control. Accordingly, when a product is scheduled and run, it may not be produced. For example, in the production of specialty plastic resins or synthetic rubbers, the plant may schedule a target grade. However, in attempting to make this target grade, a highly variable amount of lower quality fallout grades may also be produced.

A characteristic of some process industry manufacturing environments is the large demand for intermediate products. For example, a manufacturer of primary metals may sell some ingots and process other ingots into sheet and plate, bar stock, or wire.

Production of coproducts complicates inventory management for some process industries. In these industries coproducts are produced in proportions determined by chemical and natural characteristics. When producing caustic soda and chlorine by electrolysis of a salt brine, the proportions of caustic soda and chlorine produced are fixed by chemical relationships and cannot be varied by changes in operating conditions or ingredients. Imbalances in demand for coproducts can limit production of one product or create large inventories of the other.

Some process industry groups, such as food and pharmaceuticals, produce products or use raw materials with shelf lives. For example, canneries must process fruits and vegetables while they are fresh, and pharmaceuticals must be used before their expiration date.

COORDINATING MARKETING AND MANUFACTURING STRATEGIES

A firm's manufacturing facilities need to be consistent with its marketing environment. Figure 1 shows a product-process matrix. Horizontal positions on the matrix represent the degree of product differentiation discussed in the above section on marketing environment. Vertical positions on the matrix represent the material flow spectrum from a job shop to a flow shop discussed in the above comparison of job shops and flow shops. As shown in Figure 1, most industries tend to fall along the principal diagonal of the product-process matrix. Note that some fabrication and assembly industry groups, like containers and steel products, tend toward the commodity and flow shop part of the matrix, while some process industry groups, such as drugs and specialty chemicals, are in the center of the matrix. An industry group's position on the product-process matrix is an important factor in the design of a production and inventory management system.

An individual firm's position on the product-process matrix relative to the position of its competitors can be an important factor in a firm's corporate strategy [1], [2]. A number of firms in the central portion of the matrix are attempting to improve their manufacturing efficiency by moving downward toward the flow shop end of the process spectrum.

FIGURE 1
Product - Process Matrix

PRODUCT

	CUSTOM	LOW VOLUME DIFFERENTIATED	HIGH VOLUME DIFFERENTIATED	COMMODITY
JOB SHOP		AEROSPACE		
		INDUSTRIAL MACHINERY APPAREL		
		MACHINE TOOLS		
			DRUGS	
			SPECIALITY CHEMICALS	
			ELECTRICAL & ELECTRONICS	
			AUTOMOBILE TIRE & RUBBER STEEL PRODUCTS	
			MAJOR CHEMICALS	
			PAPER CONTAINERS BREWERS	
				OIL STEEL FOREST PRODUCTS
FLOW SHOP				

PROCESS

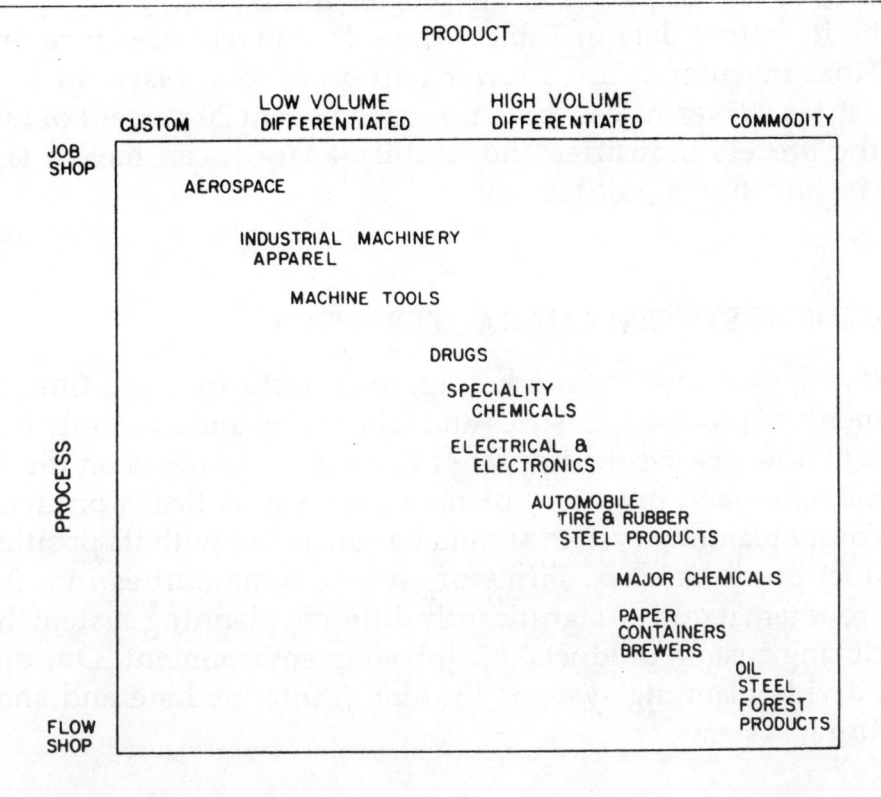

The recent emphasis on group technology illustrates this movement. On the other hand, when a firm moves toward a flow shop, it may lose some of its flexibility to produce many products, or it may need to enforce scheduling sequences which could reduce its ability to respond to rush orders.

FINANCIAL ENVIRONMENT

An industry group's or a firm's financial structure is closely related to its marketing and manufacturing environment. Table 4 gives financial data for process industry groups and for fabrication and assembly industry groups. The data show significant differences between process industries and fabrication and assembly industries, as well as significant differences among industry groups within the process industries or within fabrication and assembly industries.

In general, process industries are more capital intensive than fabrication and assembly industries. This is demonstrated in Table 4 which shows that the process industries have a ratio of 1.8 dollars of sales for every dollar of gross plant investment, compared to a ratio of 3.1 for fabrication and assembly industries.

Process industries are less labor intensive than fabrication and assembly industries. Table 4 shows that the process industries have $95,000/yr. of sales for each employee while fabrication and assembly industries have $47,000/yr. of sales per employee. Thus two employees are required by the fabrication and assembly industries to generate the same sales revenue as one employee in the process industries.

The inventory data in Table 4 show that inventories turn over faster and that inventories are a lower portion of total assets in the process industries. Nevertheless, inventories represent 20 percent of total assets for the process industries and, if mismanaged, can have a significant impact on a firm's profitability.

PLANNING SYSTEM CHARACTERISTICS

Having examined the marketing, manufacturing, and financial environments of process industries and fabrication and assembly industries, we will now discuss the impact of these environments on the design of a production and inventory planning system. A firm's production and inventory planning system should be consistent with its position on the product-process matrix. Firms producing commodities in a flow shop environment require a significantly different planning system than firms producing custom products in a job shop environment. Our discussion will divide planning systems into long, intermediate and short range planning systems.

TABLE 4
Industry Financial Characteristics

Industry	Sales/ Gross Plant	Sales/ Employee (1000$)	Inventory Turns	Inventory/ Total Assets (%)
PROCESS				
Chemicals-Major	1.0	83	6.3	17
Steel-Major	1.0	75	8.3	14
Paper	1.1	76	9.1	13
Brewers	1.2	120	10.0	12
Forest Products	1.3	84	8.3	14
Oil-Integrated Intl	1.8	315	10.0	13
Tire & Rubber Goods	1.8	50	5.6	26
Textile Products	1.8	38	5.2	29
Chemicals-Specialty	2.8	80	6.7	22
Drugs-Medical & Hospital Supply	2.9	47	4.6	28
Soap	3.1	110	6.7	27
Average	1.8	95	7.3	20
FABRICATION & ASSEMBLY				
Containers	2.1	64	7.1	20
Home Furnishings	2.3	48	5.9	28
Machine Tools	2.3	48	3.5	37
Leisure Time Products	2.5	45	4.4	31
Electronics-Semicond & Comp	2.9	32	6.3	24
Automobile	3.0	48	5.6	29
Aerospace	3.3	52	5.9	27
Industrial Machinery	3.3	49	3.3	39
Elect. Household Appliances	3.4	51	4.4	33
Electric Equipment	3.4	47	4.6	33
Apparel	5.7	34	4.6	37
Average	3.1	47	5.1	31

SOURCE: *Financial Dynamics,* Standard and Poor's Compustat Services, Inc. 1979.

LONG RANGE PLANNING

The process industries develop extensive long range resource requirements plans. Because the process industries are more capital intensive than fabrication and assembly industries, capital budgeting decisions have a greater impact on financial performance in the process industries. Accordingly, more attention is given to facilities decisions in the process industries.

Two important long range decisions are plant capacity and plant location. In the process industries, plants are designed for a specified throughput. All equipment is sized for this design capacity. Since the plants generally run seven days a week and three shifts per day, it is impossible to significantly increase capacity with overtime or extra shifts. Thus, increases in manufacturing capacity require the design and construction of new facilities. Since highly specialized, automated equipment is required, lead times of three or more years are often required for significant capacity increases.

Plant location is another important long range planning area. Process industries often transport high volumes of materials which have low values relative to their weight. Thus, transportation costs will represent a higher portion of the cost of goods sold for these industries. In order to minimize transportation costs, firms may use multiple plant locations and break bulk operations through distribution centers. Since products of competing firms have little differentiation, price is a very important factor in marketing these products. A poor plant location can increase transportation costs to the point where a plant cannot compete.

Long range plans for materials, manpower, energy, and waste disposal are also important in the process industries. In order to assure a long range supply of key raw materials, process industries frequently arrange long range supply contracts. Many firms in the process industries require a highly specialized work force. Accordingly, long range manpower plans must be developed to hire and train these workers. Since process industries tend to be energy intensive, long range energy plans are also required. Many process industries have waste products which must be disposed of in a manner consistent with environmental laws. Plans must be developed and permits obtained for emission and disposal of waste substances.

Fabrication and assembly industries which produce custom products in a job shop environment tend to have less emphasis on long range resource planning and more emphasis on product design. In this portion of the product-process matrix, product features are a key factor in corporate strategies. A flexible manufacturing facility which can quickly produce new product designs is important for these firms. Although they must develop plans for equipment, manpower, materials, energy, and waste disposal; fabrication and assembly job shops tend to acquire new resources in less time than process industries. Thus, these firms have less emphasis on long range process planning and more emphasis on product planning.

INTERMEDIATE RANGE PLANNING

Intermediate range production plans are concerned with developing plans for the utilization of resources. Production plans generally cover time horizons between three and eighteen months. A company may have more than one production plan. For example, during the annual budgeting period, production plans by quarter may be developed. Subsequently, during each quarter, monthly production plans may be developed. Table 5 summarizes areas which are emphasized in process industry production plans.

TABLE 5
Areas Emphasized In Process Industry Production Plans

- Sourcing Decisions
- Sequencing Products Through Facilities
- Optimizing Product Blends
- Determining Target Safety Stocks
- Coordinating Production and Maintenance Plans
- Temporary Shutdown of Plant or Line to Reduce Inventory
- Exchange or Swapping Agreements
- Determining Material Requirements
- Developing Aggregate Production Plans

Sourcing decisions are concerned with assignment of customers to warehouses and assignment of warehouses to plants. Since the process industries tend to have more plants, more warehouses, and spend a higher percent of their sales dollar on transportation; sourcing decisions are generally more important in the process industries than in fabrication and assembly industries. Linear programming is frequently used in the process industries to help develop sourcing plans.

In many process industries, products are made on a regular cycle. The sequence of products is often dictated by product or process technology. For example, products may be sequenced from light to dark, high viscosity to low viscosity, or wide to narrow. Determining the target sequences and cycle lengths is an important production planning problem in the process industries.

Some process industries manufacture blended products, such as gasoline or cattle feed. These industries are concerned with developing a minimum cost blend of ingredients which meets product specifications. Linear programming is frequently used, particularly in the oil industry, to develop minimum cost blends.

Process industries have a tendency to produce products to stock and, as a result, have a large percentage of their inventory investment in finished goods inventory. One function of finished goods inventories is to buffer the plant from variations in product demand. This is accomplished with a safety stock of finished product. The use of statistical techniques to size safety stocks is an important part of process industry production plans.

In a process industry plant, periodic shutdowns are required to perform maintenance. Process industries tend to operate three shifts per day and seven days per week. Thus it is impossible to perform maintenance during an off-shift or on weekends. In addition, process industries have less work in process. Thus when one process unit shuts down, the preceding and succeeding processing units must shut down. Accordingly, when major maintenance is scheduled, the plant or line is not producing. This interruption in production must be accounted for in plant production plans.

When forecasted demand is less than plant capacity, production must be reduced or inventories will build. Two strategies for reducing production are: (1) throttle the plant back to a rate equal to demand, or (2) run the plant at full capacity and periodically shut down to reduce inventories. One major area of cost savings from using periodic shutdowns to control inventory is a reduction in certain energy costs. Since process industry plants tend to be more energy intensive, there is a greater use of the shutdown strategy in process industries than in fabrication and assembly industries.

Process industries tend to produce products at the commodity end of the product differentiation spectrum. When a firm produces an undifferentiated product, it can enter exchange or swapping agreements with competitors in order to reduce transportation costs. Exchange or swapping agreements are a common practice in the petroleum, commodity chemical, and primary metal industries. These agreements are an important factor in developing production plans for these industries.

Some process industries develop material plans for key raw materials directly from their production plans. The production plan sets the rate at which the plant will operate. Some key raw materials are required for every product grade produced. Therefore, after setting the aggregate production rate for the plant, a material plan can be developed for these key raw materials.

Process industry flow shops tend to develop aggregate production plans. It is generally easier to define aggregate capacity for a flow shop than for a job shop. Flow shops have line flow and the capacity of the bottleneck operation limits the capacity of the production line. In addition, flow shops are designed to produce a closely related group of products. Thus, it is easier to aggregate product demands for a flow shop than for a job shop. Accordingly, production plans for job shops tend to have more product and process detail than for flow shops.

Production plans for the labor intensive fabrication and assembly industries require greater coordination with manpower plans than in the process industries. Production plans for fabrication and assembly industries often adjust plant capacity by changes in the work force. This is accomplished by changing the amount of overtime or the number of shifts scheduled.

In reviewing the above differences in the production planning process, it is seen that process industry flow shops must place a greater emphasis on production plans than fabrication and assembly job shops. This is because the marketing and manufacturing environments both allow and require a greater emphasis on intermediate range planning.

SHORT RANGE PLANNING

Short range plans are concerned with developing operating schedules. These schedules should be consistent with the intermediate range production plans but should have more product, process and time detail. There is often more than one operating schedule. One schedule might cover a period of a month or more, while another schedule might only cover a week but have detailed schedules for each shift within the week.

Scheduling Methods

The major difference between process industries and fabrication and assembly industries is in the approach to master production scheduling. Fabrication and assembly industries are less capital intensive and more material intensive than the process industries, as shown previously in Table 4. In order to minimize investment in materials, the need date for each order is determined and then the need dates for components (intermediate products) and purchased parts (raw materials) are determined by backward scheduling from the finished product due date. Having determined a schedule of material requirements, the feasibility of the schedule is then checked against equipment and manpower capacities. This approach is a material-oriented master production scheduling method, because materials are scheduled first and then capacities checked. This is the approach used in the closed loop MRP system.

Process industries are concerned with achieving high equipment utilizations. In addition, process industries usually have a good estimate of the capacity of a production line or plant. Thus, process industries tend to first schedule capacity and then materials. This is called a capacity-oriented master production scheduling procedure. A capacity-oriented procedure schedules production runs of various products on each production line such that capacity is utilized at the rate specified in the production plan. Having determined the production schedule, raw material requirements are then determined.

In a scheduling system, both materials and capacity must be planned. The question to be answered is which to do first. To minimize material investment, a material-oriented procedure such as a closed loop MRP system should be used. To efficiently utilize equipment, a capacity-oriented technique should be used. For a job shop producing custom products, a material-oriented scheduling method is appropriate. For a flow shop producing commodity products, a capacity-oriented scheduling method is appropriate. However, as shown by the product-process matrix given in Figure 1, many process industry groups and fabrication and assembly industry groups are not at either of these extremes, but somewhere in between. Nevertheless, firms in these industries must choose either a material-oriented or a capacity-oriented scheduling method.

At the present time, a great deal has been written about material-oriented scheduling methods (closed loop MRP) and many software packages are available. However, there is a general lack of literature and software for capacity-oriented scheduling methods. One of the most promising areas for expanding the body of knowledge in production and inventory control is in the development of capacity-oriented scheduling techniques. Even more exciting and difficult is the possibility of a scheduling system which simultaneously schedules both capacity and materials.

Scheduling System Characteristics

Table 6 lists characteristics of process industry scheduling systems. The first of these is a greater use of capacity-oriented master production scheduling methods, which has been discussed.

Since the process industries have more plants and warehouses, they place a greater emphasis on distribution requirements planning and interplant transfer planning. In the process industries, the master production schedule tends to be driven more by production plans, short-range demand forecasts, and distribution requirements plans than by customer orders. Because the master production schedule in the process industries is often buffered from customer orders by a finished goods inventory, there tends to be less customer interference in the master production schedule in the process industries.

Lot sizes in some process industry groups may be dictated by facilities design or by manufacturing practices for insuring product quality. For example, a lot size may depend on the capacity of a batch reactor or storage tank. In other cases, such as in canning of meat products, manufacturing practices require a daily washout to maintain product quality.

TABLE 6
Process Industry Scheduling System Characteristics

- Greater Use of Capacity-Oriented Master Production Scheduling Methods
- More Emphasis on Distribution Requirements Planning and Inter-Plant Transfer Planning
- Closer Coupling of Master Production Schedule with Forecasts, Production Plans, and Distribution Requirements Plans
- Less Customer Interference with Master Production Schedule
- Lot Sizes May be Dictated by Facilities Design or by Manufacturing Practices for Insuring Product Quality
- Schedule Is the Authority to Produce
- Sequencing Is Generally Accomplished in the Production Plan or Master Production Schedule
- Schedules Generally Have Smaller Time Intervals

These washouts provide logical lot sizes. Nevertheless there are many other situations in the process industries where lot sizes are not constrained. In these plants, lot sizing techniques are an important tool in developing production plans and schedules.

Fewer items, well defined capacity, and fixed routings make scheduling generally easier in the process industries. In many firms the schedule is the authority to produce and manufacturing orders are not issued. Furthermore, since sequencing is generally accomplished in the production plan or the master production schedule, daily dispatch lists are not required. However, since there is no dispatch list, schedules often have time intervals of days, shifts, or hours.

SUMMARY

The product-process matrix shows why some process industry groups are similar to many fabrication and assembly industry groups and why many process industries are different than most fabrication and assembly industry groups.

Because of differences in the marketing, manufacturing and financial environments, the emphasis on production and inventory management techniques differs between industry groups. The process industries are more capital intensive and place a greater emphasis on long range facilities planning and intermediate range production plans. In addition, in order to achieve high utilizations of expensive equipment, capacity-oriented master scheduling procedures are required.

REFERENCES

1. Hayes, Robert H. and Steven C. Wheelwright. "Link Manufacturing Process and Product Life Cycles," *Harvard Business Review,* January-February, 1979.
2. Hayes, Robert H. and Steven C. Wheelwright. "The Dynamics of Process-Product Life Cycles," *Harvard Business Review,* March-April, 1979.
3. Taylor, S. G., S. M. Seward, S. F. Bolander, and R. C. Heard. "Process Industry Production and Inventory Planning Framework: A Summary," *Production and Inventory Management,* First Quarter, 1981.

ABOUT THE AUTHORS—

SAM G. TAYLOR is a member of the industrial management faculty of the University of Wyoming. He is also a partner in Taylor and Bolander Associates, a consulting firm specializing in seminars and materials management consulting for the process industries. He is a frequent speaker at regional and national conferences and has published articles in *Production and Inventory Management, AIIE Transactions,* and *Chemical Engineering Magazine.*

SAMUEL M. SEWARD is an Associate Professor at the University of Wyoming teaching production and operations management courses in the Cheyenne MBA Program. The majority of his consulting and contract research has focused on operational problems in the public sector, including planning for such organizations as fire departments, city and state patrols, and social welfare agencies.

STEVEN F. BOLANDER is an Associate Professor at Colorado State University. He is also the Manager for Manufacturing Systems Development and formerly a Program Manager for Rockwell International in charge of designing and implementing a computer-based production and inventory management system. In addition, Dr. Bolander is a partner in the consulting firm of Taylor and Bolander Associates which conducts public and private seminars on inventory management for process industries. He is past president of the Colorado APICS Chapter and now serves on its board of directors.

INPUT/OUTPUT CONTROL
A REAL HANDLE ON LEAD TIME

OLIVER WIGHT

Symptoms of Uncontrolled Lead Time

The Board of Directors of the Manufacturing Association of a midwest city got together recently to plan their programs for the coming year. They decided to try to arrive at common problems first and then have their speaking program address these problems. Five of the problems that were universal to each company represented weren't problems at all. They were *symptoms:*

1. Excessive inventories of parts and finished material combined with poor off-the-shelf service.
2. Inability to make realistic delivery promises and meet them.
3. Excessive expediting.
4. Chronic lack of space in the plant.
5. Plants that are always behind schedule.

Why should serious problems like these go unsolved for years in manufacturing plants even with the advent of much improved inventory management techniques, better scheduling techniques, and computers to implement them? The answer is simple:

With all the fancy tools that have been developed, industry has failed to learn the fundamentals of lead time control.

Most books on scientific inventory management, for example, start out by saying, "Lead time is assumed to be known". They then proceed to develop scientific approaches to inventory management that will certainly not be able to generate anything like their potential benefits if lead times are long and erratic.

Why don't people like to address the lead time problem? Perhaps because it is almost totally ignored in the literature of production and inventory control; perhaps because it is not a problem that a convenient set of mathematical equations can solve. The lead time problem, as it manifests itself in most American manufacturing companies, is basically a problem of management. The solutions to it are not difficult to understand; in fact, they are deceptively simple. The biggest difficulty in making these solutions work is in changing the traditional thinking of manufacturing people. The Board of Directors of the Association mentioned earlier *should be* concerned about this problem: a dramatic change in the way a company operates can only be implemented if top management understands the principles and educates other members of the company to be sure they are observed religiously.

What is Lead Time?

Before discussing some of the principles of lead time control, it is worth reviewing the basic concepts. Lead time can be defined as that time that elapses between the moment it is determined that an item is needed and ordered to be replenished and that moment when the item is available for use. Lead time can include all the elements of order entry time, such as preparing input data for the computer, waiting for the computer to process batches of input data, review of orders for credit check, engineering, etc. Often there is a fertile area for lead time improvement in order entry. Among other elements in the lead time cycle that can be excessively long are backlogs in production scheduling. Particularly in make-to-order plants, it is traditional to run with consistent backlogs behind starting operations in the factory. This is ostensibly because the amount of work coming in each week cannot be predicted and tends to be erratic. Most companies, however, seldom measure this incoming work rate or know how erratic it is and they usually carry excessive backlogs to "protect" themselves. An example of the application of the basic principles of lead time control to this type of situation will be given below.

But what about the manufacturing lead time itself? The actual amount of elapsed time in the factory takes place from the moment that a shop order is released to the factory to the time it is completed. This lead time can be broken into the following elements:

LEAD TIME = SET-UP TIME + RUNNING TIME + MOVE TIME + WAIT TIME + QUEUE TIME

Set-up time is the time when the job is sitting behind the machine and the machine is being set up with the proper tooling for this job.

Running time is the actual time the job is at the machine and being worked on.

Move time is the actual time that a job spends in transit. In most job shops, this could be defined as the time the job actually spends on the fork of the forklift truck.

Wait time has been separated from Queue Time so that it could be arbitrarily associated with move time since, in many factories, the dispatching job is not highly organized and the forklift truck operators usually don't get to a job as soon as it is ready to move. In some plants, an operator of a forklift truck may "clean out" one department once a day. This could mean an average wait time of half a day and if there were 10 moves in the operation sequence, 5 days of time could be expended in waiting for a move.

Queue time is that time that the job spends waiting to be worked on because another job is already being run on that machine center.

Elapsed lead times are always far greater than actual set-up and running time. It is hard to believe that any substantial amount of the elapsed lead time is truly spent "in transit"—on the forks of the forklift truck. A substantial amount of the time *could* be spent waiting for moves. In actual practice, most of the lead time turns out to be queue time. A simple experiment can verify this for any company. Taking some samples from completed shop orders, determine the date the job started in the first department and the number of elapsed working hours that took place in the first department (counting only *manned* shifts during the week). If, for example, Job A takes one week to go through Department No. 1, this amounts to forty hours of elapsed manned time. If Job A has two hours of set-up and two hours of run time, then the set-up and running time are 10% of the elapsed time.

A continuing survey of manufacturing companies indicates that ten per cent—or less—of the total lead time in the average company is actual working time! How can that be? It would seem that queues are completely out of control. And, of course, in practice *they are!* There is overwhelming evidence in most manufacturing companies to indicate that the amount of backlog that exists is as much as the company can possibly tolerate. Backlogs on the factory floor are in evidence everywhere and there seems to be a variation of Parkinson's Law at work in the typical manufacturing shop, since:

"work-in-process normally tends to expand to fill the space available".

What plant foreman doesn't feel that he is crowded for space? What shop doesn't occasionally run out of skids, pallets, shop boxes? What shop has open spaces out on the factory floor? In the typical job shop, work-in-process tends to be piled everywhere and the oldest jobs always seem to get up against the wall so that the newer ones are the only ones that can be worked on. This "Last-in-first-out" effect tends to keep customer service low, in spite of high inventories and high expediting efforts. In most shops, even a small capacity bottleneck will cause some queueing and as queues build, expediting becomes frantic.

Backlogs are the problem

Since backlog is a fundamental cause of long lead time and lead time can only be controlled if backlog is controlled, lets look at the three major causes of large backlogs.

1. Lead time inflation.
2. Erratic input to the plant.
3. Inability to plan and control output effectively.

No. 1 *LEAD TIME INFLATION*—Take the example of a company that plans to have its product manufactured in a six week lead time. As business picks up they manage to put more into the factory than they take out. This builds up the shop backlogs and, as a result, they find that their lead times are increasing from six weeks to eight weeks. The plant always feels that if they had just a little more lead time it would be a simple matter to get jobs completed on schedule. They cite the fact that many jobs come through two weeks after their schedule date as a reason for allowing two weeks more in the lead time. When the historical "facts" show that lead time is actually closer to eight weeks, they assume that this lead time should be built back into the inventory planning. Any inventory system assumes some length of lead time in its re-ordering mechanism. An order point system tries to forecast demand over *lead time* plus some safety stock. A requirements planning system tries to determine *when* requirements will fall, and then, in backing off in time to account for the *lead time*, it determines when orders should be placed. Either basic type of inventory system relies heavily on lead time estimates.

Ironically, *as planned lead times are increased, orders will be generated sooner, thus increasing backlogs in the shop.*

In our example, an increase in the planning lead time from six weeks to eight weeks would immediately generate an extra two weeks worth of work for the shop which would increase the backlogs and thus increase the lead times. If the actual lead times are observed now, they will be longer than ever. If they are once again built into the inventory plans, orders will be generated sooner again thus increasing backlogs and increasing lead times once again. This, then, is one of the most dangerous and most common misconceptions in the industry, yet many companies have even developed sophisticated computer programs to average historical lead times so that these can be built into their planning systems! Unfortunately, a computer is amoral; it can be used to do the wrong thing faster than it was ever possible to do it manually.

An even worse situation exists between vendors and their customers. It is aggravated by the fact that purchasing people often have no real understanding of the ill effects of long lead times. Some even encourage vendors to quote longer lead times in the belief that these longer lead times will be more reliable. They seldom are. Unfortunately, even if they were, the people generating the orders, usually in inventory control in the company purchasing material, find that their ability to forecast their needs accurately goes down dramatically as they forecast farther in advance. Thus they have to carry higher safety stocks and/or reschedule frequently to protect against forecast error as vendors increase their lead time. This can readily be seen in most companies by examining their open purchase order file. The bulk of the orders are late, but *are not needed*, while other orders, some of which were just placed recently, are being expedited because they *are* needed! Part of this problem could be caused by an ineffective inventory system, but even this is going to be aggravated if lead times are long and unreliable.

Many vendors quote longer lead times in the belief that this will give them a better chance to get the product out the door on time. It never works that way. In fact, when a vendor quotes longer lead times to his customer, he almost always winds up with a bigger backlog of orders. If, for example, a vendor had been quoting a ten week lead time and now quotes a fifteen week lead time, his customers will have to plan to cover all of their requirements five weeks farther out than they normally did. This will result in sending the vendor an extra five weeks worth of purchase orders, thus increasing the vendor's backlog and his lead time. If he once again quotes a longer lead time, most of his customers will send him more purchase orders until they get throughly disgusted with him and start going to his competition. In many industries, however, such as the gray iron foundries in the United States, capacity is often tight. As one foundry increases its lead time and customers start placing orders with competitors, the competitors wind up in a capacity squeeze and then start increasing their lead time. A small increase in lead time can easily be escalated into a total lead time that is patently absurd. It is not uncommon for gray iron foundries to be quoting lead times of 36 to 48 weeks to make castings that can easily be produced in five working days!

What happens to the vendor when this small capacity bottleneck is finally eliminated? Under extreme pressure from his sales department, he reduces his quoted lead time from 48 weeks to 40 weeks. The salesman is delighted to convey this information to the customer's purchasing department. They convey it to production and inventory control who then build it back into their inventory control system. Since lead time is shorter than it was before, there is really very little they need to order right now!

Back at the vendor, the flow of incoming orders slows down. The sales department is panic stricken and decides that the competition must be getting the business. They insist upon a further reduction in lead time. When this is relayed to the customers inventory control group, they further reduce their planned lead times. This generates fewer orders and reduces the input to the vendor which further reduces his backlog of orders! One bearing manufacturer was quoting a forty-eight week lead time in one product line and twelve months later could quote a three week lead time in the same line. Three weeks is probably pretty realistic for assembling a bearing from stocked parts, but what happened to the forty-five week backlog? It seems difficult to believe that this company could have produced fifty-two weeks of normal production and also produced enough to eliminate forty-five weeks work of backlogs. This would be equivalent to ninety-seven normal weeks of production in a year! They really went through the lead time "deflation" cycle after having previously had their lead times inflated to forty-eight weeks (probably because of a *small* capacity bottleneck).

The role of lead time inflation has never been thoroughly explored in the study of business cycles. It certainly has made an important contribution, particularly since the increase in backlog tends to increase the real volume that a company has to handle because as people try to forecast their requirements farther and farther out into the future, they are less and less accurate. They suddenly find things that they need very quickly that they were not able to anticipate. When they go to order these from their suppliers, the suppliers quote them extremely long lead times *principally because they currently have backlogs made up of other items that this customer and other customers tried to forecast far in advance of requirements.*

Most systems have good expediting capability but very little "unexpediting" capability. Since the customer seldom has a good enough inventory system so that he can see what he doesn't need today, he almost always winds up adding the new item that he knows he needs to an existing backlog which has many items in it that he no longer needs. The result is a very real increase in volume just when capacity is tightest. The correct technique to handle this problem will be discussed below, but certainly one thing should be obvious to the reader:

if the reaction to longer lead times is to order material farther in advance, this will only increase backlogs and increase lead times.

No. 2 *ERRATIC PLANT INPUT*—Releasing jobs to the manufacturing floor as the system generates requirements always results in a highly erratic input to the shop. Witness these figures from a company that has an extremely stable assembly production rate. These figures represent the number of standard hours of work generated over a ten week period for parts made on one particular group of screw machines:

Week	Standard Hours
1	286 hours
2	50 hours
3	147 hours
4	176 hours
5	695 hours
6	531 hours
7	139 hours
8	321 hours
9	61 hours
10	284 hours

This is truly random input and consists of total hours generated each week. No attempt has been made to show the number of pieces or the number of shop orders created each week, since that is not relevant to the discussion. The important point to see is the tremendous variation in input rate. If a foreman is to run his department on schedule, he should produce fifty hours worth of work in one week and in another week he should make 695 hours worth of work. This type of thinking might have been reasonable during the 30's. Indeed, much of our production control technology being used today—even that being implemented on computers—dates back to the 30's when dramatic changes in capacity were not only possible but were quite economical because there was such a large surplus of available labor. Obviously, no plant today could produce the hours as input in this example. Any foreman in his right mind would try to run a fairly stable production rate. But how could he possibly run at a stable rate with this erratic input? The obvious answer is that he cannot; therefore, he does the best he can: he tries to run at a stable rate by running in a perpetual behind schedule condition. Obviously, in a week like Week No. 5, when 695 hours are required, somebody will have to make a decision as to which hours are required first. When the inventory planner passes that burden to the foreman, he has insured that an expediter will have to come into the picture to straighten out the mess which production and inventory control should have straightened out in the first place by recognizing the necessity to run the plant at a fairly stable rate. Erratic input of this type makes it necessary for the foreman to run in a constant behind schedule condition and, since he is never sure how much work is coming to him in the future, he always feels that large backlogs are necessary and the best guarantee of steady work rates in the future.

This belief coupled with production control's usual abdication of responsibility for keeping work flowing to the foreman at a steady rate, tends to aggravate the problem of backlogs out on the factory floor. This is where backlogs really cause the most problems. *How many expediters would really be necessary in a company where there was only one job behind each operation?* In most companies, expediters are constantly reshuffling the backlog that never should have been allowed to get into the factory in the first place.

In fact, as production control continues to put jobs into a plant that is already far behind schedule, their entire scheduling system ceases to function with any degree of effectiveness. Whenever there is a capacity bottleneck, the most important question to ask is, "Which job should be done first?" The production and inventory control system in many companies would be able to give only one answer under these circumstances, "They're all late—we need them all". This is why expediting has become such a frantic effort in most manufacturing companies. The cycle can be predicted very reliably: any small capacity bottleneck will be followed by an aggravation of the backlog situation in the factory and this will be followed by increasing amounts of expediting. Expediting seems to fit one definition of fanaticism:

"A fanatic is a man who redoubles his efforts when all hope of reaching the goal has been lost".

Obviously, putting orders into a shop on the date when they are supposed to be started, regardless of capacity, doesn't really make a great deal of sense. If the shop is behind on capacity, and input exceeds output, the orders will all show up late and it will be very difficult to determine what the real priorities are, particularly since these are quite likely to have changed since the orders were originally released. If the inventory system doesn't generate orders one week, it behooves people in production and inventory control to try to smooth out the input. If they don't, the foremen will have to. A brief acquaintance with any foreman, or for that matter, any production worker, will convince the observer that he has no confidence that anything but big backlogs out in the factory will guarantee a steady flow of work for him. A low level of shop backlog can be maintained only if jobs are released to the plant at a steady rate. This means that some jobs will have to be started somewhat earlier than their normal release dates and occasionally some will have to be started somewhat later. The calculations that are made to determine lead time are approximate and it is reasonable and right to juggle the actual starting time of an order to smooth the input.

No. 3 *INABILITY TO PLAN AND CONTROL OUTPUT RATES*—Figure 1 shows a typical machine load report. There would usually also be detailed load information showing order by order the jobs that constitute the load in each week. While the format has been simplified, nothing has been left out that would bear on the current discussion. Note that the load shows the weekly capacity. This is usually adjusted to reflect the shop's ability to convert actual working hours into standard hours. For example, if it takes forty hours of actual time to produce thirty-two standard hours of work, the shop is said to be working at 80% of capacity and that figure is reflected in the capacity figure shown on the machine load report. Note that the machine load report also shows the production for last week, which, in this case, was quite a bit below what is obviously required. It shows a very erratic workload with the load tapering off dramatically after the bulge in Week 726. This report in its raw form is practically useless for the following reasons:

```
MACHINE LOAD REPORT

Work Center 5910
(All figures in standard hours)

WEEKLY CAPACITY  240 HR.
PRODUCTION LAST WEEK  205 HR.
```

Week Ending	Load	Over/Under Load
Past Due	824	+ 584
706	286	+ 46
711	50	− 190
716	247	+ 7
721	196	− 64
726	690	+ 450
731	130	− 110
734	139	− 101
739	27	− 213
744	68	− 172
749	84	− 156

Figure 1

1. It doesn't project capacity requirements far enough into the future to be of real value to the foreman in making economical changes in capacity; i.e., hiring and training of people, buying new machinery, etc.
2. It shows work scheduled to be produced at widely varying rates week to week with a limited number of machines and a limited number of men. Because this is certainly not the way production will actually run, it is not a realistic plan for the foreman.
3. It does not provide a workable "norm" against which a department's performance can be measured. Since we don't really expect the foreman to produce at these weekly rates, how do we measure him?
4. It doesn't really tell us very much about what the actual capacity is. It tells us the theoretical capacity and the actual output for one week, typically.
5. It is almost impossible to learn anything about the input/output relationship that actually controls the backlog (and, in turn, controls the lead time) from a machine load report.

Machine load reports are a tool that was probably moderately effective in the past. In the 30's, manpower was readily available and capacity could be expanded or contracted on very short notice. During the 40's and 50's, large backlogs of orders existed. Even though manpower was not readily available, plenty of time was available to make significant adjustments in capacity. Today, the need to keep people working at a stable rate is recognized by practically every company. We have two conflicting pressures:

the pressure to plan farther ahead at the same time that there is less backlog that can be used for planning purposes.

These, then, are three problems that aggravate the backlog—and thus the lead time—problem:

1. Lead time inflation.
2. Erratic input.
3. Inability to plan and control output rates.

Our classical production control techniques were not designed to address these problems. Machine loading has been adopted and discarded by many companies. Yet, machine loading approaches, particularly if done by computer, *can* be used effectively to plan and control capacity—but only if they are used in conjunction with a new kind of report—the input/output report.

Input/Output Controls

There is one simple rule for controlling backlogs and thus controlling lead time and that is:

THE INPUT TO A SHOP MUST BE EQUAL TO OR LESS THAN THE OUTPUT.

There is practically nothing in any of the classical production or inventory control systems that focuses anyone's attention on the relationship of *input* to *output*, yet it is this fundamental relationship that is the most important one, not only in getting production under control but in stabilizing lead times so that inventories can be managed effectively. Input/output control is the only way to control backlogs and thus control lead time.

This tool *has* been developed by some companies. But not enough manufacturing executives today have even recognized how critical it is to have a tool that:

1. Projects capacity requirements far into the future.
2. Shows them at a level rate.
3. Shows the relationship between input and output.

Figure 2 shows an input/output report. The work rate at a work center has been planned and in the planning, the rate has been levelled out. Note that this was planned without actually scheduling individual orders. If schedule dates were put on orders far in advance, the dates would be meaningless by the time these orders were due to be released. Because it is possible to do a reasonable job of forecasting when larger groups are forecast, the total production rate required for a work center can usually be predicted with reasonable accuracy. In Figure 2, the output rate has been pegged at 300 hours per week for the first four weeks

INPUT/OUTPUT CONTROLS

Work Center 0138
(All figures in standard hours)

	Week Ending	505	512	519	526	533	540	547	554	561	568
Unreleased Backlog 0	Planned Input	270	270	270	270	270	270	270	270	270	270
	Actual Input	270	265	250							
	Cumulative Deviation		−5	−25							
Released* Backlog 120 HR.	Planned Output	300	300	300	300	270	270	270	270	270	270
	Actual Output	305	260	280							
	Cumulative Deviation	+5	−35	−55							

*Above desired level of work-in-process (standard queue) at this work center as of start of plan.

Figure 2

and then 270 hours per week. Note that the input rate is planned to be 270 hours per week as far out as the plan goes. (These plans have been abbreviated. Most of them would tend to go out twelve to twenty-five weeks into the future to give an adequate planning horizon to enable foremen to adjust capacity.) The planned output is higher than the planned input for the first four weeks. This is intended to reduce the existing released backlog by 120 standard hours.

Note that this input/output report shows the planned output at a fairly level rate. It also shows the actual output rather than the theoretical capacity and the output for one week as the machine load report did. We can get a far better idea from it of whether or not we have adequate capacity in this particular work center. The report also clearly indicates whether or not backlog, and consequently, lead time in this work center is building up. If this work center is a starting work center and it is fed by the inventory control or scheduling system, the input can be regulated to meet the planned rate. There is no need to continue to put work into the shop at a faster rate than they are taking it out. Many production control people tend to do this because *their present systems only show a capacity deficit when they have actually overloaded the shop.* Note that the input/output report will show that output has been insufficient *even if load has not been released to the shop.*

One of the rules that is usually used with this type of report is that input in any given week cannot exceed output the previous week. Note that in Week 519, the scheduler looking at the output from the previous week released only 250 hours of work (theoretically, he would have released 260, the same rate that was put out the previous week, but lot sizes will generally make it necessary to adjust this slightly upward or downward in real life). He can hold back work—as he should when the shop cannot produce it—and still see that the shop is not producing on schedule. By holding orders in production control, he can be sure that the priority on orders when they are released is the very latest. This will also avoid building the large in-plant queues that *always* generate excessive expediting.

The input/output report meets all the requirements for good lead time control. It shows a production plan far out into the future, since it shows it in total only. It measures capacity in terms of total hours rather than late orders out in the shop.

What's the "input" to the input/output report? The same computer program that is used to create the classical machine load can be used to create the input/output planning information. This planning information consists of a forecast of the usage of parts over the next few months. The planning horizon can be at the company's option. Most companies like to see an idea of what they're going to need in the way of manpower at least twelve to thirteen weeks ahead of time; therefore, production plans are usually reviewed monthly and extended out ninety days into the future. This does not include the less frequent, usually quarterly, production plans that are used to plan facilities requirements and extend out one to two years.

A company that has a time phased requirements planning system can periodically put their best estimate of future schedules into the computer program and then put the planned orders into a machine load program to generate a report like that shown in Figure 3. This machine load projection isn't a real load report—it's a *forecast* of the total amount of work that will be required in a work center over a period of time. The objective is *not* to schedule and load the individual orders. Capacity will be *planned in total hours* and then this plan will be levelled out to give the planned output rate for a work center. With input/output control, the machine load report has two functions:

1. When forecasts are put into the machine loading program, the average required production rate can be set up as the "planned output" requirement.
2. Once input/output control reports are established, the machine load report *can* be used to show where short term bottlenecks are developing. In most companies, the input/output reports will do this job without additional machine load reports.

Machine loading without input/output control is a poor tool for keeping lead time under control in a manufacturing company. Input/output—used properly—will enable a company to control lead times.

```
                    MACHINE LOAD PROJECTION

               ........ 100 ........ 200 ........ 300 ........ 500
            Week                 1st              2nd
             45   XXXXXX
             46   XXXXXXXXXXXX
             47   XXXXXXX
             48   XXXXXXXXXXXXXXXXXXXXXXXXXXXXXXXXXXXXXXXXXXXX
             49   XXXXXXXXXXXX
             50   XXXXXXXXXXXXXXXXXXXXXXX
             51   XXXXXXXXXXXXXXXXXXXXXXXXXXXXXXXXXXXXXXXXXXXXXXXXXXXXXX
             52   XXXXXXXXXXXXXXXXXXXXXXXXXXXXXXXXXX
             53   XXXXXXXXXXXXXXXXXXXXXXXXXXX
             54   XXXXXXXXXXXXXXXXXXXXXXXXXXXX
             55   XXXXXXXXXXXXXXXXXXXXXXXXXXXXXX
             56   XXXXXXXXXXXXXXXXXXXXXX
             57   XXXXXXXXXXXXXXXXXXXXXXXXXXXXXXXXXXXXXXXXXXXX
             58   XXXXXXXXXXXXXXXXXXXXXXXXXXX
  45 & 65    59   XXXXXXXXXXXXXXXXXXXXXXX
    TON      60   XXXXXXXXXXXXXXXXXXX
   PUNCH     61   XXXXXXXXXXXXXXXXXXXXXXXXXXXXXXXX
   PRESS     62   XXXXXXXXXXXXXXXXXXXXXXX
             63   XXXXXXXXXXXXXXXXXXXXXXXXXXX
             64   XXXXXXXXXXXXXXXXXXXXXXXX
             65   XXXXXXXXXXXXXXXXXXXXXXXXXXXXXXXXXXXXXXXXXXXXXXXXXXXXXXX
```

Figure 3

Controlling Input

Once capacity plans have been established, the individual items to be scheduled must be put into the plant *at the planned rate and at the last possible moment* so that their schedule dates can be made more accurate by forecasting over a shorter period of time. This can result in more accurate dates on shop orders. Highly inaccurate dates exist in most companies today because lead times are extremely long and it is, therefore, necessary to forecast individual item completion dates far out into the future. Because of this, it is common to walk into any manufacturing department and find that many jobs are well behind schedule, yet if you ask the foreman about these jobs, he'll tell you that nobody is looking for them. This indicates that the original dates on the orders were forecast sometime in the past and are no longer valid or it would be a symptom of a *very* poor inventory system!

The techniques for controlling input to meet a planned rate are not difficult to implement, particularly when a machine load program is available on a computer. The approach varies depending on the inventory system being used, the availability of a machine load report with planned orders (usually generated by a material requirements planning computer program) shown on it, and the type of work center involved. There are many work centers out in the shop where it is possible to plan the required input/output rates, but it is difficult to control the input since this is fed in from previous work centers. There are other work centers that are the "gateways" to the shop. These are starting operations like turret lathes, screw machines, presses, and work is fed into them from scheduling or often from inventory control itself.

STOCK STATUS REPORT

Item	Total Invent	Order Point	Ratio	E.O.Q.	E.O.Q. in Hours
1	4817	2730	1.77	1500	7.4
2	2056	1436	1.43	2500	8.6
3	5963	4242	1.41	1000	3.6
4	2851	1386	2.06	2700	12.8
5	8771	6250	1.40	500	2.4
6	9894	6768	1.46	2250	10.0
7	4080	3346	1.22	1000	7.0
8	1781	866	2.06	2500	9.8
9	192	239	.80	500	2.8

Figure 4

Figure 4 shows one approach to handling this problem. In this case, the inventory control system is an order point system and the ratio of order point to the inventory on hand and on order ("total" inventory) is shown. This facilitates picking which job to put into production next since it is not at all unusual to have a situation where, due to seasonal inventory build-ups, most items are above order point. The ratio then tells which item ought to be scheduled into production first. In this case, Item 9 should go in first, Item 7 should go in second, etc. The order quantity is shown in pieces and also in hours. Where a planned input rate must be attained, the inventory control man can determine which items to put into production to hit the planned rate. Obviously, if there is not enough capacity to handle all of the items that he would like to run, he must decide which ones are most important. This works out far better in practice than having him order everything he wants and then having expediters trying to sort it out after it has hit a badly overloaded factory.

In a company using a requirements plan generated by computer, the inventory report shows "planned order releases" for past due, current, and future periods. If these planned orders are then put into a machine load program, the detailed load report will show the number of hours that are planned to be released to the gateway work centers each week. When these hours do not meet the planned input rate, the scheduler can go back to the inventory planners and ask them to move some orders up a week or back a week. Since the material requirements plan should have been used to project the planned input rates, any variation in input rates should be purely random. In practice, if this is done well, there are far fewer occasions than most production control people imagine where orders have to be moved up or pushed back more than a week to keep the input rates steady.

Inventory control people frequently rebel at the idea of keeping the input rate steady. Somehow they feel that the starting date on any order is inviolable. Anyone who knows how lead times are calculated in most scheduling systems knows that even in the best run companies they are an approximation at best. Smoothing out the input rates makes a lot more sense than trying to put orders out into a shop that is overloaded or holding orders back from a shop that is running out of work.

Still another approach can be taken to controlling input. It really amounts to controlling input by exception. With this approach, orders are released to the gateway work centers as they come out of the inventory scheduling system, unless the input/output report shows a substantial deviation in actual input from planned input. When this occurs, action is taken to search out orders that can either be held back or pulled up to correct the input deviation.

There's plenty of good reason for smoothing input so that it's not erratic. Erratic input requires large queues of work to absorb the ups and downs in the workload. Many people ask, "How much work-in-process *should* we have?" The answer is that queues exist in the factory primarily to absorb the fluctuations in input rates. One company, for example, sampled the backlogs behind a particular operation over a long period of time and found that the greatest number of containers of work they ever had behind that operation was 125. The smallest number they ever had was 75. This means that the fluctuation rate was within the range of 50; in fact, this is what the normal allowed queue should have been. At a gateway work center, this fluctuation rate can be reduced to practically nothing and *there is no excuse for having large queues of released orders in front of these gateway operations.*

How can we control the input to intermediate operations? This is a far more difficult proposition since the workload is coming in from many diverse areas typically. Nevertheless, the input/output report can be used to monitor input rates and when these are dropping or falling, the machine load report can be used to pinpoint jobs in preceding operations that should be rescheduled to smooth out the input. One approach that has occurred to a few companies is to analyze their capacity requirements by key work center. They usually find that a little scheduling attention to a small number of items can do quite a bit to take some of the peaks and troughs out of the input to intermediate work centers.

Why all the attention to smoothing input? Obviously, the smoother the input rate, the less backlog the shop must have and the shorter their lead time can be. By not releasing work into the gateway work centers from the scheduling or inventory control systems at a higher rate than previous weeks output, backlogs are held in production and inventory control rather than released to the shop. This reduces expediting and confusion. It places the decision for which item to run when capacity is tight in the hands of the inventory planner who is best equipped to do it. Forcing him to decide how he can best use his limited capacity resources when output is falling behind the plan or what he would like to start first when the inventory system must be forced to generate some input to meet the plan.

Input/output control is a far cry from the classical approaches to production and inventory control. Some companies have applied input/output controls already and the results have been dramatic.

Some Examples of Input/output Control

The General Manager of one medium sized manufacturing company decided that the principles of input/output control made some sense in his plant. Lead time on a particular product line was running six weeks and, while this was not abnormally high or uncompetitive, it seemed to him that it could be reduced. He set up input/output controls and planned the output at a level that would reduce the in-plant backlog from the normal six weeks of work-in-process to five weeks. He then went to the inventory control people and told them that lead time in the future would be five weeks instead of six weeks. In spite of his high position in the company, he was greeted with a degree of skepticism. The inventory people felt that he was tampering with some of the natural laws of nature! One was heard to remark, "The next thing he'll be telling us is that we can't have rainy weather".

By setting his output slightly higher than his input and reducing backlogs, he was able to reduce lead time from six weeks to five weeks, in spite of the skeptics. In fact, by telling inventory control that their lead time was only five weeks, he got an almost perfect reduction in input, since they released very few orders the first week the shorter lead time was in effect. This general manager also charged his inventory control people with keeping a smooth flow of work into the shop. He told them it was their responsibility to decide which orders had to be done first. They couldn't just send them all out into the shop regardless of the shop's capacity, and thus automatically create the need for expediting.

Having been successful in reducing lead time from six weeks to five weeks, he proceeded to reduce it to four weeks by increasing the output rate above the input rate once again. Again, he told the people in inventory control that their lead time would be reduced from five weeks to four weeks. Again, they were skeptical; but again, because he did bring the backlogs down in the factory from a five week level to a four week level, lead time was reduced to four weeks, which to him seemed very satisfactory. He had done it all empirically; he had found that there was really very little increase in the amount of idle time for lack of work out in the shop. Without any attempt to be scientific, he feels now that this 50% reduction in lead time represents a very satisfactory achievement in a few short month's time.

While very few companies have ever done anything scientific to decide on the level of work-in-process that they should have, many manufacturing oriented people within the companies feel that the level of work-in-process they have is just barely adequate. Most foremen are deathly afraid that they will run out of work—and for good reason. The foreman has little or no control over the flow of work into his department. The control of input lies with other departments or with production control itself. Very few foremen have any confidence that production control will keep work flowing to them at a steady rate and they're usually justified in this feeling. Therefore, the presence of physical backlogs in the factory is the only security they know.

Management has aggravated this problem considerably. One of the fundamental rules of management is to measure people on those functions that they truly control. The foreman feels that he is measured on idle time for lack of material. If a man is standing around, a great deal of pressure is on him to get rid of the man. On the other hand, the production control man feels he is responsible for getting work out the door on schedule. *Doesn't it make better sense to put the responsibility for hitting the schedule on the foreman and the responsibility for keeping work flowing through the shop at a steady rate on production control?*

Some companies today charge all idle time for lack of work to production control. Other companies say they never have idle time for lack of work, but the fact of the matter is, they have many indirect charges such as broken tools, looking for skids, etc. that tend to grow drastically when workers see backlogs on the floor decreasing. They would probably be better off to pay these people for standing around than to hide their heads in the sand over the very real problem of idle time for lack of material. By the same token, trying to carry enough work-in-process so that there will never by any idle time generates excessively long lead times. It is discouraging to see company policies that are aimed at making it impossible to have a man occasionally standing idle for lack of material while they spend large amounts of money on:

1. Work-in-process inventory.
2. Inventories to protect against the large forecast errors that result when lead times are long.
3. Excessive expediting.
4. Missed schedules because large queues make it so difficult to make the *right* item.

The problem of educating machine operators so that they will not be afraid of running out of work when they see shop floor backlogs decrease is a real one. It is necessary to assure them that the work flow will continue to come or they will tend to slow down. Even companies with an incentive system can have a dramatic slowdown without the employee losing much in wages, as any man who has filled out a time ticket can attest! Some companies have fought this problem by posting on the departmental bulletin board the planned production rates as in-plant backlogs were reduced. Others have done it through education programs and by informing employees that indirect charges were going to be watched very closely as the new program was instituted. Others *pay* operators for idle time due to lack of material. Obviously, education is extremely important when a work-in-process reduction is generated. A serious work slowdown—often unconscious—can result if the education program is neglected.

Let's look at another example to illustrate the input/output relationship. A company installed the Critical Ratio priority system. This priority system is a dynamic priority system which gives a good updated relative priority for every job in the shop. Lead time quickly decreased and jobs seemed to be coming out on schedule far better than they ever had before. They were delighted with the results of Critical Ratio. Unfortunately, a short time later, things started to deteriorate and they couldn't understand it. Analyzing the problem, it was found that at the same time they instituted their Critical Ratio program, they added 40 direct labor people to the second shift. This resulted in an increase in output at the same time that input wasn't increasing dramatically. Later on, an increase in sales caused an increase in input. The increase in input built up backlogs again and lead times once again got longer. As longer queues built up in the shop, job selection became a much more difficult problem and more and more jobs came through behind schedule. The Critical Ratio technique is an excellent priority technique, but this company mistakenly assumed that it could control lead time with a priority technique. Only input/output controls can really control lead time.

Many companies have problems with their vendors. One midwest company, recognizing the importance of input/output controls and the basic principle that capacity should be forecast without committing themselves to actual orders, set up a very effective program with one of their foundries. They commit themselves to run a given number of molds down each line in the foundry as far out as the foundry would like to have this commitment. They do not specify the actual orders they're going to run. Six weeks ahead of time they specify the actual orders they're going to run. In effect, they have blocked out capacity at the foundry and committed themselves to it, but they haven't committed themselves to forecasting far in advance which orders they want to run within that capacity.

This approach also forces their inventory control people to take a look at the requirements for castings every week and determine what they think they need six weeks ahead of time. They're in a position at the present time where they can get any casting they want from this foundry in six weeks. Any of their competition ordering castings from the same foundry would have to wait twenty-two weeks! Ironically, if this company had done what the foundry had originally requested them to do, they would have increased their lead time in their inventory system until they had actual orders out at the foundry twenty-two weeks in advance. If they then needed an order in a hurry, the foundry would honestly have told them that it would take twenty-two weeks to get it! The logic of projecting capacity requirements and then scheduling actual orders to meet these plans seems to be hard to get through to manufacturing people, but its benefits are dramatic.

The production control manager of one midwest company was told by one of his vendors that lead time had increased from twelve weeks to twenty weeks. He put this information into his computer and the computer promptly reacted by generating orders for eight additional weeks. The production control manager boxed these orders and shipped them by freight to the vendor. The vendor called and asked where all the orders came from. The production control manager told him that these were orders to cover the extra lead time that had been requested. The vendor indicated that he already had file drawers full of orders and had hired two clerks to file these orders and re-file them as customers called in schedule changes. Our astute production control manager told his vendor that it was his experience that as lead time increased, the number of reschedules went up geometrically! (He was right. This is the result of the inability to forecast in detail far into the future with any degree of accuracy). The production control manager volunteered to give the vendor any "further help" that he might require. He asked if perhaps the vendor would like to have orders covering thirty weeks lead time, or forty weeks, or fifty. It's a simple matter to put this information into a computer and to generate bales of paper representing orders which probably will have to be rescheduled many, many times before they are actually delivered. Yet the number of manufacturing executives who realize the folly of increasing planning lead times when their capacity thightens up is still very small indeed!

The lead time that people use to plan has a very significant effect upon the rate of input itself. Using shorter lead times also helps people to forecast over a shorter period of time and to predict more accurately what their detailed requirements will be.

The production control manager of a sizeable company that makes carpets and carries them in inventory was very unhappy because his plant could not produce according to schedule. The order points on the carpets were based on a lead time given to him by the factory plus a safety stock to cover forecast deviation over lead time. When the loom capacity proved to be inadequate to meet his requirements, a great many orders fell past due in the factory and the actual manufacturing lead time increased. A great many people pressured this production control manager to increase his planning lead times. Recognizing that this would only generate more orders to an already overloaded shop, he decided to do exactly the opposite! He decreased his lead times in the inventory control system.

This generated less input, allowed the shop to clear up most of the backlog that they had in-process, and enabled him to predict more accurately the items that he really needed to get through his limited capacity since he was predicting his requirements over a shorter span into the future! Without any increase in capacity or any increase in finished goods inventory, he was able to generate a very substantial increase in customer service level by making more of the *right* items.

Many people would question the logic of reducing lead time to less than the actual manufacturing lead time, but there are really *two lead times* in production and inventory control. One is the *actual lead time* that it takes to produce a product and another one is a *control* that we can use in the system that will enable us to cut back on input and to forecast over a shorter period in the future what we actually need. When lead times in the factory increase because of inadequate capacity, the solution is not to increase planning lead times, since this will simply increase backlog. Increasing backlogs will increase expediting. This problem will be aggravated because we will be predicting less accurately what we actually need. The real answer is to introduce input/output controls, and a reduction in the planned lead time can help by getting the *right* items into production.

The relationship of lead time to backlog is seldom really understood, but it was brought into sharp focus in one company with the introduction of input/output controls. One significant manufacturing process had a lead time of six weeks. There was two weeks of backlog behind a badly bottlenecked starting operation. By using the input/output controls, they held back work and put in no more than the operation had turned out in the previous week. They showed the deficiency in capacity through the input/output report rather than through backlogs of actual orders. After a short period of time, they found their actual manufacturing lead time was not six weeks as they originally thought but was, in fact, two weeks. The input/output control had reduced the in-plant backlog so dramatically that, in spite of the capacity bottleneck, the work that was released to the shop was going through in a shorter period of time. Since lead time had been reduced to two weeks, they reflected this back into their inventory control system. As a result the inventory control system then did not release any substantial number of orders over a four week period of time and the company found that an operation that they thought had a two week backlog of unreleased work behind it, in fact, had no work behind it. They had to force orders out of their inventory control system to keep work flowing into what had been a badly bottlenecked operation a few weeks before! Obviously, when capacity is really needed, holding input down does not really solve the capacity problem; it does enable you to do a better job of getting the *right* items. Too often, however, the lack of input/output controls and lead time inflation can create artificial backlogs. Many companies sub-contract, work overtime, and add people just to handle backlogs created by lead time inflation.

Another company that manufactures a product sold almost exclusively to customer order found that their 8 1/2 week quoted lead time consisted of four weeks for scheduling and four and 1/2 weeks for manufacturing. By measuring the *rate* of incoming orders from customers, they found that there wasn't a very substantial variation in input rate. The random variations really tended to cancel each other over a short period of time. By monitoring the input rate, they could see trends up or down and actually plan and control their capacity more effectively than by holding big backlogs of customer orders. They also found that when they needed to make work because incoming orders were low, they could pull ahead orders for many of their larger customers who gave them schedules well into the future. The result in this company was to reduce their lead time from 8 1/2 weeks to five weeks. They found that they only needed to maintain 1/2 week of backlog of orders when they started using input/output controls to control capacity rather than using backlogs. There is an important concept here: our classical approaches to production control muddle the problems of getting "enough" and getting the "right ones". Input/output control forces us to look at each separately.

The Basic Principles of Input/output Control

There are really only two basic questions to be addressed in production control.

1. ARE WE GETTING *ENOUGH?*
2. ARE WE GETTING THE *RIGHT ONES?*

Think about the typical job shop with 30 or 40% of the jobs past due—yet no one is even expediting most of them—they aren't really needed! When this kind of situation exists we don't know where we stand. Are we really short of capacity—then why don't we seem to need the late jobs? Are we getting the right ones—if they are late and not needed it doesn't even seem that we are *asking* for the right ones!

The solutions to these two problems—"enough" and the "right ones" are very different. If we are not getting enough output, we need more capacity. If we are not getting the right ones, either our inventory control system is poor (not an uncommon problem) or we don't work on the right jobs in the plant. If we don't know which problem we have, the odds are great we won't solve it very effectively.

At the root of the input/output concept are two forecast characteristics (Figure 5).

Forecasts are more accurate over short periods of time and less accurate over long periods of time. If we try to predict our sales for next week, we can do this with a greater degree of accuracy than we can predict sales for a week, six months out into the future. Forecasting is like aiming a gun—the closer you get to the target, the closer you are likely to come to the bullseye.

	ACCURATE	INACCURATE
HORIZON	SHORT	LONG
GROUP	LARGE	SMALL

Figure 5

Forecasts are more accurate for larger groups of items than they are for smaller groups of items. If you were to try to forecast the height of the next man you might meet, your chances of being accurate would be considerably less than if you tried to forecast the height of the next ten men that you might meet.

The marketing department, for example, can always do a better job of forecasting total dollars of sales than they can of forecasting individual items.

In practically every company, trying to determine how much is "enough" and which ones are the "right ones" implies some sort of forecasting. Obviously, then, we ought to recognize these forecast characteristics in the design of our inventory and production management systems. A second glance at the forecast characteristics above makes it obvious that when we are trying to plan capacity ("enough") where we must, by definition, extend our forecast out over a fairly long horizon, we should never try to firm up our plans for manufacturing individual items over that same horizon. The chart shows us that long horizon forecasts tend to be inaccurate. The worst possible situation is to try and forecast small groups of items over a long horizon, or individual items over a long horizon. Far better to forecast a large group of items over the long horizon. The group being the items that go through a particular work center, for example.

Let's try to express, then, the basic principles of input/output control:

1. *Separate the planning and control of capacity from the planning and control of mix.*
2. *Plan capacity requirements in the largest possible groups of items.*
3. *Put the required date on individual items at the last possible moment, i.e., forecast over the shortest possible horizon.*
4. *Never put into a manufacturing facility or to a vendor's facility more than you believe that he can produce. Hold backlogs in production and inventory control.*

The reasons behind these principles should be apparent to the reader at this point. The fourth principle in particular will be hard to teach to many inventory control people. It is difficult for them to understand that when a shop is behind they should not release their backlogs to it. The minute they do, they lose control over getting the right ones through. Expediters must take over and the result is expense, chaos, and confusion. This doesn't say that we shouldn't do our best to have the plant meet our capacity requirements. It does say that using the input/output concept, we can measure capacity deficiencies without releasing backlog to the shop. It also recognizes that when capacity is tight, nobody is in a better position than the inventory planner or scheduler to determine exactly which items should be run within the limited capacity.

Any executive who assumes that these principles are understood in his production and inventory control department or even by higher level manufacturing executives should first look at the literature and education available to manufacturing people. Little of it has ever discussed lead time! He should then look at his production and inventory control system quickly. Are there input/output controls? Are there techniques that show this vital relationship clearly or are the production control techniques classical techniques that tend to obscure the relationship of input and output and to allow backlogs to develop and to get out onto the factory floor where they can't really be controlled but can only generate excessive expediting?

He should be particularly on guard when people tell him that lead time should be increased. Increasing lead times used to order inventory will only result in the increased backlog and expediting. As inventory people try to forecast farther in advance to cover the longer lead times, their guesses get worse. This means more wrong items get made. When capacity is tight, it's *essential* to get the *right* items made or purchased.

The executive should be particularly concerned when computer systems are being applied. Many computer technicians feel that putting any system on a computer will improve it. They pick up "cookbook" techniques and apply them blindly. Unfortunately, unsound applications on computers tend to be as bad or worse than unsound applications manually and to draw attention away from the real problems.

Because an article must necessarily be brief, it is easy to leave the impression that the solution proposed is the complete solution to a problem. Let me hasten to emphasize that, while lead time control is essential to good inventory control, a good inventory control system is also needed. Far too many companies that make assembled products, for example, try to order parts based on historical averages rather than projected assembly requirements. This approach can also contribute to having many "late" jobs in process that are not really needed. Input/output control without a good inventory control system is only half a loaf.

Dramatic new approaches require management understanding and support if they are to work. Plant supervision that is used to living with big in-plant backlogs, workers who are afraid of layoffs when work piles dwindle, and production control people who are used to classical concepts like machine loading will have to be educated, directed, and reassured as lead times are reduced. They will have to be reminded that they cannot really cite any instance where lengthening lead times really made things better and taught to understand what lead time really is.

Control of lead time is vital to any scheduling and to any form of inventory control. Every inventory control system has as its foundation some assumption as to what the actual lead time will be. Very few production control systems actually have the tools in them to bring backlogs sharply into focus and to keep them under control. The introduction of input/output controls and the training of people to use these effectively can be a major step in improving customer service, reducing inventory, and stabilizing production rates in a manufacturing company.

About the Author—

OLIVER W. WIGHT *is President of OLIVER WIGHT, INC. and a partner in Plossl and Wight Associates, management counling and education firms. He is also co-author of the book: PRODUCTION AND INVENTORY CONTROL: Principles and Techniques, Prentice-Hall, July 1967, now in its sixth printing.*

Mr. Wight was formerly Industry Education Manager — Manufacturing for IBM's Data Processing Division where he was responsible for the content of all IBM internal training and customer executive courses on manufacturing applications of the computer. In this position, he also advised many major U.S. companies on systems design. Prior to this, he held positions as Staff Production Control Consultant for a multi-division corporation and Inventory Manager for a major automotive parts manufacturer.

A graduate of New England College, he has long been active in APICS as National Seminars Chairman, College Education Chairman, Director of Educational Policies, and Vice President of Education and Research. He was awarded the APICS certificate of recognition at the 1960, 1963, 1965, and 1966 National Conferences. He is a member of the Fairfield County Chapter of APICS where he is one of the Directors.

Mr. Wight has written and published many articles on production and inventory management. He has been a frequent speaker at such organizations as APICS, SPA, and NAA around the country. He is also a Chapter Editor for the new APICS Production and Inventory Control Handbook, recently published by McGraw-Hill.